Environmental Scenario in India

India has moved along an impressive growth path over the last decade, marked with a falling share of agriculture, stagnating manufacturing, an expanding services segment, growing trade orientation, enhanced FDI inflows, etc. The consequent growth implications are obvious as far as numbers like the GDP growth rate and per capita GDP trend are concerned, but how sustainable is the associated development with respect to resource management and environmental governance?

This book captures the economy-wide impacts of various activities on the environment in India. The environmental impacts on water, air, soil quality and human health are captured through case studies from different parts of India. Analysing separately the concern areas within agriculture (cultivation, aquaculture), manufacturing (industrial pollution, power generation), services (waste management, bio-medical waste, e-waste recycling) and the external sector (agricultural trade, FDI inflow, trade in waste products) performance of India, the book attempts to find an answer to that crucial question. The methodology adopted to capture the environmental impacts of the various economic activities is derived from relevant branches such as environmental economics, agricultural economics, and water resources economics. The book, focusing on these particular sectors, indicates the concern areas and possible ways to enhance environmental governance.

Sacchidananda Mukherjee is an Assistant Professor at the National Institute of Public Finance and Policy (NIPFP), New Delhi. Before joining NIPFP, he was with the International Water Management Institute (IWMI), Hyderabad and the World Wide Fund for Nature – India, New Delhi. He has worked on public finance, environmental economics and water resources management issues in India for the last decade. Dr Mukherjee has studied at the Madras School of Economics, Chennai (PhD in Environmental Economics) and Jawaharlal Nehru University, New Delhi (MA in Economics). He has conducted research projects funded by the Planning Commission, Government of India; IWMI, Colombo; British High Commission and published his research papers in national and international journals. He has been consulted by the Indian Institute of Foreign Trade, New Delhi and the Madras School of Economics, Chennai. Dr Mukherjee is a life member of the Indian Society for Ecological Economics, and a reviewer (ad hoc) of *Water Resources Management*, *Water Policy*, *Environment and Development Economics*, *Urban Water Journal*, and *International Journal of Global Environmental Issues*.

Debashis Chakraborty is currently an Assistant Professor of Economics at the Indian Institute of Foreign Trade, New Delhi. Before joining IIFT, he worked for five years in the Rajiv Gandhi Institute for Contemporary Studies. He received his Doctorate Degree from Jawaharlal Nehru University, New Delhi. His research interests include international trade policy and WTO negotiations, environmental sustainability and Indian economic development. He has presented and published his research in various academic and policy forums in India and abroad. He is also reviewer of several national and international journals.

Environmental Scenario in India

Successes and predicaments

**Edited by Sacchidananda Mukherjee
and Debashis Chakraborty**

Routledge
Taylor & Francis Group

LONDON AND NEW YORK

First published 2012
by Routledge
2 Park Square, Milton Park, Abingdon, Oxon OX14 4RN

Simultaneously published in the USA and Canada
by Routledge
711 Third Avenue, New York, NY 10017

Routledge is an imprint of the Taylor & Francis Group, an informa business

British Library Cataloguing in Publication Data
A catalogue record for this book is available from the British Library

Library of Congress Cataloging in Publication Data
Environmental scenario in India: successes and predicaments/edited by
Sacchidananda Mukherjee and Debashis Chakraborty.
    p. cm.
Includes bibliographical references and index.
1. Water resources development–Environmental aspects–India. 2.
Groundwater–Pollution–India. 3. Groundwater ecology–India. 4. Water-
supply–Management–Environmental aspects–India. I. Mukherjee,
Sacchidananda. II. Chakraborty, Debashis.
HD1698.I5E58 2012
333.70954–dc23

                                                              2011029341

ISBN: 978-0-415-66655-8 (hbk)
ISBN: 978-0-203-13703-1 (ebk)

Typeset in Times
by Wearset Ltd, Boldon, Tyne and Wear

Contents

Figures and maps

Figures

Maps

Tables

Contributors

Paul P. Appasamy is Vice Chancellor of Karunya University, Coimbatore and has worked on environmental economics, urban economics and water resources management issues for more than three decades. He is a member of the Scientific Programme Committee of Stockholm International Water Institute, Stockholm, Sweden.

Rachna Arora is a Project Officer in the Indo German Environment Programme (ASEM) of Deutsche Gesellschaft fuer Internationale Zusammenarbeit GmbH, New Delhi. Her research interests include electronic waste management, climate change adaptation, environmental fiscal reforms, industrial pollution monitoring and system closure.

R. Balasubramanian is Professor of Agricultural Economics at Tamil Nadu Agricultural University, Coimbatore, India and currently a Visiting Professor at the Department of Livestock Business Management and Marketing Economics, Konkuk University, Seoul (South Korea).

Ramachandra Bhatta is currently Professor of Fisheries Economics and Head of the Fisheries Sciences Division at Karnataka Veterinary, Animal and Fisheries Sciences University, College of Fisheries, Mangalore. His research interests include economic valuation of marine biodiversity, coastal policy and management, assessment of the impact of development projects and action research on conservation and development.

Debashis Chakraborty is Assistant Professor of Economics at the Indian Institute of Foreign Trade (IIFT), New Delhi. His research interests include WTO Negotiations and Environmental Sustainability.

Ashish Chaturvedi is Senior Technical Expert with the Deutsche Gesellschaft fuer Internationale Zusammenarbeit GmbH, New Delhi. He manages projects related to environmental governance and climate change and he has presented/published papers at various policy forums in India and abroad.

Ierene Francis is a Researcher at the Ecological Economics unit of the Ashoka Trust for Research in Ecology and the Environment, Bangalore. She has obtained her MSc (Economics) from the Madras School of Economics, Anna University and is working on environmental economics issues in India.

Vinish Kathuria is an Associate Professor at the SJM School of Management of the Indian Institute of Technology (IIT), Bombay (India) and has been working on environmental economics and industrial economics for the last two decades.

Ulrike Killguss is currently working as Climate Policy Advisor, Climate Task Force, Environment and Climate Change division of Deutsche Gesellschaft fuer Internationale Zusammenarbeit (GIZ) GmbH. Her research interests include electronic waste management, climate change negotiations and sustainable industrial development.

Bimlesh Kumar is an Assistant Professor at the Department of Civil Engineering, Indian Institute of Technology (IIT), Guwahati (India). His main areas of research are environmental fluid mechanics, sediment transport and energy planning for renewable sources.

M. Dinesh Kumar is Executive Director of Institute for Resource Analysis and Policy (IRAP), Hyderabad, and has worked on water management (technology, institutions and policy) issues in India for last two decades. He is an Associate Editor of the *Water Policy* (an IWA journal).

Sacchidananda Mukherjee is an Assistant Professor of Economics at the National Institute of Public Finance and Policy (NIPFP), New Delhi and has worked on environmental economics, public finance and water resources management issues in India for more than a decade.

Shrabani Mukherjee is an Associate Fellow at the National Council of Applied Economic Research (NCAER), New Delhi, and she works on energy economics.

Achanta Ramakrishna Rao is Professor in the Department of Civil Engineering, Indian Institute of Science (IISc), Bangalore, India. His main areas of research are environmental fluid mechanics and sediment transport.

Prasenjit Sarkhel is an Assistant Professor of Economics at Kalyani University, West Bengal. His research interests include environmental regulations and conservation of natural resources.

S. Srividhya has completed her MSc in Economics from Madras School of Economics, Chennai.

Amita Shah is Professor and Director of the Gujarat Institute of Development Research (GIDR), Ahmedabad. She has been working on issues related to natural resource development with a special focus on dry land agriculture and forestry, environmental impact assessment, gender and environment, agriculture–industry interface, small scale and rural industries, diffusion of technologies, and employment–livelihood issues for more than two decades.

L. Venkatachalam is an Associate Professor at the Madras Institute of Development Studies (MIDS), Chennai. His areas of interest include environmental economics and behavioural economics. He was a Fulbright Senior Researcher at the Department of Agricultural and Resource Economics, University of California, Berkeley, USA.

Foreword

India's policy goal is to achieve a sustained and inclusive GDP growth of 8–10 per cent per annum in order to tackle poverty alleviation and improve the livelihood opportunities of the masses. At present the environmental costs of pollution and natural resource degradation are around 5 per cent of the GDP. It is well known that the poor are more affected by natural resource degradation than the rich because of their greater dependence on natural resources for livelihoods, and they bear the impact of environmental pollution of water, air, and land heavily because of their inability to incur the necessary averting expenditures. Therefore, in order to maintain the economy on a sustainable and inclusive growth path, we must address market failures, government failures and institutional failures which result in environmental pollution and natural resource degradation' and integrate environmental considerations fully into decision making by all economic units.

This book is a compendium of 13 chapters dealing with India's current environmental scenario with suggestions for achieving sustainable development. It is organized in four parts covering agriculture, manufacturing, services and trade. A noteworthy feature of this compendium is that most of the chapters are based on primary data collected by the authors with sound conceptual frameworks and well designed surveys using structured questionnaires. The data are analysed carefully with appropriate quantitative tools – statistical, econometric, social cost–benefit analysis – depending on the nature of the problem under consideration. Each chapter provides information about the institutional setting of the environmental problem, the factors responsible for the environmental pollution/ natural resource degradation, the environmental impact, the expected compliance cost and policy suggestions for sustainable development of the sub-sector. The knowledge generated from these grass-root level studies will be useful not only in filling the empty boxes in environmental accounting, but also for policy makers on what needs to be done to achieve the goal of sustainable development in each sub-sector.

Dr Sacchidananda Mukherjee and Dr Debashis Chakraborty are budding researchers with strong motivation to produce high quality policy-oriented research. I congratulate them for their efforts in bringing out this excellent compilation with a lucid introduction. I am sure this book will fill our gaps in knowledge about sources and extent of pollution/natural resource degradation and also stimulate young researchers to undertake sound applied socio–economic research on local environmental problems. I recommend this scholarly yet readable book for environmental policy makers, researchers in environmental economics and environmental management, and students studying the environmental economics course at Master's level.

U. Sankar
Honorary Professor
Madras School of Economics, Chennai

Acknowledgements

An edited volume is perhaps the best example of teamwork in the academic world. The editors are sincerely grateful to all the contributors of this volume for their constant support at each stage. No word of praise would be enough for them. They have each taken time out of their busy schedules, professional as well as family commitments, to author an extremely well-researched chapter and gladly cooperated on every occasion.

The editors are also extremely grateful to Professor U. Sankar for his constant encouragement, and also for writing the foreword of the present volume. Special thanks go to Professor Asok Barman for the inspirations coming from him from time to time. The enlightening discussions with our colleagues at the National Institute of Public Finance and Policy and the Indian Institute of Foreign Trade are also gratefully acknowledged. The editors are particularly thankful for the constant support from Ms Lam Yong Ling of Routledge, who has kept her faith in our efforts since the proposal stage. Finally we would like to thank our family members for their understanding of our cerebral absence from time to time over the last calendar year!

Sacchidananda Mukherjee
Debashis Chakraborty

Abbreviations

AAA	Analytical and Advisory Assistance, World Bank
ADB	Asian Development Bank
AID	Association for India's Development
AOA	Agreement on Agriculture (under WTO)
AP	Andhra Pradesh
APSRAC	Andhra Pradesh State Remote Sensing Applications Centre
AR	Annual report
ARWSP	Accelerated Rural Water Supply Programme
ASEAN	Association of Southeast Asian Nations
ASEP	Asian Society for Environmental Protection
ATREE	Ashoka Trust for Research in Ecology and the Environment
BAN	Basel Action Network
BAT	Best available technologies
BTA	Border tax adjustment
B/E	Biological/ecological
BFR	Brominated flame retardant
BMP	Best management practice
BMW	Bio-medical wastes
BOD	Biological oxygen demand
Ca	Calcium
CAC	Command and control approach
CAGR	Compound annual growth rate (alternatively compounded annual growth rate)
CAR	Central Asian Republic
CEA	Central Electricity Authority, Government of India
CEPI	Comprehensive Environmental Pollution Index
CERCLA	Comprehensive Environmental Response, Compensation and Liability Act
CETP	Common effluent treatment plant
CFC	Chlorofluorocarbon
CGWB	Central Ground Water Board, Government of India
CH_4	Methane
CIBA	Central Institute of Brackishwater

CIESIN	Center for International Earth Science Information Network
CIFT	Central Institute of Fisheries Technology
CIWMB	California Integrated Waste Management Board
CMFRI	Central Marine Fisheries Research Institute
CNG	Compressed natural gas
CO	Carbon monoxide
CO_2	Carbon dioxide
CO_{2e}	Carbon dioxide equivalent
COD	Chemical oxygen demand
CPCB	Central Pollution Control Board
CPHEEO	Central Public Health and Environmental Engineering Organization
CPP	Captive Power Plant
CPUE	Catch per unit effort
CRES	Centre for Resource and Environmental Studies
CRT	Cathode ray tube
CRZ	Coastal regulation zone
CSE	Centre for Science and Environment
CSO	Central Statistical Organization
CV	Coal vision
CWC	Central Water Commission
CZMP	Coastal zone management plan
DDWS	Department of Drinking Water Supply, Government of India
DIL	Direct industrial licences
DIPP	Department of Industrial Policy and Promotion
DISHA	Direct Initiative for Social and Health Action
DO	Dissolved oxygen
DSD	*Duales System Deutschland GmbH* (Dual System Germany GmbH)
DSM	Demand side management
DSR	Distribution system rehabilitation
DWAF	Department of Water Affairs and Forestry, South Africa
EAP	Environment Action Programme
EAERE	European Association of Environmental and Resource Economists
EC	European Community
EEE	Electronic and electrical equipments
EIA	Environmental impact assessments
EIP	Eco-Industrial Parks
EKC	Environmental Kuznets Curve
E/O	Economical/operational
EPA	Environmental Protection Agency
EPI	Environmental Performance Index
EPR	Extended producer responsibility
ES	Environmental classification

ESG	Environmentally sensitive good
ESI	Environmental Sustainability Index
ETS	Effluent treatment system
EU	European Union
FAO	Food and Agricultural Organization of UN
FDA	Forest Development Agency
FDI	Foreign direct investment
Fe	Iron
FYM	Farmyard manure
GAP	Ganga Action Plan
GATT	General Agreement on Tariffs and Trade
GDI	Gender-sensitive Development Index
GDP	Gross domestic product
GEP	Ganga Expressway Project
GFCF	Gross fixed capital formation
Gg	Gigagram (10^9 gram or 1,000 tonne)
GHG	Greenhouse gas
GMO	Genetically modified organism
GNP	Gross national product
GoI	Government of India
GR	Green revolution
Gt	Gigatonne
GTZ	Deutsche Gesellschaft fuer Technische Zusammenarbeit (GTZ) GmbH (in English German Society for Technical Cooperation)
Gw	Gigawatt
HACCP	Hazard analysis critical control point
HDR	Human development report
HSMD	Hazardous Substances Management Division
HTL	High tide line
HYV	High yielding variety
ICAM	Integrated coastal area management
ICAR	Indian Council for Agricultural Research
ICM	Integrated Coastal Management
ICMAM	Integrated Coastal and Marine Area Management
IDRC	International Development Research Centre
IEA	International energy agency
IEM	Industrial entrepreneur memorandum
IETP	Individual effluent treatment plant
IGES	Institute for Global Environmental Strategies
IGIDR	Indira Gandhi Institute of Development Research
IGNP	Indira Gandhi Nehar Yojna
IHD	Institute for Human Development
IIED	International Institute for Environment and Development
IIT	Indian Institute of Technology
IMF	International Monetary Fund

INCCA	Indian Network for Climate Change Assessment
INCOIS	Indian National Centre for Ocean Information Services
IPCC	Intergovernmental Panel on Climate Change
ISI	Indian Standard Institute (renamed Bureau of Indian Standards, BIS)
IT	Information technology
IUWM	Integrated urban water management
IWMI	International Water Management Institute
IWRM	Integrated water resources management
IUFRO	International Union of Forest Research Organizations
IUSM	Integrated urban storm water management
JCAHO	Joint Commission for the Accreditation of Hospitals and Healthcare Organizations
JCI	Joint Commission International
JFMC	Joint Forest Management Committee
K	Potash
kWh	Kilowatt-hour
LBP	Lower Bhavani Project
LBR	Lower Bhavani River
LDC	Less developed country
LEA	Loss of ecology authority
LEIA	Lift and Escalator Industry Association
LNG	Liquefied Natural Gas
LOI	Letters of intent
LPCD	Litre per Capita per Day
LPUE	Landing per unit effort
LULUCF	Land use, land use change and forestry
MAIT	Manufacturers' Association of Information Technology
MBI	Market-based instrument
MDG	Millennium development goal
MEA	Multilateral Environmental Agreement
MEY	Maximum economic yield
Mg	Magnesium
Mld	Million litre per day
Mn	Manganese
MNC	Multi national corporation
MOCP	Marginal opportunity cost of production
MoEF	Ministry of Environment and Forests, Government of India
MPEDA	Marine Products Export Development Authority
MPP	Mini Power Pump
MSE	Madras School of Economics
MSME	Micro, Small and Medium Enterprise
MSP	Minimum support price
MSW	Municipal solid waste
MSWMH	Municipal Solid Waste Management and Handling

MSY	Maximum sustainable yield
MT	Metric tonne
MW	Megawatt
N	Nitrogen
NAAS	National Academy of Agricultural Sciences
NACA	Network of Aquaculture Centres in Asia
NAP	National Afforestation Programme
NAPCC	National Action Plan on Climate Change
NCR	National capital region
NCRPB	National Capital Region Planning Board
NEAA	National Environment Appellate Authority
NEERI	National Environmental Engineering Research Institute
NEP	National Environment Policy, Government of India
NGO	Non-governmental organization
NHS	National Habitations Survey
NIC	National Informatics Centre
NIUA	National Institute of Urban Affairs
NO	Nitric oxide
NO_x	Nitrogen oxides
NO_2	Nitrite
NO_3	Nitrate
NO_3-N	Nitrate-nitrogen
NPK	Nitrogen, phosphorous, potash
NPS	Nonpoint source
NPV	Net present value
NRCH	Natural Resource Curse Hypothesis
NRCP	National River Conservation Project
NRSA	National Remote Sensing Agency
OECD	Organization for Economic Co-operation and Development
OHS	Occupational health and safety
P	Phosphorous
P/C	Physical/chemical
PCA	Productivity change approach
PCB	Poli-Chlorinated Biphenyls
PCC	Pulverized Coal Combustion
PCI	Per capita income
PDS	Public distribution system
pH	Potential hydrogen
PH	Porter Hypothesis
PHH	Pollution Haven Hypothesis
PRO	Producer responsibility organization
PVC	Polyvinyl chlorides
PWD	Public works department
RC	Replacement cost
RCA	Replacement cost approach

RCRA	Resource Conservation and Recycling Act
REACH	Registration, evaluation, authorization and restriction of chemical substances
RGNDWM	Rajiv Gandhi National Drinking Water Mission
RIAM	Rapid impact assessment matrix
RSPM	Respirable suspended particulate matter
RTP	Rural town panchayat
S	Sulphur
SADA	Shore Area Development Authority
SAP	Structural adjustment programme/policies
S/C	Sociological/cultural
SCPS	Super Critical Power Station
SDT	Special and differential treatment
SERI	Sustainable Europe Research Institute
SIA	Secretariat for Industrial Assistance
SIDA	Swedish International Development Agency
SIDBI	Small Industries Development Bank of India
SIWI	Stockholm International Water Institute
SMC	Surat Municipal Corporation
SME	Small and Medium Enterprise
SMF	Sundaram Medical Foundation
SO	Sulphur oxide
SO_2	Sulphur dioxide
SO_x	Sulphur oxides
SOM	Soil organic matter
SPCB	State pollution control board
SPM	Suspended particulate materials
SPS	Sanitary and phytosanitary measures
SPV	Special Purpose Vehicle
SSI	Small Scale Industry
SSLUO	Soil Survery and Land Use Organization
STEP	Solving the E-waste problem
TBT	Technical barriers to trade
TDS	Total dissolved solids
TED	Turtle excluder device
TEDDY	TERI Energy Data Directory and Yearbook
TEI	Thailand Environmental Institute
TERI	The Energy and Resources Institute
TFP	Total factor productivity
Tg	Teragram (10^3 gigagram)
TN	Tamil Nadu
TNPCB	Tamil Nadu Pollution Control Board
TPG	Thermal power generation
TPP	Thermal power plant
TSDF	Treatment, storage and disposal facility

TWAD	Tamil Nadu Water Supply and Drainage Board
UAE	United Arab Emirates
UK	United Kingdom
ULB	Urban local body
UN	United Nations
UNCED	United Nations Conference on Environment and Development
UNDP	United Nations Development Programme
UNEP	United Nations Environment Programme
UNFCC	United Nations Framework Convention on Climate Change
UP	Uttar Pradesh
VA	Voluntary approach
VP	Village panchayat
WB	West Bengal
WCD	World Commission on Dams
WDR	World Development Report
WEE	Waste Electrical and Electronic Equipments
WELL	Water and Environmental Health at London and Loughborough
WEO	World Energy Outlook
WHO	World Health Organization
WRI	World Resources Institute
WSD	White spot disease
WSP	Water and Sanitation Programme, The World Bank
WTO	World Trade Organization
WWF	World Wildlife Fund
WWT	Wastewater treatment
YAP	Yamuna Action Plan
YCELP	Yale Center for Environmental Law and Policy

Editors' introduction

The Indian growth story: towards a sustainable development?

Sacchidananda Mukherjee and Debashis Chakraborty

India's journey to prosperity: explosive growth or sustainable development?

Development economics literature clearly underlines the difference between economic 'growth' and 'development'. 'Economic growth' occurs with mere improvement of key indicators in a macro sense, e.g. augmentation of real national income, gross domestic product (GDP), per capita income (PCI), etc. However, 'economic development' takes place when improvements in GDP or PCI are associated with improvements in human development, quality of life, reduction in environmental degradation, infrastructure augmentation, etc. The received wisdom is that, defining economic achievements only with respect to broad economic indicators like GDP growth may in the long run create adverse repercussions and endanger sustainable development in a country.

India, with its unique development experience, provides a classic example in this regard. The country witnessed a sluggish growth rate for four decades in the period preceding the structural adjustment programme (SAP) initiated in 1991, which facilitated major trade and industrial policy reforms. As a result, the archaic import-substituting economic growth model was replaced by an export-promotion led growth philosophy. The resulting policy reform helped India to double its share in global merchandise export from 0.62 per cent in 1999 to 1.3 per cent in 2009, while its share in global service export increased from 1 per cent to 2.61 per cent over the same period. The continuous reforms undertaken by India's trade partners since the Uruguay Round of General Agreement on Tariffs and Trade (GATT) and later as part of their World Trade Organization (WTO) commitments contributed significantly in this regard. Moreover, the inflow of imports in the country increased considerably owing to India's tariff and procedural reforms since initiation of the SAP. As a result, the country has integrated itself closely with the global production network, resulting in greater trade flows, including trade flows in intermediate and semi-processed goods across categories.

The stability of Indian growth paradigm has been critically tested during the recent global recession, and the near 8 per cent growth even in this turbulent period vindicated its strength. The country's growth path is likely to be maintained in the future as well, given several qualitative changes taking place in the economy. First, India traditionally has been a labour-surplus economy, with a dearth of productive capital and technical expertise. The problem of capital accumulation witnessed in the pre-SAP period has been solved to a considerable extent, with a vibrant entrepreneur class fast emerging. The foreign direct investment (FDI) coming from abroad has also played a crucial role in this regard. Second, development of the critical infrastructure in terms of road, port and power network with private partnership has further widened the growth potential. The tier-two Indian cities, recently better connected with existing growth centres and ports, are driving the growth engine with enormous potential. Third, the knowledge of English and presence of a relatively young workforce has provided India a huge 'demographic dividend'. Buoyed by this edge, knowledge-intensity of the service sector has increased, which is partially reflected in the continuous double digit growth experienced by this sector. Hence the more crucial question in the present context is, whether this 'economic growth' is being translated into 'economic development', in particular with respect to environmental sustainability.

The existing literature indicates that the environmental sustainability of a country/region can be influenced by economic growth or vice versa through several routes. First, analysing the relationship between income level of a country and its environmental sustainability (Cole *et al.* 1997), the Environmental Kuznets Curve (EKC) hypothesis notes that a growing income level beyond a threshold might be associated with demand for a better environment and the consequent adoption of a superior governance mechanism (e.g. better pollution abatement practices). Second, the Pollution Haven Hypothesis (PHH) explores the depth of the trade–investment–environmental degradation nexus in a country, i.e. whether the FDI flow in a country is directed more towards the pollution-intensive sectors/regions and influencing the production pattern negatively (Cole *et al.* 2011). Third, the Natural Resource Curse Hypothesis (NRCH) proposes a negative relationship between resource endowment and growth scenario in a country (Dietz *et al.* 2007). In other words, countries with a rich resource base often witness lower growth experience. Finally, the Porter Hypothesis (PH) deals with the micro perspective on the environmental regulation and competitiveness of a firm, arguing that stringent environmental regulation (under the condition that it is efficient) could lead to technological innovation in firms, thereby enhancing their competitiveness (Porter 1991). At a macro level, the PH effect is likely to be growth-augmenting.

So, which environmental effect so far dominates India's growth path? Before going into micro perspectives, a macro overview would not be inappropriate here. The Environmental Sustainability Index (ESI) published by the Center for International Earth Science Information Network (CIESIN), Columbia University and the Yale Center for Environmental Law and Policy (YCELP) reveals that in 2001 India was ranked ninety-third among 122 countries with a composite score of 40.9, which changed to 101st among 146 countries in 2005 while its ESI score improved to 45.2. After 2005, CIESIN and YCELP have been publishing Environmental Performance Index (EPI) instead. It is observed that in 2006, India was ranked 118th among 133 countries, with an EPI score of 47.7. In 2010, India registered a marginal growth in its EPI index (48.3), while its relative rank improved to 123rd among 163 countries. In other words, India's performance looks quite humble on this front.

Estimation of the EKC hypothesis at the cross-state level is a well-researched area in the Indian context. Since time series data on various pollutants are not available for Indian States, the estimations have generally produced cross section models (Mukherjee and Kathuria 2006; Mukherjee and Chakraborty 2009; Mythili and Mukherjee 2011; Managi and Jena, 2008). The results indicate that states register high economic growth at the cost of their environmental quality. Evidently economic growth alone cannot take care of the consequent environmental degradation.

The key concern that emerges from this observation is which factors constrain better environmental performance in India? It is difficult to arrive at a direct answer to the question, as every development initiative is notionally associated with potential environmental repercussions as well. For instance, on the agricultural front a major concern for Indian policymakers during the 1960s was ensuring food security for the masses. The scenario improved considerably in the aftermath of introducing the irrigation-dependent green revolution (GR) policy, but the development came at a high cost of groundwater depletion in various pockets of major agricultural states like Punjab (Sidhu 2002). Second, fertilizer and insecticide usage in India increased multiple times as a result of the GR, with potential harmful implications for water pollution and human health through a biological magnification effect (Mukherjee 2008). For instance, India was initially not in favour of banning the insecticide endosulfan at the recent discussion under the Stockholm Convention in April 2011. Third, it was agreed to ban the insecticide over an 11-year period, after it was isolated at the negotiating forum (Haq *et al.* 2011). Fourth, the presence of low capital formation and a high volume of wastage due to the lack of a direct marketing network, paved the way for contract farming and other innovative forms of farmer–corporate house direct linkage in recent years. However, the time to decisively comment on maintaining environmental sustainability from these arrangements is yet to come. Finally, an internal debate is growing on the desirability of allowing the cultivation of genetically modified crops for enhancing agricultural productivity. The cultivation of Bt cotton has been allowed more by an accident, with the cultivation preceding the permission. However, the strong protest against cultivation of Bt brinjal shows growing concerns over environmental sustainability (Haq 2010).

The industrial growth process in India has been associated with their share of 'cleanliness' issues. The liberalization measures following SAP removed the industrial licensing requirement for all industries, barring defence-related ones, thereby increasing the number of players in the market. The consequent growth in the number of firms increased the degree of competition, leading to efficiency as well as emissions, and tackling the latter emerged as a major challenge. The government network for regular inspection of the operational units in 17 polluting industries[1] has been expanded over the period. While the 1997–98 Ministry of Environment and Forests (MoEF) inspection covered 1,551 such units, the number increased to 2,678 in 2005–06 and the proportional number of defaulting units were gradually controlled (Chakraborty 2009). Nevertheless, several concern areas propelled by economic growth remained. For instance, the illegal mining of coal, iron and steel to fuel the growth engine has emerged as a serious challenge, despite government alertness on this front. Similar problems arise from coal mining in general as well (Krishnamurthy 2004). Second, the growth of the intra-industry trade has also enhanced the volume of imports for recycling. The increased import of second-hand lead acid batteries and other similar waste and scrap products can be noted in this regard. Third, the cheap labour cost has helped Alang port in India to emerge as a major global ship-breaking hub, with environmental consequences. Fourth, increasing computerization has also generated an astounding volume of electronic waste in the country, the recycling of which poses a severe environmental challenge in various parts. Finally, the presence of a largely unregulated and dispersed unorganized manufacturing sector with limited financial ability considerably constrains the ability of the regulators to enforce sustainable production methods (D'Souza 2001).

The fast-growing tertiary sector is also not necessarily environment-friendly all the time. For instance, the health infrastructure in the country has improved considerably, but the growing population and medical tourism increases the pressure on this sector. Careful disposal of medical waste, which has grown many-fold over the last decade, is one of the newer challenges being faced by the country. A similar problem is being observed with respect to the tourism sector as well, where growing pressure of the tourist inflow might render the ecology vulnerable. Finally, the rapid urbanization drive both in the metropolitan cities and tier-two towns with the growth in construction service has been achieved at a heavy expense, as the water table is steadily receding in various parts including the national capital region (NCR).[2]

The recent infrastructure augmentation drive in the country has played a key role in connecting the relatively backward regions with growth hubs, but not without environmental shortcomings. It has often been alleged that the infrastructure projects (including road, dam or power generation) have been implemented without detailed environmental accounting. For instance, the 1,047 km long Ganga Expressway Project (GEP) launched in Uttar Pradesh in 2007 connecting the eastern and western boundaries of the state can be quoted here. Once completed, the project would ensure an eight-lane expressway running along the Ganga River, but in the process destroying thousands of trees and natural habitats of several animal species. Second, the experience of the Sardar Sarovar Dam on the Narmada river as a part of the Narmada Valley Project can be considered here as a representative example. While the benefits in terms of the irrigation network and hydroelectric infrastructure creation would be significant, the environmental adverse impacts are not to be trivialized. The second interim report (2010) of the Experts' Committee set up by MoEF has reported that compliance with various environmental parameters has been highly unsatisfactory (AID 2010). It is feared that future infrastructure initiatives may also suffer from similar shortcomings. For instance, in 2010 the nuclear power plants in India generated 4,780 MW power, which is expected to reach 63,000 MW by 2032 through the construction of newer plants. However, the environmental consequences are being questioned, especially in the aftermath of the Fukushima nuclear power plant in Okuma, Japan. Disposal of the generated nuclear waste would be another problem (Ramana *et al.* 2001).

Insufficiency of legal framework?

The environmental degradation witnessed and being projected in the country is not the result of the lack of environmental regulations, but rather by insufficient enforcement of them. The legal framework on environmental pollution in India is quite comprehensive. The Water (Prevention and Control of Pollution) Act (1974) was among the earlier regulations in India to protect the domestic environment, which was instrumental in the creation of the central and state pollution control boards (CPCB and SPCBs) for the prevention of water pollution. The framework was subsequently strengthened through the Water (Prevention and Control of Pollution) Rules and the Water (Prevention and Control of Pollution) Cess Act in 1975 and 1977 respectively. The Air (Prevention and Control of Pollution) Act of 1981 empowered the CPCB and its state counterparts to deal with air pollution, with the right to investigate and impose penalties. The Rules under the Forest (Conservation) Act of 1980 were notified in 1981, which restricts the state governments or other authorities from encouraging activities like de-reservation, leasing of forest land to private initiatives, etc. without the approval of central government. In a related context, the Wild Life (Protection) Act of 1972 empowers the state governments to declare specific areas as 'sanctuaries', 'national parks', 'game reserves', etc. and bans the hunting of wild animals (with a few exceptions) and trade in wild animals and animal articles (Antony 2001).

The Environment (Protection) Act of 1986 is the most relevant provision, it enables the government to implement all measures necessary to protect and improve the quality of the environment. The provisions enable the government to determine the permissible level of emissions or discharge of pollutants from various sources and to order the closure of any plant or modification of its production process if it is found in violation of prescribed norms. To supplement this framework, the National Environment Appellate Authority (NEAA) has been established under the National Environment Appellate Authority Act (1997) for hearing concerned appeals (Antony 2001). Environmental clearance is provided to the industries under this Act.[3]

Among other environment-related policies under the MoEF, the National Forest Policy (1988), National Conservation Strategy and Policy Statement on Environment and Development (1992), Policy Statement on Abatement of Pollution (1992), National Water Policy (2002), etc. deserve special mention. However National Environment Policy (NEP) 2006 can be considered as the most important policy document in the current context. NEP is an attempt by the government for securing a holistic approach in environmental policymaking as the document seeks to ensure deeper coordination between the existing policies. Ensuring human well-being, especially people dependent on a particular environmental resource, through their conservation is the central point of the NEP. It also intends to encourage partnerships of different stakeholders like public agencies, local communities, academic and scientific institutions and international development partners for securing their respective forte for environmental management (MoEF 2006).

The philosophy of the NEP is guided by 'precautionary approach', as prescribed by the Cartagena Protocol on Biosafety (2003). According to the principle, if credible threats of irreversible damage to key environmental resources exist, lack of full scientific knowledge should not limit government's ability to prevent environmental degradation. The NEP also relies heavily on the economic efficiency argument, the polluter pays principle and cost minimization becomes the two cornerstones, under this provision. The former principle makes the polluter responsible for bearing the cost of pollution with due regard to the public interest without disrupting normal trade and international investment flows. The latter principle in the broader sense ensures environmental governance by streamlining processes and procedures in order to minimize costs and delays (MoEF 2006). Presently the government intends to prevent pollution through a combination of regulations, legislations, agreements, fiscal instruments,[4] preparing a zoning atlas for deciding locations of industries based on environmental considerations, setting up of waste minimization circles, etc. (MoEF AR various issues).

The 'greening' of the industrial sector in India has received considerable support from judicial interventions from time to time (Antony 2001). The mandatory introduction of common effluence treatment plants (CETPs) in the leather sector in Tamil Nadu as a result of farmer complaints of groundwater pollution can be mentioned in this regard. Similarly in one instance in West Bengal, the Green Bench ordered the closure of 30 large industries, including nine transnational corporations, and also imposed daily fines on the defaulting companies through the non-exercised Environmental (Protection) Act, 1986 until the installation of pollution abatement equipment (Lal and Jha 1999).

Apart from the unilateral actions, the imposition of trade sanctions by partners has also helped several environmentally sensitive sectors in India to upgrade to a 'greener' and 'cleaner' production process. For instance, the US sanction on import of Indian shrimp and shrimp products on the grounds that the fishing nets that are used by the trawlers also kill turtles, an endangered species, could be cited here (WTO DS Case 58). Though the WTO Dispute Settlement Panel ruled that the United States indeed imposed the measure in a WTO-inconsistent manner, the basic principle underlying the sanction was not entirely rejected. Following the dispute, the Marine Product Export Development Authority (MPEDA) was entrusted with the introduction and promotion of turtle excluder devices (TEDs) in Indian fishing vessels, and shortly afterwards the commercial production of TED, designed by Central Institute of Fisheries Technology (CIFT) was introduced (Chakraborty 2009).

Towards improvement?

Will the recent procedural changes following NEP (2006) be instrumental in improving environmental governance in India? There is a need to understand that any static policy regime would never solve the environmental challenges faced by the country. India is presently home to around 16.7 per cent of the global population, while it accounts for only 2.4 per cent of its land area, thereby putting tremendous pressure on existing diverse natural resources. Therefore, only a dynamic and constantly evolving framework can respond to the pressing challenges. A quick overview of air pollution, water pollution, land (soil) and forest degradation in the country supports this contention.

The major reasons behind air pollution in India include developmental activities at various levels including emissions from vehicular, industrial and domestic activities. Air quality of the major cities/towns is regularly monitored with respect to several criteria of pollutants (SO_2, nitrite (NO_2), suspended particulate matter (SPM), respirable SPM (RSPM)) by state pollution control boards (SPCBs) and the number of monitoring stations for this purpose is increasing over the period. It is observed from various annual reports (AR) of MoEF that the percentage of cities with relatively lower SO_2 and NO_2 emission is increasing, but there is ample scope to improve SPM and RSPM emissions control. The *State of the Environment Report* (2009) published by MoEF noted that a significant proportion of the premature deaths in the world owing to outdoor and indoor air pollution occurs in India.

Three concern areas do remain in this context. First, total absolute emissions of carbon dioxide (CO_2) from the power sector in India have increased from 382.31 million tonne per year in 2000–01 to the corresponding figure of 495.54 in 2006–07. However, the high capital costs associated with replacement by cleaner technology are likely to delay closure for many of India's highly polluting coal-fired power plants. As a result, CO_2 emissions from India may increase at least in the near future. This puts India in an uncomfortable position in international negotiations, apart from domestic concerns.[5] Second, rural air pollution is another concern area. Total emissions calculated from wheat crop residue burning as reported in MoEF (2009) noted that in May 2005 the activity contributed to about 113 gigagram (Gg) of CO (carbon monoxide), 8.6 Gg of NO_x, 1.33 Gg of CH_4 (methane), 13 Gg of PM_{10} (smoke) and 12 Gg of $PM_{2.5}$. Similarly, the estimated emissions from burning paddy fields were 261 Gg of CO, 19.8 Gg of NO (nitric oxide), 3 Gg of CH_4, 30 Gg of PM_{10} and 28.3 Gg of $PM_{2.5}$ during October 2005. Indoor air pollution due to combustion of biomass fuels (wood, dung and crop residues) and coal among rural households in India is a major health concern for women and children (Balakrishnan *et al.* 2004). Making the rural population aware of best environmental practices would be a major challenge for the government. Finally, to mitigate vehicular pollution, the government has regularly upgraded the auto fuel policy by introducing a globally compatible standard (e.g. Bharat Stage IV equivalent to EURO IV, etc.) for cities and towns in India. Among other measures the greater use of compressed natural gas (CNG) as fuel can be quoted (Narain 2008). However, after the introduction of CNG in Delhi, the ambient concentration of CO has gone down significantly, whereas NO_x has gone up and concentrations of SPM and PM_{10} have gone down marginally (Kathuria 2004). Nevertheless the growing number of vehicles as a result of urbanization makes effective control of air pollution a challenging exercise (Kathuria 2002; Sinha 1993).

The pollution of water resources, both surface and groundwater, poses another challenge. The Central Water Commission (CWC) monitors the surface water quality across major rivers in India, through 123 water flow cum water quality monitoring stations and another 218 water flow cum silt cum water quality monitoring stations. The CPCB also monitors the surface water quality of rivers and tanks across states as well as medium and minor river basins and lakes under the Monitoring of Indian National Aquatic Resources programme. Though the findings are regularly published, the time lag between observation and publication of the report is around two to three years, which makes the reports outdated, and the consequent policy response inadequate. The growing pollution in rivers, especially through release of wastewater from industries along the riverbank has caused the government to initiate the National River Conservation Project (NRCP) recently, which covers 165 towns along polluted stretches of 36 rivers spread over 20 states (Maria 2003). For instance, the Ganga Action Plan (GAP) and Yamuna Action Plan (YAP) under the NRCP have created a sewage treatment capacity of 869 Mld (million litre per day) and 753 Mld respectively (MoEF AR various issues).

A similar scenario is observed in the case of groundwater pollution, which has increased considerably in recent periods, owing to several reasons including excessive use of fertilizer, unsustainable industrial wastewater disposal, mining activities, etc. (CPCB undated). The ramifications are far-reaching. First, 25 million people residing in 8,700 villages spread over 17 states in India are affected by fluorosis, caused by excess fluoride in groundwater and the scenario is particularly dire in populous states like Uttar Pradesh, Rajasthan, Gujarat, Andhra Pradesh and Tamil Nadu. Second, arsenic pollution in groundwater has emerged as a major concern in several populous districts of West Bengal, where an approximately $34,000 \, km^2$ area is witnessing a high concentration of arsenic in drinking water abstracted from tubewells. Third, nitrate pollution in groundwater is being observed in several parts of India, and the problem is quite acute in another densely populated state, Maharashtra, with a number of areas showing a nitrate content above the permissible limit. Last but not the least; the problem of groundwater pollution is magnified by the indiscriminate disposal of untreated industrial effluent, sewage and garbage associated with increasing urbanization in all parts of the country (CPCB undated, Mukherjee and Nelliyat 2007). Clearly there is room for greater vigilance by all agencies involved in preventing groundwater pollution; namely, the Central Ground Water Board, State Groundwater Departments, Public Works Department, water supply agencies, Public Health Engineering Department, etc.

Land degradation is another area of concern for India at present, owing both to natural as well as man-made reasons. In India approximately 144 million ha of land are affected by wind or water erosion. Also 15 per cent of the world's cattle and 46 per cent of the world's buffalo are present in India, which leads to severe overgrazing (FAO undated). Other factors responsible for land degradation could be linked with the level of development among a major section of the farming community, i.e. a lesser degree of exposure to best farm practices. The reasons include growing pressure on land as a result of population growth and increased use of pesticides and fertilizers, improper crop rotation, improper planning and management of irrigation systems (Reddy 2003). In addition, disturbances of hydrological equilibrium from inefficient use of irrigation water, seepage from unlined water courses, poor drainage, etc. also increases salinity in the soil and causes degradation (MoEF AR various issues). The land degradation process often escalates with deforestation, as rain then infiltrates the soil which in turn encourages erosion. This in turn leads to increasing sedimentation in rivers and blocks navigable waterways, leading to newer environmental and developmental problems (Iyenger 2003).

Finally, population pressure is felt most intensely in the forest sector, considered to be the lungs of a country. MoEF AR (2001) notes that per capita forest land in India is only 0.08 ha as compared to the requirement of 0.47 ha to meet basic needs. As a result, the pressure of timber, firewood, and fodder extraction from the forests is often unsustainable (Davidar *et al.* 2010; Reddy *et al.* 2001). For instance, in India an average of 42 animals graze in a hectare of land against the threshold level of five animals per hectare (Sahay 2000). MoEF AR (2001) noted that approximately 100 million cows graze in forests against a sustainable level of 31 million per annum. The occurrence of frequent forest fires in many parts of the country poses another major challenge. The receding forest cover also bears crucial implications for maintaining the biodiversity, including the survival of species like rhinoceros or tigers. Both species are presently vulnerable to loss of natural habitat as well as poaching.

The country has adopted various steps to protect its forest cover in recent period. First, it has taken extensive measures to protect its mangrove forests in coastal regions, which provides safety to coastal ecology. Though the Tsunami in December 2004 destroyed a major proportion of the mangrove cover in Andaman and Nicobar Islands, the mangrove cover in the rest of the country has improved considerably. Second, in the earlier period afforestation was considered to be a government responsibility. Since 2000–01, 795 Forest Development Agencies (FDAs) have been operationalized under the National Afforestation Programme (NAP). FDAs function as a federation of Joint Forest Management Committees (JFMCs) at the Forest Division level to protect the forests with people's participation, both in planning and implementation, to improve forests and livelihoods of the people living in and around forest areas (MoEF AR various issues). It is expected that the introduction of JFM would provide long-term solutions to long-standing problems like unsustainable fuelwood and fodder extraction, encroachment into forest lands, forest fires and overgrazing.

The current volume

The above discussion clearly underlines the environmental consequence of development in India. Given this background, the basic objective of the current book is to capture the impacts of various sectoral activities on the environment by using simple methodology available within the discipline of environmental economics through empirical/primary survey-based case studies. Several case studies included in this volume attempt to capture the environmental costs of various economic activities according to the fate of pollutants through alternative perspectives – e.g. 'cost of inaction' and 'cost of replacement'. In line with the concerns raised earlier, the chapters are arranged within four parts; namely, agriculture, manufacturing, services and trade, to distinguish the environmental dynamics in each of them.

The chapters in the volume focus on the environmental impacts of agriculture, fisheries (both inland – shrimp culture – and marine fisheries), generation of electricity (thermal power and hydropower), service sectors (water supply for urban areas, municipal solid waste (MSW) disposal, biomedical waste (BMW) disposal and electronic waste recycling) and the environmental impacts of trade (on agriculture and the existence of PHH). While several case studies have been conducted in Tamil Nadu, a state characterized by vibrant agricultural, manufacturing and service sectors; other studies have focused on the Indian scenario as a whole. The sectoral analysis provides a deeper insight to the environmental concerns as compared to analysing the environmental status of various environmental media where pollutants are actually received – say, water (surface water and groundwater), land and air.

Pollution abatement strategies for water resources in India and other developing countries have given priority to point sources of pollution. However, it is becoming increasingly evident that improvement of quality of surface and groundwater requires pollution control from nonpoint sources (NPS) as well. Controlling NPS pollution is particularly crucial in rural areas where groundwater is an important source of drinking water. Chapter 1 by Sacchidananda Mukherjee notes that in several parts of India, growing access to irrigation facilities along with unbalanced and overuse of nitrogenous fertilizers, unlined and open storage of livestock wastes, and insanitary disposal of human wastes have led to a high concentration of nitrate in groundwater. The survey covers six villages in the Lower Bhavani River basin in Tamil Nadu for analysing long-term groundwater nitrate concentrations and sources of irrigation. The results indicate that farmers' perceptions of risks related to groundwater nitrate pollution vary across the villages, and mimic the actual groundwater nitrate situation. Estimated results of binary choice Probit models show that households depending on their socio-economic characteristics, social- and information-network and the characteristics of the resource derive a subjective risk perception about their groundwater quality. Moreover, farmers' knowledge about impacts of agricultural practices on groundwater quality significantly influences their perceptions about groundwater quality and willingness to protect groundwater.

Coastal shrimp aquaculture has evolved as a major economic activity in Andhra Pradesh, contributing significantly to the income and employment of the region through forward and backward linkages. However, failure to integrate shrimp farming with other livelihood activities and undermining the externalities of shrimp farming on ecology and socio-economic aspects have led to many problems, including off-site and on-site water pollution. Chapter 2 by Ramchandra Bhatta attempts to evaluate the growth of shrimp farming and suggest suitable methods to integrate this with other activities and resources of coastal areas. Reviewing the existing organizational and institutional structure and the gaps in the decision support system, the analysis recommends various institutional measures for improvement. The need to develop a comprehensive integrated coastal land use plan is strongly felt, which should consolidate the responsibilities and powers of more than a half dozen ministries and authorities. The proposed unified authority vested with powers to direct a meaningful policy supported by stakeholders' interests will improve the performance of the sector. In addition, internalization of the external costs of developing sustainable shrimp farming based on scientific principles is argued essential in determining the optimum land allocation for shrimp farming.

Once thought to be inexhaustible, several species of marine fish and other sea creatures are now feared to reach extinction over next few decades and hence their conservation to maintain biodiversity is obtaining greater attention. As mentioned earlier with respect to the India–US shrimp–turtle dispute, trade partners like the United States have at times imposed unilateral sanctions on imports on this basis. In other words, both internal realization and external compulsions in the recent period have played crucial roles in ensuring best fishing practices in developing countries like India. The trawl net is the most destructive type of fishing gear, and a temporary ban on trawling during the monsoon is thought to allow fish stocks to rejuvenate. The third chapter by Ierene Francis notes the environmental consequences of mechanized trawling and attempts to evaluate the effects of an annual 45-day ban on trawling on the Tamil Nadu coastal region. The chapter analyses the effect of the ban in light of fish landings, change in the landings' composition and the ratios of landings to effort. The results on changes in the composition of landings are varied, but identify no significant evidence for an increase in fish catch due to the ban. The finding indicates that either the 45-day ban period is insufficient for fish to breed and rejuvenate, or the difficulties in regulation of mesh size of trawler nets might undo any benefits the ban brings into place.

Industrial pollution in India is on the rise, despite the recent introduction of policies for ensuring greater abatement. Such pollution in a fertile river basin can produce far-reaching consequences, given the potential negative repercussions on cultivated crops and water resources. Chapter 4 by L. Venkatachalam deals with two aspects of the economics of 'not' controlling pollution in the context of industrial pollution in the Noyyal River Basin in Tamil Nadu, India. First, within the conventional social cost–benefit setting, it attempts to estimate the economic value of agricultural damage caused by an act of 'not' controlling industrial pollution, and compares this value with the economic cost of control-ling the same ex-ante. The findings suggest that the value of reduced agricultural damage is greater than the cost of controlling pollution and therefore, it is con-cluded that controlling pollution is Pareto efficient. Second, within the 'non-conventional' institutional setting, this chapter analyses the 'economic reasons' for pollution 'not' having been controlled in the past, despite the existence of potential Pareto improvements in the system. The chapter demonstrates that poli-cymaking in this sphere still suffers considerably from moral hazard and adverse selection.

Power sectors in developing countries, especially traditional coal-based sectors, are generally major contributors to environmental degradation owing to flying ash, CO_2 and other harmful emissions. India unfortunately is not an exception to this trend. Therefore assessment of the costs of environmental degradation of energy generation is very important for policy analysis on one hand and ensuring proper management of the environment on the other. An attempt is made in Chapter 5 by Shrabani Mukherjee to analyse the environmental costs of coal-based thermal power generation in India. The study initially covers the background to the thermal energy generation process, energy efficiency in production, greenhouse gas (GHG) emissions and its repercussions on the global environment. It then attempts to eval-uate the status of current emissions from total thermal energy generation in India. Finally, on the basis of the observations, policy prescriptions for immediate action to slow down and stabilize the concentration of GHG emissions to eventually reach sustainable development are drawn.

The removal of topsoil for urban uses, mainly for brick-making, is growing rapidly due to increased urbanization and industrialization in many developing countries including India. Unfortunately, brick kilns are mostly situated on fertile agricultural land, as brick manufacturers need silty clay loam to silty clay soils with good drainage conditions. As a result, environmental degradation is unavoidable. Under this backdrop, the main focus of Chapter 6 by Vinish Kathu-ria and R. Balasubramanian is to quantify the agricultural impacts of topsoil removal for brick-making. The quantification is carried out using a replacement cost approach for the state of Tamil Nadu in India. The results using soil samples in two regions of Tamil Nadu reveal that the total cost of replacing the nutrients, levelling the land and application of tank silt works out to be nearly Rs.2,600 in the south and Rs.2,350 per acre in the north with an inter-regional average of Rs.2,475 per acre. The study observed that most farmers believed soil to be an infinitely renewable resource both in terms of quality and quantity, which ration-alizes their decision to sell the soil on an economic plane. Since only about 3.3 per cent of the average revenue from the sale of soil is being spent on remedial measures to improve the fertility status of the soil, the environmental repercus-sions could be far-reaching.

Hydropower projects are likely to cause severe environmental, economical and social impacts both at the local and regional levels. The practice of perform-ing environmental impact assessments (EIA) while constructing dams in order to prevent or mitigate these impacts is a commonly followed practice nowadays.

EIAs are important both for being able to better perform future EIAs and for being able to add new mitigation efforts to the investigated project if necessary. Chapter 7 by Bimlesh Kumar and Achanta Ramakrishna Rao addresses these concerns and presents a viable procedural layout on EIA for implementing such a project. The rapid impact assessment matrix was used to get numerical impacts (adverse or beneficial) of different parameters. This method analyses and presents in a structured, friendly and transparent environment the numerous parameters and alternatives of an EIA, by considering all four components: physical/chemical, biological/ecological, social/cultural and economic/operational. Based on the analysis, the findings indicate that such a project will be positive economically but negative otherwise considering the other three components.

As the urban population is growing rapidly, with a resultant exponential increase in demand for municipal water supplies and environmental management services, urban water management is adding many new dimensions to India's water crisis. Unlike the case of rural water management, sustainable urban water management calls for not only managing water supplies for various needs such as drinking, domestic, commercial, manufacturing, urban forestry, recreation and environmental management, but also collection, treatment and disposal of wastewater, solid waste management, flood control, apart from protecting the integrity of the hydrological system from which various water demands are met. Integrated urban water management (IUWM) as an extension of the broader concept of integrated water resources management (IWRM), is gaining acceptance in developing as well as developed economies. Chapter 8 by M. Dinesh Kumar discusses the over-arching principles of IUWM and its working at the operational level; provides a generic operational framework of IUWM; and analyses the key challenges in implementing its various components in Indian cities/towns, which are related to scientific and technical knowledge, human resources, institutional capabilities and finance. The chapter concludes that the policymakers need to create dedicated agencies responsible for development and allocation of water resources and the agencies need to function in a coordinated manner.

Per capita generation of MSW in India has increased at an alarming rate in recent times owing to an improved standard of living and higher rate of urbanization. Traditionally, for most Indian municipalities the collection and disposal practices were inadequate and imposed health and aesthetic costs on the residents. Recognition of these social costs led to the formulation of the Municipal Solid Waste Management and Handling (MSWMH) Rules (2000) that streamlined an environmentally safer practice of collection and disposal that the local bodies in India must abide by. Unfortunately, almost a decade later compliance with the MSWMH Rules among the local bodies is not yet satisfactory. This necessitates further policy interventions, particularly in the form of institutional reforms for service delivery, to ensure successful adoption of the proposed disposal norms. Chapter 9 by Prasenjit Sarkhel seeks to analyse such policy prerogatives by assessing the evolution of waste management regulations and identifying the institutional reforms that are taking shape to minimize the cost of compliance among the stakeholders in urban India.

Population growth in India has been associated with growth in the public and private health network. However, the growth necessitates disposal of the generated BMW by hospitals and similar institutions in an environmentally sustainable manner, as insanitary disposal of biomedical wastes pose serious environmental and health repercussions. To fulfil this objective, the BMW (Management and Handling) Rules were promulgated by the Ministry of Environment and Forests, Government of India in 1998. The BMW Rules require segregation of infectious and non-infectious waste streams at source since the disposal methods are different for the two streams. The tenth chapter by S. Srividhya and Paul P. Appasamy estimates the costs of collection, transport and disposal for each stream and expresses the same as a cost per bed for a private hospital in Chennai, which are extrapolated to get an estimate of the total cost of BMW management in the city. It is observed that disposal of infectious waste is increasingly being outsourced to take advantage of economies of scale.

Electrical and electronic waste (e-waste) is one of the fastest growing waste streams in the world. It is estimated that approximately 95 per cent of e-waste generated in India is recycled in the informal sector. Though e-waste recycling in the informal sector provides jobs to thousands of people, this simultaneously deals with potentially hazardous material in an environmentally unfriendly manner. The recent entry of formal sector players in this sphere has created widespread expectation that they would be able to manage e-waste in an environmentally sound manner by using best available technologies (BAT) leading to better environment and enhanced resource recovery. However, it is not clear whether the advent of formal sector recycling would come at the expense of informal sector recycler. The eleventh chapter by Ashish Chaturvedi, Rachna Arora and Ulrike Killguss argues that social welfare is enhanced by this interaction between the formal and informal sectors through reduced pollution, better resource management and creation of green jobs in the recycling sector. The chapter recommends that the collection, segregation and primary dismantling of non-hazardous portions of e-waste can be undertaken in the informal sector while the higher end processes can be concentrated in the formal sector. The discussion also recommends that the informal sector needs to be organized in associations before they enter into a trading relationship with the formal sector to secure a greater bargaining power as well as reducing transaction costs for the various stakeholders in the e-waste value chain.

The growing concern over sustainable development is one of the most important phenomena of the last century. However, the search for a new economic order, through the Rio Summit (1992) on Environment and Development, has clearly brought out a divide between the industrialized economies in the north and the primarily agrarian economies in the south. Arguably, sustainable development meant different challenges as well as developmental outcomes for the two sets of economies. In this background, on the basis of the secondary data analysis, the twelfth chapter by Amita Shah attempts to analyse patterns of agricultural production, input-use, and major environmental impacts thereof. After examining the policies for promoting agricultural production, especially in the wake of the new challenges from trade liberalization, it attempts to draw policy implications for trade negotiations in a north–south context. It is noted that Indian agriculture is still at the initial stage of growth trajectory with half the rate of fertilizer use and lower use of pesticides per hectare of net cultivated area as compared to similar figures for EU. The productivity differences are enormous with India being almost three times less productive vis-à-vis the EU in terms of cereals. The chapter concludes that enhancing access to water and a shift in cropping patterns in favour of lesser water use as well as nutrient intensive crops such as oilseeds, coarse cereals, and pulses may be an important strategy for moving in this direction.

PHH in international trade literature indicates that foreign investment in dirty industries may occur in greater proportions in developing countries/provinces characterized by relatively weaker environmental standards/policy, or with lesser willingness and capacity to enforce them. The motive behind such a move is to exploit the associated cost advantage. Since the initiation of economic reform in the 1990s, the FDI inflow in India has increased considerably, while export of environmentally sensitive products explains a significant proportion in India's export basket. In this background, the thirteenth chapter by Debashis Chakraborty attempts to verify the existence of PHH in India in a cross-state framework by focusing on the relationship between FDI inflows in a state with its environmental quality. The study concludes that the linkage between cross-state pollution levels and FDI inflow in India is not obvious for all selected categories, and PHH phenomenon may not be operational in the country across the board. However, as reflected from the analysis conducted with import figures in waste and scrap products, there exist several concern areas which require attention of the policymakers.

In light of the discussions undertaken by the individual chapters, the final chapter attempts to chalk out the future path for the policymakers to combat the identified challenges.

Relying on GDP and other macro-level income aggregates for representing economic growth and development has long been questioned, and one such quest has led to the development of the Human Development Index by the UNDP. The other approach is to ensure clean economic growth by taking care of environmental degradation or natural resources depletion, i.e. Green GDP. The United Nations is the fore runner of this approach. The UN has developed the System of Integrated Environmental and Economic Accounting (SEEA) in 1993 (UNSD 1993), which is being implemented by several countries. The system brings together economic and environmental information in a common framework to measure the contribution of the environment to the economy and the impact of the economy on the environment.

Notes

1 The polluting sectors include aluminium, caustic, cement, copper, distilleries, dyes and dyeing industry, fertilizer, iron and steel, leather, pesticide, petrochemicals, pharmaceuticals, pulp and paper, refineries, sugar, thermal power plants and zinc.

2 The NCR Planning Board (NCRPB) reveals that the water table in Delhi was dipping by two metres every year (Dash 2010).
3 Analysis of the data from MoEF reveals that during 2005–06 and 2006–07 the maximum number of clearances under Environmental Protection Act (1986) in manufacturing has been granted in Tamil Nadu (148), Andhra Pradesh (140), Haryana (93), Maharashtra (66) and Gujarat (56). Similar clearance in the case of mining has been granted in Rajasthan (139), Karnataka (88), Goa (55), Maharashtra (40), Madhya Pradesh (34), Andhra Pradesh (32), Orissa (32), Chattisgarh (26) and Tamil Nadu (25) (Chakraborty 2009).
4 The fiscal incentives provided to industries for pollution control include tax exemption, depreciation allowance, investment allowance, etc. (Chelliah *et al.* 2007).
5 In early 2008, the EU stressed at the greenhouse gas emission discussion forum that economically more advanced developing countries should contribute adequately according to their responsibilities and respective capabilities. Brazil and India were the target countries.

References

Antony, M.J. (2001) *Landmark Judgments on Environmental Protection*, New Delhi: Indian Social Institute.
Association for India's Development (AID) (undated) 'MoEF Environmental Experts Committee Concludes Gross Non-Compliance on Sardar Sarovar and Indira Sagar Projects. Online, available at: http://aidindia.org/main/content/view/1226/39/ (accessed 15 April 2011).
Balakrishnan, K., Mehta, S., Kumar, P., Ramaswamy, P., Sambandam, S., Kumar, K.S. and Smith, K.R. (2004) *Indoor Air Pollution Assessment with Household Fuel Use in India*, ESMAP Report, Washington, DC: World Bank.
Chakraborty, D. (2009) 'Sanctions and their Effects on Trade Flows and Environmental Quality: The Indian Experience', unpublished thesis, Jawaharlal Nehru University.
Central Pollution Control Board (undated) 'Groundwater Pollution – Areas of National Concern'. Online available at: www.cpcb.nic.in/oldwebsite/News%20Letters/Archives/Groundwater/ch18-GW.html (accessed 12 April 2010).
Chelliah, R.J., Appasamy, P.P., Sankar, U. and Pandey, R. (2007) 'Ecotaxes on Polluting Inputs and Outputs', New Delhi: Academic Foundation.
Cole, M.A., Rayner, A.J. and Bates, J.M. (1997) 'The Environmental Kuznets Curve: An Empirical Analysis', *Environment and Development Economics*, 2(4): 401–416.
Cole, M.A., Elliott, R.J.R. and Zhang, J. (2011) 'Growth, Foreign Direct Investment, and the Environment: Evidences from Chinese Cities', *Journal of Regional Science*, 51(1): 121–138.
Dash, D.K. (2010) 'Delhi Water Table Falling by 2m/yr', *Times of India*, 22 March, New Delhi.
Davidar, P., Sahoo, S., Mammen, P.C., Acharya, P. Puyravaud, J., Arjunan, M., Garrigues, J.P. and Roessingh, K. (2010) 'Assessing the Extent and Causes of Forest Degradation in India: Where do we Stand?', *Biological Conservation*, 143(12): 2937–2944.
Dietz, S., Neumayer, E. and Soysa, I. De (undated) 'Corruption, the Resource Curse and Genuine Saving'. Online, available at: http://129.3.20.41/eps/dev/papers/0405/0405012.pdf (accessed 5 February 2010).
D'Souza, C. (2001) 'Integrating Environmental Management in Small Industries of India', *Electronic Green Journal*, 1(14): 1–11.

European Commission (2008) 'Amending Directive 2003/87/EC so as to Improve and Extend the Greenhouse Gas Emission Allowance Trading System of the Community', 23 January, Brussels, COM(2008) 16 final, 2008/0013 (COD).

FAO (undated) 'The Problem of Land Degradation'. Online, available at: www.fao.org/docrep/v9909e/v9909e02.htm (accessed 15 April 2011).

Haq, Z. (2010) 'Expert Trashes Bt Brinjal Report', *Hindustan Times*, 25 September, New Delhi.

Haq, Z., Chauhan, C. and Choudhury, G. (2011) 'India has 11 Years to Ban Endosulfan', *Hindustan Times*, April 29, New Delhi.

Iyenger, S. (2003) 'Environmental Damage to Land Resource: Need to Improve Land Use Data Base', *Economic and Political Weekly*, 38(34): 3596–3604.

Kathuria, V. (2002) 'Vehicular Pollution Control in Delhi', *Transportation Research Part D: Transport and Environment*, 7(5): 373–387.

Kathuria, V. (2004) 'Impact of CNG on Vehicular Pollution in Delhi: A Note', *Transportation Research Part D: Transport and Environment*, 9(5): 409–417.

Krishnamurthy, K.V. (2004) 'Environmental Impacts of Coal Mining in India', Proceedings of the National Seminar on Environmental Engineering with special emphasis on Mining Environment, Indian School of Mines, Dhanbad.

Lal, P. and Jha, V. (1999) 'Judicial Activism and the Environment in India: Implications for Transnational Corporations'. Online, available at: http://openarchive.cbs.dk/bitstream/handle/10398/6956/lal_judicial.pdf?sequence=1 (accessed 11 January 2011).

Managi, S. and Jena, P.R. (2008) 'Environmental Productivity and Kuznets Curve in India', *Ecological Economics*, 65(2): 432–440.

Maria, A. (2003) 'The Costs of Water Pollution in India', Paper presented at the conference on Market Development of Water and Waste Technologies through Environmental Economics, 30–31 October 2003, Delhi. Online, available at: www.cerna.ensmp.fr/Documents/cerna_globalisation/maria-delhi.pdf (accessed 15 May 2010).

Ministry of Environment and Forest (undated) 'Ministry of Environment and Forest Annual Report', (various issues), New Delhi: MoEF, Government of India.

Ministry of Environment and Forest (2006) 'National Environment Policy 2006', Government of India. Online, available at: http://envfor.nic.in/nep/nep2006e.pdf (accessed 25 March 2011).

Ministry of Environment and Forest (2009) 'State of the Environment Report', New Delhi: MoEF, Government of India.

Mukherjee, S. (2008) 'Economics of Agricultural Nonpoint Source Water Pollution: A Case Study of Groundwater Nitrate Pollution in the Lower Bhavani River Basin, Tamil Nadu', unpublished PhD thesis, University of Madras (Madras School of Economics), Chennai, India.

Mukherjee, S. and Chakraborty, D. (2009), 'Environment, Human Development and Economic Growth: A Contemporary Analysis of Indian States', *International Journal of Global Environmental Issues*, 9(1/2): 20–49.

Mukherjee, S. and Kathuria, V. (2006), 'Is Economic Growth Sustainable? Environmental Quality of Indian States after 1991', *International Journal of Sustainable Development*, 9(1): 38–60.

Mukherjee, S. and Nelliyat, P. (2007) *Groundwater Pollution and Emerging Environmental Challenges of Industrial Effluent Irrigation in Mettupalayam Taluk, Tamilnadu*, Discussion Paper No. 4, Comprehensive Assessment of Water Management in Agriculture, Colombo, Sri Lanka: IWMI.

Mythili, G. and Mukherjee, S. (2011) 'Examining Environmental Kuznets Curve for River Effluents in India', *Environment, Development and Sustainability*, 13(3): 627–640.

Narain, U. (2008) 'Urban Air Pollution in India', *Review of Environmental Economics and Policy*, 2(2): 276–291.

Porter, M.E. (1991) 'America's Green Strategy', *Scientific American*, 264(4): 168.

Prasad, P.M. (2004) 'Environmental Protection: The Role of Liability System in India', *Economic and Political Weekly*, 39(3): 257–269.

Ramana, M.V., Thomas, D.G. and Varughese, S. (2001) 'Estimating Nuclear Waste Production in India', *Current Science*, 81(11): 1458–1462.

Reddy, V.R. (2003) 'Land Degradation in India: Extent, Costs and Determinants', *Economic and Political Weekly*, 38(44): 4700–4713.

Reddy, V.R., Behera, B. and Rao, D.M. (2001) 'Forest Degradation in India: Extent and Determinants', *Indian Journal of Agricultural Economics*, 56(4), October–December 2001.

Sahay, K.B. (2000) 'Problem of Livestock Population', *Tribune*, April 11, New Delhi.

Sawhney, A. (2003) 'Managing Pollution', *Economic and Political Weekly*, 38(1): 32–37.

Sidhu, H.S. (2002) 'Crisis in Agrarian Economy in Punjab: Some Urgent Steps', *Economic and Political Weekly*, 37(30): 3132–3138.

Sinha, R.K. (1993) 'Automobile Pollution in India and its Human Impact', *Environmentalist*, 13(2): 111–115.

United Nations Statistics Division (UNSD) (1993) *Integrated Environmental and National Accounting*, Interim Version, Handbook of national Accounting, Series F, No. 61, Department of Economic and Social development, UNSD, New York.

Yale Center for Environmental Law and Policy, Yale University and Center for International Earth Science Information Network, Columbia University, 'Environmental Sustainability Index' (various years), New Haven and New York.

Yale Center for Environmental Law and Policy, Yale University and Center for International Earth Science Information Network, Columbia University, 'Environmental Performance Index' (various years), New Haven and New York.

Part I

Agriculture sector and environment

1 Issues and options to control agricultural nonpoint source pollution

A case study from India

Sacchidananda Mukherjee

Introduction

Pollution abatement strategies for water resources in India and other developing countries have given priority to point sources of pollution (Banadda *et al.* 2009; Ongley 1996). However, it is increasingly becoming evident that improvement of the quality of surface and groundwater will also require the control of pollution from nonpoint sources (NPS) (Ribaudo 1992).[1] Controlling NPS pollution is particularly crucial in rural areas where groundwater is an important source of drinking water. Groundwater nitrate (NO_3) concentration can be considered as an indicator of NPS pollution (Engel *et al.* 1996).

In several parts of India, growing access to irrigation facilities along with unbalanced use and overuse of nitrogenous fertilizers, unlined and open storage of livestock wastes, and insanitary disposal of human wastes have led to high concentrations of NO_3 in groundwater. There is limited information on the level of pesticide contamination of water sources. However, information on the level of NO_3 in groundwater as well as surface water across Indian States is available to some extent. In India, 85–90 per cent of the rural population depends on groundwater for drinking purposes (DDWS 2008). Consumption of NO_3-contaminated drinking water poses various short- and long-term health hazards to various age groups (WHO 2004). NO_3 concentration in water used for drinking should be less than 50mg/l (milligram per litre) (WHO 2004). In India, according to the Bureau of Indian Standards (BIS 1991), the maximum acceptable limit of NO_3 in drinking water is 45mg/l (which is equivalent to 10mg/l of NO_3-N, nitrate-nitrogen). However, the maximum permissible limit of NO_3 is set at 100mg/l, provided there are no alternative source(s) of drinking water (BIS 1991).

Access to safe drinking water is vital for human well-being (UNDP 2006). One of the targets of the United Nations' Millennium Development Goals (MDGs) is to 'halve by 2015 the proportion of people without sustainable access to safe drinking water and basic sanitation' (Target 10). Pollution from NPS makes groundwater resources unsuitable for drinking. Thus the environmental sustainability of safe sources of drinking water for future generations is at stake. People exposed to polluted drinking water are vulnerable to various water borne diseases. It is primarily the poor and marginal section of the population who suffer the most, as they cannot afford to protect themselves from the impacts of pollution. Costs associated with mortality and morbidity of water-borne diseases are high. For example in India water-borne diseases annually put a burden of US$3.1 billion to US$8.3 billion in 1992 prices (Brandon and Hommann 1995). A recent study conducted by the Water and Sanitation Programme of the World Bank estimates that the total economic impacts of inadequate sanitation in India amounts to Rs.2.44 trillion (US$53.8 billion) a year – this is equivalent to 6.4 per cent of India's GDP in 2006 (Water and Sanitation Programme undated).

In India, water supply authorities mostly prefer curative measures (e.g. *ex post* treatment or source substitution) at a higher incremental cost of water supply as compared to precautionary measures (e.g. *ex ante* protection of drinking water sources). Therefore, major challenges that the rural water supply sector in India is facing today are not only to meet the large investment requirement to augment the water supply, but also an additional investment burden to tackle the water quality related problems. This has led to an astronomical demand for investment in infrastructure to supply drinking water to the rural populace (Mukherjee 2008). For example, release of funds by the Department of Drinking Water Supply (DDWS), Government of India (GoI), under the Accelerated Rural Water Supply Programme (ARWSP) has gone up from Rs.1,440 crore in 1998–99 to Rs.7,056 crore in 2008–09, which shows a 390 per cent increase (DDWS 2008). The DDWS has allocated Rs.735.67 crore during 2006–07 to tackle water quality related problems under ARWSP, which is 21 per cent of the total release of funds under ARWSP for the year (i.e. Rs.3,532 crore). According to the estimate released by the Rajiv Gandhi National Drinking Water Mission on 31 March 2004, in India 13,958 habitations are affected by drinking water affected by NO_3 pollution. The number of NO_3-affected habitations has gone up from 4,003 as on 1 April 1999 to 19,387 as on 1 April 2006.

Status of nonpoint source groundwater pollution in India

Paucity of data is the major challenge to understanding the degree and extent of exposure to drinking water NO_3 pollution in India. The information available on habitations affected by NO_3 as a percentage of total water quality affected habitations is shown in Table 1.1, which indicates the gravity of the problem. The data shows that semi-arid and arid states like Rajasthan, Gujarat, Tamil Nadu (henceforth TN) and Karnataka are largely affected by NO_3 pollution.

State governments need to monitor regularly and report groundwater quality information in terms of the number of habitations affected by various pollutants (e.g. fluoride, salinity, iron, arsenic, NO_3, multiple pollutants and total number of water quality affected habitations) to the DDWS. However, in most cases, the information is not disseminated in time or properly due to various reasons: sample survey and testing of water samples is often not completed in time; an absence of information on actual number of water quality affected habitations, data is often estimated; difficulty in identification of water quality affected

Table 1.1 Number of nitrate affected habitations and as percentage of total water quality affected habitations across selected Indian States

States/UTs (1)	As on 01.04.1999 (2)	As on 04.03.2003 (3)	As on 31.03.2004 (4)	As on 01.04.2005 (5)	As on 01.04.2006 (6)	As on 01.04.2009 (7)	As on 27.07.2010 (8)
Bihar	762 (53.25)	50 (12.76)	12 (15.33)		56 (17)	223 (23.52)	191 (34.92)
Gujarat		603 (19.41)	1,336 (6.44)	748 (1.55)	838 (8.09)	655 (5.21)	655 (7.45)
Karnataka	4,077 (19.48)	4077 (9)	2,480 (19.41)	2,000 (8.58)		53 (0.65)	
Kerala		78 (9)	79 (9.11)	33 (9)	81 (4.31)		6 (0.18)
Madhya Pradesh					6 (0.86)	6 (0.11)	
Maharashtra		296 (7.82)	521 (7.82)	4,552 (13.76)	1,210 (40.59)	1,225 (30.33)	1,225 (29.72)
Orissa			1 (0)	0 (0)	52 (20.21)	28 (0.22)	28 (0.16)
Rajasthan	3,862 (29.73)	7,882 (8.54)	6,742 (19.19)	7,693 (16.42)	927 (24.13)	856 (2.46)	856 (2.45)
Tamil Nadu	4,000 (8.54)	6,933 (42.17)	237 (4.25)	104 (1.87)	104 (7.32)		5 (0.51)
Uttar Pradesh		1 (0.02)	15 (0.02)	11 (0.3)	15 (0.17)	2 (0.25)	
All India	4,765 (2.19)	15,499 (11.83)	13,958 (6.43)	10,764 (4.96)	19,387 (9.9)	2,571 (1.43)	3,032 (2.1)

Sources: www.indiastat.com, National Habitations Survey (NHS 2003), Ministry of Rural Development (2010a; 2010b).

Note
Figures in the parentheses show the percentage of total water quality affected habitations of the respective states. For All India, figures in the parentheses show the percentage of total water quality affected habitations in India.

habitations leads to over or under reporting; number of habitations affected by various water quality pollutants are not reported properly; submission of back-dated information on water quality affected habitations, etc. As a result the number of NO_3-affected habitations varies significantly within a short period of time (as in Table 1.1). The information presented here is only indicative of the problem of NO_3 pollution in drinking water across selected states in India and should be assessed keeping in mind the above data limitations.

A recent study conducted by the Central Ground Water Board (CGWB 2010) finds that groundwater quality of shallow aquifers of Andhra Pradesh, Haryana, Maharashtra, Punjab, Rajasthan and TN are highly affected by NO_3 (Table 1.2). The report attributes the incidence of a high concentration of NO_3 in groundwater to leaching of chemical fertilizers, animal manure and septic and sewage discharges.

Figure 1.1 shows that there is a relationship between average nitrogen application on farmland (in kilograms per hectare of gross cropped area) and average groundwater NO_3 concentration. CGWB (2010) reports the NO_3 concentration of the shallow wells which cross the acceptable limit of 45 mg/l. A similar relationship was also observed by Tirado (2009) in Punjab. A survey conducted by the Public Works Department of Government of TN (PWD 1992) to study

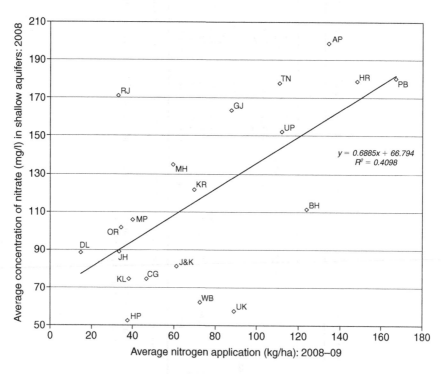

Figure 1.1 Average nitrogen application and average nitrate concentration across Indian States (source: CGWB 2010, and Department of Agriculture and Cooperation 2010).

Table 1.2 State-wise groundwater nitrate pollution in shallow aquifers

State	Number of observation wells	Nitrate concentration above 45 mg/l		Nitrate concentration above 45 mg/l	
		No. of observations	Average nitrate concentration	No. of observations	Average nitrate concentration
Andhra Pradesh (AP)	981	355 (36.2)	198.6 [46–1,300]	246 (25.1)	253.8 [100–1,300]
Bihar (BH)	373	15 (4.0)	111.1 [48–228]	6 (1.6)	166.5 [109–228]
Chhattisgarh (CG)	516	43 (8.3)	74.7 [45–240]	7 (1.4)	141 [100–240]
Delhi (DL)	87	23 (26.4)	88.4 [47–218]	6 (6.9)	142.5 [107–218]
Gujarat (GJ)	966	112 (11.6)	163.3 [45–840]	87 (9.0)	190.9 [100–840]
Haryana (HR)	426	102 (23.9)	178.9 [48–1,292]	56 (13.1)	267.5 [104–1,292]
Himachal Pradesh (HP)	85	4 (4.7)	52.5 [45–65]	–	–
Jammu and Kashmir (J&K)	206	13 (6.3)	81.2 [45–150]	4 (1.9)	119.5 [100–150]
Jharkhand (JH)	208	32 (15.4)	88.7 [46–230]	12 (5.8)	133.6 [101–230]
Karnataka (KR)	1,499	165 (11.0)	121.7 [46–1,420]	81 (5.4)	179.2 [100–1,420]
Kerala (KL)	864	34 (3.9)	74.5 [45–167]	6 (0.7)	128 [105–167]
Madhya Pradesh (MP)	1,325	270 (20.4)	105.5 [45–367]	107 (8.1)	165.2 [100–367]
Maharashtra (MH)	1,496	340 (22.7)	134.9 [45–1,750]	171 (11.4)	199.7 [100–1,750]
Orissa (OR)	1,214	112 (9.2)	101.5 [46–272]	42 (3.5)	163.5 [100–272]
Punjab (PB)	261	59 (22.6)	180.4 [45–1,180]	34 (13.0)	265.2 [104–1,180]
Rajasthan (RJ)	1,373	496 (36.1)	171.3 [46–1,150]	270 (19.7)	256.4 [100–1,150]
Tamil Nadu (TN)	906	152 (16.8)	178 [45–644]	107 (11.8)	223.4 [100–644]
Uttar Pradesh (UP)	1,218	88 (7.2)	152 [47–1,162]	43 (3.5)	238.7 [100–1,162]
Uttarakhand (UK)	44	6 (13.6)	57.5 [45–75]	–	–
West Bengal (WB)	909	8 (0.9)	62.5 [46–81]	–	–
All	14,957	2,429 (16.2)	149.6 [45–1,750]	1,285 (8.6)	222 [100–1,750]

Source: CGWB (2010).

Notes
Figures in parentheses show the percentage of total number of observation wells.
Figures in brackets show the range for the corresponding average value.

the effects of the application of fertilizers and pesticides on groundwater across six locations in the state reported the influence of fertilizers on groundwater. Though the study could not attempt to study the impact of pesticides on groundwater due to a lack of infrastructure, it found that soil texture and irrigation scheduling influenced NO_3 leaching into groundwater.

Status of nonpoint source groundwater pollution in Tamil Nadu

District-wise data on groundwater quality for 2004 is available from DDWS, which is analysed to identify the NO_3-affected districts in TN (DDWS 2004). The analysis showed that 792 habitations in TN, with a population of more than 3.9 lakh are affected by drinking water NO_3 pollution alone, and another 902 habitations with a population of more than 3.56 lakh are affected by NO_3 along with other pollutants. NO_3-affected habitations mostly fall in the northern and north-western districts of TN. The NO_3-affected population of Coimbatore district is 60,635 and Erode district is 33,947, which contributes 8.1 per cent and 4.5 per cent respectively of the total NO_3-affected population of TN. Large parts of Erode and Coimbatore districts fall within the Bhavani River Basin. Similar situations also prevail in several other parts of India and other developing countries (Mukherjee 2008).

During 2001–02, the Tamil Nadu Water Supply and Drainage (TWAD) Board carried out an extensive groundwater quality survey for shallow (149,457 samples from hand pumps) and deep aquifer (36,418 samples from power pumps). The results show that in Dharmapuri (26.22; 25.46),[2] Coimbatore (24.02; 18.04) and Vellore (20.62; 15.7) both shallow and deep aquifers are equally polluted. For Erode (10.25; 42.97), Karur (1.21; 25.04), Salem (8.57; 10.37) and Thiruvellore (2.46; 11.08), the pollution levels in deep aquifers are higher than shallow aquifers. The deep leaching of NO_3 salts could be the reason for this result. In Perambalur (20.02; 5.59) the shallow aquifer is polluted, whereas the level of pollution is low for the deep aquifer.

Foster and Garduño (2004) reported an elevated concentration of NO_3 in drinking water wells during the dry season at numerous locations in TN. The NO_3-affected belt mainly covers the north and north-western districts of the state. In the Coimbatore and Dharmapuri districts of the western zone, more than 20 per cent of drinking water wells had a NO_3 concentration greater than 50 mg/l, and in a large number of wells the same exceeded 100 mg/l. Infiltration or leaching of NO_3 from human and animal excreta appeared to be the major cause of groundwater NO_3 in those areas. The current study considers the Lower Bhavani River (LBR) basin in TN as a case study of NPS pollution.

Status of nonpoint source groundwater pollution in the lower Bhavani River Basin, Tamil Nadu

The Bhavani River is the second largest perennial river of TN, and one of the most important tributaries of the Cauvery River. The Bhavani Sagar reservoir, the Bhavani River and three diversions from the river; namely, Arakkankottai,

Thadapalli, Kalingarayan (known as old system) and a canal from the reservoir are known as the Lower Bhavani Project (LBP) canal, form the lower Bhavani River Basin (Maps 1.1 and 1.2).

To capture the temporal, spatial and seasonal variations of groundwater NO_3 concentration in the basin, groundwater quality information (for the regular observations wells) was collected from the TWAD Board, Chennai for the period May 1991 to May 2005.

Figure 1.2 indicates that the difference across pre- and post-monsoon average groundwater NO_3 concentration is discernable except for the year 1999. It also

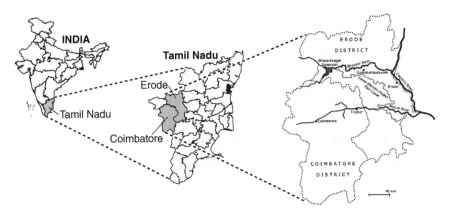

Map 1.1 Location map – the Lower Bhavani River Basin, Tamil Nadu (not to scale) (source: GIS/TWAD Board, Chennai and Mats Lannerstad).

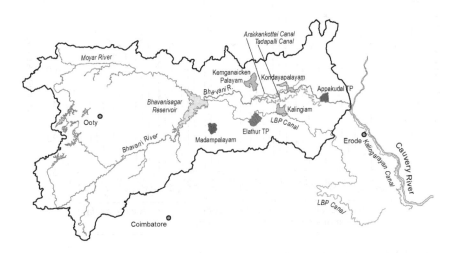

Map 1.2 Study villages in the Lower Bhavani River Basin, Tamil Nadu (not to scale) (source: GIS/TWAD Board, Chennai and Mats Lannerstad).

shows that in some years, pre-monsoon average concentration is higher than post-monsoon average concentration. Therefore, rainfall alone cannot be a decisive factor behind groundwater NO_3 concentration. Except for a few years, both pre- and post-monsoon average concentrations were higher than 40 mg/l. In 1996, both pre- and post-monsoon average concentrations were higher than 100 mg/l, which is higher than the preceding periods. This perhaps results from the severe drought in 1995 followed by heavy rainfall during 1996, leading to leaching of mineralised nitrogen into the aquifer. In 2004 and 2005, due to considerably higher rainfall, the groundwater average NO_3 concentration had declined.

Due to growing incidence of groundwater NO_3 concentration in the basin, the environmental sustainability of safe drinking water sources is at stake. In some instances the public water supply authority has provided drinking water from alternative sources to NO_3-affected rural habitations. However, a large section of the society is still dependent on decentralized drinking water systems and exposed to high NO_3-contaminated drinking water, drinking which may cause various short- and long-term health impacts. However, due to inadequate secondary health information, the same cannot be confirmed.

Options to control nonpoint source pollution

Due to the large number of sources and diffused entry points, it is technically infeasible and financially unviable to monitor the contribution of individual NPS to the ambient concentration (say, groundwater quality). Though monitoring and

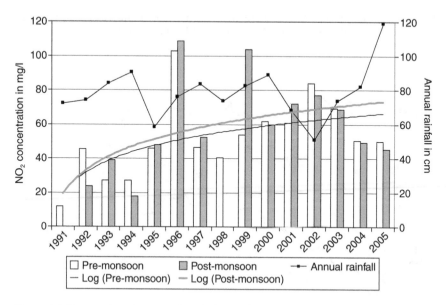

Figure 1.2 Temporal and seasonal variations of groundwater nitrate concentration – regular observation wells data (May 1991 to May 2005) (source: TWAD Board, Chennai).

using regulatory measures to protect groundwater quality is the responsibility of the central and state pollution control boards (Trivedy 2000), there is no legal provision to regulate individual agricultural polluters. As a result, NPS pollution control is, on the whole, neglected in India.

In developed countries NPS pollution control became a serious issue when it was observed that even after substantial improvement in controlling the pollution from point sources (Shortle and Abler 1997) most of the ground and surface water resources remained polluted. During the same period, the growing demand for environmental quality from civil society groups forced the environmental agencies to go in for second-generation environmental policies, i.e. NPS pollution control. As a result most of the polluted water bodies got a fresh lease of life. Environmental assessments show NPS to be a major cause of environmental damage not only for developed countries but also for developing countries (Panda and Behera 2003; Agrawal *et al.* 1999; Duda 1993; Handa 1986). Beyond limiting the extent of potential environmental quality improvements, the failure to extend pollution control to NPS increases the costs of environmental protection by precluding efficient allocation of control between point sources and NPS (Freeman 1990). Taking the cue from developed countries, it will be imperative for developing countries to initiate NPS pollution control measures as early as possible.

It is not possible to use *regulatory instruments* such as command and control measures and economic instruments like pollution charges to control NPS pollution due to the large number of sources and diffuse entry points (Dosi and Zeitouni 2001; Shortle and Horan 2002; Shortle and Abler 1997). It is also difficult to monitor discharges by individuals at a reasonable cost. In the case of groundwater, there is also the problem of accumulation of pollutants over time. *Economic instruments* like nitrogen and pesticide taxes are not feasible in the Indian context at this time, although they have been practised in some European countries (Zeijts and Westhoek 2004; Rougoor *et al.* 2001; Chelliah *et al.* 2007). In India, nitrogenous fertilizers have been subsidised to encourage their use by farmers. This has led to overuse of fertilizers by farmers and the consequent problem of NO_3 pollution of the groundwater (NAAS 2005). Proper pricing of fertilizers may lead to more careful use (Chelliah *et al.* 2007) and access to basic agricultural extension services could encourage farmers to adopt agricultural best management practices (BMPs) (Mukherjee 2010). Rules and regulations alone cannot control pollution from NPS. *Voluntary approaches* (VAs) like voluntary cooperation of the stakeholders in the adoption of agricultural BMPs may be the long-term solution to control NPS pollution of groundwater within the existing regulatory and institutional framework of India.[3] Collective action is needed to ensure that restraint in the use of fertilizers is practiced by all the farmers in a particular aquifer.

Voluntary approaches

A quite general and comprehensive definition of VAs in environmental protection is provided by Lévêque (1997), which describes VAs as 'commitments of polluting firms or sectors to improve their environmental performance'.

According to Brau and Carroro (1999), these commitments can be placed into three categories: *unilateral commitments* – which consist of environment friendly adjustments established by firms themselves; *public voluntary schemes* – in which participating firms agree to standards developed by public bodies; and *negotiated agreements* – specific contracts between public authorities or other intermediate subjects and polluting firms, e.g. agreements between community drinking water supplying authorities and farmers operating within or near drinking water catchment area to adopt agricultural BMPs to protect groundwater from NPS pollution (Brouwer *et al.* 2003).

In considering the potential effectiveness of a VA to reduce agro-chemical contamination of groundwater, following Padgelt (1994) at least five questions need to be addressed. The answers to these questions will assist in determining whether a particular environment is conducive to voluntary change. The questions are as follows:

a What is the degree of consensus among farmers about groundwater pollution?
b Is there consensus about the causes of the pollution?
c Do individuals link their own situation and behaviour to the pollution?
d Do farmers sense that viable alternatives to current practices exist?
e If alternative practices are modelled and nurtured, do they become acceptable?

The current study attempts to address these questions, as protection of groundwater can be seen as a collective responsibility of the farmers and households of the affected regions. Since long-term environmental and human health risks/implications of drinking NO_3 and pesticide contaminated water are uncertain, and *ex post* treatment and remedial measures are costly and technically/financially unviable, it is imperative to follow the 'precautionary approach' related to groundwater pollution in general and agricultural NPS water pollution in particular.

Objectives

Community participation in environmental conservation (or protection) is a new research area and it is in this context that this study attempts to understand (in *ex ante*) individual farmers' perceptions about groundwater quality, and factors which influence his/her individual decision to protect groundwater either individually (through adoption of agricultural BMPs) or collectively (by supporting local government to supply safe drinking water through alternative arrangements). This is the first step to study the possible emergence of collective action institution to protect groundwater from NPS pollution. The decision to cooperate in collective action is an individual's decision where his/her economic motives, socio-economic background and other factors play a crucial role. Apart from individual specific factors, social connectivity (social capital) and factors like information/consultation sources are expected to play a crucial role in his/her decision.

Methodology and study location

To capture the spatial variations across the basin, we have selected six villages on the basis of their sources of irrigation, long-term groundwater NO_3 concentration and level of urbanization. Among the six villages two are from the LBP canal command area (Elathur (ELA) at the head reach of the canal and Kalingiam (KAL) at the middle reach of the canal); two are from the old system (Kondayampalayam (KDP) depends on Arrakankottai canal for irrigation and Appakoodal (APP) depends on the Bhavani River for irrigation); and the final two are from rain-fed and groundwater irrigated area (Madampalayam (MDP) and Kemganaicken Palayam (KNP)). Apart from the sources of irrigation, the villages differ with respect to their level of urbanization. APP, ELA and KNP are town panchayats (TP) and KAL, KDP and MDP are village panchayats (VP) (Map 1.2).[4] Out of six sample villages from three irrigation systems – old system, new system and rain fed area – one TP and one VP falls under each of the systems (Table 1.3). Groundwater data analysis shows that APP, KNP and MDP have comparatively higher groundwater NO_3 concentration – more than 50 per cent of the samples have NO_3 concentration more than 50 mg/l. ELA, KAL and KDP have comparatively lower groundwater NO_3 concentration – less than 25 per cent of the samples have NO_3 concentration less than 50 mg/l.

A detailed questionnaire survey has been carried out among 395 farm households spread across six villages in the Lower Bhavani River Basin during June to July, 2006. Both qualitative and quantitative information were collected through face-to-face interviews with the head of the farm households. An average of 60 farm households were selected randomly from each of the six villages on the basis of their availability of own agricultural land and interest in the subject of the current research. Both the information leaflet and household questionnaire schedule were translated into Tamil, and a background of the objectives, scope and coverage of the study was described before starting the interviews. Apart from the household questionnaire survey, relevant information related to land use patterns and drinking water schemes/systems of the villages were collected from the village agriculture office and village panchayat office respectively.

Results and discussion

Sources of drinking water

It is observed that, 27.95 per cent (11.62 per cent in KAL to 60.29 per cent in KNP) of the sample households depend on their open wells (average depth of the well varied from 12.5 m to 15.8 m) to meet drinking water needs. Only 49 per cent of the households have supplied water, either through house connection (only 10.53 per cent) or through stand posts (38.5 per cent). Table 1.4 shows that 50 per cent of our sample households depend on groundwater (shallow or deep

Table 1.3 Groundwater nitrate pollution in the study villages

Name of the sample location	Source(s) of irrigation	NO$_3$ concentration (in mg/l)		Percentage of observation having NO$_3$ concentration		No. of sample household
		Mean	Range	>50 mg/l	>100 mg/l	
Appakoodal (APP) (TP)	The Bhavani river and groundwater (open wells and deep bore wells)	50.0	10–105	53.8	3.8	65
Elathur (ELA) (TP)	The LBP canal and groundwater (open wells and deep bore wells)	34.5	1–120	23.1	11.5	72
Kalingiam (KAL) (VP)	The LBP canal and groundwater (open wells and deep bore wells)	24.3	0–134	13.0	4.3	66
Kemganaicken Palayam (KNP) (TP)	Small dam, groundwater (open wells and bore wells) and river pumping	47.9	0–106	50.0	4.5	68
Kondayampalayam (KDP) (VP)	The Arakkankottai canal and groundwater (open wells and deep bore wells)	49.7	2.7–115	44.0	4.0	64
Madampalayam (MDP) (VP)	Mostly rain fed and groundwater (open wells and deep bore wells)	128.7	0–320	77.3	54.5	60

Source: Census of India (2001), TWAD Board, Chennai (Year) and Primary Survey.

Table 1.4 Sources of drinking water (in percentage of sample households)

Village name (1)	Own hand pump (2)	Own power pump (3)	Own open well (4)	Supply water – house connection (5)	Supply water – stand post (6)	Public hand pump (7)	Community well (8)	Water tanker (9)	Number of respondents (10)
Appakoodal	0.00	3.59	19.74	0.77	71.28	0.00	0.00	4.62	65
Elathur	2.43	16.20	23.26	14.93	36.69	2.08	4.40	0.00	72
Kalingiam	31.06	1.52	11.62	36.36	0.00	14.14	2.78	2.53	66
Kemganaicken Palayam	2.21	18.38	60.29	0.00	17.65	0.00	1.47	0.00	68
Kondayampalayam	1.30	11.72	32.03	9.11	42.71	2.08	1.04	0.00	64
Madampalayam	3.89	8.89	19.44	0.83	66.39	0.56	0.00	0.00	60
All villages	6.81	10.21	27.95	10.53	38.46	3.16	1.69	1.18	395

Source: Primary Survey.

aquifers) to meet drinking water needs (sum of columns 2, 3, 4, 7 and 8), which varies from 23 per cent in APP to 82 per cent in KNP. Though KNP is a rural town panchayat (RTP), it cannot provide drinking water due to its sparsely settled population and inadequate supply network. Since APP has an independent water supply scheme, which draws water from the Bhavani River (1.6 million litre per day), the dependence on groundwater as a source of drinking water is comparatively less (23 per cent). However, in APP almost 5 per cent of households are dependent on water tankers provided by local industry, as they are not under the centralized drinking water network.

Farmers' perceptions about groundwater and drinking water quality

Researchers often argue that the costs of supplying drinking water from alternative safe sources in India (mostly from surface water from reservoirs, rivers, infiltration wells, etc. after treatment) are efficient as compared to protection of groundwater from NPS pollution. In their views, the drinking water component constitutes only a miniscule amount of the water that needs to be withdrawn from surface water sources, and the investment required in the treatment and supply network is not so substantial that the government cannot afford it for public interest. But they often forget that providing access to safe drinking water to all rural population is a challenge not due to financial constraints but due to a sparsely settled population, including other physical and infrastructural constraints to bring them under centralized water supply networks. However, in the absence of strict regulation and monitoring of drinking water quality, having access to a centralized water supply network does not ensure access to adequate safe drinking water. When access to safe drinking water is not adequate, people collect water from alternative sources or depend on their own sources. As the quality of those sources is unmonitored and unregulated, they become vulnerable to various water-borne diseases. Even in the urban centres of India, the demand for safe drinking water by a large section of the population is not entirely met (Mukherjee *et al.* 2010), forcing them to depend on informal (untreated, unregulated and unmonitored) sources.

Since a substantial part of the rural population depend on groundwater as a source of drinking water, it is imperative to protect groundwater from all possible sources (point and nonpoint) of pollution. During summer months, when surface water flow reduces and competition across the sectors (agriculture, urban water supply, industrial water supply and environmental health of the water bodies) makes little water available to withdraw for the drinking water supply; it becomes difficult for people to meet their demand for drinking water.[5] The same situation also prevails in various other parts of rural India. The focus of this study is to protect groundwater from NPS pollution, as developing countries like India can neither afford to invest in a corresponding treatment infrastructure (like NO_3 and pesticides), nor have the financial capacity to investment in research and development to provide alternative low cost technology for water treatment.

Farmers' perceptions about groundwater water quality

Through four different questions the present study attempts to capture individual farmer's perceptions (subjective) about groundwater and drinking water quality. A disagreement with the second question and agreement with the other questions as shown in Table 1.5 indicates that water quality is polluted. An average of 84 per cent of the sample households are satisfied with their drinking water quality (WQS in Table 1.5), and an average of only 28 per cent of the sample households think that their groundwater quality is polluted (GWQP). However, in the case of APP, KNP and MDP more than 40 per cent of the sample households responded affirmatively for GWQP. An average of 45 per cent of the households collect water as their own source(s) of drinking water is polluted. In the case of ELA, though it is moderately polluted, 54 per cent of the sample households collect water due to water quality problems. In KNP and MDP, more than 60 per cent of the households collect water. In APP, 43 per cent of the sample households collect water, which goes against the actual groundwater quality perception as revealed to us. It is mainly due to the fact that respondents are reluctant to reveal the actual groundwater quality situation to us for fear of intimidation from local industry. Farmers' perceptions vary across the study villages significantly. On an average, 24 per cent of the sample households purified their water after collection for drinking and cooking purposes. In KAL, only 8 per cent, and in KNP 34 per cent of the households purified their water before use. However, the purification methods adopted by the sample households (boiling and using plain cloth as filter) would not reduce the presence of NO_3 in water. Further, boiling increases the concentration of NO_3, and therefore is not recommended if there is presence of NO_3 in the water.

Table 1.5 Farmers' perceptions about groundwater quality (in percentage of total number of sample farmers)

Criteria (1)	APP (2)	ELA (3)	KAL (4)	KNP (5)	KDP (6)	MDP (7)	ALL (8)
Do you think groundwater quality is polluted? (*GWQP*) (1 if 'Yes', 0 otherwise)	43	25	8	44	11	40	28
Are you satisfied with your drinking water quality? (*WQS*) (1 if 'Yes', 0 otherwise)	85	81	100	60	92	88	84
Do you collect water due to quality problem of your own drinking water source? (*CLCTWAT*) (1 if 'Yes', 0 otherwise)	42	54	21	65	30	60	45
Do you purify/treat water after collection for drinking and cooking purposes? (*PURIWATR*) (1 if 'Yes', 0 otherwise)	18	26	8	34	27	28	24

Source: Primary Survey.

Farmers' perceptions about drinking water quality

Respondents were asked to rank their drinking water quality according to their perceptions. A five-point Likert-type scale was constructed on the basis of five categories of perceptions; namely, very good (5), good (4), fair (3) bad (2) and very bad (1). The average drinking water quality scores with respect to the farmers' perceptions are presented in Figure 1.3 within three categories; namely, drinking water quality of supplied water (DWQSW), where both house connection and stand post are taken into consideration; drinking water quality of their own sources (DWQOS), which covers own hand pump, power pump, open well; and drinking water quality of public hand pump (DWQPHP). The average score of supplied water quality is 3.9 (3.6–4.0), which implies that supplied water quality lies between fair (3) to good (4) quality. However in four out of six villages some farmers also report that drinking water quality is bad (2), for example in APP and MDP, 72 per cent and 67 per cent respectively of the respondents – despite being dependent on supplied water (columns 5 and 6 in Table 1.4), their level of water quality satisfaction (WQS) is not that much higher than the average (84 per cent, column 8 in Table 1.5). The average score of own source drinking water quality varies from 2.9 to 3.9, which implies that it lies between bad (2) to good quality (4), depending on the place of residence. As for example, in KNP 66 per cent of the respondents collect water from alternative sources as their own sources of drinking water is polluted (CLCTWAT). On average, 46 per cent of the respondents collect water, as their own drinking water sources are not potable.

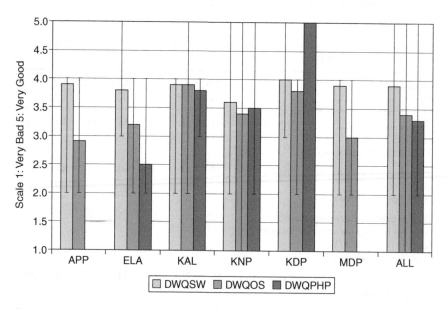

Figure 1.3 Farmers' perceptions about drinking water quality: average score (source: Primary Survey).

Factors influencing farmers' perceptions about groundwater quality

To understand the farmers' perceptions about groundwater quality in their area, in the primary questionnaire survey the respondents were asked to reveal their opinion for the following binary choice question:

Do you think groundwater quality is polluted? (GWQP)

GWQP = 1 if 'Yes'
      0 otherwise

To capture the factors influencing farmers' subjective risk perceptions about groundwater quality (GWQP), binary choice Probit models are estimated using the data collected through the primary survey and the results show that households with larger per capita landholding are more likely to perceive that their groundwater quality is polluted. Per capita landholding is a measure of a household's income, which shows that higher income households perceive a greater risk of groundwater pollution. Farmers having knowledge about impacts of agricultural practices on groundwater quality are more likely to perceive that their groundwater quality is polluted. Farmers' knowledge about agricultural practices (agriprac) and environmental BMPs (knowbmp) positively influences their perceptions.[6] However, farmers having latrine and biogas plant, using bio-fertilizers and practicing organic farming (defined as pro-environment farmers), are less likely to accept that their groundwater quality is polluted. Irrespective of sources of drinking water, farmers perceive that their groundwater quality is polluted. Households having a higher number of children, less than 5 years of age, are less likely to perceive that their groundwater quality is polluted. Sample households from comparatively highly NO_3-affected villages; namely, APP, KNP and MDP, are more likely to perceive that their groundwater quality is polluted, the opposite is true for other villages; namely, ELA, KAL and KDP. The results indicate that farmers' subjective perceptions about groundwater quality mimic the actual groundwater NO_3 situation of the villages.

Factors influencing farmers' perceptions about drinking water quality

To understand the farmers' perceptions about drinking water quality of their own sources, in the primary questionnaire survey the respondents were asked to reveal their opinion for the following binary choice question:

Do you collect water due to quality problem of your own drinking water source? (CLCTWAT)

CLCTWAT = 1 if 'Yes'
              0 otherwise

To capture the factors influencing farmers' perceptions about drinking water quality of their own sources, binary choice Probit models are estimated. The results show that:

- Farmers' perceptions about groundwater quality positively influence their decision to collect drinking water. Collection of drinking water from alternative sources and purification of water are the major coping mechanisms adopted by the households. Farmers who purify drinking water are more likely to collect water as their own sources are polluted.
- Irrespective of sources of drinking water, farmers agree that they collect water as their own sources are polluted. Farmers who are satisfied with their own drinking water quality are less likely to collect water from alternative sources.
- Households having a higher number of children (less than five years of age) and more economically active persons are less likely to collect water. Therefore, those families are more vulnerable to groundwater pollution, as they cannot collect water from alternative safe sources.
- Sample households from KNP and MDP are more likely to collect water as their own sources are polluted. In ELA, households collect water given limited access to safe drinking water and relatively better supplied water quality.
- Farmers from KAL and KDP are less likely to collect water, as their own source(s) of drinking water are comparatively less polluted. In APP, households collect drinking water from stand posts as their own sources are polluted; however due to fear of facing intimidation from local industry, households are reluctant to reveal that to us.

Factors influencing farmers' willingness to protect groundwater

To understand the factors influencing farmers' willingness (or reluctance) to protect groundwater from agricultural NPS pollution, in the questionnaire survey respondents were asked to reveal their response for the following statement:

> Since groundwater is a major source of drinking water in this area, it should be protected from agricultural chemicals (WTPGWQ)

WTPGWQ = 1 if agrees
                 0 otherwise (no response)

To capture the factors influencing farmers' willingness (or reluctance) to protect groundwater quality from agricultural NPS pollution, binary choice Probit models are estimated. The results show that:

- Farmers having better knowledge about impacts of agricultural practices on groundwater quality (agriprac) are willing to protect groundwater from NPS.
- Farmers who are staying for a long time in the sample villages and have a larger per capita landholding are reluctant to protect groundwater quality.

- Farmers' membership in participatory social institutions (e.g. Cooperative Milk Producers' Association, Farmers' Association, etc.) positively influences their willingness.
- In all comparatively NO_3-polluted villages (APP, KNP and MDP), farmers are willing to protect groundwater quality, whereas in other villages (ELA, KAL and KDP) farmers are reluctant.
- Farmers' having knowledge about agricultural BMPs and their environmental impacts (benefits) are more likely to protect groundwater quality.

Factors influencing farmers' willingness to support local government

To understand farmers' willingness (or reluctance) to support local government to supply safe drinking water (demand for safe drinking water), in the primary questionnaire survey the respondents are asked to respond to the following binary choice question:

> *Since you collect water due to quality of your own drinking water sources being problematic, will you support local government to supply water from alternative safe sources or to set up state-of-the-art water treatment plant, by contributing, supporting and taking initiative? (WTSGOVCW)*

WTSGOVCW = 1 if Yes
          0 otherwise

The results show that an average of 38 per cent (minimum 20 per cent in KAL to maximum 58 per cent in MDP) of the sample farmers are willing to support local government, which varies significantly across the sample villages. To capture the factors influencing farmers, binary choice Probit models are estimated, which show that:

- Irrespective of sources of drinking water, farmers are willing to support local government in terms of initiatives and contribution to supply safe drinking water.
- Farmers having access to relatively good quality drinking water are reluctant to support the local government. Farmers' perceptions about their groundwater quality influence their willingness, and the households who purify water are also willing to support.
- Households from APP, KAL and KDP are less likely to support government, as their own sources of groundwater quality are comparatively less polluted (KAL and KDP) or they already have good access to supplied water (APP).
- Households from ELA, KNP and MDP are willing to support government, as their own sources of drinking water are comparatively polluted (KNP and MDP), and they want to improve the access to supplied water (ELA).

Summary and conclusions

The present analysis attempts to understand the farmers' perceptions about groundwater quality in their area through a primary survey. On average, 28 per cent of the sample households perceived that their groundwater quality was polluted, which varied significantly across the villages from the minimum 8 per cent in KAL to the maximum 44 per cent in KDP. In the case of APP, KNP and MDP more than 40 per cent of the sample households responded affirmatively to perceiving groundwater pollution. Among six villages selected for our primary questionnaire survey, three villages; namely, APP, KNP and MDP, had comparatively higher groundwater NO_3 concentration, which was also reflected in the perception survey. Farmers from these three villages thought that their groundwater quality was polluted, whereas the farmers from other three villages responded negatively. The estimated results show that:

- Farmers from comparatively high groundwater NO_3-contaminated villages correctly perceive (subjective) their groundwater quality and they are willing to protect groundwater quality as compared to farmers from less affected villages. *Therefore, it shows that any groundwater quality protection programme from NPS pollution should take into consideration the site characteristics and socio-economic characteristics of the stakeholders.*
- Farmers' groundwater quality perceptions vary across the villages and mimic the actual groundwater NO_3 situation. Households depending on their socio-economic characteristics, social- and information-network and the characteristics of the resource (alternative sources and quality of drinking water) derive a subjective risk assessment of their groundwater quality. *Regular monitoring of groundwater quality, assessment (objective) of risks of consuming contaminated groundwater and communication of risks to the stakeholders could help the farmers to take measures/initiatives either individually or collectively to protect groundwater from NPS pollution.*
- Demand for safe drinking water varies across the villages, based on the variations of socio-economic characteristics of the sample households and groundwater quality. However, their willingness to support local government initiatives in this regard shows different results. For example, farmers from villages having higher concentration of groundwater NO_3 are willing to protect groundwater quality and reluctant to support local government. *However, adoption of a demand driven approach for provision of drinking water may not be suitable specifically when the risk of consuming contaminated drinking water is not commonly perceived by the consumers, as the presence of NO_3 does not change the taste, odour, colour or any other commonly perceivable quality/characteristics of drinking water.*
- Farmers' knowledge about impacts of agricultural practices on groundwater quality significantly influences their perceptions about groundwater quality and willingness to protect groundwater. Therefore, *provision of agricultural information and education along with basic agricultural extension services could induce the farmers to protect groundwater from NPS pollution.*

- Both socio-economic characteristics of the households and the character-istics of the subject (groundwater or drinking water) significantly influence the farmers' perceptions. Knowledge of agricultural BMPs and their impacts on environment positively influences farmers' perceptions and willingness.
- Memberships in social participatory institutions and sources of agricultural information significantly influence farmers' perceptions and willingness.

Since long-term environmental and human health risks/implications of drinking NO_3-contaminated water are uncertain, and *ex post* treatment and remediation measures are very costly and technically/financially unviable, it is imperative to follow the precautionary approach related to groundwater pollution in general and agricultural NPS water pollution in particular. Taking the cue from developed countries, it will be imperative for developing countries to initiate NPS pollution control measures as early as possible. Developing countries like India cannot afford (technically or financially) to rely solely on curative meas-ures; therefore it is imperative that they should protect drinking water sources by controlling pollution from NPS. Since, groundwater is a major source of drink-ing water, protection of groundwater quality from NPS should be an integral part of managing sustainable access to safe drinking water.

The role of stakeholders and their voluntary participation in agri-environmental management in general and water resources conservation/ management in particular is a new area of research, at least for a developing country like India. It is important to stress the linkages between water quantity and quality problems in river basin management. The issue of groundwater pol-lution from NPS is a growing concern not only for relatively water-scarce coun-tries like India, but also for water abundant countries around the world, which needs to be addressed by policymakers in an expeditious manner to protect the health and welfare of the citizens.

Notes

1 Ongley (1996) notes that,

> Nonpoint source water pollution arises from a broad group of human activities for which the pollutants have no obvious point of entry into receiving watercourses. In contrast, point source pollution represents those activities where wastewater is routed directly into receiving water bodies by, for example, discharge pipes, where they can be easily measured and controlled. Obviously, NPS pollution is much more difficult to identify, measure and control than point sources.

2 Numbers in parentheses show the percentage of NO_3-affected samples to total number of samples drawn from hand pumps and power pumps respectively.

3 Voluntary cooperation 'involves individuals or groups moving in concert in a situation in which no party has the power to command the behaviour of others' (Wondolleck and Yafee 2000).

4 A place satisfying the following three criteria simultaneously: (a) a minimum popula-tion of 5,000; (b) at least 75 per cent of the male working population engaged in non-agricultural pursuits; and (c) a density of population of at least 400 per km^2. can be classified as a town panchayat.

5 If demand for safe drinking water in rural areas cannot be met with local sources (pre-dominantly from groundwater), it will put additional burden on surface water sources (rivers, lakes and reservoirs, etc.), which are under stress (Mukherjee *et al.* 2010).

6 To capture farmers' knowledge on farm management practices, a composite index has been constructed by using indicators of farmers' knowledge about: crop-wise recommended doses of fertilizers suitable for their soil; organic farming; bio-fertilizers; bio-gas plant and bio-composting of animal waste. A composite index of farmers' knowledge about agricultural practices and their impacts on groundwater quality (agriprac) has been constructed by using indicators of farmers' understanding on: crop-wise, land-to-land variations of recommended doses of fertilizers (based on soil quality testing); impacts of over application of fertilizers and pesticides on soil and groundwater quality; impacts of cutting down of fertilizers' application on productivity of crops; impacts of recommended doses of fertilizers on environment; impacts of unlined and open storage of livestock waste on groundwater quality; impacts of open defecation and toilet on groundwater quality; and impacts of unlined storage of human waste on groundwater quality.

References

Agrawal, G.D., Lunkad, S.K. and Malkhed, T. (1999) 'Diffuse Agricultural Nitrate Pollution of Groundwater in India', *Water Science and Technology*, 39(3): 67–75.

Banadda, E.N., Kansiime, F., Kigobe, M., Kizza, M. and Nhapi, I. (2009) 'Landuse-Based Nonpoint Source Pollution: A Threat to Water Quality in Murchison Bay, Uganada', *Water Policy*, 11(Supplement 1): 94–105.

BIS (1991) *Indian Standard Specifications for Drinking Water: IS 10 500*, New Delhi: Bureau of Indian Standards.

Brandon, C. and Hommann, K. (1995) 'The Cost of Inaction: Valuing the Economy-Wide Cost of Environmental Degradation in India', paper presented at the conference on Modelling Global Sustainability, United Nations University, Tokyo.

Brau, R. and Carraro, C. (1999) 'Voluntary Approaches, Market Structure and Competition', Note di Lavoro 52.99, Milan: Fondazione Eni Enrico Mattei (FEEM).

Brouwer, F., Heinz, I. and Zebel, T. (eds) (2003) *Governance of Water-related Conflicts in Agriculture: New Directions in Agri-Environmental and Water Policies in the EU*, Dordrecht: Kluwer Academic Publishers.

Census of India (2001) *Village and Town Directory under District Census Handbook*, Chennai: Directorate of Census Operations, GoI.

CGWB (2010) 'Ground Water Quality in Shallow Aquifers of India', Faridabad: Central Ground Water Board, Ministry of Water Resources, GoI.

Chelliah, R.J., Appasamy, P.P., Sankar, U. and Pandey, R. (2007) *Ecotaxes on Polluting Inputs and Outputs*, New Delhi: Academic Foundation.

DDWS (Department of Drinking Water Supply) (2004) *List of Water Quality Affected Habitations as Reported by States (as on 31 March 2004) – As Per Quality Survey 2000*. Online, available at: http://ddws.nic.in/WQ/main.asp (accessed 5 May 2006).

DDWS (2008) 'Annual Report – 2007–08', New Delhi: Ministry of Rural Development, GoI.

Department of Agriculture and Cooperation (2010) *Agricultural Statistics at a Glance 2010*, New Delhi: Ministry of Agriculture, GoI.

Dosi, C. and Zeitouni, N. (2001) 'Controlling Groundwater Pollution from Agricultural Non-point Sources: an Overview of Policy Instruments', in C. Dosi (ed.) *Agricultural Use of Groundwater: Towards Integration between Agricultural Policy and Water Resources Management*, Dordrecht: Kluwer Academic Publishers.

Duda, A.M. (1993) 'Addressing Nonpoint Sources of Water Pollution Must Become an International Priority', *Water Science and Technology*, 28: 3–5.

Engel, B., Kumar, N. and Cooper, B. (1996) 'Estimating Vulnerability to Nonpoint Source Pollution from Nitrate and Pesticides on a Regional Scale', paper presented at Vienna Conference on HydroGIS 96: Application of Geographic Information Systems in Hydrology and Water Resources, April.

Foster, S. and Garduño, H. (2004) *India – Tamil Nadu: Resolving the Conflict Over Rural Groundwater Use Between Drinking Water and Irrigation Supply*, Case Profile Collection Number 11, Sustainable Groundwater Management Lessons from Practice, Global Water Partnership Associate Program, Washington, DC: World Bank.

Freeman, M. (1990) 'Water Pollution Policy', in P. Portney (ed.) *Policies for Environmental Protection*, Washington, DC: Resources for the Future.

Handa, B.K. (1986) 'Pollution of Ground Waters by Nitrates in India', *Bhu-Jal News: Quarterly Journal of Central Ground Water Board*, 1: 16–19.

Lévêque, F. (1997) 'Voluntary Approaches', in *Environmental Policy Research Briefs*, no. 1, produced within the framework of the EU Concerted Action on Market Based Instruments.

Ministry of Rural Development (2010a) *Quality Affected Habitations*, Department of Drinking Water, GoI. Online, available at: http://indiawater.gov.in/IMISWeb/Reports/rws/Rep_QualityAffectedHabitationSelection.aspx?Rep=Y (accessed 5 May 2006).

Ministry of Rural Development (2010b) *Problem of Contaminated Drinking Water*, PIB Press Release, 3 August 2010. Online, available at: http://pib.nic.in/release/release.sp?relid=64016 (accessed 3 August 2010).

Mukherjee, S. (2008) 'Economics of Agricultural Nonpoint Source Water Pollution: A Case Study of Groundwater Nitrate Pollution in the Lower Bhavani River Basin, Tamil Nadu', unpublished PhD thesis, University of Madras (Madras School of Economics).

Mukherjee, S. (2010) 'Nutrient-Based Fertiliser Subsidy: Will Farmers Adopt Agricultural Best Management Practices?', *Economic and Political Weekly*, 45(49): 66–72.

Mukherjee, S., Shah, Z. and Kumar, M.D. (2010) 'Sustaining Urban Water Supplies in India: Increasing Role of Large Reservoirs', *Water Resources Management*, 24(10): 2035–2055.

NAAS (2005) 'Policy Options for Efficient Nitrogen Use', Policy Paper No. 33, New Delhi: National Academy of Agricultural Sciences.

National Habitations Survey (2003) *Contamination-Wise Number of Quality Affected Habitations*. Online, available at: http://ddws.gov.in/habquery/rep_affected_group.asp (accessed 5 May 2006).

Ongley, E.D. (1996) 'Control of Water Pollution from Agriculture', FAO irrigation and drainage paper 55, Rome: Food and Agriculture Organization.

Padgelt, S. (1994) 'Groundwater Pollution Prevention: Voluntary BMPs for Agriculture', *Water Quality Update*, 4(3–5), University of Idaho. Online, available at: www.uidaho.edu/wq/wqu/wqu44.html#art4 (accessed 15 May 2005).

Panda, R.K. and Behera, S. (2003) 'Non-Point Source Pollution of Water Resources: Problems and Perspectives', *Food, Agriculture and Environment*, 1(3/4): 308–311.

Public Works Department (PWD) (1992) 'Report of the Study of Effect of Intensive Application of Fertilizer and Pesticide on Groundwater Quality in Agricultural Fields', Chennai: Office of the Chief Engineer, Ground Water, PWD, Government of Tamil Nadu.

Ribaudo, M.O. (1992) 'Options for Agricultural Nonpoint-Source Pollution Control', *Journal of Soil and Water Conservation*, 47(1): 42–46.

Rougoor C.W., Zeijts, H. Van, Hofreither, M.F. and Bäckman, S. (2001) 'Experiences with Fertilizer Taxes in Europe', *Journal of Environmental Planning and Management*, 44(6): 877–887.

Shortle, J.S. and Abler, D.G. (1997) 'Nonpoint Pollution', in H. Folmer and T.H. Tietenberg (eds) *The International Yearbook of Environmental and Resource Economics 1997/98*, Cheltenham: Edward Elgar.

Shortle, J.S. and Horan, R.D. (2001) 'The Economics of Nonpoint Pollution Control', *Journal of Economic Surveys*, 15(3): 255–289.

Tirado, R. (2009) *Chemical Fertilisers in our Water: An Analysis of Nitrates in the Groundwater in Punjab*, New Delhi: Greenpeace India.

Trivedy, R.K. (2000) 'Legislation Controlling Quality of Freshwater in India', *Journal of Industrial Pollution Control*, 16(1): 131–143.

UNDP (2006) 'Human Development Report 2006 – Beyond Scarcity: Power, Poverty and the Global Water Crisis', New York: United Nations Development Programme.

Water and Sanitation Programme (undated) *The Economic Impacts of Inadequate Sanitation in India*, New Delhi: The World Bank.

WHO (2004) *Guidelines for Drinking-water Quality – Recommendations*, Volume 1, Geneva: World Health Organization.

Wondolleck, J.M. and Yaffee, S.L. (2000) *Making Collaboration Work: Lessons from Innovation in Natural Resource Management*, Washington, DC: Island Press.

Zeijts, H. van and Westhoek, H. (2004) *Experiences with Taxes/Levies on Fertilisers and Pesticides in European Countries*, The Hague: Netherlands Environmental Assessment Agency.

2 Economics of sustainable shrimp aquaculture in India

Ramachandra Bhatta

Introduction

Shrimp aquaculture in India has evolved from a mere subsistence industry in the 1980s to one of the world's leading producers of cultured shrimp by the mid-1990s. In 2003, India was world's second-largest producer of cultured shrimp at 115,320 tonne with 152,000 ha under shrimp culture (MPEDA 2004a). Experts believe that the industry is still in its infancy, occupying only 15 per cent of India's total coastal area identified as suitable for land-based aquaculture. Yet, Indian aquaculture has already emerged as one of the largest export-earning sectors, with total shrimp exports reaching 134,815 tonne in 2003 valued at Rs.4,608 million out of which 82 per cent was contributed by cultured shrimp. Favourable climatic conditions, availability of natural brood stock, ample trained manpower, technological advancements, and concessions have contributed to the industry's rapid expansion. Total cultivated shrimp production increased from 35,500 tonne in 1990–91 to 102,940 tonne in 2001–02 with an annual compound growth rate of 8.8 per cent. However, average yield per hectare, which reached its peak during 1994–95 to 819 kg/ha, started declining due to both health and disease problems and the reduction of intensive shrimp farms in the coastal regulation zone (CRZ) from 2000 onwards. Cultured shrimps currently contribute around 30 per cent of total fisheries gross national product (GNP), with ample employment opportunities. Andhra Pradesh (henceforth AP) contributes more than half of country's shrimp production and exports.

Difficulties linking individual shrimp farm practices and ambient water quality makes shrimp farming a typical non-point source (NPS) of pollution. Wastewater discharge by a large number of individual small and medium farms at irregular times and levels makes controlling pollution very difficult. Developmental pressures pose an important policy question regarding the ability of the government to rationally allocate the finite coastal lands between aquaculture and traditional uses so as to produce crops, quality water and shrimp in sustainable manner. With large untapped areas having potential for shrimp aquaculture, the government may find it hard to resist the industry lobbying to develop the remaining land. In AP out of 85,000 ha of shrimp area developed during the last decade, only 53,000 ha is currently under operation (Government of AP 2004).

Arriving at an optimal land allocation decision requires recognition of coastal land as a complex resource with both renewable and non-renewable components. As Swallow (1990) points out, 'failure to recognize resource interactions leads to excessive [coastal land] development'. The renewable components include, among others, the land's intrinsic quality to produce food and its ability to filter undesirable salt (a pollutant) leaching into groundwater in the region. The non-renewable component is the finite surface area for which there are conflicting uses (crop production versus shrimp aquaculture). Needless to say, the renewable and non-renewable components are interdependent. The use of the non-renewable portion of the resource for shrimp aquaculture can adversely affect the environmental bases (e.g. land quality and salinity assimilation capacity) of renewable resource production. Unfortunately, there is a lack of empirical research in developing a decision-support system in the Indian context which could help coastal land-use agencies to evaluate alternative land-use options in terms of their ecological and socio-economic merits. Specifically, the policy-makers require a decision support tool enabling them to make informed decisions on the allocation of limited resources to various land-use options through an integrated approach.

Integrated coastal area management (ICAM) is a component of the Food and Agriculture Organization's code of conduct for responsible fisheries that develops an optimization framework and integrates the environmental and technical dimensions of the land management plan within the broader socio-economic and ecological considerations. The adoption of best management practices (BMPs) may affect current income and yield. However, the small farmers are mostly averse to risk factors related to changes in their management practices. Therefore, in the absence of a good institutional and organizational mechanism, the adoption of BMPs becomes very slow. Organizing the small farmers through farm clubs and producer associations requires strengthening of the organizational set-up.

The specific objectives of the current study are:

- To study the changing structure of shrimp farming and its implications on governance;
- To review the existing institutional arrangements of the coastal aquaculture sector with specific to AP and suggest an appropriate institutional framework for the regulation of aquaculture;
- To review the AP coastal zone management plan (CZMP) and suggest ways and means to further strengthen the implementation of aquaculture activities within the CZMP through ICAM.

In order to make a comprehensive review of the existing scenario, the current study critically analyses the existing literature on the ICAM framework, coastal shrimp farming, CZMP, etc. Moreover, expert consultations and discussions with various organizations, authorities and NGOs on the positive and negative aspects of the existing framework have been conducted to derive policy suggestions.

Current status of coastal shrimp farming in Andhra Pradesh

AP is the fourth-largest state in India in terms of geographical area (8.4 per cent of the country's territory) and fifth-largest in terms of population. The state is divided into three regions and the coastal region consists of nine districts covering a coastal length of 980 km along the Bay of Bengal with a total area of 9.24 million ha. The normal rainfall of the coastal districts ranges from 750 mm to 1,160 mm with an average rainfall of 1,024 mm, which is slightly higher than the state's average of 925 mm. The irrigated area is only 2.11 million ha and the groundwater availability is estimated to be 12,637 million m^3.

Coastal shrimp farming has been undergoing structural changes in AP. The shrimp farming industry was initially developed with support from the State Fisheries Department and Marine Products Export Development Authority (MPEDA), under the Ministry of Commerce, Government of India. With the entry of corporate players, the shrimp farming industry witnessed substantial growth during late 1980s and early 1990s. The environmental and socio-economic problems culminated to the Supreme Court judgment in 1996 prohibiting intensive and semi-intensive shrimp farming within the CRZ and constituted Aquaculture Authority to prohibit modern shrimp farming within CRZ and promote only improved extensive shrimp farming practices outside of CRZ. The recent shrimp farm area developments in AP indicate the need for serious land use planning.

The area under shrimp culture has declined from 78,702 ha in 1994 to 53,246 ha in 2004, indicating a 32 per cent decline (Table 2.1). The number of farms has declined by only 16 per cent, indicating that much of the decline in the farm area was among the larger farms. In districts like Krishna and Nellore a large area has been abandoned where the density of farms was also very high. Thus those regions with a higher density of farms suffered considerably. On the other hand in Srikakulam, Prakasham, East and West Godavari districts, the number of farmers has

Table 2.1 Changes in the shrimp culture area in Andhra Pradesh

Districts	Area under culture (ha)			No. of farmers		
	1994	2004	% change	1994	2004	% change
Srikakulam	647	451	−30	211	326	55
Vizianagaram	101	29	−71	7	6	−14
Visakhapatnam	1,759	792	−55	208	140	−33
East Godavari	7,821	9,253	18	4,814	9,454	96
West Godavari	14,374	14,577	1	16,179	21,806	35
Krishna	32,968	14,767	−55	37,495	18,853	−50
Guntur	8,821	4,177	−53	10,669	4,060	−62
Prakasam	5,105	4,442	−13	1707	2,842	66
Nellore	7,105	4,759	−33	2,050	4,326	111
Overall	78,702	53,246	−32	73,340	61,813	−16

Source: MPEDA (2004b).

increased by 55, 66, 96 and 35 per cent respectively as potential existed for the expansion of the shrimp farm area with a lower density of farms. Interestingly, in Nellore district although the total area has declined by 33 per cent the numbers of farms have doubled, showing an increase of 111 per cent. Thus most of the corporate farms have dismantled into small farms.

During 1993–94 to 2003–04, the number of farmers with less than 5 ha land under shrimp culture has declined by 25 per cent. The number of farms with a greater than 5 ha size has declined by 65 per cent (Table 2.2). The trend indicates that the large farms have become economically un-viable. The management implications of declining farm size is that it has led to an increased non-point source of pollution leading to an increased transaction cost of implementation of BMPs and other eco-friendly farm management practices such as limited use of approved chemicals, disease free seeds, formation of bio-ponds for the settlement of the wastewater, planting of mangroves around inlets and outlets and effluent treatment systems (ETS).

There has been a growth in small-sized farms in Srikakulam, East Godavari, Prakasham and Nellore districts, although overall the 0–5 ha size category has declined by 14 per cent. The number of farms greater than 5 ha farm-size has declined by 70 per cent. The observations indicate that the corporate farms have become unviable due to several reasons such as self-pollution (release of effluent water from the neighbourhood aquaculture ponds), non-availability of fresh water on large scale and compliance cost of pollution control measures.

With the increasing density of shrimp farms, over the years their water quality and surrounding environment has degraded and compelled the farmers to abandon the large number of developed areas as shrimp farming in those areas was economically unviable. Table 2.3 presents the district-wise shrimp developed area, the area within the CRZ 500 m from the high tide line (HTL) and the abandoned/un-utilized area. The table shows that a major section of the

Table 2.2 Changing farm-size structure in Andhra Pradesh

Districts	0–5 ha			>5 ha		
	1994	*2004*	*% change*	*1994*	*2004*	*% change*
Srikakulam	194	312	61	17	14	−18
Vizianagaram	3	3	0	4	3	−25
Visakhapatnam	118	102	−14	90	38	−58
East Godavari	4,696	9,400	100	118	54	−54
West Godavari	16,158	21,764	35	21	42	100
Krishna	37,466	18,767	−50	29	86	197
Guntur	10,643	4,021	−62	26	39	50
Prakasam	1,516	2,719	79	191	123	−36
Nellore	879	4,223	380	1,171	103	−91
Overall	71,673	61,311	−14	1,667	502	−70

Source: MPEDA (2004b).

Table 2.3 Shrimp farming and coastal land degradation in Andhra Pradesh

District	Area developed (ha)	Percentage of area developed within CRZ	Percentage of area under Shrimp culture within CRZ	Percentage of abandoned area within CRZ	Percentage of abandoned area to total developed area
Srikakulam	663	68	67	34	23
Vizianagaram	102	30	30	–	–
Visakhapatnam	2,074	4	0	100	4
East Godavari	10,085	72	71	10	7
West Godavari	24,049	45	12	84	38
Krishna	28,906	87	87	48	42
Guntur	6,294	100	100	34	34
Prakasam	5,173	99	99	14	14
Nellore	6,816	56	54	32	18
Overall	84,162	70	62	44	31

Source: MPEDA (2004b).

shrimp farms developed within the CRZ (fragile and sensitive area) has now degraded within a period of ten years of shrimp farming. The percentage of abandoned area within CRZ is twice that of the overall abandoned area, indicating that the earlier developed areas have been degraded and the farmers have been moving away from CRZ area for shrimp farming.

As per the latest estimation nearly 31,000 ha (37 per cent of the total developed area) is currently un-utilized (MPEDA 2004a). Pond abandonment, crop holidays, crop diversion, fallows and settlements are some of the reasons behind the non-use of developed land for shrimp farming. Conversion of shrimp ponds for crop farming is observed at times, but rice yield in such converted farms is only one-third that of traditional cropland. Further the farmer has to forego two to three crops to bring them to normal yield level apart from land development costs, which acts as a disincentive for such conversion.

Socio-economics of shrimp farming

The following section present the results of the socio-economic survey conducted during 2003 among the shrimp farmers of AP, Karnataka and West Bengal (henceforth WB). Shrimp farming unlike freshwater aquaculture is purely a commercial enterprise undertaken by educated and skilled individuals and firms (partners). The years of education ranges from nine to 13 years, indicating that the shrimp farmers have completed a minimum of secondary education (Table 2.4). Most of the sample farmers have been practicing shrimp cultivation during the last 6–8 years. The size of shrimp farms among the sample ranges between 0.9–13.0 ha, signifying the presence of small and marginal farmers on one hand and capitalistic firms on the other. Since shrimp farmers specialize only in shrimp cultivation, entire land area is utilized for shrimp ponds leaving very little area for other activities like wastewater treatment, etc.

The farmers of AP have utilized the entire land area for shrimp farming unlike Karnataka and WB. Thus there is no scope for planting mangroves and forming bio-ponds for the settlement of the wastewater. The stocking density, as measured by number of seeds per ha, was two to three times higher in AP as

Table 2.4 Socio-economic profile of shrimp farmers in Andhra Pradesh, Karnataka and West Bengal

Particulars	Andhra Pradesh	Karnataka	West Bengal
Sample size	144	121	70
Level of education (years)	13	10	9
Years of experience in shrimp farming (years)	6	6	8
Area under shrimp farming (ha)	9.0	2.9	6.1
Total land area (ha)	9.0	3.6	8.3

Source: Bhatta (2003).

compared to Karnataka and WB. This indicates that advanced pond management practices are followed in AP. The feed, fertilizer, lime and chemicals use is also much higher in AP as compared to other two states (Table 2.5).

The cost incurred by AP farmers is around twice that incurred by each of the other two selected states. It is observed that more than 75 per cent of the total cost is spent on seed and feed followed by labour and other costs (Table 2.6). One of the most controversial issues concerning shrimp farming is that it leads to a loss of employment as compared to agricultural crops. On an average, the shrimp farms generate 156 labour days per crop per ha, whereas the comparable figure for paddy cultivation is 220 man-days (Bhatta 2005). However, the wage rate in shrimp farms and paddy cultivation on average are Rs.50–60/man-day and Rs.40–45/man-day respectively. Thus, although there is a small decline in labour itself, the labour payment is higher in shrimp farming, resulting in an improvement in the socio-economic status of the fish farmers.

Table 2.5 Input use pattern in different shrimp farms (per crop/ha)

Particulars	Andhra Pradesh	Karnataka	West Bengal
Seeds (no)	73,083	31,889	26,089
Feed (kg)	130	50	60
Labour (days)	161	161	135
Fertilizers (kg)	247	40	24
Organic fertilizers (kg)	213	17	1
Chemical fertilizers (kg)	34	23	23
Lime (kg)	978	521	754

Source: Bhatta (2003).

Table 2.6 Cost profile of shrimp farming (in per cent of total cost)

Particulars	Andhra Pradesh	Karnataka	West Bengal
Seeds	17.0	16.4	23.1
Feed	55.8	35.6	41.5
Labour	8.2	21.0	9.7
Fertilizers	1.2	0.3	0.4
Chemicals for pond preparation	1.7	2.8	5.1
Hormones and vitamins	0.4	0.4	0.2
Fuel	5.3	3.6	5.6
Rent (farm and equipment)	1.5	2.8	8.4
Depreciation and interest*	7.8	16.3	5.0
Incidentals	1.0	0.8	0.9
Total	100	100	100
Total cost (Rs./ha)	1,14,628	70,257	72,398

Source: Bhatta (2003).

Note
* The rate of depreciation and interest rate is 10 per cent.

A comparison of costs and returns of shrimp farming across the states also shows that the yield and net revenue is substantially higher in AP due to a more intensive method of farming.

An analysis of cost of production and returns per kilogram of shrimp is presented in Table 2.8. The table shows that the cost per kilogram is lowest in Karnataka with extensive pond management practices.

Health management

In order to address the problem of shrimp diseases, MPEDA, Cochin, in association with the Network of Aquaculture Centers in Asia (NACA), Thailand, instituted a study involving a detailed epidemiological survey and concluded that much of the disease outbreaks could be prevented by farm level managerial interventions (Hossain et al. 2003). White spot disease (WSD), caused by White spot syndrome virus, affects 80 per cent of the health problems in shrimp farms. Other serious diseases include loose-shell syndrome and stunted growth (causes could be malnutrition, bacterial and viral infections). Mass mortalities due to high ammonia and low dissolved oxygen in farms are another problem in improved traditional farms. Risk factors faced by farmers for good production are as follows:

- Disease;
- Very poor water qualities in the source (Creek/drains);
- Irregular farming without any discipline for follow up of practices, e.g. stocking time stretched from January to April instead of the optimum time of February first week to March second week.

Table 2.7 Cost and returns of shrimp farming (Rs. in lakh/ha/crop)

Particulars	Andhra Pradesh	Karnataka	West Bengal
Yield (kg/ha)	811	620	626
Total cost	1.15	0.70	0.72
Gross returns	2.69	1.58	1.84
Net revenue	1.55	0.88	1.11
Benefit cost ratio	2.35	2.25	2.53

Source: Bhatta (2003).

Table 2.8 Cost and returns of shrimp farming (Rs./kg/crop)

Particulars	Andhra Pradesh	Karnataka	West Bengal
Average price received (Rs./kg)	332	255	293
Total cost	141	113	116
Gross returns	332	255	293
Net revenue	191	142	177

Source: Bhatta (2003).

- Poor seed quality – most of the seed batches (more than 50 per cent) from hatcheries are infected with deadly pathogens;
- Introduction of pathogen carriers like zooplankton, wild shrimps, etc. into the pond due to no use of water filter;
- High amount of sludge inside the ponds due to non-cleaning of pond bottom for long periods;
- Benthic algal growth and subsequent decomposition leading to fall in dissolved oxygen;
- Excessive feeding leading to feed wastage and fall in dissolved oxygen.

Table 2.9 shows that the financial loss due to disease is increasing rapidly. The loss incurred per hectare has increased by Rs.2,500 within a period of three years. The declining economic viability of shrimp farming due to health and poor growth problems is affecting small and medium farmers more severely than large farmers since they are more vulnerable to risk factors. The highest quality seeds and feeds are sold to corporate farms and the small farmers depend on poorer quality seeds (sold at lower price), which are susceptible to disease and poor growth. Technical measures such as crop holidays, crop alternation, alternative canals for intake and discharge of water, regular flushing out of water from the creek, development of secondary aquaculture, cultivation of mangrove forests around shrimp ponds, and following BMPs are suggested to make shrimp farming more sustainable. However, there is no clear demonstration of the ecological and economic benefits of such measures at the farm level, leading to reluctance and slow adoption among the farmers.

Shrimp farming and the environment

The earlier belief that aquaculture will relieve pressure from marine biodiversity is not necessarily true. Some intensive methods of aquaculture have worsened marine biodiversity through their unsustainable demand for water, seed and food resources, and also because of the release of wastewater. For example, in order to produce 1 tonne of cultured shrimp it is estimated that an almost equal quantity of wild fish is required in the form of aqua feed. Fishmeal and fish oil, have

Table 2.9 Financial loss due to shrimp diseases in Andhra Pradesh

Particulars	2000–2001	2003–2004
Area under culture (ha)	97,137	115,143
Total area affected (ha)	19,444	28,682
Total yield loss (tonne)	18,551	30,921
Loss/ha (kg)	19	27
Loss (Rs./ha @ Rs. 331/kg)	6,308	8,964
Total loss (Rs. Lakh)	6,127	10,321

Source: MPEDA (2004b).

become major ingredients for industrially produced aqua feeds since they provide the same composition as the natural food consumed by carnivorous fish. The dependence on marine fish catches for producing aqua feed and shrimp feed for aquaculture may put pressure on wild fish stock, and that could also put pressure on the availability of fish which are now used for human consumption, as in the future they could be used for fishmeal production. This raises considerable concern regarding trends in 'biomass fishing' in India which involves highly non-selective fishery techniques involving small-mesh sizes for the single purpose of catching as many marine organisms as possible; after the valued commercial catches are removed the remaining majority of fish is utilised for fish meal production.

Some of the major environmental concerns of aquaculture are:

- Conversion of mangrove forests and other wetlands to aquaculture farms and thus leading to a decline in the area available for wild shrimp and fish breeding grounds;
- Eutrophication of natural waters by effluents from aquaculture operations leading to decline in availability of dissolved oxygen required for healthy fish production;
- Increased sedimentation in natural water bodies as a result of shrimp pond effluents and disposal of pond sediment, poor water storage level and increased cost of water exchange system;
- Salinization of fresh water by pond effluents and seepage into aquifers and loss of drinking water sources;
- Use of potentially toxic and bio-accumulative chemicals in production;
- Excessive use of resources such as fresh water, feed ingredients, electricity, etc.;
- Negative effects on native fisheries and biodiversity through habitat destruction, water pollution, impingement by pumps, uses of wild-caught brood stock and larvae, and introduction of non-native species

There should be no conflict between shrimp growers and non-shrimp growers regarding organic loading, pollution and enrichment. Aquaculture is unique, as unlike other industries it is also adversely and directly affected by self-generated waste. The shrimp growers should realize that effective waste treatment and pollution abatement can be considered as the core of sustainability, which also enhances community welfare. Limiting the stocking density within farms or limiting the number of farms within an area will doubtlessly work, but four questions need to be answered:

- How can farms be monitored for compliance with the density limits?
- How can the size of farms (in hectares) to be allowed in an area be determined?
- Is it feasible or even technically possible to determine the carrying capacity in all the shrimp growing areas?

- Imposing limits on stocking density stifles productivity and efficiency; should we be content at producing a few hundred kilograms per hectare when potential production can be several metric tonne? There is also insufficient baseline data to compute carrying capacities of a given area.

Viewed objectively, it is not the number of shrimps per se, but the amount of waste generated by the shrimp stock, which has a negative impact on environment. If a shrimp farm can successfully manage its waste so that it no longer affects the environment, should it still be punished for exceeding the imposed limits? Just as the government does not normally dictate the output of manufacturing plants (leaving it to the discretion of the operator who would consider the plant capacity and market) no limits should be imposed on shrimp stocking density. However, the government in the interest of public health and safety should have the right to impose standards on the waste discharges, be it from a manufacturing plant or a shrimp farm.

Certain aquaculture practices also reduce wild supplies through excessive seed stock collection. The salinization of coastal cropland owing to unregulated shrimp cultivation has generated its own crisis. There are ample evidences that the common water bodies have been shrinking through degradation, encroachment and siltation, etc. which is not properly reflected in the official data. Another threat to fisheries and aquaculture is from industrial pollution. Both biological oxygen demand (BOD) and total coliform are found to be rising in many rivers of Karnataka (Central Water Commission 1996). As reported by the Central Pollution Control Board (1997), in AP out of 2,466 million litre of wastewater discharged every day 2,116 million litre are from aquaculture, where there has been maximum growth of aquaculture.

Economic feasibility of sustainable shrimp farming

The Food and Agricultural Organization (FAO), Aquaculture Authority and the state Department of Fisheries are advocating the adoption of best pond-management practices for sustainable shrimp farming. The guidelines on ETS issued by the Aquaculture Authority (2003) stresses the need for ETS in large shrimp farms and also a common ETS for clusters of small shrimp farms. In order to educate the shrimp farmers about the need for sustainable and eco-friendly shrimp farming practices, the State Department of Fisheries, Central Institute of Brackish-water Aquaculture and MPEDA regularly conduct awareness camps and training workshops.

In small shrimp farms, since each pond will have an independent discharge point, they could be connected to a common discharge channel leading to a settlement pond for treatment. Such discharge points should be sufficiently away from the culture ponds. The Aquaculture Authority has made it mandatory for all large shrimp farms, with a greater than 5 ha area within CRZ or 10 ha outside the CRZ, to implement ETS. For promoting cooperative approaches to introducing common management practices among small cluster farmers such as water management, seed stocking, procurement and maintenance of quality seeds, feeds, health management, and other related issues the Department of Fisheries has promoted aqua clubs. One of the objectives of these clubs is to set up settlement ponds. So far 126 aqua clubs have been established with 3,321 members in AP. Table 2.10 presents the capital and operational cost of maintaining an ETS with 0.5 ha of settlement pond area, which can cater to the needs of 5 ha of land under shrimp farming. MPEDA has taken up the promotion of such a system by providing a capital subsidy of Rs.150,000 for each ETS established by the shrimp farmers.

The small farmers cannot afford to adopt eco-friendly pond management practices. Further, due to large number of small farms, the institutional cost of mobilizing farmers for the adoption of community managed practices such as common ETS would be higher. It is estimated that at least six or seven farmers have to join together to adopt and operate one common ETS with an additional capital cost of Rs.64,000 and an operating cost of 28,000 per crop per farm apart from other transaction costs. The indiscriminate use of chemicals, pro-biotics, concentrated feeds and fertilizers in excess of the required quantity, results in environmental degradation. In the absence of strong extension services and crop insurance against health risks, farmers adopt measures which lead to adverse impacts on water quality of the common water bodies and also on pond management.

Table 2.11 shows that due to the adoption of ETS, the expected decline in net revenue per hectare for the small farms is high as compared to large farms. The small farmers tend to lose a larger share of net revenue which acts as a disincentive for them to invest in the adoption of eco-friendly management systems.

Institutional development

Shrimp farming is basically a state subject as far as its development and monitoring is concerned. For example, the government of AP is responsible for

Table 2.10 Cost of effluent treatment system (0.5 ha, for a farm area of 5 ha)

Particulars	Amount in Rs.
Capital cost	550,000
Subsidy available from MPEDA	150,000
Net capital cost	400,000
Fixed cost	
Depreciation on capital cost	55,000
Interest	40,000
Electricity/fuel	6,500
Loss in revenue due to loss in farm area	75,000
Total cost	176,500
ETS cost per ha	35,300

Source: Based on primary survey.

planning coastal resource utilization. However, environmental protection is a central subject and all developmental activities are expected to adhere to the central environmental rules and regulations. The implementation of an integrated management system of coastal resources for sustainable development depends on choices in the use of fresh water among various uses such as crop and shrimp farming, mangroves, forestry, drinking water supply and domestic uses. Such a system needs the integration of shrimp farming in the watershed as per the carrying capacity of the region. Further sustainable shrimp farming practices should be made economically more attractive to farmers. In order to make such an integrated system work, an analysis of state as well as district/block level policies and underlying legal and institutional framework is required. Research on the carrying capacity of each basin could be a starting point, followed by an analysis of the existing type of organizational set-up and proposed set-up for proper implementation.

Institutions for the approval of shrimp farming

As directed by the Supreme Court in December 1996, an aquaculture authority has been set up through a notification dated 6 February 1997 under the provisions of the Environment (Protection) Act, 1986. The planning commission of India has defined the coastal zone as 20 km on either side of the HTL (Mani 1997).

As per the procedure, the shrimp farmer submits an application for approval in the prescribed proforma, furnishing information on the farm area and location, commencement of the farm operations and technology followed, etc. The concerned fisheries officer forwards the application to the revenue officer of the taluk. The standing committee – consisting of the representatives of agriculture, forestry, groundwater, revenue and fisheries under the chairmanship of the

Table 2.11 Cost and return of shrimp farming with and without ETS in Andhra Pradesh (Rs. in lakh/ha/crop)

Particulars	<2 ha	2–5 ha	>5 ha	All farms
Cost of culture	1.30	1.45	1.10	1.15
Cost of ETS	0.35	0.35	0.35	0.35
Total cost	1.65	1.80	1.45	1.50
Gross returns	3.07	3.04	2.64	2.69
Net revenue				
Without ETS	1.77	1.59	1.54	1.55
With ETS	1.42	1.24	1.19	1.19
Benefit cost ratio				
Without ETS	2.36	2.09	2.39	2.35
With ETS	1.86	1.69	1.82	1.79

Source: Based on primary survey.

revenue divisional officer and representative of the district collector – meets whenever there is requirement and forwards the application to the district level body along with their recommendation. The district level committee forwards the application to the central aquaculture authority through a state level committee under the Commissioner of Fisheries. The entire process, which is expected to finish within a period of three months, normally takes between six and ten months. The main drawbacks of the system is that the approval committee at the grassroots level does not have technical expertise regarding site-selection, deciding on the suitability of the soil and water quality, or assessment of the impact of shrimp farming on other crops and livelihoods. The concerned departmental representatives look into the matter as a routine activity and they are alerted only if there is some objection raised from the public or the neighbourhood. Further, there is no scope for public participation in the process either through the NGOs or elected representative of the panchayat.

The Aquaculture Authority has so far issued approvals for around 7,000 farmers, out of more than 100,000 farms operating in India, which indicates the ineffective implementation of the approval process. The farmers do not perceive any major advantage in registering and getting approval from the Aquaculture Authority. Second, there is no economic incentive for the farmers to follow the stipulated farm management practices. The state Revenue and Fisheries Departments, which are entrusted with the implementation of the registration of the shrimp farms, are already overburdened with other activities and are not able to supervise the work. Although the Supreme Court judgment clearly ordered for payment of compensation for the closure of modern shrimp farms within CRZ, there are no instances of such closures and payment of compensation during the last five years. Apart from these issues, many questions arise from the recent developments:

- When the corporate shrimp farms are closed due to un-sustainability (disease or on-site pollution), in respect of the payment of compensation to workers and also to land owners: Who should make the payment? Who should ensure payment is made? Who should be paid?
- Can the polluter-pays-principle be extended to include all the stakeholders responsible for land degradation? For example, when shrimp ponds are abandoned, the restoration cost and loss of income should be compensated not only by the shrimp farms but also MPEDA and state Department of Fisheries as they provided technical, policy and financial support to motivate the farmers to undertake the shrimp farming.

Stakeholders' initiatives

One of the significant developments in AP's shrimp sector is the growth of shrimp farmer's trade associations, traders, hatcheries, processors, feed distributors and exporters, which are linked vertically and horizontally. These trade associations are organized at the district, state and national levels and act as a pressure group of the stakeholders to protect their economic interests. The district level associations are generally registered under the Societies Act and interact with other associations to highlight their problems and issues. For example the Nellore Prawn Farmers Welfare Association was formed in 1997 with a 15-member working committee and 3,000 farmers. The association is headed by a president and has been lobbying with the state government to include shrimp farming as one of the permitted activities within the CRZ through the forthcoming Aquaculture Bill in parliament. Apart from protecting the interest of the members, the association is also fighting against the establishment of other polluting industries such as thermal power, tanneries and plastic manufacturing industries nearer the creeks. The association periodically arranges meetings and consultations with the hatchery and feed distributors for the supply of quality inputs. The laboratory owners are also consulted to prevent the outbreak of diseases. The association has been successful in mobilizing state support for promoting scampi production in the district.

Implementation of technical measures requires community participation and use of common property resources. The concept of sustainable development recognizes public opinion as an essential element in decision making. The views of experts could be different from the way citizens feel about the sustainability of an economic activity. The participation of stakeholders in the planning of projects results in two important outcomes: (*a*) active involvement of the people; and (*b*) reduction in criticism against the proposed activity. The amendments brought to environmental impact assessment notification under the Environment Act (1986) in 1997, 2001 and 2002 have made public hearing mandatory for undertaking any new establishment. However, such public hearing is applicable only for establishments with an investment greater than Rs.50 crore. In planning for small-scale activities also it is important to involve the stakeholders so that both positive and negative impacts are fully assessed/realized. Crop versus shrimp production, mangrove conservation and management, river water sharing and maintenance, soil and groundwater management are some of the aspects where there is a need for the participation of all the stakeholders and the entire community.

Public participation in decision making for development and implementation of ICAM by creating appropriate organizations should lead to effective management of private and collective resources together. Although at the highest level there are multiple organizations responsible for coastal area management such as the National and State Coastal Zone Management Authority, Shore Area Development Authority, Aquaculture Authority, National Biodiversity Authority, State Biodiversity Board, and biodiversity management committees at the local level, and state government departments such as fisheries, agriculture, irrigation, groundwater, revenue, forests and rural development and panchayat raj are functioning parallel, there is no horizontal and vertical integration among them. ICAM as an institutional instrument for decision making requires closer interaction among these bodies at different levels for proper planning of various activities. The restoration and maintenance of mangrove forests and the institutions involved in such an exercise provides a useful example of institutional development. The mangroves of AP occupy an area of $582\,km^2$ in coastal districts, which has degraded due to various anthropogenic activities, including aquaculture. The livelihood of fishers is directly and indirectly dependent on mangroves. The unsustainable harvesting of mangroves and clearing of mangrove forests in private lands for aquaculture has led to land degradation. It was estimated that the restoration of degraded mangrove forests through community participation and involvement would cost Rs.12,000 to 18,000 per hectare and could generate an employment of 200 man-days for men and 20–30 man-days for women (Ravishankar and Ramasubramanian 2003).

Equitable distribution of the benefits of shrimp farming among all the stakeholders is an important issue that the policymakers need to address during the development of strategies. The issue of safeguarding the coastal wetlands and ecosystem and the interest of local communities needs to be negotiated with the perspective of developing alternative shrimp farm management scenarios. At the planning stage various scenarios could be developed with plausible alternative features. In order to build such a scenario, stakeholder workshops are highly useful.

The general business scenario is based on the assumption that the current trend will continue in the future. Accordingly state policies are envisaged to continue in the existing set-up. In the industry-led alternative scenario the shrimp industry will be shaped by the importers undermining the local impact. Although the domestic industry will have to adopt higher standards to meet foreign criteria it would need high levels of investment and result in an oligopolistic market structure marginalizing small farmers and processors. The participatory scenario incorporates the prerequisites of sustainability. The economic issues that prevent shrimp farmers participating in public action to internalize the externalities are as follows:

- Exposure on the various ecological and social problems associated with shrimp farming;
- Farmers perceive that the current returns from investment on water quality improvement and conservation are too small;
- There are too many institutional and organizational problems that divert the attention of the farmers from undertaking community based conservation programmes;
- The absence of full property rights on resources affects the investment;
- Farmers prefer private initiatives to group initiatives and thus the organization of small farmers for common programmes suffer from lack of interest among the farmers on group activities;
- The priorities and opinion of specialized experts for practicing sustainable shrimp farming differ from the experience of farmers.

In a conflicting situation over the use of coastal resources, stakeholder participation provides an extremely useful framework to discuss following issues:

- Understanding the actual land-use pattern changes;
- Understanding how the introduction of coastal shrimp farming has contributed to increase/decrease of income and employment of the local communities;
- Assessment of the defaulters of various regulations and their negative impact on other users;
- Finding ways for halting further degradation of coastal resources and to develop strategies;
- Turning situations of conflict into opportunities for overall development.

The process of bringing all stakeholders together is possible within the existing organizational framework, with proper modifications. It is important to note that such a stakeholder dialogue will not yield instant results. The participation of stakeholders may result in some tangible outcomes in those watersheds where the threshold level of disaster has been reached (for example Kandaleru watershed in Nellore district) and/or there is severe competition for the freshwater resources between crops and shrimp farming. Hence the policy issue is:

- Whether shrimp farming should be promoted by extensive use of the remaining unused land areas and in their hinterlands, or
- Whether to intensify shrimp farming by limiting it to coastal zones and in degraded coastal land itself.

The policy research should guide the state planners to continue shrimp farming in a sustainable manner. Since the expansion of shrimp farming results in a sharp decline in crop, livestock production, forest and grazing land, it would be wise to promote intensive shrimp farming based on modern technology and limit the incursions into crop land areas and cause damage to ecology and environment.

Conclusions and recommendations

The suggestions for the implementation of an ICAM plan are based on the premise that there are enough administrative, legal and institutional mechanisms and enforcement powers. However, in the absence of strong linkages and coordination among multiple organizations and multiple stakeholders it will only cause confusion, ambiguity and inefficiency. It is important to recognize that each of the watersheds in coastal regions is ecologically different as per the resource characteristics; type of resource use and prioritization of the stakeholders is concerned. The pond management practices, input use and yield differ widely across the clusters, river basins and distance from the sea. There is a major need for local level planning that is supported by state and central policy initiatives. Some of the suggestions mentioned below are based on the field study and literature search on the existing institutional framework.

1 Restructuring of national and state level coastal zone management authori-

ties to include all stakeholder organizations and related departments, especially some of the newly created authorities such as water users/watershed associations, aqua clubs, biodiversity management committees, *grama sabhas* (village councils), development commissioner of the special economic zones, concerned state departments (revenue, agriculture, fisheries, water, shipping and transport, industries and commerce, and environment and forests).

2 Formulation of a site-specific expert committee that could link institutes which are functioning independently and generating crucial data and information. Currently there is no coordinating agency, which collects exclusive data for monitoring and evaluation of environmental changes in the coastal zone. Hence, a separate mandate should be created within the existing organizational structure to generate and disseminate exclusive data on the coastal zone.

3 Technical measures such as crop holidays, crop alternation, alternative canals for intake and discharge of water, regular flushing out of water from the creek, development of secondary aquaculture and cultivation of mangrove forests around shrimp ponds, and following BMPs are suggested to make shrimp farming more sustainable. However, there are no clear demonstrations of the ecological and economic benefits of such measures at the farm level, leading to reluctance and slow adoption by the farmers. It is important to demonstrate to the farmers how they would become economically less vulnerable, and more viable, by adopting BMPs in the long run.

4 There is a clear case for developing institutional mechanism to realize benefits of economies of scale and monitoring the NPS pollution with an increasing number of smaller farms. Such a development can take place within the existing organizational structure modelled on water users' associations among shrimp farmers of a watershed.

5 At present the aqua clubs share and exchange only technical information but do not coordinate with non-members within the watershed. Similarly trade associations such as prawn farmers' welfare associations are effective only in lobbying with the government and state agencies but do not take the initiative to manage water quality. Hence, there is a strong case for initiating a water users' association among the shrimp farmers on the lines of the model suggested in the AP Farmers Management of Irrigation Systems Act (1997), with appropriate modifications.

6 The increase in shrimp production costs due to the adoption of ETS and BMPs (capital cost, operation and maintenance costs and transaction costs of organizing small farmers) have resulted in undermining the importance of adopting eco-friendly farm management practices. The increased profitability, reduction in the cost and health risks have made it economically lucrative to convert cropland for shrimp farming. However, such conversions should consider the cost of other environmental damages.

7 The increase in water salinity due to reduced water inflow from upstream and decline of flush-out into the sea has resulted in increased health

management costs and production risks. Hence any further expansion of shrimp farming in a watershed should consider an optimal land use plan and the carrying capacity of the watershed. As the state continues to exploit the untapped potential for aquaculture, public agencies must address among other things two main issues: impact of shrimp farming on other livelihood activities of the region; and increased self-pollution problems. The sustainable pond management practices that minimize both off-site and on-site pollution may be essential to justify any further expansion.

8   The economically optimal expansion of the shrimp farm area even by following BMPs does not address the concerns of other stakeholders. Hence existing forms of the organizational structure and institutional model could be modified and utilized to include all resource users.

9   The existing programmes and organizations are attempting to encourage BMPs and are partially successful in minimizing the on-site pollution wherever it is implemented. However, controlling off-site pollution needs support from all the stakeholders, which requires the design of a new institutional framework.

10   Development of shrimp farming could be achieved either through intensification by adopting a modern technology or by extension to hinterland and new areas. It was observed that intensification of shrimp farming and limiting it to the coastal zone would be a better option, considering the resource use costs and its competition with other sectors.

11   The extent of soil degradation due to shrimp farming and its impact on shrimp and crop yield may be assessed by the Central Institute of Soil Salinity and Land Use Planning could undertake the assessment of soil degradation due to shrimp farming and also crop yield.

References

APSPCB (2000) *State of Environment in Andhra Pradesh*, Hyderabad: Andhra Pradesh State Pollution Control Board.

Bhatta, R. (2003) S*ustainable Development and Management of Shrimp Aquaculture in India* (unpublished), Mangalore: Department of Fisheries Economics, College of Fisheries.

Central Pollution Control Board (1997) *Pollution Potential from Coastal Aquaculture*, New Delhi: MoEF, Government of India.

Central Statistical Organization (1997) *Compendium on Environmental Statistics*, New Delhi: Government of India.

Central Water Commission (1996) 'Annual Report of the Central Water Commission 1996', New Delhi: Government of India.

Government of Andhra Pradesh (2003) *Andhra Pradesh Water Vision: Methods, Position Papers and District Reports vol. II*, Hyderabad: Mission Support Unit, Water Conservation Mission, Government of Andhra Pradesh, p. 203.

Government of Andhra Pradesh (2004) 'Fisheries Action Plan 2004', Hyderabad: Department of Fisheries, Government of Andhra Pradesh.

Government of India (2001) 'Guidelines: Effluent Treatment System in Shrimp Farms', Chennai: Aquaculture Authority.

Hossain, Md. Zakir, N.K Tripathi and W. Muttitanon (2003) 'Carrying Capacity Study of Kandaleru Creek: An Integrated Approach for Sustainable Shrimp Farming in Andhra Pradesh', Proceedings of the Workshop for MPEDA–NACA Project on Shrimp Disease and Coastal Management, Chennai.

Mani, J.S. (1997) Coastal Zone Management Plans and Policies in India. *Coastal Management*, 25(1) 93–108.

Marine Products Export Development Authority (2004a) 'MPEDA – An Overview', Kochi: Marine Products Export Development Authority, p. 64.

Marine Products Export Development Authority (2004b) 'Data on Shrimp Farming of Andhra Pradesh', Personal Communication of the Office of the Deputy Director, MPEDA, Vijayawada, AP.

Ravishankar, T. and R. Ramasubramanian (2003) 'Community Based Reforestation and Management of Mangroves for Poverty Reduction in the East Coast of India', in H.C. Sim and S. Appanah (eds) *Forestry for Poverty Reduction: Can Community Forestry Make Money*, Bangkok: Food and Agricultural Organization, Regional Office.

Swallow, S.K. (1990) 'Depletion of the Environmental Basis for Renewable Resources: The Economics of Interdependent Renewable and Nonrenewable Resources', *Journal of Environmental Economics and Management*, 19: 281–296.

3 Impact of the monsoon trawling ban on marine fisheries in Tamil Nadu

*Ierene Francis**

Introduction

Marine fisheries, once considered inexhaustible, are presently under severe stress. Marine fishing has transformed from a means of livelihood to an industry, and there is now a scientific consensus that the fisheries sector has been plagued by problems of overexploitation and pollution. Overfishing in the global fisheries was confirmed by the fact that there has been an annual decline in world fish catch of 0.36 million tonne per year since 1988 (Watson and Pauly 2001). The Food and Agricultural Organization (FAO) of the United Nations estimates reveal that 70 per cent of the world's fish stocks are affected by overfishing. Increasing adoption of destructive fishing techniques like bottom trawling further threatens marine wildlife and ecosystems. Recent predictions indicate that if global fishing activities continue at the present pace, there will be a 'global collapse' of all species currently fished, possibly around 2048 (Worm *et al.* 2006).[1]

Fisheries in India constitute an important sector with regard to livelihood, nutrition and food security. After independence in 1947, fisheries gained importance and were given the status of a sector capable of accelerating the growth of the rural economy (Kurien and Achari 1990). From the 1950s onwards, the focus for marine products shifted from the domestic to the international market, with the government promoting this sector in a response to address the severe shortage of foreign exchange in the country. Exports initially focused on frozen shrimp, the success of which led to the 'prawn rush' or 'pink gold rush' in the following decades.

In line with the global trend, India initially experienced a rapid growth of its fisheries sector with the introduction of bottom trawling in the 1950s and 1960s (Ammini 1999). Marine fish landings have increased by five times in the period 1950–2000 (Bhathal 2004). India is now the third largest producer of fish in the world. Marine fish production had increased to 2.92 million tonne in 2007–08 and earnings from marine exports were estimated at Rs.7,621 crore (Department of Animal Husbandry, Dairying and Fisheries 2008–09). In India, the total population involved in marine fisheries is more than eight million (Kocherry 2000). While the artisanal sector contributes to a very small part of landings, trawl net (mechanized) and gillnet (motorized) are the important gears in the Indian Coast.

The trawl net is the most common method of fishing and offers high returns. Yet, it is the most destructive type of fishing gear because trawling involves scraping the seabed, and apart from drawing large volumes of by-catch it destroys habitats, shelter and suitable breeding areas for the fish, and disturbs fish larvae and eggs.

With respect to the Indian state of Tamil Nadu, in the 1990s it was argued that increase in trawler efficiency was posing a threat to the sustainability of fisheries in the state and that 'the trawling effort of daily and multi-day trawlers have to be reduced to obtain maximum sustainable yield' and consequently, an 'implementation of a comprehensive fishery management policy for the coastal trawl fishery' was suggested (Vivekanandan and Meiyappan 1999). Upon the advice of the Central Marine Fisheries Research Institute (CMFRI), a 45-day ban from 15 April to 29 May on mechanized trawling and fishing has been implemented on the east coast of India since 2001.[2] The problems associated with trawling bans in India often take on a socio-political hue (Bavinck 2001; van Haastrecht and Schaap 2003).

Objective

The present analysis intends to examine the effect of the controversial 45-day monsoon ban on mechanized fishing and trawling in Tamil Nadu. The growth rate of certain groups of fish in four sub periods during 1985–2004 is compared for this purpose. An attempt is also made to analyse the change in the landings composition as well as ratios of landings to effort during this period. Moreover whether the ban has had any effect on the overall landings, and the landings of certain important fish groups is also explored.

Review of literature

The term 'overfishing' was first used by Samuel Cleghorn in 1854, and until then, it was generally believed that the resources of the sea were inexhaustible (Smith 2002). Gordon (1954) demonstrated that the 'overfishing problem' has its roots in the economic organization of the industry, because the natural resources of the sea yield no economic rent.

One of the earliest and most popular models of fishery resources management is the 'bioeconomic' model (Gordon 1954; Schaefer 1957), which postulates a nonlinear relationship (inverted 'U'-shaped relationship) between effort (measured on the X axis) and catch (measured on the Y axis). According to the model, as effort increases, catch at first increases, reaches a maximum and then falls for any additional increases in effort beyond the maximum point, known as the maximum sustainable yield (MSY). The model can be extended to incorporate cost factors too, to derive the maximum economic yield (MEY) point, where profits in the fishery are maximized.

While overfishing is widely reported (Watson and Pauly 2001; Worm *et al.* 2006), measuring the extent of it is often constrained by the lack of proper knowledge of the complex interaction of various biological processes in the marine ecosystem and uncertainty of biological parameters, which are usually estimated from economic data on catches and fishing inputs. Zhang and Smith (forthcoming) address some of the empirical issues by proposing a two-stage procedure to estimate the biological parameters using a panel-data model. The stock is first estimated from production parameters, which in the second stage is substituted into the state equation that captures the biological dynamics.

Analysing fishing impacts on marine seafloor biodiversity, particularly in soft-sediment habitats that comprises 70 per cent of the seafloor; Thrush and Dayton (2002) find that effects are not always consistent across regions. Given that the impact of the gear varies in different habitats, obtaining precise data from these complex ecosystems is also difficult. The literature on the effect of legal bans on trawler fishing suggests a positive impact of it from both social and ecological perspectives. Chong *et al.* (1987) note that the Indonesian trawl ban initiated in 1980 resulted in a positive contribution towards stock recovery, raising fish landings and export revenue from shrimp within five years. Pipitone *et al.* (2000) analyse the effect of a year-round trawl ban in the Gulf of Castellamare in Sicily, Italy by comparing catch per unit effort (CPUE) from experimental trawl surveys carried out before the ban and the same four years later. The study reveals that the catch of nearly all the considered species underwent an increase after the four-year ban, with an eight-fold increase in biomass.

In the Indian context, Kurien and Achari (1990) noted that very large pelagic fish were caught in the state of Kerala after the trawl ban in 1988. Although the event cannot be completely attributed to the ban, the phenomenon is suggestive. Positive effects of Kerala's trawling ban have been noted in terms of production and sustainability (Ammini 1999; Kurup 2001). The present analysis aims to contribute to the literature by focusing on the impact of the trawler ban in the coastline along Tamil Nadu, which is a relatively less researched area.

Review of the fisheries of India and Tamil Nadu

The coast of Tamil Nadu is around 1,076 km long along the Bay of Bengal and is affected by two distinct monsoons, the north-east monsoon (October–December) and the south-west monsoon (June–September) contributing about 60 per cent and 28 per cent of the total annual rainfall respectively. Tamil Nadu occupies the third place with respect to marine landings in India and contributes significantly to India's exports (Bavinck 2001). Figures 3.1 and 3.2 show the trends in total fish catch in Tamil Nadu and India.

Trawling was first introduced in Tamil Nadu during 1965–66 and it worsened the prolonged conflict that existed along the Coromandel Coast between the artisanal fishermen and mechanized fishermen since the 1960s (Bavinck 2001). The conflicts peaked in the 1970s but declined later. The main incentive for trawling was that the annual return on capital investment for trawlers was initially quite high (up to 32.6–38.2 per cent in 1993–94), which led to an increase in effort in the inshore areas (Devraj *et al.* 1996).

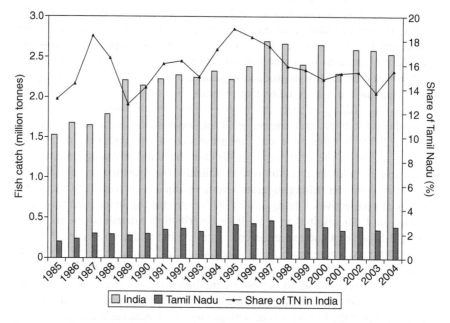

Figure 3.1 Fish catch in India and Tamil Nadu (source: computed by the author).

van Haastrecht and Schaap (2003) noted that trawler fishermen in Tamil Nadu understand the need for a ban but do not agree with the timing of the same. The study concluded that ecological justification of the ban is blurred due to lack of information and a lack of consensus on breeding periods among the scientific communities. However the analysis supported continuation of the ban, until further research provides more evidence to support or reject this measure.

Analysing the effects of fishery regulations on other sectors of the economy, Bhat and Bhatta (2006) show, using a dynamic input–output model, that primary fishing and processing sectors eventually realize significant wage and profit gains after a period of transition, during which there are no significant benefits to them.

The trawling ban and the legal instrument

On 5 January 2001 the Tamil Nadu government issued the order concerning the 45-day trawling ban along the entire eastern coastline. The main reason for the installation of an annual trawling ban is the conservation of fishery resources. Another objective of the uniform ban was to end clashes with regard to different ban periods between the fishermen of the different states.[3] The CMFRI and the Fishery Survey of India conducted research to provide scientific backing about breeding periods of commercially important fish species to determine the right period for the enforcement of a ban (van Haastrecht and Schaap 2003).

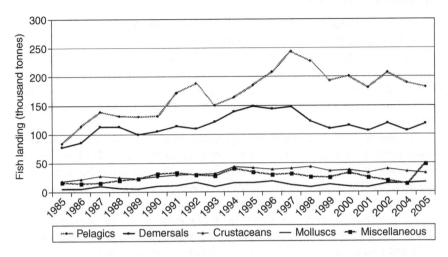

Figure 3.2 Category-wise fish landing in Tamil Nadu (source: computed by the author).

One major concern for the government has been to address the associated socio-economic problems like the loss of livelihoods of fishermen during the ban period, for which several schemes were introduced. There is a lack of scientific consensus about the breeding time of fish and hence the appropriate ban period; breeding seasons are known to differ between regions and species. Political pressures further compounded the problem; a ban must be uniform for the entire East Coast, and governments are reluctant to impose a strict or lengthy ban due to vote-bank pressures. For example the CMFRI initially recommended, among other measures, two bans – during both the north-east monsoon and the south-west monsoon. This was not accepted by the government fearing unpopularity among the masses and the present ban mainly protects commercial fish species like seerfish and tuna (van Haastrecht and Schaap 2003).

Fishery in India is a state subject and in the light of the conflicts between artisanal and mechanized fishermen, the Tamil Nadu Marine Fisheries Regulation Act of 1983 (henceforth referred to as 'the Act') was introduced. The Act (1983) governs marine fisheries management in Tamil Nadu, and forms the legal basis of the 45-day trawling ban. The Act was brought in to protect artisanal fishermen (by creating separate zones for mechanized and artisanal fishermen), to conserve fish and to maintain law and order at sea. It was brought in when measures like peace committees and minor regulations failed to quell discord between mechanized and artisanal fishermen (Bavinck 2001). The Act (1983) calls for registration and licensing of all fishing vessels in the state; regulates mesh-size and type of fishing gear; and gives regulations regarding designation of the different types of fishing vessels.

Methodology and data

In order to understand the effectiveness of the ban in checking the dwindling fish stock, there is need to look at the historical data of the fish stock in the region. This would explain how the stock composition has changed over years. The analysis needs to be carried out at a disaggregated level in order to understand varied growth and exploitation patterns amongst different groups of fish over the years. This exercise would be instrumental in isolating the impact of the ban on the fish stock.

The source of the secondary disaggregated data on fish landings estimates (annual and quarterly) in Tamil Nadu over 1985 to 2004 is CMFRI at Cochin, Kerala, which only provides data on landings, i.e. the difference between catch and discards. The available data for several resources of fish were added up into sub categories for ease of calculation. For example, the landings of sharks, skates, rays and eels were added up to get the landings of *Elasmobranchs*.

The data on proxies for effort; namely, numbers of mechanized boats, country crafts and catamarans, total fishermen population and number of active fishermen was obtained from 'Endeavors and Achievements'[4] published by the Office of the Directorate of Fisheries of Tamil Nadu. Annual time series information is avail able from 1992 onwards.[5] Regression models are estimated to study the growth rates, composition of landings and the effect of the ban on fish landings, etc.

Growth rates

The growth rates of the fish stock are estimated using data on landings. A posit- ive relationship between fish stocks and landings is assumed, which is logical given the present interest in the direction of change than absolute numbers of the stock. The growth rate of various categories is computed for four sub-periods of five years each (1985–89, 1990–94, 1995–99, 2000–04). Growth rate estimates of five major categories, demersals (fish that thrive at the sea floor), pelagics (fish at shallow depths), crustaceans (prawns, etc.), molluscs (shell fish) and miscellaneous fish are computed. The sub period 2000–04 is of particular inter- est, for understanding the change in growth rates in the post-ban period. The growth rate is estimated using the following model:

$$\ln X_{it} = a + bt \tag{3.1}$$

where X_{it} is the landing of the ith group of fish in tth time period, which is regressed on time variable t. The average annual growth (r) is calculated as $r = \{\exp(\hat{b}) - 1\}$, where $\hat{b}$ is the estimated value of b in Equation 3.1.

Composition

To test the statistical significance of change in composition of fish landing over the period, the methodology adopted by Bhatta *et al.* (2003) has been followed.

The percentage composition of each group is regressed on a time trend. Change in composition of landings is analysed for categories of fish and individual types of fish. The change in composition of fish landing is estimated using the following model:

$$Y_i = \alpha + \beta t + \varepsilon \tag{3.2}$$

Where Y_i is the percentage composition of the ith group of fish, t is the time trend and ε is the error term.

The null hypothesis for the regression is that the composition has not changed. If the estimated coefficient of β is significant, the null hypothesis can be rejected, which implies that composition has indeed changed.

Analysis of the effect of the ban on fish landings

The landings (Y_t) of both individual groups of fish and total fish landings are regressed on a time trend (t) and a dummy variable to capture the effect of the ban (D_1). The regression (Equation 3.3) is run on quarterly data for 20 years after checking for the stationarity of the series. The model is specified as below:

$$Y_t = \beta_0 + \beta_1 D_1 + \beta_2 t + \varepsilon_t \tag{3.3}$$

Where, D_1 takes value 1 if ban is in the existence and takes value 0 otherwise. ε_t is the standard error.

Impact of the ban and effort on total landings

To control the effect of effort variable on the catch, an alternative specification for the model presented in Equation 3.3 is estimated (see Equation 3.4). In Equation 3.4, total catch is regressed on the dummy variable for ban, time trend, and effort variables – number of mechanised boats (mech), catamarans (catam) and country craft (countr), for the years 1992–2004. To avoid multicollinearity, the data on fishermen is not used in the regression as it was estimated using the data on country crafts.

$$Totalcatch = \alpha + \beta_1 D_1 + \beta_2 t + \beta_3 mech + \beta_4 catam + \beta_5 countr + \varepsilon \tag{3.4}$$

Ratios of landings per unit effort

The total catch of any fish resource does not usually measure the size of the population available to the fishermen. The size of the total catch depends on the relation between the numbers of fish in the available population and the amount of effort expended. The present analysis notes the ratios between landings and effort variables like number of fishermen, number of catamarans, number of country boats, and number of mechanised boats the years between 1992 and 2004.

Results

Growth rates

Individual groups of fish

The growth rate estimates for individual groups of fish show varying trends, but a general pattern can be drawn from them (Table 3.1). While growth rates were largely positive for the first two sub periods; they have fallen and even turned negative for the last two sub periods. However, there is some indication of a recovery during 2000–04. When the same analysis is carried out for total fish landings, it reveals that the growth rate has been progressively declining over the four sub periods. It has picked up over the last sub period, albeit marginally, going from −2.67 per cent to 0.1 per cent.

Table 3.1 Period-wise growth rates for individual groups of fish (percentage)

Category	1985–89	1990–94	1995–99	2000–04
Elasmobranch	9.7	13.7	−4.2	5.3
Clupeid	8.9	6.85*	4.0	0.2
Anchovy	17.7*	−5.8	−1.6	−12.2*
Lizard Fish	20.2*	8.2	−31.48*	9.2
Half Beak and Full Beak	16.0	2.6	32.96*	−21.77*
Flying Fish	96.8	−34.5	−5.4	3.0
Perch	10.84*	8.9*	−7.78*	3.0
Goatfish	56.36*	−9.4	17.7*	−5.1
Threadfin	8.3	−11.9	−16.9	−6.6
Catfish	0.8	8.2	−3.4	−4.7
Croaker	14.97*	0.2	−10.6*	−5.9*
Ribbon Fish	−33.6	−3.5	−3.4	1.1
Carangid	12.4	0.7	−3.1	6.6*
Silverbelly	−0.6	9.7*	−7.9*	−2.0
Big-Jawed Jumper	−13.9	−20.6	−16.5	−18.1
Pomfret	40.1*	8.3	−11.25*	−5.2
Mackerel	8.2	18.3	−9.03*	11.5
Seerfish	5.7	12.54*	15.8	−11.0
Tunny	26.5*	4.0	11.7*	−3.2
Bill Fish	−20.2	26.7*	54*	22.9
Barracuda	33.4*	−4.6	3.3	−11.7
Mullet	0.1	3.8	8.0	−12.4*
Flat Fish	17.3*	−10.29*	−9.73*	−3.8
Crustacean	5.5	11.19*	−1.5	−2.7
Mollusc	3.1	6.5	−10.9	17.7*
Miscellaneous	9.8*	3.4	−7.5*	1.0
Overall	9.2*	5.17*	−2.7	0.1

Source: author's calculations.

Note
* Estimated coefficient of time variable (as shown in Equation 3.1) is significant at 0.05 level.

Categories

For clarity, the landings are divided into categories of pelagic, demersal, crustaceans and molluscs. The estimates of growth rates of landings that are aggregated into these categories are depicted in Table 3.2. The trend clearly shows that, except for pelagics and crustaceans, growth rates have increased in the last sub period, during which the ban was in effect. The interesting observation is that demersals (which are found at the bottom of the sea, and hence most affected by trawlers) have benefited from the trawl ban, as reflected through their growth rates. The available literature shows that demersal stocks exhibit limited recoverability after over-exploitation (see Hutchings 2000 as cited in Thrush and Dayton 2002). Interestingly, the estimates of growth rates for crustaceans show a declining trend while the ban was mainly imposed to rejuvenate the catch of prawns.

Category-wise composition of landings

The average landings are noted for the four sub-periods and are decomposed into the categories of pelagic, demersal, crustaceans, molluscs and miscellaneous (as illustrated in Table 3.3). These results reveal that the percentage share of pelagics has increased from 45 per cent in 1985–89 to 50 per cent in 2001–04, while the same for demersals has declined from 37 per cent to 30 per cent over the same period.

The increasing share of pelagics in landing is a possible indication of 'fishing down', although this can be better shown through the changes in trophic levels of landings of fish, which is beyond the scope of the present analysis due to unavailability of data.[6]

Change in resource wise composition of landings

The estimated regression models as represented in Equation 3.2 are presented in Table 3.4. A significant 'beta' indicates that the null hypothesis that composition is the same can be rejected. In other words, it can be inferred that the composition has changed. The composition analysis shows that the presence of groups

Table 3.2 Category-wise compounded annual growth rate of fish landing (percentage)

Category	1985–89	1990–94	1995–2000	2001–04
Pelagic	10.84	3.11	0.26	−0.74
Demersal	8.25	6.55	−6.23	1.85
Crustaceans	5.52	11.19	−1.52	−1.79
Mollusc	3.12	6.45	−10.13	22.67
Miscellaneous	9.82	3.36	−2.28	17.22
All categories	9.16	5.17	−2.59	2.27

Source: author's calculations.

Table 3.3 Category-wise average fish landing (in tonne)

Category	1985–89		1990–94		1995–2000		2001–04	
Pelagic	120,311.2	(45.12)	161,337.4	(45.27)	209,866.17	(49.54)	189,881.5	(50.32)
Demersal	97,946.4	(36.74)	118,097.4	(33.14)	131,423	(31.02)	112,369	(29.78)
Crustacean	23,373.8	(8.77)	32,294	(9.06)	39,763.833	(9.39)	34,991	(9.27)
Mollusc	6,817.2	(2.56)	12,461.8	(3.5)	12,675.833	(2.99)	13,509.25	(3.58)
Miscellaneous	18,177	(6.82)	32,183.8	(9.03)	29,884.833	(7.05)	26,587.5	(7.05)
All categories	266,625.6	(100)	356,374.4	(100)	423,613.67	(100)	377,338.25	(100)

Source: author's calculations.

Note
Figures in parentheses show the percentage share in total fish landing.

like clupeids, anchovies, half beaks, full beaks, perches, threadfins, croakers, ribbon fish, silverbellies, big jawed jumper, pomfrets, seerfish, tunnies, bill fish, barracudas and flatfish in the total catch have changed significantly over the 20-year period.

The effect of the ban on fish landings

From Table 3.5 it is observed that 'ban' has a negative and significant coefficient in catch of catfish, clupeids, half and full beaks, perches, croakers, silver bellies, seerfish, barracudas, mullets, flat fish, crustaceans and most importantly total fish landings. In fact all the categories characterized by significant coefficients are found to be negative (12 out of the 27 groups studied).

The negative coefficient of 'ban' indicates that the fish that breed during the monsoon time have not been able to increase their stock during the ban period.

Table 3.4 Regression results for analysis of change in composition

Category	Beta	t-value	Composition status
Elasmobranch	0.002	0.05	Same
Clupeid	0.603	5.08	Changed (+)
Anchovy	−0.244	−4.85	Changed (−)
Bombay duck	−0.001	−0.96	Same
Lizard Fish	−0.014	−0.62	Same
Half Beak and Full Beak	0.029	3.03	Changed (+)
Flying Fish	−0.004	−0.1	Same
Perch	0.156	4.83	Changed (+)
Goatfish	−0.035	−1.09	Same
Threadfin	−0.006	−3.53	Changed (−)
Catfish	0.008	1.26	Same
Croaker	−0.097	−6.64	Changed (−)
Ribbon Fish	−0.181	−2.87	Changed (−)
Carangid	0.053	1.35	Same
Silverbelly	−0.481	−7.5	Changed (−)
Big-Jawed Jumper	−0.007	−2.83	Changed (−)
Pomfret	0.024	4.77	Changed (+)
Mackerel	0.011	0.21	Same
Seerfish	0.055	3.08	Changed (+)
Tunny	0.038	2.24	Changed (+)
Bill Fish	0.011	3.63	Changed (+)
Barracuda	0.033	2.63	Changed (+)
Mullet	0.004	1.63	Same
Unicorn Cod	−0.001	−1.48	Same
Flat Fish	−0.015	−2.69	Changed (−)
Crustacean	0.040	1.37	Same
Mollusc	0.040	1.35	Same
Miscellaneous	−0.022	−0.28	Same

Source: author's calculations.

The significance of the trend variable indicates the importance of increasing catch effort and demand generation in fisheries. It is observed that trend coefficients are generally positive and significant for most fish categories.

In particular for elasmobranchs, carangids, pomfrets, tunnies, barracudas and molluscs, it is observed that the increase has been caused by the effect of trend, and in these cases the ban is not significant. Moreover, the trend coefficient is found to be positive and significant.[7]

Regression results of total landings on trend, ban and effort

In the next part of the analysis, total catch is regressed on the ban's dummy variable (D_1), time trend (t), and effort variables like number of mechanised boats (*mech*), catamarans (*catam*) and country craft (*countr*), for the years 1992–2004,

Table 3.5 Results of the regression showing effect of ban on landings

Category	Estimated coefficient of ban variable	Estimated coefficient of time trend
Elasmobranch	−763.6	31.8*
Catfish	−277.2*	9.2*
Clupeid	−10,776.4*	360.1*
Anchovy	−1,349.7	6.5
Lizard Fish	−524.1	9.2
Half Beak and Full Beak	−478.6*	14.7*
Flying Fish	752.3	−6.2
Perch	−1,654.7*	86.8*
Goatfish	−649.3	8.7
Threadfin	−28.7	0.1
Croaker	−1,031.3*	7.9
Ribbon Fish	862.1	−33.3*
Carangid	−263.4	43.7*
Silverbelly	−2,238.5*	−4.1
Big-Jawed Jumper	−1.1	−0.5
Pomfret	−125.2	9.1*
Mackerel	−988.5	31.1
Seerfish	−785.9*	30.8*
Tunny	−232.8	16.9*
Bill Fish	100.7	1.8
Barracuda	−403.9*	18.1*
Mullet	−123.8*	3.2*
Flat Fish	−267.4*	3.6*
Crustacean	−3,014.1*	92.1*
Mollusc	−590.6	31.8*
Miscellaneous	−2,766.5*	66.9*
Total	−52,066.5*	1,724.9*

Source: author's calculation.

Note
* Implies the estimated coefficients (as presented in Equation 3.3) are significant at 0.05 level.

in line with the regression analysis proposed under Equation 3.3. It was done with annual data as effort data was only available annually and the sample size is only 13 (data on effort variables is available for 1992–2004 only).

The regression results shown in Table 3.6 reveal that in the given period, only catamarans are found to be significant, yet they are negative. The observation implies that an increase in the number of catamarans does not contribute to the increase in catch, on the contrary the landings are reduced.

Estimates of landings per unit effort

The changing ratios of landings per unit effort (LPUE) over 1992–2004 is presented in Table 3.7. Although conventionally 'catch-per-unit-effort' is analysed, given access to data on landings and not on catch, the current study uses LPUE. The measures of effort are the numbers of mechanised boats, catamarans and country boats and number of fishermen. It is observed that LPUE has declined over the years, implying an increase in effort does not lead to proportionate increase in landing. Declining LPUE is a reality in the fisheries sector across the world, and hence the results are not surprising.

Conclusions

The fact that marine fisheries all over the world are overexploited is well documented by many studies. In this background, the present study attempts to undertake a closer investigation into the growth and dynamics of the fish-stock composition over 1985–2004, for examining the effectiveness of the 45-day ban on trawler fishing in Tamil Nadu which was initiated in 2001.

Landings for India as a whole, and for Tamil Nadu in particular, have increased around the late 1990s and fell thereafter. It was observed that the estimates of growth rates had fallen over the 20-year period between 1985 and 2004,

Table 3.6 Regression results of total landings on trend, ban and effort

Variable	Coefficient	t-value
Ban	−64,482.22	−1.71
Trend	16,099.28	0.94
Mechanised boats	19.34	0.8
Catamarans	−5.66*	−2.91
Country craft	−12.16	−1.21
Constant	481,893**	3.51
R^2	0.73	
N	13	

Source: author's calculations.

Notes
* Indicates significance at 95 per cent level.
** Indicates significance at 99 per cent level.

although there has been a surge in the second sub-period (1990–94). In addition, for several groups there was an increase in growth rates during the last period (2000–04). The increase in growth rates for demersals is an encouraging sign, as this is witnessed largely during the period when the ban on trawling was in place, and demersals are affected by trawling. It is however an area of concern that the estimates of growth for crustaceans have been progressively dipping, especially because the ban was specifically brought into place to benefit the prawns and shrimp, which are a major component of crustaceans. Despite increases in effort, landings have not gone up proportionately, but LPUE appears to have stabilized, or at least have not fallen drastically after the ban.

The analysis on composition of landings show that landings of certain groups of fish, as percentage of total landings have changed for 15 of the 27 groups of fish studied. It is also seen that the proportion of pelagics in landings has been increasing while that of demersals is falling, which is a possible indication of 'fishing down'.

The negative coefficient of 'ban' observed from the regression analysis reveals that the fish that breed during the monsoon time have not been able to increase their stock during the ban period. The coefficient of the ban is found to be significant and negative for 12 out of the 27 groups studied. Regarding the effectiveness of the ban, it is difficult to conclude on the basis of the present analysis that the ban has led to increase in fish catch. The ban period of 45 days may not be sufficient for fish to breed and rejuvenate. The difficulty in regulation of mesh size of trawler nets constitutes another major cause for catching juveniles, which could undo any benefits the ban brings into place.

Since the livelihood of so many people depend on fisheries sector, it is important to conserve the very resource they depend on, even if it means temporarily disrupting their activity. Many studies have stressed the importance of a

Table 3.7 Landings per unit effort (1992–2004) (tonne)

Year	Landings/ fishermen	Landings/ countrycraft	Landings/ catamarans	Landing/ mechanised boats
1992	0.838	45.884	14.495	68.394
1993	0.674	29.612	12.559	53.461
1994	0.769	31.827	24.970	55.802
1995	0.779	30.744	22.989	51.267
1996	0.761	28.137	19.114	48.744
1997	0.798	28.448	22.928	52.554
1998	0.708	25.064	16.460	42.706
1999	0.573	18.667	11.556	35.168
2000	0.595	19.189	11.821	37.992
2001	0.518	16.334	12.683	34.122
2002	0.577	17.934	12.574	34.736
2003	0.503	15.369	10.750	29.873
2004	0.557	17.061	12.392	32.814

Source: author's calculations.

fishing holiday. With respect to the Tamil Nadu ban, even though the 45-day period may not be sufficient to rejuvenate stocks, perhaps some ban is nevertheless better than indiscriminate fishing. Regulation of mesh size would also be helpful to reduce by-catch, thereby allowing juveniles to escape.

Highlighting a few areas of future research, given the limitations of the present study, would not be inappropriate here. First, this study does not take into account factors like temperature, rainfall, etc. which affect landings. Second, the growth rates calculated for the fish groups were not all statistically significant, and could not be compared with intrinsic growth rates of the fish species, which would have verified if the resource was being exploited at a sustainable level.

The analysis assumes that landings are a function of stock of fish, and does not identify if the *stock* of fish has changed due to the ban. Third, data limitation has been a major issue. For instance, as only an annual estimate of effort was available; CPUE could be computed only annually. It is quite plausible that the catch could have fallen due the fall in effort during the ban (mechanized vessels abstaining from fishing). Fourth, breeding times for fish are uncertain and change along the coast and from species to species, so it is hard to identify a uniform period for all species. Therefore, caution should be exercised while interpreting the results regarding the effectiveness of the ban since this intervention could possibly have lagged effects on stock composition and growth rate, which requires some gestation period. Hence any future research should necessarily focus on detailed analysis of ban periods and breeding times.

Notes

* The author is grateful to Dr Paul. P. Appasamy for his comments and suggestions.
1 The study was based on all data on fish and invertebrate catches from 1950 to 2003 within all 64 large marine ecosystems worldwide. Collectively, these areas produced 83 per cent of global fisheries' yields over the past 50 years.
2 The west coast of Tamil Nadu has a different ban (15 June to 29 July – same as Kerala's trawl-ban) from the east coast (15 April to 29 May). The west coast ban has not been taken into account in the present study. However, this does not change the results, because the length of the Tamil Nadu's west coast (Kanyakumari district) has a coastline of about 60 km which is only 5.6 per cent of the total coast line of Tamil Nadu.
3 The East Coast states could not arrive at a consensus regarding the ban period. Tamil Nadu was initially reluctant to impose a ban during April–May, as it is affected more by the north-east monsoon in October–November (Schaap and van Haastrecht 2003). The time of the ban was later accepted on the basis of a CMFRI (2000) report.
4 Due to lack of any other data on effort, the data from Directorate of Fisheries is used despite its inconsistencies. The potential bias that could arise due to a plausible forced artificial upward trend in variables which are crucial for measuring achievements by the department is acknowledged.
5 Due to inconsistencies in the data available on the population of fishermen, the population variable had to be constructed using a regression. It was observed that there was a high correlation (94 per cent) between country craft and the existing data on fishermen. So to estimate fishermen population from data on country craft, the following regression equation is used: $(totalfishermen) = \beta_0 + \beta_1(Countrycraft) + \varepsilon$ where the variables are self-explanatory. The estimated series of fishermen population comes from substituting the existing values of numbers of country crafts in Equation 3.3.

6 For a detailed study, see Bhathal (2004).
7 Of all the significant trend coefficients, only that of ribbonfishes is negative. This is because over the 20-year period, landings of ribbonfish have fallen to almost half of the initial amount, after peaking sharply in 1986 and again in 1992. Ribbonfish are considered a low value or trash fish in India, and are not commercially important.

References

Ammini, P.L. (1999) 'Status of Marine Fisheries in Kerala with Reference to Ban of Monsoon Trawling', *Marine Fisheries Information Service T and E Series*, 160: 24–36.

Bavinck, M. (2001) *Marine Resource Management-Conflict and Regulation of Fisheries of the Coromandel Coast*, New Delhi: Sage.

Bhat, M.G. and Bhatta, R. (2006) 'Regional Economic Impacts of Limited Entry Fisheries Management: An Application of Dynamic Input–Output Model', *Environmental and Development Economics*, 11: 709–728.

Bhathal, B. (2004) 'Historical Reconstruction of the Indian Marine Fisheries Catches 1950–2000, as a Basis for Testing the Marine-Trophic Index', unpublished Master's thesis, University of British Columbia.

Bhatta, R., Rao, A.K. and Nayak, S. (2003) 'Changing Composition of Marine Fish Production in Karnataka: Symptoms of Fish Famine'. *Economic and Political Weekly*, 38(44): 4685–4693.

Chong, K.C., Dwiponggo, A., Ilyas, S. and Martosubroto, P. (1987) 'Some Experiences and Highlights of the Indonesian Trawl Ban: Bioeconomics and Socioeconomics' Paper Presented at the Symposium on the Exploitation and Management of Marine Fishery Resources in Southeast Asia, Darwin (Australia), February.

CMFRI (2000) 'Spawning Season of Marine Fishes and Ban on Fishing along Tamil Nadu Coast', Official document prepared by the Madras Research Centre of CMFRI, Chennai: ICSF Documentation Centre Chennai.

Department of Animal Husbandry, Dairying and Fisheries (2008–09) 'Annual Report 2008–09', Ministry of Agriculture, Government of India, New Delhi.

Devraj, M., Paul Raj, R., Vivekanandan, E., Balan, K., Sathiadas, R. and Srinath, M. (1996) 'Coastal Fisheries and Aquaculture Management in the East Coast of India' *Marine Fisheries Information Service T and E Series* 141: 1–9.

Gordon, H. Scott (1954) 'The Economic Theory of a Common-Property Resource: The Fishery'. *Journal of Political Economy*, 62(2): 124–142.

Government of India, 'Annual Report 2008–09', New Delhi: Department of Animal Husbandry and Dairy.

Haastrecht, E. van and Schaap, M. (2003) 'A Critical Look at Fisheries Management Practices: The 45-day Ban in Tuticorin District, Tamil Nadu, India' unpublished MSc thesis, University of Amsterdam.

Hutchings, J.A. (2000) 'Collapse and Recovery of Marine Fishes', *Nature*, 406:882–885.

International Collective in Support of Fishworkers, 'Tamil Nadu Marine Fishing Regulation Rules 1983'. Online, available at: www.icsf.net (accessed 6 October 2010).

Kocherry, T. (2000) 'Indian Fisheries over the Past 50 Years', *Kachappa*, 2: 3–7.

Kurien, J. and Achari, T.T.R. (1990) 'Overfishing along Kerala Coast: Causes and Consequences', *Economic and Political Weekly*, 25(35/36): 2011–2018.

Kurup, B.M. (2001) 'Experiences from the Seasonal Closure of Bottom Trawling in Kerala (South India) on the Exploited Marine Fisheries Resources', in S. Goddard, H.

Al-Oufi, J. McIlwain and M. Claereboudt (eds) *Proceedings of 1st International Conference on Fisheries, Aquaculture and Environment in the NW Indian Ocean*, Muscat: Sultan Qaboos University, Oman.

Pipitone, C., Badalamenti, F., D'Anna,G. and Patti, B. (2000) 'Fish Biomass Increase after a Four-Year Trawl Ban in the Gulf of Castellammare (NW Sicily, Mediterranean Sea)', *Fisheries Research*, 48: 23–30.

Schaefer, M.B. (1957) 'Some Considerations of Population Dynamics and Economics in Relation to the Management of the Commercial Marine Fisheries', *Journal of Fisheries Research Board Canada*, 14(5): 669–681.

Smith, T.D. (2002) 'A History of Fisheries and their Science and Management' in P.J.B. Hart and J.D. Reynolds (eds) *Handbook of Fish Biology and Fisheries* 2, Oxford: Blackwell Publishing.

Thrush, S.F. and Dayton, P.K. (2002) 'Disturbance to Marine Benthic Habitats by Trawling and Dredging: Implications for Marine Biodiversity', *Annual Review of Ecology and Systematics*, 33: 449–473.

Vivekanandan, E. and Meiyappan, M.M. (1999) 'Changing Pattern of Trawling along Chennai Coast', in Proceedings of *The Fourth Indian Fisheries Forum* held during 24–28 November 1996, Kochi.

Watson, R. and Pauly, D. (2001) 'Systematic Distortions in World Fisheries Catch Trends' *Nature*, 414: 534–536.

Worm, B., Barbier, B.E., Edward B., Beaumont, N., Duffy, J.E., Folke, C., Halpern, B.S., Jackson, J.B.C., Lotze, H.K., Micheli, F., Stephen R. Palumbi, S.R., Sala, E., Selkoe, K.A., Stachowicz, J.J. and Watson, R. (2006) 'Impacts of Biodiversity Loss on Ocean Ecosystem Services' *Science*, 314 (5800): 787–790.

Zhang, J. and Smith, M. (forthcoming) 'Estimation of a Generalised Fishery Model: A Two-Stage Approach' *Review of Economics and Statistics*.

Part II
Manufacturing and power sector and environment

4 Economics of 'not' controlling pollution

A case study of industrial pollution in Noyyal River Basin, Tamil Nadu, India

L. Venkatachalam

Introduction

Industrial pollution as a negative externality is one of the major environmental problems in India, affecting especially the water resources that generate multiple benefits to both households and firms. If industrial pollution in an ill-specified policy environment is directly proportional to the level of industrial output, then any attempt to increase the latter would correspondingly raise the social costs of pollution – in most cases, *non-linearly*. This has larger welfare implications: the welfare loss would be much worse in developing countries where the standard of living of a larger labour force is determined by the growing industrial output level (Solow 2009). In other words, there is a 'trade-off' between social benefits and social costs of controlling pollution and in most cases; these benefits and costs affect diverse economic agents differently. Therefore, 'how much to pollute' becomes a normative question in any pollution control policy effort in a social welfare maximizing context. In technical terms, this determines at what pollution level a socially optimal, Pareto efficient equilibrium between gains and losses from it can be achieved in an economy. The standard Pigouvian solution suggests that an efficient level of pollution is the one at which the marginal social benefits are equal to the marginal social costs provided all the social costs and benefits are measurable in monetary terms (Pigou 1932).

The Pigouvian solution to negative externality (Pigou 1932) prescribes government intervention through a 'pollution tax' that equates social benefits and social costs at the margin. Coase (1937) on the other hand, prescribed a more market-oriented, 'property rights'-based solution to internalize the negative externality. Coasian prescription does not insist on government intervention, as such a policy may distort other types of more efficient methods of internalizing the externalities. For example, 'vertical integration' of polluted and polluting activities in a zero transaction cost regime is assumed to generate an efficient welfare outcome (Joskow 2005). The Coasian framework, therefore, does not require government agencies or any other third party, to estimate the economic value of the benefits and costs accruing to different agents to arrive at a Pareto efficient pollution control. The government agency is supposed to restrict its role only up to assigning the property rights to these economic agents – no matter to whom the property rights are assigned *initially*. If the transaction cost of negotiation is positive, then transaction cost minimizing institutions are expected to emerge, provided the negotiating agents are not guided by 'bounded rationality' (Williamson 2000).

While Coase's prescription is Pareto efficient in a well-defined property rights regime with zero transaction cost, the Pigouvian prescription is found to be more effective under the following conditions: (a) where there is substantial amount of uncertainty over the welfare impact of the environmental resources under consideration; (b) where the property rights over these resources are either 'ill-defined' or not defined at all; (c) where the polluters and receptors are large in number so that any negotiation among them becomes opportunistically costly (Nalebuff 2000); (d) when the resource conflict is so intense that the agents will not have any economic incentives to bargain (Hanemann and Dyckman 2009); (e) where the transaction cost minimizing institutions do not emerge adequately; and (f) where the agents are 'boundedly' rational in designing efficient institutions and minimizing the transaction costs. Many of the environmental problems presently faced by developing countries do reflect the above characteristics and therefore, it is felt that government intervention can ensure a 'second-best solution' (Cropper and Oates 1992), though not the first-best Pareto efficient one. The monetary value of social benefits and costs are pre-requisite for a Pigouvian solution; but measuring them in monetary terms is a great challenge, as these benefits and costs are 'social' in nature and most of them fall outside the market domain. However, failing to appropriately measure these values and incorporate them in environmental and development policies has been proved to be detrimental to various efforts aimed at improving the overall social welfare in developing countries (Dasgupta and Maler 2000).

It should be noted that many of the environmental policies promoting sustainable development especially in developing countries are *not* based on the economic values of the trade-off involved between economic activities and environmental pollution; consequently making policy failure a dominant feature there. However, this does not imply that environmental policies with appropriate economic values become successful in achieving the underlying welfare objectives, either. Beyond economic values, there are complex institutional constraints in implementing these policies. Therefore, the present chapter intends to address two related issues in an integrated manner: (a) estimating the economic values of costs and benefits of improvements in soil and water quality affected by industrial pollution in order to demonstrate how these values could play a distinctive role in effective environmental decision-making at regional or local level; and (b) analysing the 'institutional failure' which not only produces a negative externality problem but also sustains it over a period of time. The above issues are analysed in the context of environmental damage in the agricultural sector, caused by industrial pollution in the Noyyal River Basin in Tamil Nadu, India. It is worth mention that the knitwear-based industrial activities in and around the Tiruppur Municipal Corporation in the Noyyal River Basin generates positive benefits such as direct export earnings amounting to US$70,000 million and direct employment up to 200,000 workers per annum. Simultaneously, around 730 bleaching and dying units clustered there considerably pollute water resources through harmful effluents, mainly, total dissolved solids (TDS), which adversely affect economic activities (e.g. agriculture and animal husbandry) in downstream areas of the river basin. So, the present study is positioned within the context of trade-off between the development and environment in the study area.

Economic valuation methodology

As discussed earlier, one of the practical problems with implementing the Pigou-vian solution is that the social costs and benefits of environmental change are mainly non-marketed in nature. Hence their valuation in monetary terms for incorporating them in the decision-making processes is an empirically challeng-ing task. For avoiding this difficulty, economists developed alternative, least-cost based 'second-best' solutions for controlling pollution at efficient levels (Baumol and Oates 1988). Yet, they are not perfect substitutes for the Pigouvian first-best solution; because, the non-Pigouvian solutions are based on 'direct costs' of con-trolling pollution and do not reflect the benefit side. Given this background, the necessary condition for efficient pollution control is to estimate the marginal social benefits and costs of different levels of pollution using standard non-market valuation techniques, and then using these estimates in pollution control decisions. Since the present chapter intends to demonstrate how to estimate the economic benefits and costs of pollution control in Tiruppur region, two stand-ard non-market valuation techniques are used to measure the relevant economic values. The estimation of economic impact of the agricultural damage, due to deterioration in soil and water quality, is based mainly on the *replacement cost method.* In order to estimate the agricultural benefits due to improvements in soil and water quality, the income method has been used which analyses the possible net income generated due to reduced pollution.

Data sources

The valuation exercise is based on both secondary as well as primary data. The data on soil quality came mainly from a study conducted by the Soil Survey and Land Use Organization, Coimbatore and commissioned by Madras School of Economics, Chennai (Madras School of Economics 2002); the data on quantity of effluents and agricultural production and productivity were collected mainly from existing studies carried out by various organizations in Noyyal and neigh-bouring Bhavani River Basins. Informal interactions with different stakeholders associated with environment sector in the Tiruppur region provided useful quali-tative information on estimating the economic values.

Soil quality data

Soil quality is measured in terms of pH (potential hydrogen) level – a measure of the acidity or basicity of an aqueous solution. If the pH level ranges between 7 and 8.5, then the quality of the soil is considered 'normal' and conducive for crop production. If the pH level is less than 7, it indicates that the soil is *acidic* and if it is above 8.5, then the soil is considered to be *alkaline*. The alkaline soil is *not* conducive for agricultural crop growth; the non-alkaline soil may not affect the crop growth but may cause some other problem. Given the primary focus on agricultural damage, the present analysis is confined mainly to assessing the economic impact of alkaline soil. Existing literature confirm that the alkalinity problem in Noyyal basin is being caused by industrial pollution.

Table 4.1 describes the soil quality information across the Noyyal River Basin. For analytical purpose, the river basin is classified into four zones from its origin (Vellingiri Hills) to its confluence point (Kodumudi) at Cauvery River. While Zones I and II fall in the upstream area of Tiruppur, Zones III and IV fall in the downstream area which is claimed to be experiencing intensive pollution damage. On an average, 43 per cent of the soil samples are found to be alkaline in nature; out of this, 40 per cent is moderately affected (pH level between 8.5–9) while 3 per cent is severely affected (i.e. pH>9). Importantly, soil quality not only in the downstream of Tiruppur but also in the upstream has been affected by alkalinity problems. For example, while around 38 per cent of the soil samples in the upstream region of Tiruppur are alkaline in nature; the corresponding figure in the downstream is 46.05 per cent. Under ceteris paribus assumption, the derived conclusion is that only around 8 per cent of the alkalinity problem is due to pollution originating from industrial units in Tiruppur. Even the 8 per cent difference cannot be entirely attributed to the pollution from Tiruppur if the polluting industrial units located upstream of Tiruppur are also considered. This empirical evidence contradicts the conventional notion that the pollution damage in the Noyyal basin takes place only in the downstream area of Tiruppur, caused entirely by the polluting units located there. The 'origin' of negative externality does not affect the obtained results since the study estimates the damage cost at the river basin level.

Though the soil quality data does not reveal the extent to which the cultivable land area gets affected by the alkalinity problem, the same can be estimated by simple and realistic assumptions. Assuming that the soil samples have been randomly collected only from cultivable land area, it can be concluded that the percentage of soil samples affected exactly matches with the percentage of

Table 4.1 Soil quality details of the Noyyal River Basin

Zone	Alkaline	%	Non-alkaline	%	Total	%
I (Vellingiri Hills to Singanallur)	20	42	27	58	47	100
II (Irugur to Karumathampatty)	68	38	117	62	185	100
III (S. Palayam to Orathupalayam)	136	43	179	57	315	100
IV (Maravapalayam to Kodumudi	62	54	53	44	115	100
Total	286	43	376	57	662	100

Source: computed from MSE (2002).

cultivable land area affected. With this assumption, the total cultivable land area affected by alkalinity is estimated to be 75,336 ha. Out of this, around 93 per cent of the affected area (i.e. 70,080 ha) is classified as 'moderately affected', while the remaining area (i.e. 5,256 ha) is classified as 'severely affected' (Table 4.2).

Replacement cost – soil quality

To estimate the 'replacement cost' of soil quality deterioration, apart from economic inputs adequate scientific inputs from other disciplines such as, agronomy is also used. Consultation with the agronomists revealed that a prominent remedial measure required to restore the affected soil is to apply an appropriate amount of 'gypsum' on the land and leach it with water so that the alkalinity in the soil can be washed off. If the alkaline problem is 'severe', the above process needs to be repeated. First, the total quantity of gypsum required for restoring the entire affected area is estimated. According to agronomists, 2.5 tonne/ha of gypsum is required for moderately affected areas, and 5 tonne/ha for severely affected areas. So, the total quantity of gypsum required is 201,480 tonne. The total cost of this remedial measure is calculated by using: (a) the market value of the gypsum required; and (b) the transaction cost of transporting and applying gypsum in the soil. The market value of gypsum was Rs.1,800 per tonne (at 2002 prices) and the total cost of gypsum required is estimated at Rs.362.7 million. The transaction cost in terms of transporting and applying gypsum at the farm level is estimated to be Rs.37.7 million (at Rs.500 per ha). So, the total cost of restoring soil quality in the entire Noyyal basin, for either the government agencies or the farmers, comes to Rs.400.33 million per annum.

Replacement cost – water quality

As mentioned earlier, deterioration in soil quality is not only caused by the industrial effluents from Tiruppur but also by possible other upstream sources. While this needs to be investigated further, it can be argued that industrial effluents are causing considerable damage to the agriculture sector and therefore, their treatment up to the prescribed limits would substantially reduce the

Table 4.2 Size of agricultural land area affected by the alkaline problem

Headings	Size of the area (in Ha.)
Total geographical area of the basin	350,000
Total cultivable land area of the basin	175,200
a) Moderately affected area (@40 per cent; pH=8.5–9 range)	70,080
b) Severely affected area (@3 per cent; pH=above 9)	5,256
Total cultivable land area affected (a+b) (@43%)	75,336

Source: computed from MSE (2002).

damage. The Tamil Nadu Pollution Control Board (TNPCB) reports indicate that effluent discharge from polluting firms to the Noyyal river is around 83 Mld (million litre per day).[1] For estimating the replacement cost of water quality, only the 'variable cost' of treating the effluents is considered here. Figures provided by the government agencies indicate that till end 2008 the fixed cost incurred on pollution control measures in Tiruppur on the common effluent treatment plants (CETPs) and individual effluent treatment plants (IETPs) amounts to Rs.10,988.1 million, approximately. The already incurred fixed cost is assumed to be 'exogenous' to present estimation since it is not going to affect the marginal cost of treating the additional effluents.[2] Table 4.3 provides details about the restoration cost of effluent treatment.

With the existing technology and investment, the total cost of restoring soil and water quality in the Noyyal River Basin is equivalent to Rs.1,309.18 million[3] at 2002 prices. This estimation is based on the assumption that the polluters are willing to control pollution without 'free-riding' and similarly, the farmers and the government agencies are also willing to improve the soil quality up to its normal level. It should be noted that there is an inverse relationship between the restoration costs incurred on soil quality improvements and that of treating the effluent water: if the polluters increase their efforts to control pollution, then the efforts of the receptors to restore the quality of the soil will decline. Cost estimation in the present context captures this aspect, which is explained in the following.

Benefits of restoration measures

An important question here is to determine whether the net benefit of the required improvements in soil and water quality are accomplished by incurring scarce resources that are opportunistically costly. Since the chapter focuses on the agriculture sector, the marginal 'producer surplus' that could be recovered under the pollution control regime is estimated. To simplify the valuation

Table 4.3 Details of abatement cost of treating industrial effluents

Total amount of industrial effluent per day: 83 MLD	(Rs.)
a) Abatement cost of treating biological oxygen demand (BOD), chemical oxygen demand (COD) and colour up to the prescribed level (@1 paise per litre)	830,000
b) Abatement cost of removing total dissolved solids (TDS) up to the prescribed level (@ 2 paise per litre)	1,660,000
Total abatement cost per day	2,490,000
Total abatement cost per year*	908,850,000

Source: computed by the author.

Note
*The cost figures in the table are estimated at 2002 prices.

exercise a 'direct method' of estimating the marginal benefits in the agriculture sector is used, which involves estimating the 'net farm income' in the non-polluted areas and then using this as an indicator for estimating the producer surplus foregone in the affected areas. The intuition here is that ceteris paribus, the farm incomes in both affected and non-affected areas would have been equal if pollution had been absent in the affected area. Using farm income data from the non-affected areas both in the Noyyal basin as well as the Lower Bhavani Project (LBP) area in the neighbouring Bhavani basin (where the irrigation water is of better quality), the marginal difference in the net farm income between the two areas is estimated at Rs.18,750 per hectare per year (at 2002 prices). Based on this information, the estimated total marginal net benefit that could be regained in the affected areas in the Noyyal basin comes to around Rs.1,412.55 million per year. Table 4.4 provides the 'net present value' (NPV) of the costs and benefits of the restoration measures in the Noyyal basin, estimated at 6 per cent discount rate for the initial four years of the pollution control activities at constant prices.

It should be noted that the cost of soil quality improvements, though it declines rapidly, continues to be positive till end of the third year because the quality of the soil does not improve within a year of initiating the remedial measures. This suggests that the remedial measures will have to continue for at least three years during the initial period of restoration, so that the alkalinity in the soil can be eliminated completely. However, in each subsequent year the cost required is only 50 per cent of the total cost incurred in the previous year because of substantial improvements (here, 50 per cent improvement is assumed) in the soil quality in the next year. The above rate of reduction in the restoration cost can be realized only if a constant effort is taken to control pollution, which shows up in the NPV of the stream of pollution control cost. The NPV of net benefits becomes positive in the third year and the maximum net benefit is realized in the fourth year. The estimation results indicate that a constant effort on pollution control activities will yield a NPV value of Rs.1,547.44 million as

Table 4.4 Net present value of the costs and benefits of improved soil and water quality in the Noyyal River Basin

	Cost (Rs. million)				Benefits (Rs. million)	
	Soil (i)	Control %	Water* (ii)	Total (iii) = (i) (ii)	Total (iv)	Net (v) = (iv) − (iii)
Year 1	400.30	100	908.85	1,309.15	353.13	−956.02
Year 2	178.13	50	808.90	987.03	628.58	−358.45
Year 3	84.02	25	736.08	820.10	889.50	69.40
Year 4	00.00	Not needed	719.90	719.90	1,118.83	398.93

Source: computed by the author.

Note
* Water, 100 per cent control.

benefits during the next ten years in the agricultural sector alone. The findings suggest that once the water quality is improved up to the prescribed limit, the quantum of social benefits restored can be many times higher due to other associated benefits such as, health benefits, biodiversity and recreation.

Institutional issues

As noted earlier, till end of 2008, approximately Rs.10,988.1 million has been invested on CETPs and IETPs; a huge amount of public money has been additionally invested on primary institutional measures such as, running the pollution control board. The estimates of this study suggest that there are improved social benefits which could be regained if the investment already incurred is put into proper use. A profound question that arises here is: Why is pollution not being controlled adequately despite the enormous amount of investment incurred, various institutional arrangements put in place and sizable potential social benefits that could be restored by controlling the same? According to Coase theorem, the negative externality will continue to persist if the transaction cost of reducing it is prohibitively high; which implies that pollution in the Noyyal region would have been controlled with negligible transaction cost. Coase theorem can also be interpreted to state that if the transaction cost is exorbitant, then new institutions will emerge to minimize it. But measuring the transaction cost to verify the Coase contention – in the presence of uncertainty, information asymmetry and bounded rationality regarding efficient institutions (Williamson 2000) – is a huge task, and an area of future research in the context of Tiruppur. Following North (1994) the present study argues that 'institutions do matter' in the economic analysis of pollution control and proceeds to analyse different sources of 'institutional failure' that have contributed to the negative externality problem in the Noyyal basin.

Command and control approach – a misused approach

The history of environmental regulation adopted in the Tiruppur region indicates that the 'command and control approach' (CAC) followed by pollution control authority had not produced any efficient outcomes, despite ample opportunities to achieve such outcomes. Rather, implementation inaccuracies in this approach encouraged inherent inefficiency in the system. Under this approach, the options given to the polluters are mainly 'discrete' in nature – i.e. all the polluting firms are required to either adopt 'end-of pipe treatment' (either through CETPs or IETPs) or face punishment. However neither option worked efficiently. During the initial years, CAC in general (in particular the end-of pipe solution) was considered to be the only option for controlling industrial pollution, since very limited alternatives were available to the pollution control authority owing to lack of experience. The end-of-pipe solution within the CAC approach was the outcome of 'demonstration effect', replicating practiced procedures in other developing countries. However, over time, the limitations of this approach were realized. Interestingly, no effort has been made to revamp this approach or to introduce better efficient pollution control methods when other developing countries changed their pollution control strategies.

The end-of-pipe solution created not only a 'lock-in effect' in the system but also provided opportunities for firms to use it strategically for enhancing their opportunistic behaviour, at the cost of social welfare. For example, empirical studies on pollution control in other industries demonstrated that within the 'end-of-pipe' technological regime, the cost of controlling pollution through CETPs was less than that of IETPs due to economies of scale, reduction in transaction cost, etc. (Sankar, 2000). Nevertheless, a considerable number of firms in Tiruppur opted for establishing their own IETPS, instead of joining the CETPs. Out of 729 polluting firms, a total of 495 firms (67.9 per cent) joined the CETPs while the remaining 234 firms (32.1 per cent) installed their own IETPs. The obvious question is why a considerable number of 'rational' (cost-minimizing or profit maximizing) firms are encouraged by existing regulations to adopt a relatively costly pollution control technology rather than selecting a cheaper available option? The underlying reasons can be the following: (a) while the 'transformation cost of pollution' control is low, the firms' transaction cost of joining the CETPs may be high; (b) firms might be adopting IETPs as a business strategy to maximize their own profits by eliminating competition in the industry. For example, if the marginal cost of reducing the pollution is inversely related to the size of the members of the CETPs and the marginal producer surplus is also inversely related to the level of competition in the output market, then some of the firms may try to strategically eliminate those firms from the industry by increasing their relative cost through establishing IETPs. Though it is sound in principle, it seems that this kind of strategy does not work well in Tiruppur because of inefficient regulation. Moreover, the high cost firms joining CETPs are still enjoying their stake for reasons such as, free-riding behaviour of the firms,[4] collective action on not controlling pollution, etc; and (c) the IETP firms might think that the probability of non-compliance may be increased significantly in the case they adopt IETPs rather than joining CETPs. This is because, the transaction cost of monitoring and enforcement by the authority is inversely related to the number of firms being monitored. Since a high transaction cost will reduce the amount of monitoring, the probability of non-compliance firms getting caught becomes less. So, more IETPs will lead to more non-compliance which in turn will lead to more pollution. However, this kind of strategy of an IETP firm depends mainly on how other firms also behave – if other firms also follow the same strategy, then non-compliance is the Nash equilibrium outcome.

In Tiruppur, a considerable number of firms have established their own IETPs and therefore, it will be interesting to study how a 'spontaneous order' emerged among a sizeable number of firms to establish their own IETPs and the strategies being followed by these firms. The behaviour of the firms in selecting the technological options that differ in terms of cost indicates that the actual cost of pollution control at firm level varies across these firms. The existing CAC does not recognize this difference and has also completely failed to exploit this important factor to control pollution in an efficient manner. Instead the current CAC approach taxes the low cost polluters and subsidizes the high cost polluters, ultimately affecting the incentive for the low-cost polluters to control more pollution at lesser cost. This is obvious from the experience of CETPs where the firms are charged on the basis of the average cost and not on the basis of marginal cost of pollution control. Moreover, the polluters have used the CAC strategically to reduce the competitiveness in the output market to gain more profits, rather than controlling pollution to minimize the social cost. This is one of the major reasons why the pollution problem has become inherent in the Tiruppur region.

The CAC provides ample opportunity for the regulatory authority to maximize its own benefits at the cost of social benefits. It should be noted that the cost of pollution control is blamed as the major culprit for the existing level of pollution in Tiruppur. The 'rent seeking behaviour' of the regulatory authority makes the compliance cost 'relatively higher' by strategically fixing the amount of 'bribe' at a lower level; since the polluters are rational, they find 'bribing' to be cheaper than compliance. So, the 'maximizing behaviour' of the authority as well as the polluters results in 'non-zero sum outcomes' for both of them, but at a 'zero sum outcome' to the society as a whole. This implies that not only the polluters, but also the authority, utilize the CAC as an effective strategic instrument to generate private benefits, rather than generating social benefits.

Evolution of pollution control policy – a chaos

The previous section notes that the CAC in general, and end-of pipe solution in particular, did not work well, leading to the argument that pollution control policies should have evolved clearly with the inefficient components being replaced by the efficient ones. Rather, the policy prescriptions during the past 20 years or so created more 'chaos' than they improved the situation. For example, during the initial policy regime the industrial units were required to treat only three parameters in their effluents; namely, colour, BOD (biological oxygen demand) and COD (chemical oxygen demand). Reduction of TDS, a major culprit, was not a priority item in the prescription since it was believed that reducing TDS would increase the operational cost of the firms tremendously. Subsequently the adverse impact of TDS was strongly opposed by farmers' groups downstream of Tiruppur, causing the authorities to instruct the polluting units to reduce TDS as well. But the polluting units, citing cost as the reason, refused to comply with the standards. During the mid-2000s, the farmers filed a case with the high court, Chennai and the court verdict instructed the polluters: (a) to pay Rs.125 million for cleaning up the Orathupalayam dam in the downstream of Tiruppur and Rs.240 million as 'compensation' to the farmers for the damage caused (Eswaramoorthi *et al.* 2003)[5]; and (b) to go in for 'zero-discharge', which essentially means that no effluent is to be released into the Noyyal river; all the effluents are to be treated and the treated water is to be recycled within the industry (Eswaramoorthi *et al.* 2003; Madhav 2008). The concept of 'zero discharge' is not economically viable since the marginal social cost of achieving zero effluents becomes greater than the corresponding marginal social benefits. Moreover, the zero-effluent policy does not provide any incentive for the firms to recycle and re-use the treated water within the prevailing institutional structure. This is because, the bleaching and dying units require 'fresh water' for processing, which is available at a much cheaper rate from other sources such as, private lorry tankers, and not recycled water. Firms are thus more likely to access cheaper water from these sources than to use the relatively costly treated water. Moreover, the recently implemented water supply programme under the public–private partnership arrangement in the Tirupur region (Madhav 2008) has made 'fresh water' even much cheaper. So, there are economic reasons why the zero-effluent policy prescription will not bring the expected change in the behaviour of the firms. Of late, the policy prescriptions are centred on a concept called 'marine discharge'. Under this, the effluents will be transported through pipe-lines for a distance of 250 km and discharged into the Bay of Bengal. The total cost of this project is estimated to be Rs.7,000 million and a company called, Textile Eco Solutions Tamil Nadu Limited, has been established to implement this project. The chief minister of Tamil Nadu assured that out of the total cost of the proposed scheme, 25 per cent would come as a grant from the centre and 15 per cent from the state, while the remaining 60 per cent of the cost would be borne by the firms themselves (Gunasekaran, 2007). This proposal leaves the following profound questions unanswered: (a) what will happen to the huge amount of investment already incurred on existing pollution control measures in Tiruppur? (b) what is the guarantee that the effluents will be properly treated before release into the ocean, under the proposed scheme? and (c) what kind of the impact it will have on the marine ecosystem and what is the cost of the impact? The history of pollution control in the Tiruppur region indicates that the firms and regulatory authorities will use this new scheme also as an instrument for opportunistic behaviour (Davis 2004), merely 'transferring' pollution from land to ocean. So, the conclusion that is derived from the analysis is that there is complete 'policy chaos' in Tiruppur, and this kind of chaos has created 'procras-tination' among the firms in decision-making regarding pollution control. The ad hoc polices of the authority have not 'fooled' the firms; rather, they have strengthened the 'rational expectation' of the firms in terms of not controlling pollution.

Emerging institutions – no way-out

In recent years, judicial intervention in pollution-related matters has introduced some institutional changes in the handling of these problems in the Tiruppur region in particular. The Loss of Ecology Authority (LEA)[6] – emerged out of such an intervention – recently estimated the total accumulated damage to the agriculture sector in the Noyyal basin at Rs.24.79 million. This amount is to be collected from the polluting firms and transferred to the affected farmers as com-pensation. Though the LEA initiative in transferring resources from 'gainers' to the 'losers' – not only in the Noyyal basin but also in other basins in Tamil Nadu – is a step forward, in line with Venkatachalam (2005) certain serious problems with their approach can be pointed out. While on one hand, the LEA's effort to operationalize the 'hypothetical' Hicks–Kaldor compensation criterion is a welcome measure; on the other, this kind of ad hoc measure might worsen things in the long run by potentially creating a 'moral hazard' among the receptors and polluters. Coase theorem suggests that from a pure efficiency point of view, a socially desirable efficient outcome in internalizing the negative externality would emerge if the marginal cost of cleaning the environment is borne by all stakeholders in proportion to their pay-offs. The above principle is relevant when no one has any 'well-defined' property rights over the environment, or when the property rights are equally distributed across all members. In the Tiruppur context, the right to water in the Noyyal River is not well-defined anywhere and therefore; all parties have equal access to the services provided by the river. If the farmers have the right to use clean water for the purpose of irrigation, the industrialists also possess an equal right to use the 'eco-system services of the river as a sink of waste' of the river under the 'no property rights' regime. As both parties have an equal right to use the water resources, they also have an equal right to protect the water. If compensating the 'receptors' becomes a standard policy measure, then 'moral hazard' would become a dominant strategy among the agents. For example, if the compensation amount is smaller than the cost of controlling pollution, polluting would become a dominant strategy – the polluters would prefer to compensate the receptors and continue to pollute the river, rather than controlling pollution. Similarly, if the receptors find being compensated to be more beneficial than any other measures (e.g. punishing the polluters), they would prefer to have the pollution and continue to be compensated. So, the compensation measure resulting in a moral hazard problem will lead to sub-optimal outcomes. Similarly, Coase theorem implicitly suggests that if the transaction cost of controlling pollution is greater than that of other measures such as, compensating the receptors if they voluntarily move away from the polluted area, then a socially efficient outcome will emerge if the receptors are compensated for their voluntary movement. Since voluntary movement is not a common phenomenon, compensating the farmers should be based on their preferences and it should be adopted only in the case of damage that has already occurred. However the permanent solution to the problem is to design efficient institutional mechanisms by which the pollution impact is reduced to the socially acceptable level.

Apart from LEA, the courts are also appointing 'expert committees' to assess the environmental problems in the Noyyal basin and to make appropriate recommendations for minimizing pollution damage. However, appointment of these committees runs into the classic problem of 'adverse selection'. The members appointed in these committees often do not possess adequate scientific knowledge about the possible economic and environmental impacts of pollution, necessary institutional arrangements required for creating proper incentives and disincentives to change the opportunistic behaviour of the polluters and regulatory authorities, efficient pollution control policies conducive for the existing condition, etc.

In most cases, their decisions become both 'ad hoc' and non-scientific in nature. For example, a committee appointed recently by the High Court to look into the pollution problem in Noyyal basin visited the controversial Orathupalayam dam (which accumulates effluent water) and then asked the authorities to release the effluent water from the dam in a 'phased manner' (Eswaramoorthi and Dhanapal 2005), in order to minimize the impact of pollution in downstream areas. The committee obviously failed to comprehend that whether the effluent is released in a phased manner or otherwise, the pollution load in the river system is going to be the same under the status quo regime. The committee's suggestion is also superficial in the sense that it is supposed to provide suggestions on 'how to control effluents' and not on 'how to release effluents'.

Empirical evidences demonstrate that under the well-defined property rights regime, rules of the games designed mainly by the stakeholders themselves produce more efficient outcomes in the area of environmental management (Ostrom 1998). The committees formed through judicial intervention, consisting mainly of outside members (and not the local stakeholders) with limited local knowledge have so far failed to produce desired results. Adequate care needs to be taken in future for ensuring that these initiatives efficiently tackle the adverse selection problem.

Conclusion

The present chapter estimates the costs of controlling water pollution in bleaching and dying units and the associated benefits realized in the agricultural sector in the Noyyal basin – through improved water and soil quality measures. It is found that the NPV of the agricultural benefits is positive and significant, and the benefits of controlling pollution would be substantially larger in the coming years as well. The conclusion is that despite substantial amount of pollution control costs already incurred and a considerable quantity of net benefits that could be potentially realized, the pollution in the Noyyal basin is not being controlled adequately. This is attributed to the 'institutional failure' which is causing pervasive inefficiency in the system. The institutional and policy measures initiated so far have resulted in creating a 'chaos' in the system, rather than harmonizing it. Specific institutional interventions, such as the establishment of LEA and expert committees, have not resolved the problems because of the ad hoc nature of the decisions taken by these bodies. It is obvious that the existing CAC approach is responsible for the existing problem in the Noyyal region, which has not provided adequate incentives for the economic agents to carry out their responsibilities to reduce the pollution. In this background, a complete revamping of the current pollution control policy is warranted for achieving the desired goals in this region. There should be a policy-shift from the existing CAC regime to a more 'market-based' regime, which will bring in relatively efficient outcomes in the environment (Sterner 2002). The 'market-based instruments' (MBIs) such as, 'Pigouvian tax' and 'tradable pollution permits', which have been implemented successfully in reducing industrial pollution in other parts of the developing world, can be introduced with effective regulation. Since the 'site-specific' institutional and behavioural aspects determine the outcomes of the policy instruments at the local level, more attention needs to be paid to these issues before introducing such instruments.

Notes

1 Another source puts this figure between 100–120 Mld (Madhav 2008). Authentic information about the effluent load from all industrial units is not readily available for analysis, despite the involvement of several government agencies in the collection and maintenance of the relevant data. Due to data constraints, the treatment cost estimated in the present analysis should be regarded as providing only a conservative, lower bound estimation.
2 Technically speaking, the first order condition of the fixed cost already incurred is zero for any additional amount of effluents controlled.
3 The estimate excludes the interest paid on fixed investment.
4 Free-riding within a CETP is possible since the free-riders are charged only in respect of their average cost of controlling pollution and not their actual cost. The actual cost may be higher for these free-riders where their pollution load is treated independently of other lower cost members. For these free-riders, the average cost may be lower than the actual costs when there is a substantial number of low-cost members in the CETPs or if the actual cost of few members is too low.
5 Another report written by the first two authors of this source provides entirely different figures: Rs.60 million for clean up and Rs.1,400 million for compensation (see also, Madhav 2008).
6 See Venkatachalam (2005) for more details on LEA.

References

Baumol, William J. and Oates, Wallace E. (1988) *The Theory of Environmental Policy*, Cambridge: Cambridge University Press.
Coase, Ronald (1937) 'The Nature of the Firm', *Economica*, 4(16): 386–405.
Cropper, Maurine L. and Oates, Wallace E. (1992) 'Environmental Economics: A Survey', *Journal of Economic Literature*, 30(2): 675–740.
Dasgupta, Partha and Maler, Karl Goren (2000) 'The Resource-Basis of Production and Consumption: An Economic Analysis', in Partha Dasgupta and Karl Goren Maler (eds), *The Environment and Emerging Development Issues*, vol. 1, Oxford: Oxford University Press, 1–34.
Davis, Jennifer (2004) 'Corruption in Public Service Delivery: Experience from South Asia's Water and Sanitation Sector', *World Development*, 32(1): 53–71.
Eswaramoorthi, S. and Dhanapal, K. (2005) 'Textile Effluent and Wastewater Management in Tiruppur: Need for Government Aid', Research Report, Tiruppur: Environment with People's Involvement and Coordination in India.
Eswaramoorthi, S., Dhanapal, K. and Karpagam, J. (2003) 'Zero Discharge – Treatment Options for Textile Dye Effluent: A Case Study at Manickapurampudur Common Effluent Treatment Plant, Tiruppur, Tamil Nadu'. Online, available at: www.epicin.org/documents/zero%20discharge.pdf (accessed 20 November 2009).
Gunasekaran, M. (2007) 'Company Formed to Implement Marine Discharge Project'. Online, available at: www.hindu.com/2007/03/13/stories/2007031313970100.htm (accessed 20 November 2009).

Hanemann, Michael and Dyckman, Caitlin (2009) 'The San Francisco Bay-Delta: A Failure of Decision-Making Capacity', *Environmental Science and Policy*, 12(6): 710–725.

Joskow, Paul (2005) 'Vertical Integration', in Claude Menard and Mary M. Shirley (eds) *Handbook of New Institutional Economics*, Dordrecht: Springer, 319–348.

Madhav, Roopa (2008) 'Tiruppur Water Supply and Sanitation Project: An Impediment to Sustainable Water Management? International Environmental Law Research Centre Working Paper 2008–01. Online, available at: www.ielrc.org/content/w0801.pdf (accessed 20 November 2009).

Madras School of Economics (2002) 'Environmental Impact of Industrial Effluents in Noyyal River Basin', Project Report, Chennai: Madras School of Economics.

Nalebuff, Barry (2000) 'On a Clear Day, You Can See the Coase Theorem', in Partha Dasgupta and Karl Goren Maler (eds), *The Environment and Emerging Development Issues*, vol. 1, Oxford: Oxford University Press, 35–47.

North, Douglass C. (1994) 'Institutions do Matter'. Online, available at: http://129.3.20.41/eps/eh/papers/9411/9411004.pdf (accessed 5 December 2009).

Ostrom, Elinor (1998). 'A Behavioral Approach to the Rational Choice Theory of Collective Action', *American Political Science Review* 92(1): 1–22.

Pigou, Arthur C. (1932) *The Economics of Welfare*, fourth edition, London: Macmillan.

Sankar, U. (2000) 'Common Effluent Treatment Plants: An Institutional Arrangement for Pollution Control in Small Scale Tanneries in India'. Online, available at: www.elaw. org/system/files/India2000.pdf (accessed 20 November 2009).

Solow, Robert M. (2009) 'Imposed Environmental Standards and International Trade', in Kaushik Basu and Ravi Kanbur (eds), *Arguments for a Better World: Essays in Honor of Amartya Sen: Society, Institutions and Development*, vol. II, Oxford: Oxford University Press, 411–424.

Sterner, Thomas (2002) *Policy Instruments for Environmental and Natural Resource Management*, Washington, DC: Resources for the Future.

Venkatachalam, L. (2005) 'Damage Assessment and Compensation to Farmers: Lessons from Verdict of Loss of Ecology Authority in Tamil Nadu', *Economic and Political Weekly*, 40(15): 1556–1560.

Williamson, Oliver E. (2000) 'The New Institutional Economics: Taking Stock, Looking Ahead', *Journal of Economic Literature*, 38(3): 595–613.

5 Environmental costs of coal-based thermal power generation in India

Notion and estimation

Shrabani Mukherjee

Introduction

The recent discussions on sustainable development and climate change related challenges are centred on greenhouse gases (GHGs)[1] emissions and global warming. The discussions since the Rio Summit (1992) has culminated in the introduction of the Kyoto Protocol (1997), which enforces a binding commitment on industrialized countries to reduce their emissions of GHGs by 5.2 per cent below the level prevailing in 1990 (Gupta 2007). Though developing countries are not yet subject to a reduction commitment on this front, their developed counterparts are putting increasing pressure on more advanced developing countries (e.g. Brazil, China, India) to complement their actions (EC 2003). Given the fact that GHGs can originate from multifarious activities involving primary (e.g. agriculture and related activities), secondary (e.g. iron and steel, cement), infrastructure (power generation, transport), waste management and many other sectors, any commitment by India at the multilateral forum on reducing emissions would have long-term repercussions on the economy.[2] The emission management concern is more serious in the context of the coal-based power generation sector in a developing country like India, where the economy is still in the booming stage.

The generation of thermal power results in emissions of GHGs, with profound implications for global climate change.[3] The key emissions from coal-based thermal power plants (TPPs) include carbon dioxide (CO_2), nitrogen oxides (NO_x), sulphur oxides (SO_x), chlorofluorocarbons (CFCs), and air borne inorganic particles like fly ash, soot and other trace gases. These emissions are considered responsible for stratospheric ozone depletion and also pose various health risks. For instance, inhalation of black carbon particles (soot) causes inflammation of lung tissue and various particle bound chemicals are known carcinogens. Therefore, apart from the direct economic costs of thermal power generation (TPG) there exist indirect costs of environmental degradation (and a corresponding human health cost) which are transferred to the society as negative externalities. The command and control based approach attempts to reduce the social welfare costs associated with environmental degradation by imposing regulatory standards on emissions. But these standards are normally set with respect to estimates of allowable exposure levels, and for many significant pollutants any exposure level could be harmful (Sankar and Mathur 1998).

The challenges before the thermal power sector in India and other developing countries is not only to enhance capacity to generate more power to meet the demand from growing economic activities and to provide better access to electricity to a larger section of the populace, but also to comply with domestic regulatory standards for emissions. With the growing concern for global climate change, coal-based TPPs may have to face global scrutiny on emission standards in future. Therefore for future climate change mitigation concern, it is an appropriate juncture to redefine the country's coal-based thermal power technology trajectory. India has around 112,824.48 MW (as on 31 March 2011) installed capacity for thermal electricity generation, and more than 73 per cent of present generation of electricity is produced by coal-based power plants (CEA 2009), which also contributes a major share in total CO_2 emissions. The larger dependence on coal-based power plants and poor endowment of alternative sources of energy (like crude petroleum, natural gas, nuclear ore, water reservoirs, etc.) underlines the urgency to explore an alternative trajectory for energy security for India. However, larger dependence on energy sources (e.g. crude and natural gas) from outside could also pose a serious challenge on India's energy security (Garg and Shukla 2009). Therefore, proper assessment of the environmental impacts (costs) of coal-based power generation is of the utmost necessity, not only to control the environmental costs associated with the existing power plants, but also for efficient abatement of pollution from forthcoming power plants or for expanding the capacity of the existing plants.

This chapter makes an assessment of the environmental impacts of TPG in India by using available secondary sources of information. First, it discusses the Indian power sector scenario including different aspects of coal-based TPG, consumption, followed by a discussion on the use of coal as input. Based on this analysis, an attempt has been made to understand the direct as well as indirect costs associated with TPG. The chapter concludes with policy prescriptions to overcome the problems.

The Indian power sector scenario

As on 31 March 2011, the total installed capacity of electricity generation in India is 173,626.4 MW, of which the shares of thermal power (112,824.48 MW), hydro power (37,567.4 MW), nuclear power (4,780 MW) and other sources (18,454.52 MW)[4] are 64.98, 21.64, 2.75 and 10.63 per cent respectively. Of the total installed TPG capacity, coal-based power plants have a 83.2 per cent (93,918.38 MW) share, and gas and oil based power plants contribute 15.7 per cent (17,706.35 MW) and 1.1 per cent (1,199.75 MW) respectively. Of the total installed electricity generation capacity in the country, the state, central and the private sectors account for 47.49, 31.34 and 21.17 per cent respectively.

The above statistics underline the importance of the role of coal-based power plants in India. The source-wise installed capacity of electricity generation is presented in Table 5.1, which shows that TPG contributes approximately 65 per cent of total power generation. In addition, the coal-based power plants contribute the maximum of TPG.

Source-wise generation of electricity is presented in Table 5.2, which reveals that thermal power contributes 83 per cent of total electricity generation within the public sector. Availability of coal, as compared to other energy sources, is the major driver for larger dependence on thermal power; availability of thermal power technology is another factor influencing the growth of thermal power infrastructure in India.

Out of 593,732 inhabited villages (as per the 2001 Census of India), 55,785 (9.4 per cent) villages are yet to be electrified as on 31 March 2011 (CEA 2011). Since a considerable section of rural India is still deprived of electricity connection and there is also the problem of getting quality electricity supply round the clock, the household sector electricity demand is still unmet. The successful implementation of various rural electrification programmes (e.g. *Rajiv Gandhi Grameen Vidyutikaran Yojana*, Remote Village Electrification Programme) and improvement of basic urban infrastructure could generate additional demand for electricity. However, per capita consumption of electricity in India is estimated to be 704 kWh during 2008–09,[5] which is fairly low as compared to other developing countries (China 719 kWh; Brazil 1,783 kWh in 1997), developed countries (USA 8,747 kWh, UK 5,843 kWh in 1997) or the global average (2,300 kWh).

It is observed from Table 5.3 that during 1998–99 to 2007–08, the compounded annual growth rate (CAGR) of electricity consumption was 4.5 per cent. The major demand came from the commercial sector (14.5 per cent), followed by the domestic sector (5.4 per cent). The average share of industrial power consumption during the period was 35.5 per cent, followed by the agriculture/irrigation sector (25.1 per cent) and the domestic sector (22.5 per cent).

Importance of coal in Indian thermal power sector

Table 5.4 provides comprehensive information on the five-year average production and consumption of conventional energy in India by major sources; namely; coal and lignite, crude petroleum, natural gas, hydro and nuclear power over the last four decades. It is observed from the table that coal production increased in line with the increase in average consumption over the years, and the CAGR during 1970–71 to 2004–05 was 5.4 per cent. The dependence on coal is likely to continue in the future, given the highly volatile growth rates experienced for the crude petroleum and natural gas sector. Generation of nuclear power has increased in the recent period, but is still in the nascent stage.

Figure 5.1 demonstrates the sectoral perspective of coal use in India over the last four decades. It is observed from the figure that the proportional importance of other economic activities in coal consumption is declining. For instance, coal consumption in railways has been discontinued since the late 1990s. Similarly,

Table 5.1 Energy source-wise installed capacity of electricity in India (as on 31 March of the year) (in MW)

Energy source	2006		2007		2008		2009		2010		2011	
Coal	68,518.88	(83.1)	71,121.38	(82.7)	76,048.88	(82.7)	77,648.88	(82.8)	84,198.33	(82.2)	93,918.38	(83.2)
Gas	12,689.91	(15.4)	13,691.71	(15.9)	14,656.21	(15.9)	14,876.61	(15.9)	17,055.85	(16.6)	17,706.35	(15.7)
Diesel	1,201.75	(1.5)	1,201.75	(1.4)	1,201.75	(1.3)	1,199.75	(1.3)	1,199.75	(1.2)	1,199.75	(1.1)
Total thermal	82,410.54	[66.3]	86,014.84	[65]	91,906.84	[64.2]	93,725.00	[63.3]	102,453.98	[64.3]	112,824.48	[65]
Hydro	3,235.77	[2.6]	34,653.77	[26.2]	35,908.76	[25.1]	36,877.76	[24.9]	36,863.40	[23.1]	37,567.40	[21.6]
Nuclear	3,360.00	[2.7]	3,900.00	[2.9]	4,120.00	[2.9]	4,120.00	[2.8]	4,560.00	[2.9]	4,780.00	[2.8]
Renewable energy source	6,190.86	[5.0]	7,760.60	[5.9]	11,125.41	[5.9]	13,242.41	[8.9]	15,521.11	[9.7]	18,454.52	[10.6]
Total	124,287.17		132,329.21		143,061.01		147,965.41		159,388.49		173,626.40	

Source: TERI (various years).

Notes
Figures in parentheses show the percentage of total installed capacity for thermal electricity generation.
Figures in brackets show the percentage of total installed capacity of electricity generation.

the use of coal in sectors like cement, cotton, paper and iron and steel has increased in an absolute scale but is showing a declining trend in a proportional sense. As a result a consolidation of coal uses in the TPG sector is observed over the years, with obvious pollution implications. Alternatively, it can be argued that controlling emission from coal combustion in TPG has emerged as a major challenge in recent years.

Table 5.2 Source-wise electricity generated in India (gross) (in billion kWh)

	2004–05	2005–06	2006–07	2007–08	2008–09
(i) Utilities					
Thermal	492.8	506	538.4	585.3	617.8
	(82.9)	(81.0)	(80.3)	(81.0)	(82.7)
Hydro	84.6	101.5	113.5	120.4	114.1
	(14.2)	(16.2)	(16.9)	(16.7)	(15.3)
Nuclear	17	17.3	18.8	16.9	14.7
	(2.9)	(2.8)	(2.8)	(2.3)	(2.0)
Total	594.4	624.8	670.7	722.6	746.6
(ii) Non-utilities	71.4	73.6	81.8	90.5	95.9
	[10.7]	[10.5]	[10.9]	[11.1]	[11.4]
Grand total	665.8	698.4	752.5	813.1	842.5

Source: Government of India (2009).

Notes
Figures in parentheses show the percentage share in total of utilities.
Figures in brackets show the percentage share of the grand total.

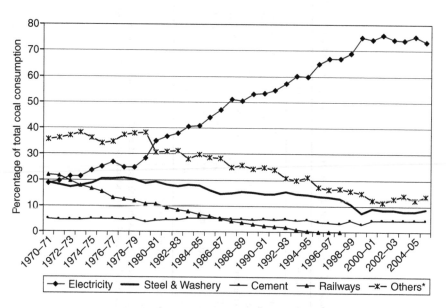

Figure 5.1 Coal use in different sectors (source: Coal Controller Organization various years).

Table 5.3 Sector-wise consumption of electricity in India (MkWh)

Year	Domestic		Commercial		Industrial		Agriculture/ irrigation		Railway traction		Others		Total
1998–99	57,553	(18.4)	15,182	(4.9)	105,207	(33.6)	93,687	(30.0)	6,660	(2.1)	34,396	(11.0)	312,685
1999–00	65,909	(16.8)	16,332	(4.2)	170,690	43.4	98,801	(25.1)	7,469	(1.9)	34,134	(8.7)	393,335
2000–01	67,061	(21.3)	16,372	(5.2)	96,026	(30.5)	91,618	(29.1)	7,241	(2.3)	36,521	(11.6)	314,840
2001–02	72,605	(22.0)	17,302	(5.2)	99,474	(30.2)	97,869	(29.7)	7,475	(2.3)	34,896	(10.6)	329,621
2002–03	77,004	(23.7)	22,988	(7.1)	114,959	(35.4)	82,238	(25.3)	8,110	(2.5)	19,391	(6.0)	324,691
2003–04	89,736	(24.9)	28,202	(7.8)	124,573	(34.5)	87,089	(24.1)	9,210	(2.6)	22,128	(6.1)	360,937
2004–05	95,659	(24.8)	31,381	(8.1)	137,589	(35.6)	88,555	(22.9)	9,495	(2.5)	23,453	(6.1)	386,134
2005–06	100,090	(24.3)	35,965	(8.7)	151,557	(36.8)	90,292	(21.9)	9,944	(2.4)	24,039	(5.8)	411,887
2006–07	111,002	(24.4)	40,220	(8.8)	171,293	(37.6)	99,023	(21.7)	10,800	(2.4)	23,410	(5.1)	455,748
2007–08	120,918	(24.1)	46,685	(9.3)	189,424	(37.7)	104,182	(20.8)	11,108	(2.2)	29,661	(5.9)	501,978
Average share		22.5		6.9		35.5		25.1		2.3		7.7	
CAGR (1998–99 to 2007–08)	8.4		14.5		5.4		0.4		6.0		–4.2		4.5

Source: TERI (various years)

Note
Figures in parentheses show the percentage share in total consumption of electricity.

Table 5.4 Average production and consumption of conventional energy sources in India (1970–71 to 2004–05)

Year	Average production (MT)				Average consumption (MT)			
	Coal and lignite	Crude petroleum	Natural gas	Electricity from hydro and nuclear	Coal and lignite	Crude petroleum	Natural gas	Electricity from hydro and nuclear
1970–75	81.1	7.3	1.7	29.3	77.34	19.96	0.77	48.55
1975–80	104.9	10.3	2.6	42.5	100.34	24.72	1.47	70.30
1980–85	138.1	20.6	4.9	52.8	127.84	31.99	2.85	96.92
1985–90	190.9	31.4	11.9	59.6	179.42	47.42	8.08	148.06
1990–95	255.9	29.9	18.5	79.4	242.59	53.50	15.40	223.37
1995–2000	312.5	33.3	25.6	86.4	303.60	68.26	21.52	295.30
2000–05	371.7	33.0	30.9	92.5	367.36	114.45	29.51	345.15
1970–2005	207.9	23.7	13.7	63.2	199.79	51.47	11.37	175.38
CAGR (1970–71 to 2004–05)	5.39	5.38	11.08	3.85	5.51	5.71	13.75	7.08

Source: Coal Controller Organization (various years).

Environmental impacts of coal-based power generation

Table 5.5 shows the trend of CO_2 emission in the Indian context, which has increased more than five-fold over the period. Interestingly, it is observed from the data that coal's CO_2 emission as a percentage of total emission is showing a declining trend, though it retains its position as the most important contributor. While pollution from coal accounted for 71.5 per cent of the total emission during 1971, the corresponding figure for 2004 stood at 66.6 per cent. The relative decline is caused by the recent increase in CO_2 emission from other sectors like oil and gas.

The estimate released by Government of India (2010) shows that the total GHGs emissions from the electricity sector in 2007 was 719.31 million tonne of CO_2 equivalent (CO_{2e}). In 2004, CO_{2e} emission from electricity was 355.03 million tonne and it has registered 5.6 per cent CAGR during 2004 to 2007. In 2007, total CO_{2e} emissions from electricity generation were 65.4 per cent of the total CO_{2e} emitted from the energy sector (i.e. 1,100.05 million tonne). The distinctive key features of the two assessments and the improvements in the 2007 assessments are indicated in Table 5.6.

Fugitive emissions from mining and extraction of coal, oil and natural gas should also be accounted as the cost of TPG. The total GHG emissions without land use, land use change and forestry (LULUCF) have grown from 1,251.95 million tonne in 1994 to 1,904.73 million tonne in 2007 at a CAGR of 3.3 per cent and with LULUCF the CAGR is 2.9 per cent. Between 1994 and 2007, some of the sectors indicate significant growth in GHG emissions such as electricity generation (5.6 per cent), waste (7.3 per cent) and cement (6.0 per cent) (Government of India 2010).

Cost analysis of thermal power generation

Evaluation of the costs of TPG depends on the four factors: capital cost; maintenance cost; fuel cost and external cost (or costs associated with externalities). The fuel and external costs are sensitive to fuel type and thermal efficiency of power plant. The total cost (tc_{it}) of TPG for ith plant at tth period can be written as:

$$tc_{it} = cc_{it} + mc_{it} + fc_{it} + sc_{it} + \sum_{j=0}^{\infty} ec_{it+j} \qquad (5.1)$$

Where, cc denotes the capital cost, covering initial capital expense for equipment, system design, system engineering and installation. This cost is considered as a single payment occurring in the initial year of the project; mc is the operation and maintenance cost expressed as the sum of yearly scheduled maintenance and operation costs, including salaries for operation, inspections, and insurance; the fuel cost fc is the sum of yearly fuel costs; salvage value of a system sc shows its net worth in the final year of the lifetime period; ec is the environmental costs including pollution abatement, or damage cost for current as well as

Table 5.5 Trends of CO$_2$ emission from India (million tonne)

Year	Total	From coal		From oil		From gas	
1971	199.1	142.3	(71.5)	55.5	(27.9)	1.3	(0.7)
1975	240.2	175.8	(73.2)	62.3	(25.9)	2.1	(0.9)
1980	294.6	205.8	(69.9)	86.1	(29.2)	2.8	(1.0)
1985	417.6	291.1	(69.7)	117.7	(28.2)	8.8	(2.1)
1990	588.3	401.5	(68.2)	164.1	(27.9)	22.7	(3.9)
1995	784.9	522.6	(66.6)	222.1	(28.3)	40.1	(5.1)
2000	971.5	625.6	(64.4)	297.4	(30.6)	48.5	(5.0)
2001	980.7	641.1	(65.4)	291.3	(29.7)	48.4	(4.9)
2002	1,011.2	657.8	(65.1)	301.5	(29.8)	51.8	(5.1)
2003	1,041.7	678.2	(65.1)	309.6	(29.7)	53.8	(5.2)
2004	1,102.8	734.2	(66.6)	314.4	(28.5)	54.2	(4.9)
% Change 1990–2004	87.5	82.9		91.7		138.4	

Source: IEA (2006).

Note
Figures in parentheses show the percentage share in the total emission.

future periods, due to emission. It is expected that the environmental impacts and damages will be approximately proportional to the emissions from the plant. Future costs in price terms must be discounted because of the time value of money.

Damages caused by the generation of thermal power are usually included only to the extent that they influence productivity. The general cost classifications of production include variable costs, fixed costs, direct costs, indirect costs or overhead costs, opportunity costs and sunk costs. Therefore, the full cost accounting of TPG includes environmental and other social costs. But the proper evaluation of true environmental cost requires a number of conceptual issues to be taken into consideration. This includes the correct estimation of emissions, choice of valuation technique, setting the time horizon, assessing distributional impacts and inter-temporal issues, and evaluating risk, uncertainty, etc. In fact, the coal-based power sector portrays a large discrepancy between internal and external costs and the area where regulation should appear. With regulation, the electricity industry should balance its objectives with both environmental quality and energy supply at minimum cost.

Given the TPG and coal consumption scenario by Indian power sector, it is important to understand the adverse effects of the inter-connected process ranging from coal mining to combustion for future generations. Ideally, in order to arrive at the true social cost of production, the environmental management and social rehabilitation cost of coal mining should also be considered.[6]

Since emissions from TPPs are generally evaluated based on the plant specifications, it is difficult to estimate a 'typical' set of emissions for any resource

Table 5.6 Comparison of GHG emissions by sector between 1994 and 2007 (million tonne of CO_2 equivalent)

Sectors	1994		2007		CAGR
Electricity	355.03	(28.4)	719.30	(37.8)	5.6
Transport	80.28	(6.4)	142.04	(7.5)	4.5
Residential	78.89	(6.3)	137.84	(7.2)	4.4
Other energy	78.93	(6.3)	100.87	(5.3)	1.9
Total energy sector	593.13	(47.4)	1,100.05	(57.8)	
Cement	60.87	(4.9)	129.92	(6.8)	6.0
Iron and steel	90.53	(7.2)	117.32	(6.2)	2.0
Other industry	125.41	(10.0)	165.31	(8.7)	2.2
Agriculture	344.48	(27.6)	334.41	(17.6)	−0.2
Waste	23.23	(1.9)	57.73	(3.0)	7.3
Total without LULUCF	1,251.95		1,904.73		3.3
LULUCF	14.29		−177.03		
Total with LULUCF	1,228.54		1,727.71		2.9

Source: Government of India (2010).

Note
Figures in parentheses show the percentage share in total GHG emissions for the corresponding year without land use, land-use change and forestry (LULUCF).

type. Emissions depend on several factors other than the plant type, such as: age and type of plant; fuel type; grade; sulphur content of fuel; installed emissions control technology; plant operating parameters like heat rate, combustion efficiency, steam temperature, furnace slagging and fouling, etc. The combustion of coal, like that of other fossil fuels, leads to CO_2 emission. Table 5.5 shows that CO_2 emission in India from coal combustion over 1971–2004 has drastically increased; though the percentage change over 1990–2004 is highest for gas sources.

The existing literature has strongly underlined the importance of power plants' efficiency in controlling CO_2 emission. Gupta (2007) estimates the marginal abatement costs of CO_2 reduction for a sample of coal-based thermal plants in India for the period 1991–92 to 1999–2000. Gupta (2007) adopted an output distance function approach where duality with the revenue function was established. The average costs of per tonne of CO_2 reduction from the then level was estimated to vary between Rs.2,402 to Rs.3,381. The analysis shows that the marginal abatement cost varies by plant depending on the plant's age, technology adopted for pollution abatement, volume of emission, etc. The study observed a strong correlation between efficiency of the power plants in terms of CO_2 emission per unit of electricity generation and marginal abatement cost of CO_2 and concluded that marginal abatement cost increases with the efficiency of the thermal plant.

Bhattacharyya (1997) assessed the environmental costs of coal-based TPG in India. The analysis noted that the costs of environmental impacts are small but not insignificant, and the estimated costs are sensitive to assumptions made with reference to atmospheric conditions and wind speed. Sathaye and Phadke (2006) estimated the cost of reducing emissions from combined cycle power plants in India, and estimated the cost at US$144 per tonne of C. They found that capital, fuel and other costs were higher for combined cycle power plants in India than in the United States, but that these costs were comparable for coal power plants in the two countries.

A study conducted by the National Environmental Engineering Research Institute (NEERI) across three coal-based TPPs (Chandrapur Super TPP (CSTPP), Maharashtra; Gandhinagar TPP (GTPP), Gujarat and Ramagundam Super TPP (RSTPP), Andhra Pradesh), one natural gas-based TPP (600 MW NTPC Ltd. in Jhenor-Gandhar, Gujarat) and one hydroelectric project (100 MW Koyna Hydro Electric Project, Maharashtra) to understand the post-clearance environmental impacts of power generation in India (NEERI 2006). The results are presented in Table 5.7. For coal-based TPPs the ambient concentration of SO_2, NO_x and SPM surrounding the plant is higher than gas-based TPP. The study found that 6.5 per cent of the population living within a 2 km radius of the RSTPP suffer from respiratory disorders, while this figure decreases to 3.2 per cent at a distance of 2.5 km and becomes 0.91 per cent at distances over 5 km from the plant. The estimated environmental cost, which includes ecosystem damage costs (loss of forests and habitats of wild animals), loss of agriculture and cost of health impairment, for coal-based TPP is higher than other plants.

Table 5.7 Comparative environmental impacts of electricity plants

Description	Ambient concentration surrounding the plant			Water requirement (m³/kWh)	Land required for the plant (ha)	Land required for disposal of fly ash (ha)	Loss of agricultural land due to plant (ha)	Environmental cost[4] (Rs./kWh)
	SO_2 (µg/m³)	NO_x (µg/m³)	SPM (µg/m³)					
Coal-based thermal power plant				0.005–0.18	0.1–4.70			0.1067
CSTPP	3.61–18.9	8.89–26.55	52.6–193.2			2,616		0.0646
GTPP	3–37	5–34	65–482			74		0.0614
RSTPP (pg/m³)[1]	20–25			0.15–0.18		321		0.1067
Natural gas-based power plant		5–7		0.003	0.26		168[3]	0.0202
Hydroelectric power plant					6.6		1,380[2]	0.0054

Source: NEERI (2006).

Notes
1 1pg $= 1.0 \times 10^{-6}$ µg; 1 µg $= 1.0 \times 10^{-6}$ gram.
2 includes 1,150 ha loss of forest land.
3 0.13 ha/MW of capacity.
4 includes ecosystem damage costs (loss of forests and habitats of wild animals), loss of agriculture and cost of health impairment.

Environmental impacts of coal mining

Mining of coal has substantial impacts on the environment which leads to air pollution, water pollution; land degradation; impacts on the ecosystem, and noise pollution (Krishnamurthy 2004). The impact of mining on health and safety of workers and the larger socio-economic and socio-cultural impact of the region is substantial (Singh 2008). Air pollution is mainly caused by emissions of particulate substances and gases like methane (CH_4), sulphur dioxide (SO_2), NO_x and carbon monoxide (CO) from mines (Ghose and Majee 2000). Opencast mining is a more severe air pollutant in comparison to underground mining, and the growing share of opencast coal mining leads to release of dust and gaseous pollutants (Ghose 2007). Opencast mining is the predominant method of mining today, and its share is likely to further increase in the future. In India a large part of the coal, lignite, iron ore, copper ore and lead-zinc ore is mined from large and deep mechanized opencast mines (Banerjee 2004). In India, the share of opencast mining for coal extraction has gone up to 87 per cent in 2007–08, recording a growth rate of 6.53 per cent over the previous year.

Coal mining also results in water pollution (Tiwary and Dhar 1994; Pathak and Banerjee 1992; Swer and Singh 2004). A high incidence of total dissolved solids, sulphate, hardness, iron and biological contamination is observed in the Damodar River Basin which holds 46 per cent of the coal reserve in India (Tiwary and Dhar 1994). Depending on the location of the mine, the hydrology, climate of the area, physical and chemical properties of the coal and reject material from the mine, the impact of mining varies across the basins (Reza *et al.* 2009). Apart from coal mining, several activities related to coal processing like coal washeries, effluents from coal beneficiation plants, workshops, vehicle wash plants, seepage and run off from waste/tailing ponds also results in substantial water pollution (Singh undated). Gupta and Singh (1995) identified coal washeries as a major source of pollution for the Damodar River in Jharia Coalfields. Effluents from coal washeries pose a serious water pollution problem with respect to suspended solids, oil and grease and chemical oxygen demand (COD). The impact of acid mine drainage results in surface water pollution problem (Equeenuddin *et al.* 2010).

Large and deep opencast mines significantly influence the hydrological conditions of a region, mainly groundwater resources. In mines, percolated water is collected in the mine sump, a part is used up in the mine, and the surplus water is discharged into the surface drainage system. The cone of depression caused by lowering of the water table by the mine excavation usually extends to a radius of 0.5–1.5 km depending upon the depth of the mine and the characteristic of aquifers present in the area (Banerjee 2004).

Coal mining alters the physical and biological nature of the mined area and causes large scale land degradation and subsidence of land. The loss of topsoil, disturbance of the water table and severe ecological imbalance are reported from coal mines in India (Singh *et al.* 2007). Sahu and Dash (2011) show that coal mining alone has resulted in 10,175 ha of land degradation in India in 2005–06.

Generation and disposal of dump waste from open cast coal mines force a change in the land use pattern of the region surrounding the dumping sites (Rai *et al.* 2010; Singh *et al.* 2007). Rai *et al.* (2010) observed that the overburden dumps (also known as mine spoil dumps) formed outside the open pits alter the surface topography and contribute to the environmental degradation. Deposition of coal particles from the overburden dumps through wind and water erosion change the physical and chemical properties of the land surrounding the mines (Shankar *et al.* 1993). Even after 20 years of natural recovery process, the topsoil of the affected land remain nutrient (nitrogen (N), phosphorous (P), potash (K), magnesium (Mg) and potential hydrogen (pH)) deficient and enriched in calcium (Ca), manganese (Mn), zinc (Zn), iron (Fe) and sulphur (S) (Shankar *et al.* 1993). A major constraint for the ecological restoration of coal mine overburden dumps, which are acidic in nature, is the low concentration of organic matters (Maiti and Ghose 2005).

An expanding mining sector will continue to seek large parcels of land and will face problems of land acquisition, involving a much larger problem of displacement. Coal Vision (CV) 2025 brought out by Ministry of Coal (Government of India) estimated that the requirement of forest land for mining would increase more than three-fold from the current 22,000 ha (15 per cent of the current total land requirement) to 73,000 ha (25 per cent of the projected total land requirement), since much of the coal resources to be exploited are located in forests. In India during 1950–91 the mining projects provided employment to only 560,000 people, but displaced nearly 2.6 million people,[7] almost 52 per cent of whom were tribal. CV 2025 estimates also suggest that 170,000 families or 850,000 displaced persons would have to be rehabilitated by 2025 when the requirement for mining land would double from the current 147,000 ha to 292,500 ha.

Concern areas

The huge ash content in Indian coal (35–50 per cent),[8] low calorific value (gross heat of combustion) and inefficient technologies for combustion jointly contribute to the emission of particulate matter and other gases, including GHGs (Sengupta 2007). Furthermore, the high ash content of coal makes it difficult to enrich the coal through beneficiation, which results in high production of fly ash and corresponding problems of disposal. Apart from fly ash, coal combustion residues contain heavy metals and several radioactive elements which are potential threats for the environment and human health (Sushil and Batra 2006; Asokan *et al.* 2005).

The burning of coal emits SO_x and NO_x –responsible for 'acid rain' and 'ground level ozone'. Acid rain due to SO_2 emissions is presently a serious concern, but increasing coal use or blending Indian coal with imported coal of higher calorific value (further increasing electricity production) needs to be carefully addressed through viable technological options. The average SO_2 emission per unit of electricity generation is 0.0069 gigagram (Gg) (1 Gg = 10^9 gram)

(Enzen Global Solutions undated). Total SO_2 emissions are estimated to be 7.33 Gg/day or 2.7 teragram (Tg) per year ($1\,Tg = 10^3\,Gg$). The nitric oxide (NO) emission per unit of electricity generation is estimated at 0.00056 Gg approximately. Total NO emissions are estimated to be 0.5 Gg/day and 0.185 Tg/year. Nitrogen oxides are responsible for the formation of smog, contribute to acidity in atmosphere and act as ancestor gases for the configuration of tropospheric ozone.

Last but not the least, incomplete and inefficient combustion processes of fossil fuel generate soot. Estimation of soot emissions in India is a relatively less researched area. Available estimations reveal that soot emissions are produced at a rate of 22.0 Gg per year from Indian TPPs (Enzen Global Solutions undated). Proper technical interference to prevent soot carbon emissions may possibly reduce the chances of soot escaping into the atmosphere (where it can potentially change the radiation balance), as well as possibly leading to further increases in electricity production.

Policy prescriptions

The search for appropriate policies for emission management and for sustainable development is a continuous process. The increasing appreciation of the need to treat environmental implications in a more effective and practical manner is a healthy sign so far. In this background, the present chapter attempts to understand the environmental costs of coal-based TPG. Since utilities burn mostly coal with approximately 10–30 per cent excess air, technological improvements in efficient combustion of coal can lead to greater production of electricity per unit of coal that will effectively reduce CO emission per unit of electricity. The policy recommendations are the following:

1   A two-pronged objective is to limit CO_2 emissions. The first is to improve generating efficiency for reducing the quantity of coal burned to produce one unit of power, and, second is to introduce extensive CO_2 capture and permanent storage.

2   Equipment required for efficient new coal-fired plants are relatively inexpensive and the technology mix can provide another solution to reduce carbon emission. Oxy-combustion and post combustion solution also makes great sense to control emission.

3   Post combustion technology is presently the most advanced method, which consists of separating pollutants from exhaust gases using chilled ammonia. Recent test results reveal that the chilled ammonia capture method could remove 90 per cent of CO_2 from combustion gases (Energy Business 2010). This technology can be used for both coal-fired power plants and combined cycle-gas fired power plants.

4   Currently national level policies for controlling emissions from power plants often depend on the use of specific technologies. But such technology-centric policies do not provide an optimal solution, since they do not take

into account the differences in marginal abatement costs across power plants. Therefore, it is necessary for policymakers to consider alternate policy tools, such as carbon tax or emissions trading, which can be more cost effective and achieve greater leverage over a regulation-based approach. When compared to a technology push policy, an emissions trading regime is likely to generate cost-savings for equivalent reductions. These savings could be invested in clean coal technologies, strengthening institutions for effective policy implementation and other air quality management measures.

5 Coal-fired power plants operate on the 'modified Rankine thermodynamic cycle'. The efficiency of the power plant can be dictated by the parameters of this thermodynamic cycle. The overall efficiency of coal-based power plant varies between 32 and 42 per cent. Conversely, hydro turbines, the most commonly used as renewable energy source, have the most efficient among all power conversion processes. The efficiency is in the range of 85 to 90 per cent and wind turbines have an overall conversion efficiency of 30 to 45 per cent.

6 Promoting renewable energy in India has received greater focus nowadays in view of the high share of coal in the increasing demand for energy. Wind energy has achieved a dramatic growth rate and success in this context. But the basic problem is that wind and solar power plants are dependent on the availability of wind and solar isolation. Thus, the generation from these plants is not controllable and varies periodically or daily.

7 Solar power generation technologies are still not economical on a stand-alone basis, with the generation cost being Rs.13–Rs.15 per kWh. Moreover, current policy framework and financial support are not adequate to enable sufficient deployments.

8 Greater focus on research and innovation of new low carbon technologies can provide a solution, which could ensure sustainable development.

At present the major available options include improving energy efficiency, power recovery using renewable energy, fuel switching, etc. but devising other alternatives to combating climate change are of utmost importance. The reason behind the absence of implementing innovative techniques might be a lack of market demand, and sometimes lenient government regulations. The changing perspective of the ultimate consumer is however the saving grace, owing to the recently growing awareness about climate change.

Notes

1 GHGs includes the common gases, namely, CO_2 and water vapour, and rarer gases such as nitrous oxide, CH_4 and CFCs, etc. The increased atmospheric presence of such gases results from the mining of raw input, burning of fossil fuels, emissions from power plants, etc.
2 India has voluntarily announced that the emissions intensity of GDP will be reduced by 20–25 per cent over the 2005 levels by the year 2020 (Planning Commission 2011).

3 The World Energy Outlook (IEA 2009) projects that global CO_2 emissions from fuel combustion will continue to grow unabated, reaching 40.2 gigatonne (Gt) of CO_2 by 2030 (1 Gt=10^9 metric tonne). Such an emission growth trend would be in line with the worst-case scenario presented by the Intergovernmental Panel on Climate Change (IPCC) in the *Fourth Assessment Report* (2007), which projects a world average temperature increase of between 2.4°C and 6.4°C by 2010.
4 The others include, renewable energy sources like small hydro projects, biomass gasifier, biomass power, and urban and industrial waste power, etc.
5 The per capita consumption of electricity has gone up from 253 kWh in 1990–91 to 631 kWh in 2005–06 (TERI various years).
6 A study on energy modelling for India, conducted by Planning Commission (Government of India) (Sengupta 1993), estimates the average cost of production of power grade (inferior non-cooking) coal is Rs.173 for open cast and Rs.293 on average for all the capacities to be created for all time to come.
7 For details, see CSE (2008).
8 According to Mishra (2004), the ash content is as high as 55–60 per cent, with an average value of about 35–40 per cent.

References

Asokan, P., Saxena, M. and Asolekar, S.R. (2005) 'Coal Combustion Residues –Environmental Implications and Recycling Potentials', *Resources, Conservation and Recycling*, 43(3): 239–262.
Banerjee, S.P. (2004) 'Mineral Availability and Environmental Challenges – A Vision 2020 Statement', Professor S.K. Bose Memorial Lecture. Online, available at: www.ismenvis.nic.in/skbose04.html (accessed 10 February 2010).
Bhattacharyya, S.C. (1997) 'An Estimation of Environmental Costs of Coal-based Thermal Power Generation in India', *International Journal of Energy Research*, 21(3): 289–298.
Central Electricity Authority (CEA) (2009) *Annual Report 2009–10*, New Delhi: CEA, Ministry of Power, Government of India.
Central Electricity Authority (CEA) (2011) 'Progress Report of Village Electrification as on 30 April 2011'. Online, available at: www.cea.nic.in/reports/monthly/dpd_div_rep/village_electrification.pdf, (accessed 10 June 2011).
Centre for Science and Environment (CSE) (2008) '*Rich Land, Poor People – Is Sustainable Mining Possible?*' New Delhi: CSE.
Coal Controller Organization (various years) *Coal Directory of India*, Kolkata: Department of Coal, Ministry of Coal and Mines, Government of India.
Energy Business, *Publishing on the Internet*, various news items. Online, available at: www.energybusiness.in (accessed 25 August 2010).
Enzen Global Solutions (undated), 'Environmental Impact of Emissions from Thermal Power Generation in India'. Online, available at: www.enzenglobal.com/pdf_downloads/environmental_impact.pdf (accessed 10 May 2010).
Equeenuddin, S.M., Tripathy, S., Sahoo, P.K. and Panigrahi, M.K. (2010) 'Hydrogeochemical Characteristics of Acid Mine Drainage and Water Pollution at Makum Coalfield, India', *Journal of Geochemical Exploration*, 105(3): 75–82.
European Commission (EC) (2003) 'Draft Commission Regulation on Directive 2003/87/EC', Brussels. Online, available at: http://ec.europa.eu/clima/news/docs/proposal_restrictions_final.pdf (accessed 10 February 2011).
Garg, A. and Shukla, P.R. (2009) 'Coal and Energy Security for India: Role of Carbon Dioxide (CO_2) Capture and Storage (CCS)', *Energy*, 34(8): 1032–1041.

Ghose, M.K. (2007) 'Opencast Coal Mining in India: Analyzing and Addressing the Air Environmental Impacts', *Environmental Quality Management*, 16(3): 71–87.

Ghose, M.K. and Majee, S.R. (2000) 'Sources of Air Pollution due to Coal Mining and their Impacts in Jharia Coalfield', *Environment International*, 26(1–2): 81–85.

Government of India (2009) *Basic Statistics on Indian Petroleum and Natural Gas: 2008–09*, New Delhi: Economic Division, Ministry of Petroleum and Natural Gas, Government of India.

Government of India (2010) *India: Greenhouse Gas Emissions 2007*, New Delhi: Indian Network for Climate Change Assessment (INCCA), Ministry of Environment and Forests, Government of India.

Gupta, M. (2007) 'Costs of Reducing Greenhouse Gas Emissions: A Case Study of India's Power Generation Sector', Working Papers No. 89, Milan: Fondazione Eni Enrico Mattei.

Gupta, R.K. and Singh, G. (1995) 'Water Pollution Profile of Coal Washeries', *Pollution Research*, 14(2): 203–213.

Intergovernmental Panel on Climate Change (2007) *Fourth Assessment Report*, Geneva: IPCC.

International Energy Agency (IEA) (2006) *CO_2 Emissions from Fuel Combustion 1971–2004*, Paris: IEA.

International Energy Agency (IEA) (2009) *World Energy Outlook*, Paris: IEA.

Krishnamurthy, K.V. (2004) 'Environmental Impacts of Coal Mining in India', Proceedings of the National Seminar on Environmental Engineering with special emphasis on Mining Environment, Indian School of Mines, Dhanbad.

Maiti, S.K. and Ghose, M.K. (2005) 'Ecological Restoration of Acidic Coal Mine Overburden Dumps – an Indian Case Study', *Land Contamination and Reclamation*, 13(4), 361–369.

Mishra, U.C. (2004) 'Environmental Impact of Coal Industry and Thermal Power Plants in India', *Journal of Environmental Radioactivity*, 72(1–2): 35–40.

NEERI (2006) 'Summary Report of the Study on Post-Clearance Environmental Impacts and Cost–Benefit Analysis of Power generation in India'. Online, available at: www.mospi.gov.in/research_studies_post_clerance.htm (accessed 17 February 2010).

Pathak, V. and Banerjee, A.K. (1992) 'Mine Water Pollution Studies in Chapha Incline, Umaria Coalfield, Eastern Madhya Pradesh, India', *Mine Water and the Environment*, 11(2): 27–36.

Planning Commission (2011) 'Interim Report of the Expert Group on Low Carbon Strategies for Inclusive Growth', Government of India, New Delhi.

Rai, A.K., Paul, B. and Singh, G. (2010) 'A Study on the Bulk Density and its Effect on the Growth of Selected Grasses in Coal Mine Overburden Dumps, Jharkhand, India', *International Journal of Environmental Sciences*, 1(4): 677–684.

Reza, R., Jain, M.K. and Singh, G. (2009) 'Impact of Mining Activities on Surface Water Quality in Angul-Talcher Region of Orissa, India', *Mining Engineers' Journal*: 22–28. Online, available at: www.ismenvis.nic.in/My_Webs/Digital_Library/GSingh/Impact%20of%20mining%20activities%20on%20surface%20water%20quality0001.pdf (accessed 10 February 2010).

Sahu, H.B. and Dash, S. (2011) 'Land Degradation due to Mining in India and its Mitigation Measures', Proceedings of Second International Conference on Environmental Science and Technology, Feb 26–28, 2011, Singapore. Online, available at: http://dspace.nitrkl.ac.in:8080/dspace/bitstream/2080/1411/1/icest2011_submission_45.pdf (accessed 31 May 2011).

Sankar, U. and Mathur, O.P. (1998) *Economic Instruments for Environment Sustainability*, New Delhi: NIPFP and MSE.

Sathaye, J. and Phadke, A. (2006) 'Cost of Electric Power Sector Carbon Mitigation in India: International Implications', *Energy Policy*, 34(13): 1619–1629.

Sengupta, I. (2007) Regulation of Suspended Particulate Matter (SPM) in Indian coal-Based Thermal Power Plants: A Static Approach', *Energy Economics*, 29(3): 479–502.

Sengupta, R. (1993) 'Energy Modeling for India', New Delhi: Planning Commission, Energy Division, Government of India.

Shankar, U., Boral, L., Pandey, H.N. and Tripathi, R.S. (1993) 'Degradation of Land due to Coal Mining and its Natural Recovery Pattern', *Current Science*, 65(9): 680–686.

Singh, G. (undated) 'Water Pollution in Mining areas – Issue Related to its Protection and Control', Paper presented at the International Symposium on Environmental Issues of Mineral Industry, Online, available at: www.ismenvis.nic.in/My_Webs/Digital_Library/GSingh/Water%20Pollution%20in%20mining%20areas%20issue%20ralated.pdf (accessed 10 February 2010).

Singh, G. (2008) 'Environmental and Social Sustainability of Mining Companies – including R&R Issues, Human Resources Development'. Online, available at: www.ismenvis.nic.in/my_webs/digital_library/gsingh/environmental%20and%20social%20sustainability%20of%20mining%20companies_.pdf (accessed 10 February 2010).

Singh, R., Singh, P.K. and Singh, G. (2007) 'Evaluation of Land Degradation to Coal Mining – A Vibrant Issue', Paper presented at the First International Conference on MSECCMI, New Delhi, India. Online, available at: www.ismenvis.nic.in/My_Webs/Digital_Library/GSingh/Evaluation%20of%20land%20degradation%20due%20to%20coal%20mining....pdf (accessed 2 March 2011).

Sushil, S. and Batra, V.S. (2006) 'Analysis of Fly Ash Heavy Metal Content and Disposal in Three Thermal Power Plants in India', *Fuel*, 85(17–18): 2676–2679.

Swer, Sumarlin and Singh, O.P. (2004) 'Water Quality, Availability and Aquatic Life Affected by Coal Mining in Ecologically Sensitive Areas of Meghalaya'. Online, available at: http://dspace.nehu.ac.in/bitstream/1/3335/1/water%20quality.pdf (accessed 10 February 2010).

The Energy Resources Institute (TERI) (various years) TERI Energy Data Directory Yearbook (TEDDY), TERI, New Delhi.

Tiwary, R.K. and Dhar, B.B. (1994) 'Environmental Pollution from Coal Mining Activities in Damodar River Basin, India', *Mine Water and Environment*, 13(1–10) June–December. Online, available at: www.imwa.info/docs/MWE130301.pdf (accessed 10 February 2010).

6 Environmental cost of using topsoil for brick-making

Vinish Kathuria and R. Balasubramanian

Introduction

The removal of topsoil for urban uses, and in particular for brick-making, is increasing rapidly due to the tremendous growth in urbanization and industrialization in many developing countries. Unfortunately, brick kilns are mostly situated on fertile agricultural land, as brick manufacturers need silty clay loam to silty clay soils with good drainage conditions. Quite often soils used in brick-making have high fertility status and their opportunity cost is also high especially when the soil/brick-earth is removed from river basins with intensive agricultural production. Another important dimension to the problem is the depth over which the soil is removed frequently exceeds the agreed depth of soil extraction, which renders land unsuitable for agriculture.

Under this backdrop, the main focus of this chapter is to quantify the agricultural impacts of topsoil removal for brick-making. The removal of topsoil has a direct impact on agricultural crop production via the reduced fertility status of soils. As the addition of organic matter in the forms of human and animal wastes and plant residues occurs only over the top layers of soil, removal of topsoil leads to loss of soil fertility. Therefore, the negative impact of topsoil removal is quantified in terms of the cost of replacing the nutrients lost. The quantification is important because while procuring brick-earth/soil, this cost is never considered, as this is a societal cost.

The quantification of the cost of topsoil removal is carried out using a replacement cost approach (RCA) for Tamil Nadu, a southern state of India. The choice of Tamil Nadu is justified because the state is in the forefront of urbanization among all the states in India, with nearly 44 per cent of its population living in urban areas.[1] Fast growing cities like Chennai, Madurai and other major cities in the state are witnessing steady growth in construction activities. As a result the Cooum River Basin around Chennai and the Tamirabarani River Basin in Tirunelveli and Tuticorin districts are the two major fertile agricultural areas facing serious challenges from brick industries. In order to compute the environmental cost of using topsoil, 60 soil samples – 30 from each region – are analysed from both types of fields, i.e. fields sold/leased land for brick-making, and virgin fields not exposed to excavation by brick manufacturers.

The organization of the remaining chapter is as follows: the following section describes the methodology to compute the environmental cost of removing topsoil. The next section looks into whether any study exists in India or elsewhere that has tried to quantify the impact of soil loss, followed by the description of study site(s) in terms of type and extent of agriculture, extent of irrigation, etc. The section also gives the characteristics of the sampled farms in terms of the land-holding pattern, type of crop, etc. An estimation of the environmental cost of using topsoil is performed in the following section. The final section draws policy conclusions.

Sampling methodology

The agricultural impact of the removal of topsoil for brick-making is two-fold; namely, (a) the costs incurred by the farmers in levelling the field and/or mitigating the hardpan[2] problem by application of tank silt; and (b) the loss of soil nutrients. The quantification of costs of levelling the field and mitigation of the hardpan problem is direct, as the actual costs incurred by the farmers in taking up these activities are directly observable. However, quantification of the loss of nutrients is not direct. It leads to a reduction in crop yield unless all the critical nutrients required for crop growth, which were lost due to removal of topsoil, are adequately replaced through application of organic matter and inorganic fertilizers. There are two methods widely used in the literature to quantify the nutrient-loss impact of topsoil removal on farm economy: (a) the RCA; and (b) the productivity change approach (PCA). RCA has been used in the present study to compute the impact of soil loss. The method essentially quantifies the additional nutrients need to be added to restore the fertility status of the soil.

Valuation of loss in soil organic matter

An important and related issue in valuing the soil fertility loss is the soil carbon or soil organic matter (SOM). SOM is complex and consists of living and dead plant and animal residues of different ages, activities and resistances. SOM contributes to soil structure, soil water-holding capacity, soil nutrient content and nutrient exchange capacity and thus soil fertility and agricultural yields in general. However, there have been few attempts in the economic literature to value it, even though SOM losses have long been recognized as a significant aspect of soil degradation in tropical environments. In contrast to the assessment of nitrogen (N), phosphorous (P), and potash (K) balances, direct measurements or estimations of carbon inputs and outputs are more difficult (Detwiler 1985). To obtain a quantifiable proxy for SOM losses, it is possible to analyse soil carbon, which makes up the majority of SOM, over time or between different treatments, with and without soil loss. Even after measuring SOM or soil carbon loss or gain, another key challenge is determining an appropriate price to apply in its valuation.

Literature review

In this section, we review studies on quantification and valuation of soil loss. It needs to be mentioned at the outset that no study exists in India or elsewhere that has tried to estimate the impact of soil loss and productivity due to brick-making. As a result, the literature review is from studies carried out elsewhere and for soil loss from reasons other than brick-making.

Replacement cost approach

The cost of replacing an ecosystem service with a man-made substitute is used in the RCA as a measure of the economic value of the ecosystem service. Consequently, it must be possible to identify a substitute for the ecosystem service. Both the cost of investment and the maintenance cost should be included in the replacement cost (RC). The method could for example be applied to value the flood protection capacity of wetlands by estimating the cost of replacing this capacity with the use of a human made protection, i.e. some kind of artificial coastal defence such as sea walls.

Gosselink *et al.* (1974) made an early attempt to apply the RCA to value the waste treatment function provided by wetlands. The value estimate was achieved by estimating the cost of sewage treatment as a replacement technique. They argued that this cost could be viewed as the value of the wetland's waste assimilation capacity. The method could also be used to estimate a value of soil fertility by looking at the cost of fertilizers needed to maintain a certain level of productivity.

Drechsel *et al.* (2004) provide a conceptual overview and empirical evidence for valuation of soil nutrients using both the PCA and the RCA. They contend that of all methods, these two have been the most commonly applied in the economic evaluation of soil services, especially as related to developing countries, by noting:

> In developing countries, and perhaps more generally, the most common methodology for the economic assessment of 1) soil nutrients specifically, as opposed to soil in general, is the RCA. The approach's popularity most likely stems from the fact that it is relatively simple to apply when nutrient loss data are available (Bojö 1996; Predo *et al.* 1997). In essence, the RCA measures the costs that are or might be incurred to replace damaged or lost soil assets, such as nutrients (Grohs 1994). ... A key advantage in using the RCA is that market prices are usually available for at least some common nutrients, making assessments simple once the nutrient database is obtained. However, in applying input prices, caution must be used as the appropriate price to apply depends on the purpose of the analysis. Local market prices might be appropriate to determine financial implications for farmers, while a world market price might be used to calculate societal impact at the national or international level.

Gunatilake and Vieth (2000) present a comparison between the RCA and the PCA. Both methods are applied to estimate the on-site cost of soil erosion in the upper Mahweli watershed of Sri Lanka. The on-site cost of erosion is defined as the value of lost future productivity due to current cultivation. To estimate the RC information on nutrient loss per ton of soil eroded, the price of nutrients and the cost of labour spreading fertilizer are required. The cost of repair and maintenance of damages due to soil erosion is also included in the RC. Fertilizers generally used in Sri Lanka are identified and the cost of nutrient replacement is calculated from market prices assuming the use of these fertilizers. The estimated on-site cost value is also used in a cost–benefit analysis and compared to the cost of soil conservation practices. Stone terraces and spill drains are two of the soil conservation measures evaluated in the study.

It is assumed that the productivity of soil can be maintained by replacing the lost nutrients and organic matters artificially. This assumption can be considered as an argument for the idea that the replacement, i.e. fertilizers, provides functions that are equivalent in quality and magnitude to the ecosystem service.

Samarakoon and Abeygunawardena (1995) have also applied the RCA to value the on-site cost of soil erosion in Sri Lanka. Two different replacement techniques are examined in their study. The cost of material used and cost of labour make up the RC. The RC is also estimated for the two main rainy seasons in the area. Fertilizers suitable to the area are used to replace lost nutrients. Costs of repairing damaged field structures are also included in the RC.

Another RC study focusing on soil erosion in Korea deserves special mention (Kim and Dixon 1986). Arable land is a scarce resource in Korea due to urbanization and industrialization. Even upland areas are used for farming. Inadequate soil management techniques have made erosion a severe problem in these upland areas. The productivity in the upland areas can be maintained either by physically replacing lost soil and nutrients or by adopting a management technique and this is compared in a cost–benefit analysis. The RCs are interpreted as a minimum estimate of the value of measures that will improve on site management practices and thereby prevent damages. The RCs are estimated by adding the cost of fertilizer, transport of organic matter, irrigation and the cost of repairing damaged field structures. It is assumed that the productivity in upland areas can be maintained by replacing lost soil nutrients with fertilizer.

In a case study of Changbaishan Mountain Biosphere Reserve in China, the value of benefits derived from the forest ecosystem has been estimated (Xue and Tisdell 2001), wherein the RCA is used to provide a monetary value of four of the ecosystem services identified. These services include water conservancy, nutrient cycling, pollutant decomposition, and disease and pest control. The role of trees in enriching the soil nutrient status has been estimated by multiplying the total net nutrient amount maintained in the standing forest by the market price of nutrients, i.e. the market price of chemical fertilizers.

Guo *et al.* (2001) estimate the value of forest ecosystem services in Xingshan County of China. In their study, the RCA is applied to estimate the value of soil conservation. The RC is interpreted as the value of the benefit of restoring the asset. The inorganic nutrients, such as N, P and K, are also lost due to soil erosion and to replace these nutrients chemical fertilizers are needed. The price of fertilizer is used to estimate this RC.

Byström (2000) provides another application of the RCA. The value of using wetlands for abatement of agricultural N load to the Baltic Sea, with regard to a reduction target of 50 per cent, is estimated. The replacement value is defined as the savings in total abatement costs that are made possible by using wetlands as an abatement measure in cost-effective reductions of N load to the Baltic Sea.

Valuation of loss in soil organic matter

Kumar (2004) in a recent study using the RCA has analysed the loss of carbon through erosion and has used the market price of farmyard manure (FYM) to estimate the price of carbon. As organic carbon is one of the most frequent elements in the topsoil, its inclusion in the valuation process more than doubled the RCs computed without including the organic carbon. In a variation to the RCA, Izac (1997) has illustrated how various functions of SOM could be substituted by differing man-made inputs. Individual SOM services could then be valued by using the market price of similar goods or by approximating the value of the next best alternative/substitute good with or without a market price or from farmers' willingness to pay for a corresponding service. In this substitute goods approach, the value of SOM could be considered equivalent to the sum of the costs of the various substitutes. In view of the complexities involved in directly valuing the SOM, one possible method for avoiding the pricing problem for SOM and soil carbon is the use of the PCA, as it values the provision of soil services in general rather than physical quantities.

Methodology

Sampling

Poonamalle taluk in Thiruvalloor district in Northern Tamil Nadu and Sri Vaikuntam taluk in Tuticorin district in Southern Tamil Nadu were selected for the study (see Map 6.1). It is to be noted that selection of these two taluks is purposive as each taluk falls within a radius of 100 km from a thermal power plant, namely, North Chennai and Tuticorin.[3] In each of these taluks the list of survey numbers (and the village name) from where topsoil has been leased/given to the brick manufacturers was obtained from the respective collector's office, from this five villages were chosen at random.

Replacement cost approach

In this method, nutrient loss due to topsoil removal is quantified by laboratory analysis of soil samples collected in plots from where topsoil was removed and from plots from where topsoil was not removed. In each region 30 soil

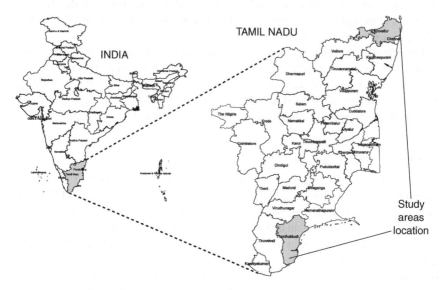

Map 6.1 Location of study areas (not to scale).

samples – comprising 15 from affected plots and 15 from unaffected plots – are analysed to quantify the differences in the three major plant nutrients: N, P, K, the important micronutrients such as iron (Fe), zinc (Zn), copper (Cu) and magnesium (Mg) as well as the organic matter content of the soils. The differences in soil nutrient status between affected and unaffected plots were valued using the current market prices of these nutrients.

Sample characteristics

The present section gives in brief the sample characteristics in the two regions.

Land holding pattern

Canals from river Tamirabarani and the system tanks linked to this river are the major sources of irrigation in the southern study area while tanks and bore-wells are the major sources of irrigation in the northern study area. Wet season paddy cultivation is predominant in both the regions. Paddy–groundnut–fallow and paddy–paddy–fallow are the major cropping sequences during a normal year in the northern study area, while paddy–paddy–fallow and paddy–banana–banana are the major cropping sequences in the southern study area. It is to be noted that in the southern region, coconut is grown by small number of farmers especially along irrigation channels. Since coconut is a perennial crop grown with very little application of man-made inputs such as fertilizers, it is practically insignificant to quantify the impact of topsoil removal on coconut yields.

The lower share of paddy in the south is because of the cultivation of banana crop by many farmers, which is an annual crop occupying land for about ten months to a full year, thereby limiting the land available for paddy cultivation. In the southern region, banana crop is usually planted during the third season, soon after the harvest of second season paddy, and hence banana is the major crop in the third season as well as in the first season of the ensuing year. In the third season, paddy cultivation is practiced in about 10 per cent of the area in the south while groundnut is the only crop cultivated during the third season in the northern region.

Sale of topsoil for brick-making

Given the objective of the study, this sub-section deals with the extent of the sale of topsoil for brick-making by the farmers. A total of 200 farmers (100 in each region) were surveyed to find out their reasons for selling topsoil. Out of the 100 farmers selected in each region, 47 farmers in the north and 55 farmers in the south turned out to be sellers of topsoil for brick-making. Both the average area and the depth over which the topsoil was mined for brick-making were higher in the northern study area as compared to the south. The average area over which topsoil was mined for brick-making ranged from 0.95 acres in the south to 1.18 acres in the north, with an average of one acre for the two regions put together. The average area over which topsoil was mined was not found to be statistically significantly different between the two regions.

It is observed that on an average approximately three acre-feet of soil has been sold by each of the farmers who resorted to selling the soil. The average quantity of soil sold worked out to about 4.1 acre-feet in the north and 2.68 acre-feet in the south, with a mean of 3.35 acre-feet for both the regions put together. The difference in the average quantity of soil sold between the two regions was found to be statistically significant at the 1 per cent level. The income realized by the sale of soil for brick-making was found to be higher at Rs.61,000[4] per acre in the north as compared to Rs.48,000 in the south, with the average income being around Rs.54,400 per farm (Table 6.1). The higher income in the north is due to the heavy demand for soil compared to the south and also higher land value in the north, as the areas from where topsoil is removed are located close to the Chennai metropolitan area.[5]

An analysis of reasons for the sale of soil reveals that about 57 per cent of the farmers in the north and 38 per cent of the farmers in the south resorted to sale of topsoil mainly to level the land (Table 6.2). An urgent need for liquidity for various purposes was the second major reason attributed for the sale of soil in both regions (row 4). About one-quarter of the farmers in the north and one-third of the farmers in the south sold soil for this reason.

Economic costs of using topsoil for brick-making

Soil samples from plots from which topsoil was sold and plots from which soil was not sold for brick-making were subjected to chemical analysis in the

Table 6.1 Details on sale of soil for brick-making (mean for farms which sold soil)

Details	North			South			Mean of two regions
	Min.	Max.	Mean (Std. Dev.)	Min.	Max.	Mean (Std. Dev.)	
% of farmers who sold soil	–	–	47	–	–	55	51
Av. land area in which soil was sold (acre)	0.10	3.50	1.18 (1.31)	0.15	2.75	0.95 (0.82)	1.06
Depth of soil sold (feet)	2.00	6.00	3.47 (2.12)	1.75	5.00	2.82* (0.97)	3.15
Quantity of soil sold (acre-feet)	0.40	14.00	4.10 (2.43)	0.25	11.50	2.68** (1.16)	3.34
Av. income from sale of soil (Rs./farm)	7,000	220,000	60,863 (29,591)	5,500	185,000	47,927** (21,564)	54,395

Source: field survey.

Notes
Figures in parentheses give the standard deviation; * and ** indicate that the figures are statistically different at the 5 per cent and 1 per cent level respectively from the corresponding figures for the other region.

soil testing laboratory to examine the loss in fertility status, if any due to the removal of topsoil. Table 6.3 reports the results of the soil analysis. The plots from which soil was removed for brick-making are found to have lost substantial amounts of N and K while the loss in P was not substantial as the P content of soils are found to be much lesser in nature. Though the topsoil in the southern region are found to be more fertile in N and K before soil mining, the impact of topsoil removal on the fertility status was found to be higher in the northern region in terms of loss in N and K. The net loss in nutrient status of the soils due to topsoil mining is given in Table 6.4. On an average removal of topsoil has resulted in a loss (per acre) of about 13 kg of N, 1 kg of P and 16 kg of K in the north, while the corresponding figures for the southern region are 10 kg of N, 1.4 kg of P and 11.5 kg of K. In percentage terms the nutrient loss was the lowest in the case of K, which varied from 16.34 per cent in the south to 25.47 per cent in the north (Table 6.3). Though the loss in absolute terms was the lowest in the case of P, the percentage loss was the highest in this nutrient between plots with and without topsoil mining.

Soil mining has also led to significant loss of micronutrients, and the percentage reduction varied from about 35 per cent for manganese (Mn) in the north to about 63 per cent for Zn in the south. The differences in the organic matter content of the soils between plots from where topsoil was removed and plots from which topsoil was not removed is very meagre probably due to the very poor base-level organic carbon content of these soils.

The costs of replacement of the nutrients were estimated using the loss in nutrient status of soils and the respective market prices of the nutrients (Table 6.4). The costs of replacement of micronutrients such as Fe and Mn were higher than the other nutrients mainly because of higher losses in these nutrients due to soil mining and also due to their higher market prices. The value of Fe lost due to soil mining was about Rs.560 per acre in the north and Rs.625 per acre in the south, while the value of Mn was Rs.185 per acre in the north and Rs.270 per acre in the south. The loss in organic matter due to soil mining was the highest in physical terms, while its monetary value was in the range of Rs.97 to Rs.130 per acre. Among the major nutrients, the average cost of replacement of N was about Rs.123 per acre, followed by K at Rs.100 per acre and P at Rs.28 per acre. The total cost of replacing the nutrients lost due to soil mining worked out to Rs.1,218 per acre in the northern

Table 6.2 Reason for sale of topsoil for brick-making (% of farmers reporting various reasons)

	Reason	North	South	Mean
1	Level the land	56.52	38.18	47.35
2	Poor quality of topsoil	13.04	20.00	16.52
3	Not interested in active agriculture	4.35	9.09	6.72
4	Urgent need for liquidity	26.09	32.73	29.41

Source: field survey.

Table 6.3 Comparison of soil fertility status in mined and unmined plots

Details	Plots from which topsoil was not removed			Plots from which topsoil was removed		
	North (N=15)	South (N=15)	Average	North (N=15)	South (N=15)	Average
Major nutrients (kg/acre)						
Nitrogen (N)	30.34	33.73	32.04	17.61 (41.96)	23.89 (29.18)	20.75 (35.23)
Phosphorous (P)	4.76	4.34	4.55	3.85 (19.22)	2.51 (42.16)	3.18 (30.16)
Potash (K)	62.47	70.51	66.49	46.56 (25.47)	58.99 (16.34)	52.77 (20.63)
Micronutrients (kg/acre)						
Copper (Cu)	2.10	1.87	1.99	1.08 (48.57)	0.82 (56.15)	0.95 (52.26)
Iron (Fe)	31.50	29.78	30.64	18.52 (41.21)	15.22 (48.89)	16.87 (44.94)
Zinc (Zn)	1.14	1.18	1.16	0.50 (56.14)	0.44 (62.71)	0.47 (59.48)
Manganese (Mn)	12.40	15.62	14.01	8.08 (34.84)	9.38 (39.95)	8.73 (37.69)
Organic matter	1,376.52	2,024.29	1,700.40	1,052.63 (23.53)	1,781.37 (12.00)	1,417.04 (16.66)

Source: computed by the authors.

Note
Figures in parentheses are percentage changes in respective nutrient levels in mined plots vis-à-vis un-mined plots.

Table 6.4 Cost of replacement of soil fertility status due to topsoil removal for brick-making

Details	Loss in nutrient status of soil due to removal of topsoil in kg/acre							Cost of replacement of nutrients (Rs./acre)		
	North			South			Average for both regions	North	South	Average
	Min.	Max.	Mean (S.D.)	Min.	Max.	Mean (S.D.)				
Nitrogen	5.31	21.65	12.73 (4.61)	4.37	18.96	9.84 (2.51)	11.29	138.28	106.88	122.57
Phosphorous	0.15	3.47	0.91 (0.23)	0.51	4.37	1.83 (0.24)	1.37	18.87	37.73	28.30
Potash	8.78	37.20	15.91 (11.96)	3.47	16.76	11.52 (4.37)	13.72	116.66	84.46	100.55
Copper	0.61	2.65	1.02 (0.13)	0.24	2.31	1.05 (0.23)	1.04	43.86	45.15	44.51
Iron	8.71	20.43	12.98 (4.61)	5.79	21.43	14.56 (4.37)	13.77	558.14	626.08	592.11
Zinc	0.14	1.35	0.64 (0.03)	0.16	1.73	0.74 (0.04)	0.69	27.52	31.82	29.67
Manganese	2.42	7.11	4.32 (0.26)	2.31	8.48	6.24 (0.42)	5.28	185.76	268.32	227.04
Organic matter	80.97	895.54	323.88 (37.79)	56.68	790.69	242.92 (16.01)	283.4	129.55	97.17	113.36
Total cost	–	–	–	–	–	–	–	1,218.64	1,297.61	1,267.33

Source: computed by the authors.

Notes

The cost of replacement of nutrients is calculated using the current market price per kg of N, P and K (N=Rs.10.86, P=Rs.20.62, K=Rs.7.33, organic matter=Rs.0.40 per kg, and micronutrients=Rs.43 per kg); The cost of nutrients were worked out using the current market prices of fertilizers supplying these nutrients and their nutrient content.

region and Rs.1,297 in the southern region with an inter-regional average of Rs.1,267 per acre. When compared to the income realized by farmers through the sale of soil, the cost of replacement of nutrients lost in the process of soil mining appears to be meagre,[6] which is probably the reason behind farmers resorting to the sale of topsoil at a moderate depth of about three feet.

The economic impacts of topsoil removal as summarized in Table 6.5, which reveals that the total cost of replacing the nutrients, levelling the land and application of tank silt worked out to be nearly Rs.2,600 in the south and Rs.2,350 per acre in the north with an inter-regional average of Rs.2,475 per acre.

Remedial measures undertaken

To offset the likely negative effect of topsoil removal on soil quality and crop yield most farmers resorted to strategies such as the application of tank silt, high doses of inorganic fertilizers in the ensuing few seasons and/or FYM and green manure. Table 6.6 provides a list of remedial measures undertaken to restore the soil quality. The table also gives the expenditure incurred to undertake these measures. Levelling the soil and overcoming the hardpan of soil layers, which are exposed for cultivation after the removal of topsoil are the most expensive remedial measures undertaken by farmers. However, this is not the case with all farmers who have sold soil. Most of the farmers resorted to deep ploughing to break the hardpan. Only about 10 per cent of the farmers resorted to the application of tank silt to overcome the hardpan problem. This accounted for an average cost of Rs.1,217 per acre. Restoring organic matter is another important remedial measure. However, as a cheaper and readily available source of organic matter, FYM is applied in higher quantities so as to offset the negative impact of topsoil removal. About 45 per cent of the farmers who sold topsoil attempted to restore the organic matter content of the soil by applying a high dose of FYM at an average additional (imputed) cost of about Rs.435 per acre (Table 6.6, row 3). These costs are not out-of-pocket expenses for the farmers as the FYM is often available within farm.

Table 6.5 Economic impact of topsoil/brick-earth removal for brick-making (Rs./acre)

	Details	North	South	Average
1	Application of tank silt for levelling and overcoming the hardpan problem	1,132	1,301	1,217
2	Cost of replacement of soil nutrients	1,219	1,298	1,268
3	Total cost of replacement, tank silt application and levelling (1+2)*	2,351	2,599	2,475
4	Economic value of yield loss due to soil mining[#]	2,585	3,928	3,256

Source: computed by the authors.

Notes
* These estimates are based on cost of replacement of nutrients lost due to soil mining; # These estimates are based on change in productivity approach i.e. the economic value of yield loss due to soil mining.

Table 6.6 Remedial measures undertaken to restore soil quality and costs incurred

Details of remedial measure	Frequency (percentage of farmers reporting)			Average additional expenditure on various measures (Rs./acre)		
	North	South	Mean	North	South	Mean
1 Application of tank silt for levelling the field	6.82	14.55	10.68	1,132	1,301	1,217
2 High fertilizer application to restore nutrient status.	25.00	29.09	27.04	167	119	143
3 Application of farmyard manure and green manure for restoring the organic matter of the soils.	47.73	45.45	46.59	489	381	435
4 None	20.45	10.91	15.68	–	–	–
5 Total expenditure	–	–	–	1,788	1,802	1,795

Source: own compilation based on survey.

Application of a higher dose of inorganic manure/fertilizer is the next important strategy to revive soil fertility, which has been adopted by little more than one-quarter of the farmers. The average additional expenditure on inorganic fertilizers purchased in the market is Rs.143 per acre. The remaining 15 per cent of the farmers resorted to a 'do nothing' strategy. On the whole, the farmers seem to have spent only a very meagre fraction of the total income from the sale of soil on remedial measures to restore soil fertility. Out of the average revenue of Rs.54,000 per acre from the sale of soil, only about Rs.1,800 per acre ($\cong$3.3 per cent) has been spent on remedial measures to improve the fertility status of the soil. Most farmers were of the firm view that soil is an infinitely renewable resource, both in terms of quality and quantity, and hence there is nothing wrong in selling the soil.

Conclusions

The economic impacts of topsoil removal in the selected regions of Tamil Nadu, an Indian state witnessing an urbanization drive, revealed that the total cost of replacing the nutrients, levelling the land and application of tank silt worked out to be nearly Rs.2,600 in the south and Rs.2,350 per acre in the north with an inter-regional average of Rs.2,475 per acre.

A comparison of the revenue realized by selling topsoil for brick-making with the economic losses associated with it reveal that the revenue from the sale of soil ($\cong$Rs.54,000 per acre) more than offsets the loss in yield and soil nutrients in the short run. Hence, it becomes economically rational to sell the soil at least in the short run, and this decision gains strength when the farmers face a liquidity crunch together with the offer of high prices for their soil. Interestingly, out of the average revenue from the sale of soil only about 3.3 per cent has been spent on remedial measures to improve the fertility status of the soil. The survey reveals that most farmers believed soil to be an infinitely renewable resource both in terms of quality and quantity, which explains their decision clearly.

One limitation of the present work is that the RCA sometimes underestimates the true loss. This is because the removal of topsoil leads to the loss of certain unquantifiable, qualitative properties of topsoil, which are not reflected in the RCA but still lead to yield loss. The method can be complemented by using PCA to quantify the exact impact.

Acknowledgement

This chapter is part of the project titled 'Utilization of Fly-ash by Brick Manufacturers – Environmental Costs vs. Benefits', awarded by the Ministry of Environment and Forests (MoEF), Government of India. We are extremely thankful to MoEF for sponsoring this study. An earlier version of the chapter was presented at the sixteenth annual conference of the European Association of Environmental and Resource Economists (EAERE) held at the School of Business, Economics and Law, Gothenburg University, Sweden during 25–28 June 2008. We sincerely thank the conference participants for their useful comments. The usual disclaimers nevertheless apply.

Notes

1 Against Tamil Nadu's urbanization rate of 44 per cent, the all India average is only 27.8 per cent. In fact, among the 16 major states of India, Tamil Nadu has the highest urbanization rate (NIUA 2002).
2 The physical structure of the top layers of the soil is generally very conducive for crop growth because of repeated ploughing and other field operations. However, when the topsoil is removed for brick-making, the deeper layers are used for crop cultivation. These deeper layers have a harder surface and are not so favourable for crop growth at least in the initial few years. This is known as the hardpan problem.
3 As per MoEF guidelines, units located within 100 km radius of a power plant are mandated to use fly ash to make bricks. Quantification of soil loss was one of the objectives of this study, the other objective being to determine the barriers in using fly ash to produce bricks from brick-kiln owners. Hence, the purposive sampling was used to pick farmers falling within the radius.
4 The approximate exchange rate of US$1 equal to INR45 has been considered here.
5 It is to be noted that the sale price in the two regions could be understated. This is because our sample consisted of farmers who engaged in these land transactions some four or five years previously, the current price is higher due to increased pressure on the land caused by urbanization. Our conjecture was verified during an interview with the secretary, Tamil Nadu Brick Field Manufacturers. According to him, the prevailing land price around Chennai region is approximately Rs.3 lakh per acre, against the stated price of nearly Rs.61,000 per acre. An understated land price will have implications for the final results.
6 It deserves mention that this is an underestimation because there is a foregone income for the period for which land is leased/sold. Inclusion of the forgone income will reflect the true cost to the farmer for leasing or selling.

References

Bojö, J. (1996) 'The Costs of Land Degradation in Sub-Saharan Africa', *Ecological Economics*, 16(2): 161–173.

Byström, O. (2000) 'The Replacement Value of Wetlands in Sweden', *Environmental and Resource Economics*, 16(4): 347–362.

Detwiler, R.P. (1985) 'Land Use Change and the Global Carbon Cycle: The Role of Tropical Soils', *Biogeochemistry*, 2(1): 67–93.

Drechsel, P., Giordano, M. and Gyiele, L. (2004) 'Valuing Nutrients in Soil and Water: Concepts and Techniques with Examples from IWMI Studies in the Developing World', IWMI Research Report 82, Colombo: International Water Management Institute.

Gosselink, J.G., Odum, E.P. and Pope, R.M. (1974) *The Value of the Tidal Marsh*, Center for Wetland Resources, Baton Rouge: Louisiana State University.

Grohs, F. (1994) 'Economics of Soil Degradation, Erosion and Conservation: A Case Study of Zimbabwe', Arbeiten zur Agrarwirtschaft in Entwicklungsländern. Kiel: Wissenschaftsverlag Vauk Kiel KG.

Gunatilake, H.M. and Vieth, G.R. (2000) 'Estimation of On-Site Cost of Soil Erosion: A Comparison of Replacement and Productivity Change Methods', *Journal of Soil and Water Conservation*, 55(22): 197–204.

Guo, Z., Xiao, X., Gan, Y. and Zheng, Y. (2001) 'Ecosystem Functions, Services and their Values – A Case Study in Xingshan County of China', *Ecological Economics*, 38(1): 141–154.

Izac, A.N. (1997) 'Developing Policies for Soil Carbon Management in Tropical Regions', *Geoderma*, 79(1–4): 261–276.

Kathuria, V. (2007) 'Utilization of Fly-ash by Brick Manufacturers – Environmental Costs vs. Benefits', Report submitted to Ministry of Environment and Forests, Government of India, New Delhi.

Kim, S.-H. and Dixon, J. (1986) 'Economic Valuation of Environmental Quality Aspects of Upland Agriculture Projects in Korea', in J. Dixon and M. Hufschmidt (eds) *Economic Valuation Techniques for the Environment – A Case Study Workbook*, Baltimore: Johns Hopkins University Press.

Kumar, P. (2004) *Economics of Soil Erosion: Issues and Imperatives from India*, New Delhi: Concept Publishing Company.

National Institute of Urban Affairs (2002) *Handbook of Urban Statistics*, New Delhi: NIUA.

Predo, C., Grist, P., Menz, K. and Rañola, R.F. Jr. (1997) 'Two Approaches for Estimating the On-Site Costs of Soil Erosion in the Philippines: The Replacement Cost Approach', *Imperata Project Paper 1997/8*, Center for Resource and Environmental Studies, Canberra: The Australian National University.

Samarakoon, S. and Abeygunawardena, P. (1995) 'An Economic Assessment of On-Site Effects of Soil Erosion in Potato Lands in Nuwara Eliya District of Sri Lanka', *Journal of Sustainable Agriculture*, 6(2–3): 81–92.

Xue, D. and Tisdell, C. (2001) 'Valuing Ecological Functions of Biodiversity in Changbasin Mountain Biosphere Reserve in Northeast China', *Biodiversity and Conservation*, 10(3): 467–481

7 Environmental impacts (costs) of hydropower generation in India

Bimlesh Kumar and Achanta Ramakrishna Rao

Introduction

For a developing country like India, energy is the fundamental input for economic growth. The current target of economic growth is 10 per cent and energy demand in various sectors such as agriculture, industry, transport, commercial and domestic is rising rapidly. Electricity is perhaps the most vital form of energy input required for infrastructural development of India's agriculture and industry, and it also plays a critical role in socio-economic development. The total installed capacity of power generation through various sources (as at February 2010) is about 156.09 Gw (Government of India, Ministry of Power). The thermal power contribution to this generation is around 63 per cent followed by hydropower contributing 25 per cent. India is endowed with rich hydropower potential; it ranks fifth in the world in terms of usable potential. This is distributed across six major river systems; namely, the Indus, Brahmaputra, Ganga, the central Indian river systems, and the east and west flowing river systems of south India. The Indus, Brahmaputra and Ganga together account for nearly 80 per cent of the total potential. The economically exploitable potential from these river systems through medium and major schemes has been assessed at 84,044 MW at 60 per cent load factor corresponding to an installed capacity of around 150,000 MW. Considering the large untapped potential and the intrinsic characteristics of hydropower in promoting the country's energy security and flexibility in system operation, the government is giving a thrust to accelerate hydropower development. When developed in accordance with good environmental and social practices, hydropower plants have the advantage of producing power that is both renewable and clean. Hydropower projects are seen as greenhouse gas reducing; industrialized countries can therefore earn emission credits by investing in such projects in developing countries (WCD 2000). Hydropower stations have an inherent ability for instantaneous starting, stopping, load variations, etc. that can help in improving the reliability of the power system and are the best choice for meeting the peak demand. The generation cost is not only inflation independent but also reduces with time. Hydropower projects have a long useful life, extending over 50 years, and help in conserving scarce fossil fuels. They are also instrumental in opening avenues for the development of remote and backward areas.

But on a local or regional scale, the environmental and socio-economic impacts can be negative and serious. The landscape and the dammed rivers often change their characteristics severely after the completion of a hydropower project. Sometimes the ability of people living in the area to use natural resources to improve their livelihood can be highly limited after completion of a project. In rural areas in developing countries, using the surrounding environment for small scale farming, hunting and fishing can be equally important as they are the means of earning a livelihood. The people worst affected by such an environmental change are often the poorest ones with the lowest safety margins. Therefore before a hydropower project is undertaken, it is important to estimate in what way the project is likely to affect the area and the people living in it, and to include actions in the project plan that will prevent, mitigate or compensate for negative impacts (Ames and Buetlkofer 2003). This is normally done by performing an environmental impact assessment (EIA). An EIA is a process of identification, prediction and evaluation of a project's impact on the environment and is, essentially, an aid to the decision-makers responsible for planning (Brismar 2003). It can also be manipulated into a management tool for environmental sustainability so that a project will be both economically and environmentally sound (Hartley and Wood 2005). An EIA particularly aims to optimize a trade-off between developmental activities and socio-ecological losses. It is a management tool to be linked closely to the project life cycle to ensure that appropriate environmental information is provided at the correct time. The overall objective of the EIA is to design developmental projects and activities taking into consideration the environmental perspective. Keeping this in mind, the current study investigates and presents a procedural layout of the environmental impacts of hydropower projects. Using the rapid impact assessment matrix (RIAM) software, analysis of a construction phase and operational phase of a hydropower plant setup is performed to analyse quantitatively the effects of different parameters.

EIA case study: hydropower project

While hydropower holds an important role in the energy and development strategies of India, such natural resource projects are inherently challenging. Environmental and social impacts – potentially both positive and negative – are inevitable (Alshuwaikhat 2005). The responsible response is to develop a clear understanding of such impacts, drawing from analytical as well as local knowledge, and to minimize the negative impacts through appropriate design. The United Nations Environment Programme (UNEP) (1988) enunciated the simplest and most important principles relating to EIA methodology:

- Focus on the main issues;
- Involve the appropriate persons and groups;
- Link information to decisions about the project, present clear options for the mitigation of impacts and for sound environmental management; and
- Provide information in a form useful to decision-makers.

Unfortunately these recommendations are not always heeded. Too much stress is often placed on mathematical modelling techniques rather than practical assessment methods, and environmental statements tend to provide enormous amounts of detailed, unnecessary information. RIAM is a method used to evaluate all sorts of environmental impacts (Pastakia 1998). It allows the completion of subjective classifications justified for each analysed item, resulting in not only a clear outcome of the assessment, but also in a register for subsequent revaluations. It analyses and presents in a structured, friendly and transparent environment the numerous parameters and alternatives of an EIA. It considers all four components: physical/chemical (P/C), biological/ecological (B/E), social/cultural (S/C) and economic/operational (E/O). The RIAM is a scoring impact of components against pre-defined criteria, transposing scores into ranges describing the degree of positive or negative impacts. Each component is evaluated against each criteria and the value recorded in the matrix. A measure of the importance of the relevance condition (A1) is evaluated according to the land boundaries or interest of those affected. The scale is defined in the following way:

0 – irrelevant;
1 – relevant just to the local condition;
2 – relevant to the areas immediately out of the local condition;
3 – relevant to the regional/national interest;
4 – relevant to the national/international interest.

The magnitude (A2) is defined as a measure of the scale of benefit/damage of an impact or condition. The scale is defined in the following way:

3 – extremely positive benefit;
2 – moderately positive benefit;
1 – lightly positive benefit;
0 – no alteration/actual state;
−1 – lightly negative damage;
−2 – moderately negative damage;
−3 – extremely negative damage.

The permanent criterion (B1) defines if a condition is temporary or permanent, and if it should only be seen as a measure of the temporary state of the condition. The scale is defined in the following way:

1 – no alteration/actual state;
2 – temporary;
3 – permanent.

The reversibility criterion (B2) defines if a condition can be changed and if it can be seen as a measure of control on effect of the condition. The scale is defined in the following way:

1 – no alteration/actual state;
2 – reversible;
3 – irreversible.

The cumulative criterion (B3) takes into account of the effect of a condition, which will have a single direct impact. Theoretically, the cumulative criterion is used to judge the sustainability of a condition, and it should not be confused with a permanent situation or reversible condition. Its scale is defined in the following way:

1 – no alteration/not applicable;
2 – non cumulative/of direct effect/singular;
3 – cumulative/of indirect effect/synergetic.

Scores for the value criteria (group (B)) are added together to provide a single sum. This ensures that the individual value scores cannot influence the overall score, but that the collective importance of all values (group (B)) is fully taken into account. The sum of the group (B) scores is then multiplied by the result of the group (A) scores to provide a final assessment score (environmental classification, ES) for the condition. The formula used to compute the ES can be expressed as follows:

$$ES = (A1 \times A2 \times \ldots AN) \times (B1 + B2 + \ldots BN) \qquad (7.1)$$

where (A1) is the individual criteria scores for group (A), B1 is the individual criteria scores for group (B) and the ES is the assessment score for the condition. The RIAM requests the definition of specific components of impact evaluation and each one of those environmental components falls into one of four categories:

- *P/C*: Covers all physical and chemical aspects of the environment, including non-renewable natural resources (no-biological) and the degradation of the physical environment through pollution.
- B/E: Covers all biological aspects of the environment, including renewable natural resources, conservation of the biodiversity, interaction between species and pollution of the biosphere.
- S/C: Covers all human aspects of the environment, including social subjects that affect the individuals and the communities; with cultural aspects, inheritance conservation and human development are included.
- E/O: To identify qualitatively the economical consequences of environmental change, temporary and permanent, as well as the complexities of administration of the projects inside the context of the activity project.

The degree of damage and benefit, according to RIAM is shown in the Table 7.1.

Table 7.1 Environmental classifications according to RIAM

Environmental classification (ES)	Value of the class	Value of the class (numerical)	Description of the class
72 to 108	E	5	Extremely positive impact
36 to 71	D	4	Significantly positive impact
19 to 35	C	3	Moderately positive impact
10 to 18	B	2	Less positive impact
1 to 9	A	1	Reduced positive impact
0	N	0	No alteration
−1 to −9	−A	−1	Reduced negative impact
−10 to −18	−B	−2	Less negative impact
−19 to −35	−C	−3	Moderately negative impact
−36 to −71	−D	−4	Significantly negative impact
−72 to −108	−E	−5	Extremely negative impact

Source: author's calculations.

The first step in the RIAM is to set up a number of different options for the assessment in question, and the RIAM program will individually process them. The present analysis is performed for a hypothetical hydropower installation project. An EIA study has been completed for the construction and operational phase of the hydropower plant. The different components and their measures taken for the site-preparation phase, construction phase and operation phase are provided in Tables 7.2a, 7.2b and 7.2c.

Table 7.2a Data for the site-preparation phase of the project

		A1	A2	B1	B2	B3
Physical and chemical components (PC)						
PC1	Changes in terrain topography	2	0	3	3	2
PC2	Changes in natural drainage	1	−1	3	3	2
PC3	Infiltration pattern	1	0	3	3	3
PC4	Metal erosion	2	−2	2	3	3
PC5	Generation of noises and air pollution	1	−1	2	2	2
Biological and ecological components (BE)						
BE1	Vegetation loss	1	−1	2	2	2
BE2	Habitat loss	1	−1	2	2	2
BE3	Flora-fauna	1	−1	3	2	3
Sociological and cultural components (SC)						
SC1	Landscape	1	1	3	3	3
SC2	Job offer	3	1	2	1	1
SC3	Loss of lands	1	−1	2	2	1
Economical and operational components (EO)						
EO1	Increment in living cost	2	2	3	2	1
EO2	Speculation in the cost of lands	3	−2	2	2	2

Source: author's calculations.

Table 7.2b Data for the construction phase of the project

		A1	A2	B1	B2	B3
Physical and chemical components (PC)						
PC1	Production of excavation materials	2	−2	2	2	3
PC2	Noise and vibration problem	1	−1	2	2	2
PC3	Changes in natural drainage	3	−1	3	3	2
PC4	Increment of eroded materials	3	−2	2	2	3
PC5	Air pollution	3	−2	2	2	3
PC6	Changes in the quality of water	3	−2	2	2	3
Biological and ecological components (BE)						
BE1	Loss of vegetation	2	−1	3	3	2
BE2	Loss of wild habitats	2	−1	3	3	2
BE3	Loss of aqua habitats	2	−2	3	2	2
BE4	Loss of species	1	−1	2	2	2
BE5	Modification of landscape	3	−2	3	3	3
BE6	Bioaccumulation	1	−1	3	3	3
Sociological and cultural components (SC)						
SC1	Increase in job	3	2	2	2	2
SC2	Loss of lands	1	−2	3	2	2
SC3	Loss of cultivations	1	−2	3	2	2
SC4	Arrive of temporary population	3	−2	2	2	2
SC5	Increase in domestic residual	2	−1	2	2	2
SC6	Increase in solid municipal residues	2	−1	2	2	2
SC7	Flooding of temporary housing construction	1	−1	3	2	2
Economical and operational components (EO)						
EO1	Modification in consumption pattern	2	−2	2	2	3
EO2	Increase in earnings	3	2	2	2	1

Source: author's calculations.

The modelling results have been shown in Figures 7.1 to 7.3.

It is to be noted that during site preparation, the following points must be considered: expropriation and acquisition of pieces of land, opening and construction of, construction of stores and workshops, water supply, supply of electric power and fuel. The construction of camps and the location and adjusting of places for dumping scrap materials must also be chosen on priority basis. RIAM indicates that the parameters in the P/C category are having negative impacts. The most adverse impact is shown by river water quality, which is obvious. A similar scenario is observed for the parameters considered in the B/E category, as hydropower constitutes a major infrastructure development. Public acceptability (local) is adverse, as the population must vacate their belongings. However, this type of electricity generation project provides a major boost to the national economy as well as local areas.

A hydropower project requires a significant amount of construction materials, which needs to be extracted from various quarry sites in and around the project area (Peirce *et al.* 2004). Normally quarrying is undertaken along the hill face

Table 7.2c Data for the operational phase of the project

		A1	A2	B1	B2	B3
Physical and chemical components (PC)						
PC1	Modification of microclimate	2	−1	3	3	2
PC2	Changes in the quality of water	3	−2	3	3	3
PC3	Modification of flow intensity downstream	3	−1	3	3	2
PC4	Erosion in the downstream	2	−1	2	2	3
PC5	Increase in seismic activity	2	−1	3	3	3
PC6	Dam failure scenario	3	−2	3	3	3
PC7	Loss of sediments and nutrients	1	−1	3	2	2
Biological and ecological components (BE)						
BE1	Modification of vegetation pattern	1	−1	3	2	2
BE2	Modification of aquatic organism	1	−1	2	2	2
BE3	Changes in aquatic ecosystems	2	−2	3	3	3
BE4	Bioaccumulation	2	−2	3	3	3
Sociological and cultural components (SC)						
SC1	Landscape modification	3	−3	3	3	3
SC2	Water availability	3	3	3	1	1
Economical and operational components (EO)						
EO1	Decrease in the level of local earnings	2	−2	2	2	3
EO2	Availability of approach roads	2	2	3	2	3

Source: author's calculations.

and left untreated after extraction of the required construction material. These sites can become permanent scars on the hill face and become potential source of landslides. During the construction phase, various equipments are brought to the construction site. The placing of these construction equipments would require significant amounts of space. Similarly, space will be required for work-shops, storing of equipments and materials, etc. In addition, land will also be temporarily acquired for the storage of quarried material before crushing, cement, rubble, sand, fuel, parking for vehicles, etc. Temporarily various storage sites need to be earmarked for this purpose. The storage site should be selected in such a way that it should lead to minimal impacts on human life and wild life. A large quantity of excavated rock is expected to be generated in any hydro-power project as a result of tunnelling operations, construction of access roads, etc. The muck so generated, which otherwise can lead to significant adverse environmental impacts, needs to be properly disposed of. Sometimes muck is disposed along the river bank, which ultimately finds its way into the water body, leading to adverse impacts on river ecology.

Construction of roads in such areas can give rise to erosion hazards if ade-quate protection measures are not undertaken. The construction of diversion weirs and storage dams for diverting discharge of hydropower generation will lead to a reduction of flow in the downstream of the weirs and dam sites up to the confluence point of tailrace discharge. However, a reduction in flow is likely

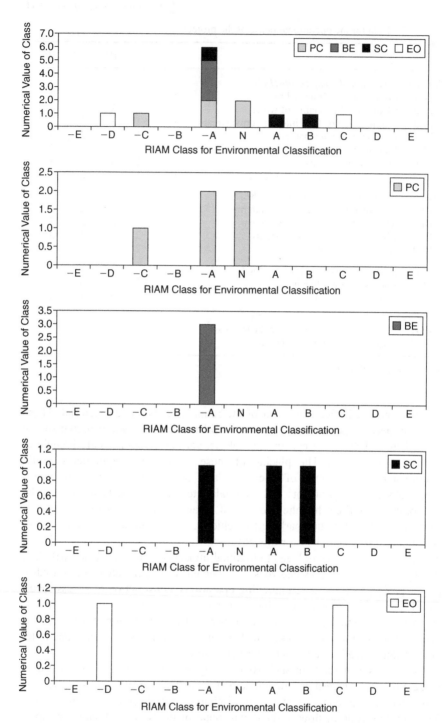

Figure 7.1 RIAM results for site-preparation phase (source: author's analysis).

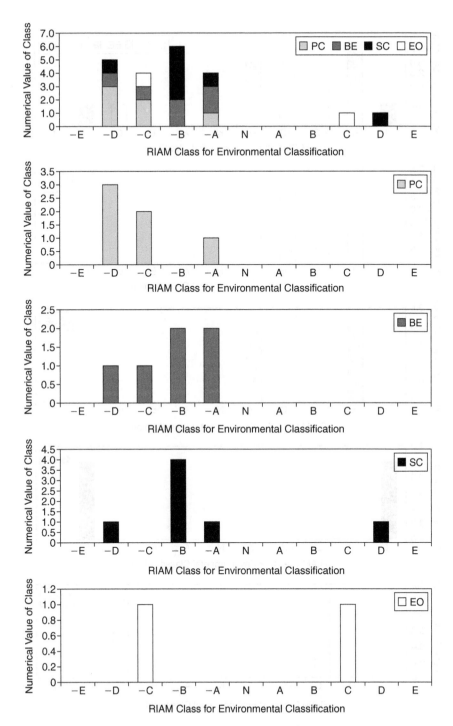

Figure 7.2 RIAM results for construction phase (source: author's analysis).

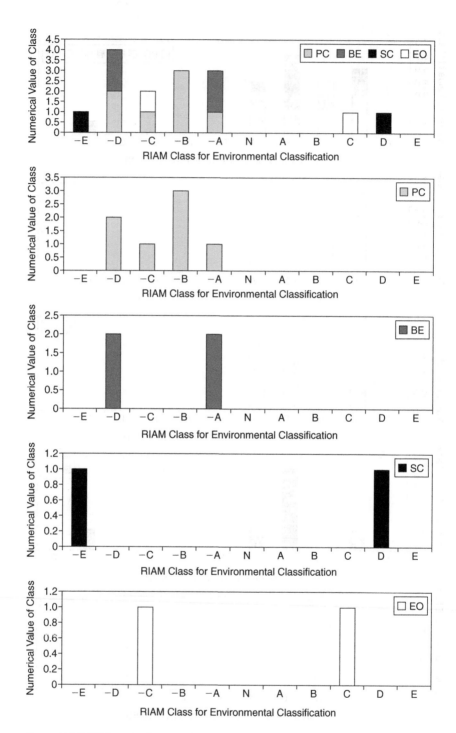

Figure 7.3 RIAM results for operational phase (source: author's analysis).

to have marginal impact, as the discharge during the lean season may be low, but the same is supplemented by contributing from intervening streams (Gilpin 2006). Any hydropower project construction is likely to last for a period of 3–4 years. Job opportunities will improve significantly in the surrounding area. This means that many people (workers, technical staff, security guards, etc.) are likely to work during the construction phase. Those who would migrate to the project area are likely to come from other parts of the country, and so have different cultural, ethnic and social backgrounds. Due to a longer residence in one place, a new culture, having a distinct socio-economic similarity will develop which will have its own identity (Gilland 1995).

The construction phase also leads to mushrooming of various allied activities to meet the demands of the immigrant population in the project area. Thus, the total increase in population during the construction phase can range from 1,000 to 1,500 for a medium to minor project (Razzaque 2004). The total quantum of sewage generated may be in the order of 0.2–0.3 million litres per day. The biological oxygen demand (BOD) load contributed will be about 200–240 kg/day. The sewage generally shall be disposed off in nearby streams or channels through open drains, where ultimately it will find its way to a river or stream. Inadequate sewage treatment and disposal facilities could lead to an increased incidence of water-borne diseases. Thus it is necessary to commission appropriate sewage treatment facilities in the vicinity of the project area.

The flooding of forest and agricultural land in the submergence area increases the availability of nutrients resulting from the decomposition of vegetative matter. The enrichment of impounded water with organic and inorganic nutrients becomes a major water quality problem immediately after commencement of operation (Marriott 1997). So detailed dissolved oxygen (DO) modelling is required to estimate its potential level, and also other physio-chemical and biological parameters in the nearby stream during the initial years of operation and thereafter. During the construction, a huge quantity of muck is generated at various construction sites which, if not properly disposed of, will invariably flow down the river during heavy precipitation. Such a condition can lead to adverse impacts on the development of aquatic life, which needs to be avoided.

Among the aquatic habitants, fish are generally worst affected. Migratory fish species are likely to be affected due to obstruction to their migratory route when any diversion structure is created. An increased noise level is anticipated only during the construction phase due to the operation of various equipment, increased vehicular movement, blasting, etc. Generally these sites belong to no man's land, so no significant human impact can be attributed due to increased noise levels. However, to conserve the river ecology and wild life, it is imperative to conduct detailed noise modelling studies on them. Normally diesel is used in construction equipment; the major pollutant which gets emitted as a result of diesel combustion is sulphur dioxide (SO_2) (Shyam *et al.* 2006). The suspended particulate materials (SPM) are minimal due to a low ash content in diesel. Hence detailed model studies should be undertaken to ascertain the increased SO_2 level. The operation of the crusher during the construction phase is likely to generate fugitive emissions, which can move even up to 1 km. Since there are no human habitants near the hydropower sites, no major adverse impacts can be anticipated on this account. Infrastructure projects are a significant component of a nation's socio-economic development, although this is still a controversial issue because of the large displacement of the local inhabitants. Lack of proper resettlement leads to impoverished situations of displaced people and this will constrain society's development (Cernea and Guggeenheim 1993). During the operational phase, the water quality of the parent river should be monitored. It will provide the basis to identify the occurrence of stratification with deoxygenated bottom layers and to adjust the reservoir management to the observed quality constraints. Monitoring of livelihood restoration should be carried out; public participation can be beneficial to the local people, helping to reduce negative socio-economic impacts from hydropower projects. Participation can also introduce a democratic element into negotiations, and agreement that may form a base for a long-term and solid relationship between the parties. It is also implied that the local people can strengthen their organizational structure which will make them better prepared to define their role in the development process (Ismode 2000).

Conclusions

The current study presents a procedural layout of EIA components to be taken during hydropower plant construction and operational phases, and what can be done in order to have minimal adverse impacts. This work uses RIAM to quantitatively judge the impacts of different parameters which might be affected due to hydropower installation. In the physical and chemical category the following parameters have been analysed: geophysics, groundwater quality and hydraulic resources, climate, air quality and the sonorous environment. RIAM indicates that hydropower plants exert negative impacts for the parameters considered in this category. The changed environment is found to be negatively affecting people living in the area, directly or through chain effects.

A hydropower project will doubtlessly cause substantial landscape changes. The most obvious landscape changes are the creation of the artificial reservoirs in the area. Other changes in the landscape are the occurrence of waste dumps, quarries, machinery parks, offices, power lines, a transformation station, a power house, access roads, the diversion canal, conduits and pressure shaft for the conveyance tunnel and tree plantations. In the biological and ecological category the following parameters had been analysed: flora, vegetation, fauna and habitats. The RIAM indicates two types of impacts in this phase: less negative impacts for fauna and habitats, and moderately negative impacts for flora and vegetation. If the characteristics of the rivers are changing, people's possibilities/options to use the rivers might deteriorate. A change in environment can be due to altered flows, deteriorating water quality and a river flow pattern change due to dam construction. Under the sociological and cultural category, RIAM indicates negative impacts. EIA suggests that there are different kind of negative impacts, which should be appropriately mitigated and compensated; with ongoing monitoring and adaptive management.

References

Alshuwaikhat, H.M. (2005) 'Strategic Environmental Assessment can help Solve Environmental Impact Assessment Failures in Developing Countries', *Environmental Impact Assessment Review*, 25(4): 319–340.

Ames, P.L. and Buetlkofer, L.B. (2003) *Environmental Audit: Estimating Hydroelectric Project*, Broomfield: MWH Americas Inc.

Brismar, A. (2003) *Environmental Consideration in the Planning of Large Dam Projects*, Linköping: Linköping University.

Cernea, M.M. and Guggeenheim, S.E. (1993) *Anthropological Approaches to Resettlement*, New York: West View Press.

Gilland, B. (1995) 'World Population, Economic Growth, and Energy Demand, 1990–2100: A Review of Projections', *Population and Development Review*, 21(3): 507–539.

Gilpin, A. (2006) *Environmental Impact Assessment: Cutting Edge for the 21st Century*, Cambridge: Cambridge University Press.

Government of India, Official Documents by Ministry of Power. Online, available at: http://powermin.nic.in (accessed 12 March, 2010).

Hartley, N. and Wood, C. (2005) 'Public Participation in Environmental Impact Assessment (EIA) Process', *Environmental Impact Review*, 25(4): 319–340.

Ismode, A. (2000) *The Social Challenge of Hydropower: The Option of Popular Participation*, Stockholm: Royal Institute of Technology.

Marriott, B.B. (1997) *Environmental Impact Assessment: A Practical Guide*, Berkshire: McGraw-Hill Professional.

Pastakia, C.M.R. (1998) 'The Rapid Impact Assessment Matrix (RIAM) – A New Tool for Environmental Impact Assessment', in Kurt Jensen (ed.), *Environmental Impact Assessment Using the Rapid Impact Assessment Matrix (RIAM)*, Fredensborg: Olsen & Olsen.

Peirce, J.J., Vesilind, A. and Weiner, R. (2004) *Environmental Pollution and Control* Hoboken: John-Wiley & Sons.

Razzaque, J. (2004) *Public Interest Environmental Litigation in India, Pakistan, and Bangladesh*, London: Kluwer Law International.

Shyam, S., Verma, H.N. and Bhargava, S.K. (2006) *Air Pollution and its Impact on Plant Growth*, New Delhi: New India Pub.

United Nations Environment Programme (UNEP) (1988) *Environmental Impact Assessment: Basic Procedures for Developing Countries*, Nairobi: Kenya.

World Commission on Dams (WCD) (2000) *Dam and Development: A New Framework for Decision-Making*, The report of the World Commission on Dam. London: Earthscan Publications Ltd.

Part III

Service sector and the environment

8 Growing environmental costs of urban water supplies

Overcoming the challenges in implementing integrated urban water management

M. Dinesh Kumar

Introduction

Growing urban water stress is one of the features of India's water crisis. Reducing per capita supplies and reliability, huge water wastages, growing inequity in access to water and its inefficient pricing across different classes are some of the problems (Mukherjee *et al.* 2010). Growing deprivation of the urban poor of water for basic survival needs is a remarkable dimension of the entire crisis, found in many cities of India and elsewhere in the developing world (UNDP 2006). This crisis has mainly stemmed from exponential growth in urban water demands, compounded by dwindling local sources of water and the increasing inability of urban water utilities to improve the water supply infrastructure (Tecco 2008).

On the demand front, over the past few decades, the urban population in India has been growing at a much faster rate than rural populations, due to rapid urbanization and industrialization. This growth is mainly concentrated in some of the naturally water scarce regions of the country, as evident from a recent research (Mukherjee *et al.* 2010). The population rise and economic growth increase urban water demands exponentially. First, the population itself increases the per capita water supply needs of municipalities due to the increasing need for sewage disposal.[1] Second, economic growth increases the per capita water demand for domestic uses (Amarasinghe *et al.* 2007) and income elasticity will be higher at lower levels of demand (Rosegrant *et al.* 1999). Also, urban growth, which comes with heavy industrialization, will increase the water supply needs for commercial activities and manufacturing units. Failure on the part of water utilities to realistically project future growth in water demands is characteristic of poor urban governance.

As regards the supplies, local water resources in urban areas are fast depleting as they come under heavy stress due to concentrated demands (Mukherjee *et al.* 2010). Over-exploitation of local aquifers due to excessive draft, compounded by problems of quality deterioration; reduced yields of surface sources such as ponds and tanks due to land use changes in catchments, and encroachment by developers; and water quality also suffers due to indiscriminate disposal of solid waste and urban domestic and trade effluents. Further, in many cities and towns, the water infrastructure is increasingly becoming inadequate to cope with the urban growth in terms of geography and demography. Lack of adequate finance is another major problem.

The traditional civil engineering approach to managing water supplies has focused on increasing the capacity of existing sources, and exploiting new sources of water in the vicinity or elsewhere without much consideration to the sustainability of a resource base, or environment or ecosystem. A lack of focus on fiscal and market instruments to manage the demand for water including pollution control is also visible. As a result, attempts to increase the supplies results in an increasing demand for water with no positive impact on scarcity mitigation, with a widening gap between the rich and the poor and growing problems of pollution. This is compounded by the sectoral and segmented approach to managing water for urban areas.[2] The overall outcome is that with growing size, urban areas are increasingly dependent on exogenous sources of water from far off regions (Mukherjee *et al.* 2010) that pose major technological, institutional and financial challenges to urban utilities.

Nearly 25 per cent of India's poor live in urban areas. Though India has made substantial progress in reducing poverty over the past 25 years (Asefa 2005),[3] improved water security is crucial to sustain the progress in human development and the current economic growth, thereby reducing poverty (Kumar *et al.* 2008a). This would require investments in water infrastructure, supported by appropriate policies and institutions. According to the Global Water Partnership, in order to achieve the Millennium Development Goals (MDG) related to water, the level of investment in the sector would have to be raised to US$180 billion per year from the current level of US$75 billion. The future would see a greater percentage of our population living in urban areas (Government of India 1999). Hence, a significant chunk of this investment will be for tackling urban water scarcity. However, comprehensive approaches to dealing with urban water problems are lacking.

Emerging concept of integrated urban water management

As Tipping *et al.* (2005) have acknowledged, 'the 2005 IWRM target offers the potential to implement the management and policy framework essential for successful achievement of water and sanitation targets'. Likewise the UN Millennium Project Task Force on Water and Sanitation (2005) recognizes the role that integrated urban water management (IUWM) could play in meeting, 'all the MDGs, not solely the one dealing specifically with water supply and sanitation'.

However, rather surprisingly, given the importance of the urban sector to the social and economic development of most countries, little appears in the integrated water resources management (IWRM) literature which explicitly considers what an IWRM approach might involve for urban centres. Moreover, few city managers or politicians have engaged with IWRM. The potential benefits of employing the IWRM concept at the intra-urban scale are at best poorly understood. IWRM is typically seen as something to do with river basins and of limited relevance as long as the city continues to be able to successfully compete to secure additional sources of water. As Molle and Berkoff (cited in Van Rooizen *et al.* 2005) point out, cities have been very effective in capturing water from agriculture using a variety of formal and informal mechanisms. Such success reduces the apparent need for urban administrations to become key actors in the IWRM process.

Literature on IWRM does, of course, refer to urban situations and many of the instruments that are of potential value when adopting an IWRM approach have been exemplified in an urban context. For example, there exists a wealth of material on urban water demand management, pollution abatement tools, leakage control, dual supply and recycling, decentralization and public–private partnerships. However, much of this literature is instrument-specific and does not explore the broader dimensions of IWRM in the urban context. Furthermore, little attention has been focused on what specific problems could arise in attempts to implement an IWRM approach in major metropolitan centres, although there are some potentially relevant lessons to be learnt from efforts to employ participatory and cooperative approaches to the solution of other urban problems. One potentially valuable set of experiences can be found in the work on sustainable cities and efforts to implement Agenda 21, a key output from the 1992 UN Conference on Environment and Development. Agenda 21 recognizes the vital role of local governments in addressing many environmental problems encountered in developing world cities, including water pollution, sanitation and vulnerability to water-related hazards.

Just as the IWRM literature has tended to neglect the urban dimension, the rich literature on urban water and sanitation provision has been largely silent on the broad role of IWRM. There are, of course, exceptions to this general statement, most obviously in countries such as South Africa and Singapore where IWRM principles are being incorporated into the strategic planning and management of urban water services (DWAF 2004; Tortajada 2006).

The urban water services literature does make reference to specific management instruments, such as demand management tools, stakeholder participation and community actions, which are potentially consistent with an IWRM approach but typically does not consider the range of cross-sectoral actions and assessments which would be involved in the implementation of an IWRM process. For example, in the UN Habitat report on Water and Sanitation in the World's Cities, which sees improving urban services provision as part of IWRM, the discussion focuses almost exclusively on specific demand management instruments (UN Habitat 2003). Although demand side management (DSM) techniques are undoubtedly of importance and the report very usefully highlights the lessons and potential tensions arising from implementation attempts, the focus on DSM gives only a partial view of the role of IWRM in urban water management. It neglects both the interrelationships between water and other urban services and the role of the latter in efficient and sustainable development of scarce natural and human capital resources.

What is integrated urban water management?

Conventional urban water management considers water supply, wastewater and storm water as separate entities, and planning, delivering and operating of these services with little reference to one another. Current urban water systems harvest large volumes of water from remote catchments and groundwater sources, deliver potable water to all urban uses and subsequently collects generated wastewater. This wastewater is removed, taken to treatment plants usually located on the fringe of the city or town, then discharged to the surrounding environment. Only 9 per cent of this wastewater is currently reused (Radcliff 2003). Large volumes of storm water are also generated within urban areas due to the increased imperviousness of urban catchments. The majority of this storm water flows out of the urban area, with little management of its quality and even less of it being used. As a result, the adverse impact of conventional urban water management on the water balance of these areas is substantial (Mitchell *et al.* 2003, 1997).

In comparison, IUWM takes a comprehensive approach to urban water services, viewing water supply, storm water and wastewater as components of an integrated physical system and recognizes that the physical system sits within an organizational framework and a broader natural landscape.

There are a broad range of tools which are employed within IUWM, including, but not limited to water conservation and efficiency; water sensitive planning and design, including urban layout and landscaping; utilization of non-conventional water sources including roof runoff, storm water, grey water and wastewater; the application of fit-for-purpose principles; storm water and wastewater source control and pollution prevention; storm water flow and quality management; the use of mixtures of soft (ecological) and hard (infrastructure) technologies; and non-structural tools such as education, pricing incentives, regulations and restriction regimes.

IUWM recognizes that the whole urban region, down to the site scale, needs to be considered, as urban water systems are complex and inter-related. Changes to a system will have downstream or upstream impacts that will affect cost, sustainability or opportunities. Therefore, proposed changes to a particular aspect of the urban water system must include a comprehensive view of other items and consider the influence on them.

Over-arching principles

The principles of IUWM can be summarized as: (a) consider all parts of the water cycle, natural and constructed, surface and sub-surface, recognizing them as an integrated system; (b) consider all requirements for water, both anthropogenic and ecological; (c) consider the local context, accounting for environmental, social, cultural and economic perspectives; (d) include all stakeholders in the process; (e) strive for sustainability, balancing environmental, social and economic needs in the short-, medium- and long-term.

Integrated urban water management at the operational level

There are five important considerations in urban water management: using various components of the urban water cycle; namely, urban storm water, runoff from roof catchment, urban wastewater, and use of both good quality and poor quality water from surface and groundwater sources for sustainable water use; treating various components of the hydrological system as part of a single system for water resource assessments and planning, by capturing surface water-groundwater interactions, catchment-stream flow interactions, and quality as well as quantity aspects; water demand management, including inter-sectoral water allocation; cost effectiveness of the water management interventions; and use of subsidiarity principle in urban water governance and management (Mitchell *et al.* 2003).

Integrated urban water management framework

Keeping in view the over-arching principles of IUWM, a generic framework for IUWM has been developed (Figure 8.1). The first component of the IUWM framework is the water use system. The second is the water supply, storm water collection, and wastewater treatment (WWT) system. The third is the water resource system, which includes water from desalination and imported water. These systems are interlinked. How much water is drawn from the water resource system depends on the demand for water in the water use system, and the network losses. The amount of wastewater generated depends on the water use.

As indicated in the schematic diagram, treated water from the conventional water treatment system, which provides water of high quality, is used to meet the water demands for domestic purpose and municipal uses. Relatively poor quality water is used for gardening, vehicle washing and toilets. The wastewater generated is either treated locally or goes to a centralized water treatment system. The treated water either joins the streams or groundwater or is available for reuse in agriculture. The storm water generated in the urban area including that from roof catchments is also collected, treated and can augment the water resources for use in urban areas.

As the box on the top right hand side indicates, the water use is a function of several complex physical, socio-economic and institutional and policy factors; namely, income level, water pricing structure and prices, supply restrictions, climate, seasons and culture, pollution tax and pollution control norms, subsidies for water conservation technologies, groundwater regulation and tax, presence of social institutions and organizations. The demand for water reduces with increases in price, and is less elastic to price changes under hot and arid climates and also when income levels are high.

On the other hand, the wastewater, if treated and recycled or reused, can reduce the effective water supply requirement in the urban areas. For instance, domestic wastewater can be reused for gardening, car washing and toilets. If not

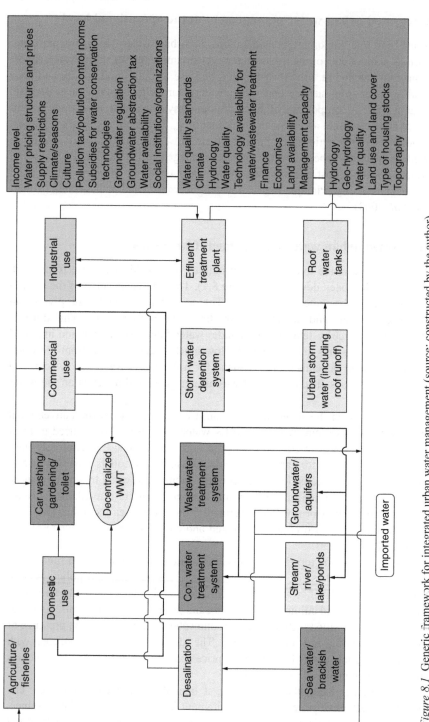

Figure 8.1 Generic framework for integrated urban water management (source: constructed by the author).

treated, it can deteriorate the quality of water in the natural systems and ecosystem health. The nature of raw water treatment, water supply and WWT systems depend on water quality standards applicable to the urban area, climate, hydrology and quality of water available from the natural system, technologies available for WWT, financial health of the water utility, economics of various water and WWT options and land availability. To elaborate, when stringent water quality (emission or effluent) standards are strictly enforced by the enforcing agencies (say the Pollution Control Board), the incentive to set up WWT systems that treat water to very high standards would be high among the water users like the municipality and industries.

The availability of water from the water resource system for supplies depends on hydrology, geo-hydrology of the basin/aquifer in which the region/basin falls, natural water quality, urban land use and land cover, type of housing stocks and topography. In addition to conventional sources of water (such as rivers/streams, lakes/ponds and groundwater), urban areas can augment their water supplies through rainwater harvesting. But, the amount depends on the rainfall (hydrology) and the total roof area and roof characteristics. Urban storm water, if collected and treated in detention systems, can be used to augment the lakes or aquifers.

Integrated urban water management practices

These practices are derived on the basis of an extensive review of national and international literature available on the physical (hydrological, geological, topographical and climatic) and economic (land use, land availability, land prices, sources of water supply and water supply-demand balance, cost of production of water) factors that influence the performance of various technological, economic and institutional interventions for urban water management. They are also grounded on thorough scrutiny of conditions under which various physical interventions with respect to water supply, WWT, storm water management and leakage reduction – and economic and institutional measures for water demand management – work effectively, distilled from research papers and articles on relevant topics (based on Baumol and Oates 1988; Chatterjee and Purohit 2009; Cropper and Oates 1992; Dussaillant *et al.* 2005; EPA 2006; Esrey 1996; Gerba *et al.* 1975; Frederiksen 1998; Gijzen 2001; Government of India 2005; Kumar *et al.* 2008a, 2008b, 2008c; Kumar 2004; Laurence *et al.* 2001; Mara 1997; Marsden Jacob Associates 2007; Misra and Eng 2007; Mukherjee *et al.* 2010; National Academy of Sciences 2008; Peña *et al.* 2002; Parr *et al.* 2004; Noll *et al.* 2000; Rose 1999; SIDA 2000; Sibly and Tooth 2007; Tsuchiya 2004; World Bank-GoI 1998; World Bank 2007).

•   In high rainfall, mountainous areas, roof water would be an important resource and source for urban water supplies from the point of view of augmenting the water supplies and also making it cost effective, and therefore should be part of the mainstream water supply system. In low-lying cities that receive very high rainfall that cause flash floods, collection of roof runoff in tanks would help reduce the intensity of floods.

- In flood-prone areas, flood management would be critical to achieve sustainable urban water supply sanitation that ensures basic survival, community health and environmental management.
- In semi-arid and arid areas, urban storm water can be detained in detention ponds, which can be used to recharge groundwater using the method of aquifer storage/recovery systems.
- In sub-humid and humid areas, urban storm water can be stored in decentralized detention ponds for sedimentation, and then discharged into natural drainage systems. This can reduce the capacity requirements of storm water drainage systems, and prevent urban floods.
- In large urban areas falling under low–medium rainfalls, with a larger proportion of the geographical area covered by 'built up area', rain gardens should be promoted.
- Leakage prevention in the water supply system would be a major consideration in water-scarce regions, and must receive high priority in large urban centres that have scattered populations.
- Land availability and land prices would be important considerations in choosing WWT technologies.
- Anaerobic treatment of wastewater is most ideal for hot and arid regions. In humid and cold areas, aerobic treatment has to be practiced. Since irrigation demand would be less in these areas, water has to be diverted for pisciculture.
- In arid and semi-arid areas with adequate sunshine, waste stabilization ponds would be ideal. The soil aquifer treatment is ideal for areas with deep water table conditions and permeable soil.
- Decentralized treatment of the domestic wastewater and its reuse in the same localities would reduce the demand for infrastructure and energy requirements for collection and disposal, while reducing urban water demand. It should be promoted in cities with scattered population and large cities.
- Decentralized sanitation systems can be encouraged only if the groundwater table is deep, or is of poor quality and not used for human consumption and will be ideal in arid climates with low rainfalls and light soils.

Key challenges

The key challenges for operationalizing IUWM concept can be classified into: institutional, administrative, financial and economic factors, concerning both supply and demand management issues.

Physical and environmental sustainability considerations in water supply

In India, urban water supply falls within the purview of the urban utilities (mostly under urban local government) or state level water supply agencies (under state government). In India, the various line agencies in the water supply sector follow a highly sectoral approach and there is no coordination amongst these agencies. As a result, they work at cross purposes. For example, a lack of coordination leads to increased withdrawal of groundwater or watershed treatment activities in the upper catchments that can affect the stream-flows during the non-monsoon season; posing a potential threat to drinking water supplies in towns and cities in the lower catchments. The challenge is to make sure that the watershed agency takes into account the planned future diversions of water from the streams. Similarly, the urban water utility while planning new supply augmentation schemes, should consider the new projects coming up in the upper catchments.

Many large urban centres are currently heavily dependent on water from distant reservoirs which are also claimed by other competing uses such as irrigation (Mukherjee *et al.* 2010). The plan for augmentation of the existing supplies from the same source in accordance with future urban growth should take into account the likely growth in the rural water demand, particularly from the irrigation sector, failing which the physical sustainability of urban water supplies would be seriously threatened in the long run affecting development and growth.

New water supply schemes to meet the growing urban water demands also mean that the quantity of wastewater generated would increase. This would pose new risks for ecological and in-stream uses in the lakes, streams and ponds which act as the natural sink for the urban wastewater and industrial effluent. Some of the in-stream uses could be washing clothes and utensils, bathing, and even drinking water supplies for communities living in urban fringes and slums. The challenge is to ensure that the wastewater generated is treated to environmentally safe standards for protecting the quality of water resources for meeting the existing and future needs.

Often excessive withdrawal of groundwater from small geographical areas within urban centres causes excessive drawdowns (Mukherjee *et al.* 2010). One illustrative example is the groundwater underlying Ahmedabad city. Such drawdown can result in a drastic increase in the cost of pumping groundwater, intrusion of water from saline formations, and negative externalities for groundwater users in the rural areas surrounding them. Such problems occur due to a lack of environmental sustainability considerations in water resource development planning. This is essentially because the agency engaged in developing and allocating the resource is not concerned with water resource management.

Integrated development of surface water, groundwater and catchments

Many urban areas are endowed with multiple sources of water (such as surface water in tanks and ponds, stream flows and groundwater) that are capable of augmenting the supplies. When these systems are often hydraulically linked, integrated planning and development is crucial for sustainable water supplies. For instance, exploitation of groundwater from shallow aquifers for municipal supplies in urban areas which have freshwater lakes, should consider the hydraulic interaction between the lake systems and the groundwater. Hence, protecting the lake system would require reducing the groundwater draft and maintaining the water table at a level if the groundwater outflows contribute to lake inflows. Conversely if lake water contributes to groundwater recharge, sustainable development of groundwater for water supplies should consider the infiltration from the lake or tank bed. This means such lakes are well protected from encroachments, and disposal of debris from construction.

In peninsular India, many cities and towns are surrounded by lakes and ponds. However, the reliability of water supplies from these ponds is low due to the high variability in rainfall and runoff that these regions experience. So, in good years, water could be imported from donor basins in almost the same quantity as is imported during normal and bad years, and the surplus amount after meeting the city demand, which is equal to the replenishments in local aquifers during the good year, can be stored in these surface structures. This will be wise from an environmental and ecological perspective also as the basin would be open. This is applicable to basins such as Krishna, and Cauvery that are 'water scarce'.

The pumping of groundwater in and around these structures would induce greater recharge of water from these ponds and lakes into the shallow aquifers, thereby increasing the storage space in them. This would act as the buffer for bad years. Hence in bad years, the dependence on exogenous sources could reduce. This could help avert the crisis that is likely to arise out of export of water from the donor basins when scarcity situation prevails in the basin.

Lack of integration of resource use can sometimes result in serious environmental problems, as was observed in Jodhpur city. The city corporation of Jodhpur used to draw water from several of the tanks surrounding the city. But, with water being made available from the Indira Gandhi Nehar Yojna (IGNP), the municipal corporation has now stopped drawing water from these tanks. The water, which remains in these tanks throughout the year, induces a lot of recharge to the shallow aquifer underlying the city. As a result, water levels have come up. The rise in water level is resulting in the flooding of the basements of houses in the city. The most ideal choice would have been the integration of the ponds with the water transfer system of the IGNP; as the tanks become dry with diversion of water for municipal use, the imported water can be used to fill them up, and water can be drawn from these tanks.

Another recent example is that of Rajkot city water supplies. The city corporation depends on Aji reservoir as its main source of water supply. The numerous check dams built by the panchayats of the upper catchment villages in recent years to augment groundwater recharge for irrigation and other uses, has drastically reduced the inflows into the reservoir (Kumar *et al.* 2008b). Such phenomena occur due to a lack of consideration of the basin hydrology in local water planning. The root of the problem lies in the 'segmented approach' wherein the agency, which is engaged in building minor irrigation structures including the check dams in small catchments, and the agency which is concerned with water resource systems in large basins under which such catchments fall, are different (Kumar 2006).

Integrated development of water resources, i.e. catchments, surface water and groundwater, would require coordination amongst the corresponding line agencies at the river basin level, where the different components of the hydrological system could be integrated. This is a great challenge, as the current institutional framework hardly provides any incentive to these agencies to work in tandem. The reason is each line agency tries to maximize its individual performance, which is assessed in relation to the total amount of water resources appropriated and supplied.

Treating storm water as a useful resource in urban water management

Integrated urban storm water management (IUSM) is a concept that has evolved in the West over the last 20–30 years, largely in response to the knowledge that rapid conveyance of urban storm water led to environmental degradation of receiving waterways (Wong and Eadie 2000). It has more recently been influenced by the growing interest in IUWM and the idea that urban storm water could provide a valuable resource. Overall, it is a concept concerned with enabling more sustainable management of urban storm water environments. However, the significance of IUSM does vary between places and it attracts more attention where the storm water drainage network system is typically separate from the wastewater network.

Separating out the storm water from the wastewater is important on two counts: (a) it prevents the dilution of wastewater, thereby help in increasing the energy recovery efficiency in WWT processes; (b) it helps in preventing contamination of storm water, which is an important resource in water-scarce regions. The benefits of sustainable storm water management are: flood reduction; pollution minimization; storm water retention; urban landscape improvement; and reduction of drainage investments.

It is not always easy to achieve these synergetic effects in storm water management in real life situations. The reason being: there is very low incidence of cities which experience problems of frequent flooding that also face a physical shortage of water, and vice versa; and issues of pollution of water bodies are least likely to be in cities which experience flooding. Because of these features, when flood control benefits of storm water management become high, the benefits of water conservation become low, as the cost of alternatives for producing and supplying domestic water supplies would be much lower. In situations where the economic benefits of creating new water sources through storm water conservation are high (in high rainfall hilly areas) due to the high cost of supplying water through alternative ways, the flood control and environmental management benefits are very low.

Storm water management systems are the key in protecting and enhancing the urban environment. The need for storm water management systems grows along with urban development. This is because, if the proportion of the built up area to the total geographical area of the urban centre increases, the storm water generation potential of the urban catchments increases.

The organizational administration of IUSM is the most challenging dimension to practical realization (Tyson *et al.* 1993; Geiger and Hofius 1996; Lawrence *et al.* 1999; Brown 2003). The organizational and administrative impediments to enable the implementation of IUSM can be typified into the characteristics relating to technocratic power and expertise, values and leadership, and structure and jurisdiction (Brown 2004). The technocratic structure of the administrative regime inherently gives emphasis to technical expertise and economic rationalism over an interdisciplinary alternative that values community participation in decision making and environmental sustainability. For instance, in India, communities do not pay for ecosystem services offered by urban lakes. Hence, the officials engaged in storm water management do not perceive any direct economic benefit arising out of storm water management interventions that would protect the lakes from contamination due to mixing with urban storm water. The result is that they tend to support only those interventions by which they can derive urban flood control benefits that exceed the costs of the interventions. Consequently, there are only minimal investments covering storm water drainage systems.

Financial and economic viability of wastewater treatment

WWT systems are expensive and hence the investments have to yield sufficient returns. They have to be both financially and economically viable. The systems become financially viable when the habitations living in the periphery of urban areas are willing to pay for the treated wastewater, which is used for agriculture, fisheries, etc. as an economic good, and the urban consumers pay for the enhanced quality of the environment resulting from the treatment of wastewater, which provides an environmental good. The systems become economically viable when the cost of treatment becomes less than the opportunity cost of polluting.

As regards economic viability, it depends on the direct economic benefits from treated wastewater and positive externality induced by WWT systems. The direct economic benefits that can be generated from use of treated wastewater for fisheries or irrigation of crops can be quite insignificant when compared to the cost of WWT. It is again a function of the physical and socio-economic condition of the region in question, with the irrigation benefits likely to be less in humid and sub-humid regions. The positive externalities can be in the form of prevention of public health hazards, conservation of fresh water for basic needs, prevention of environmental degradations and eco-system damages. The opportunity cost of not treating wastewater can also be considered as the benefit of treatment. But there are two issues involved in using these concepts for mobilizing public investments for WWT, and these issues are different for the two different situations that exist.[4]

Even if the government treats management of urban environmental quality as a public good and tries to recover the investments through general taxes, there are two issues making the investments difficult: (a) assessing the real opportunity cost of the lack of treatment or the benefits of treatment; and (b) evaluating the treatment costs. While the benefit of treatment would depend on the degree of treatment, the same would determine the cost of treatment as well. The marginal returns from treatment would ideally decline towards higher levels of treatment, while the marginal costs would increase. One reason for the earlier is the maximum ecological, environmental and direct economic benefits would result from the secondary levels of treatment of wastewater. The reason for the latter is that the higher order treatments to remove the nutrients, heavy metals and patho-gens from the wastewater are far more expensive than the secondary treatment.

Hence, the challenge is to determine the level of treatment which would produce the highest social welfare. Carrying out such analysis requires both environmental engineers and environmental economists working together to identify the best engineering solution for treatment of effluents from the point of view of environmental performance, and determine the degree of treatment which gives highest social return.

As regards financial viability, the revenue has to come from two sources: (a) the prices people pay for the treated wastewater, which would eventually be used for economic functions such as irrigation or fish production and which is a func-tion of the quantum of treated wastewater; and (b) the price people are willing to pay for the better environmental quality resulting from cleaned up streams, rivers and lakes. While pricing of wastewater could be a viable proposition in many peri-urban areas of India owing to the fact that wastewater outflows would be highly dependable and available even during summer months, and treated waste-water contains many macro nutrients such as nitrogen and phosphorous and a scarcity of irrigation water persists in many peri-urban areas, the latter is the concern area. The reason is in developing economies like India, the overall will-ingness to pay for management of environmental quality would be generally low and there are very few people in urban areas who would value such services.

Efficient pricing and metering of urban water supplies

Pricing of urban water supplies serves two purposes: (a) recovering the cost of producing and supplying water; and (b) reducing the wastage of water, which helps in managing the demand (World Bank and Government of India 1998). There are three institutional factors that influence water use in Indian cities. First, domestic water supply is highly subsidised in many Indian cities, including Kolkata, Bhopal and Indore. Second, there are problems with water supply administration. Domestic water supply is not fully metered even in large cities. In more than 50 per cent of the cities falling under Class I and Class II category, household connections are partially metered or un-metered (NIUA 2005). Third, there are problems with the way water tariff is administered. Many large cities meter a very small fraction of the water supply connections, making administra-tion of volumetric tariff difficult (ADB 2007).

An important implication of demand that exhibits some price elasticity is that a mistake in pricing can have large consequences for water use. Prices that are too low create a demand to expand water delivery beyond the efficient point. If the costs of the water system are not primarily financed by water revenues, but by general taxes or revenue from another utility, under-pricing water can be very expensive to society as it would mean massive, uneconomic expansion of the water delivery system (Noll *et al.* 2000).

The question of water pricing involves several pertinent issues. The first concerns what component of the cost should be included in water pricing. If full cost pricing is to be introduced, and if costs are high due to inefficient or corrupt management, much economically warranted water usage can be cut off (Noll *et al.* 2000). The second concerns the consumers not valuing water quality high enough. This can happen because of imperfect information.[5] In such a situation, consumers may respond to higher prices for piped water by consuming too much low-quality water from contaminated alternative sources. This can be corrected by subsidizing a minimum amount for human consumption, though subsidies may introduce other distortions (Noll *et al.* 2000).

Finally, the decision for metering, which is required for introducing volumetric block rates at the consumer level, must be subjected to cost–benefit analysis and introduced on a case-by-case basis, as installing meters and taking meter readings are costly affairs. The case for metering will become strong as both incomes, and water supply and disposal costs increase. The reasons are two-fold. First, the cost saving and social benefits from reduction of wastage and effluent load would be higher at higher marginal opportunity costs of production of water. Second, the feasibility of introducing meters and volumetric pricing would increase with an increase in income. In order to arrive at a decision on metering, the long-term marginal opportunity cost of production (MOCP) of water should be estimated (World Bank 2007). Based on these figures of MOCP, the total amount of water that can be saved through metering and volumetric pricing and the cost of metering, cost–benefit analysis can be carried out. This is a major institutional challenge to address as many towns and cities do not have proper accounts of water wastage and the direct cost of production and supply of water (ADB 2007), let alone aspects such as cost of resource depletion and the cost of environmental degradation.

Economics of integrated urban water management

In regions where local water resources are scarce and urban water demands are high, adoption of IUWM would prove to be a boon, as it would facilitate the following objectives: defer the investment in infrastructure for augmenting urban water supplies; reduce the environmental degradation problems associated with diversion of freshwater resources from rivers and aquifers for municipal uses, reduce pollution of freshwater resources that support several economic, social and ecological functions; reduce the opportunity cost of diverting water from other sectors, particularly agriculture, to urban areas; reduce the cost of damage occurring from urban floods and degradation of water bodies as a result of disposal of urban storm water. The argument is illustrated in the following.

First, the cost of production and supply of exogenous water to growing urban areas in water-scarce regions would be enormously high (Mukherjee *et al.* 2010). IUWM interventions can, on the one hand, reduce the water supply requirements through leakage reduction measures, and end use conservation with the help of appropriate water pricing policies and efficient water use technologies. On the other hand, it can increase the supplies by tapping all local water sources, and augment local water resources through the adoption of ISWM measures.

In the absence of IUWM, in addition to the direct cost of the infrastructure for supplying water, the urban utilities will put a huge environmental cost of diverting water from rivers, aquifers and streams to meet the demands, and also of degrading the urban environment with the polluted water to the society. Obviously, in water-scarce regions, the environmental degradation caused by disposal of domestic wastewater in natural water bodies would be more severe than in water-rich regions. In addition, the opportunity cost of depletion of the water would also be very high, when the resource is scarce (Kumar *et al.* 2008c). IUWM interventions can help reduce wastewater generation through measures such as pollution taxes and water pricing. It can reduce storm water generation through economic incentives and engineering measures. All these would not only save the cost of infrastructure required for their treatment, but also prevent the environmental damage caused by disposal of both into natural water bodies through proper selection of WWT and storm water management systems.

Conclusions

IUWM, as an extension of the broader concept of IWRM is gaining acceptance in developing as well as developed economies. In spite of the importance of the urban sector to the social and economic development of most countries, little appears in the IWRM literature which explicitly considers what an IWRM approach might involve for urban centres. Just as the IWRM literature has tended to neglect the urban dimension, the literature on urban water and sanitation provision has been largely silent on the broad role of IWRM in urban water management. The literature on urban water services makes reference to management instruments, such as demand management tools, stakeholder participation and community actions, which are potentially consistent with an IWRM approach. But, it does not consider the range of cross-sectoral actions and assessments which would be involved in the implementation of an IWRM process.

The present analysis discussed the over-arching principles of IUWM, and its working at the operational level. A generic operational framework of IUWM was provided, followed by the over-arching practices in IUWM. The discussion then covered the key challenges in implementing its various components in Indian cities/towns, which are related to scientific and technical knowledge, human resources, institutional capabilities and finance. The specific challenges include: (a) introducing physical and environmental sustainability considerations in urban water supply; (b) integrated development of groundwater, surface water and catchments; (c) treating storm water as a useful resource for managing urban water supplies on a sustainable basis; (d) making WWT financial or economically viable; and (e) efficient pricing and metering of urban water supplies. It is argued that IUWM would be economically more viable in water-scarce regions.

The first challenge for policymakers is to make the agencies concerned with development and allocation of water resources for various uses including municipal uses, understand the opportunity cost of using it. Second, the actions of these agencies need to be coordinated at the level of river basins. Determining the optimal level of WWT where the real costs do not exceed the net social welfare, evaluating the real marginal opportunity cost of water supply and ascertaining the economic viability of metering and making communities aware of the health benefits of using good quality water so as to increase their willingness to pay for water supplies are other important institutional challenges.

Notes

1 A similar increase in urbanization would result in a 0.68 per cent increase in per capita domestic water demand.
2 For detailed discussions on this, please refer to Kumar (2006).
3 The poverty rate in India declined from 50 per cent in 1981 to 35 per cent in 2001 (Asefa 2005).
4 In the first situation, there are a few polluters and many victims; and in the second one, there are as many polluters as victims. In the first case, like industrial pollution, if polluters are not held accountable for the costs that they impose on others, they will continue to pollute and use an inefficiently large amount of water. The Pigouvian solution here is to impose a tax on the output equal to the difference between the marginal social cost and price at the socially optimal level (Pigou 1920). The tax creates a financial penalty for water pollution, and so provides a financial reason to invest in either sewers or water treatment facilities. These investments, in turn, will raise the price of water use, and so curtail consumption and the pollution that it creates. In the second case, like in the case of municipal effluent disposal, the situation is ideal for levying 'environmental service charges' that reflect the positive externality induced by waste treatment. But, here the challenge is to make people aware of the negative externalities induced by their actions on their own life, and recover the cost of environmental degradation from them through levying charges over and above the cost of production and supply of water and the cost of its depletion.
5 Some users may lack understanding of the relationship between water quality and health. Others may understand these relationships in principle, but they cannot easily observe aspects of poor water quality such as the presence of microorganisms or trace chemicals.

References

Amarasinghe, U.A., Shah, T., Turral, H. and Anand, B.K. (2007) *India's Water Future to 2025–2050: Business-as-usual Scenario and Deviations*, Research Report No. 123, Colombo: International Water Management Institute (IWMI).

Asefa, S. (ed.) (2005) *The Economics of Sustainable Development*, East Lansing: W.E. Upjohn Institute, Michigan State University.

Asian Development Bank (2007) *2007 Benchmarking and Data Book of Water Utilities in India,* A Partnership between the Ministry of Urban Development, Government of India and Asian Development Bank, New Delhi.

Baumol, W. and Oates, W.E. (1988) *The Theory of Environmental Policy,* second edition, Cambridge: Cambridge University Press.

Brown, R. (2003) *Institutionalization of Integrated Urban Stormwater Management: Multiple-Case Analysis of Local Management Reforms Across Metropolitan Sydney,* unpublished PhD Thesis, University of New South Wales, Sydney.

Brown, R. (2004) 'Local Institutional Development And Organisational Change For Advancing Sustainable Urban Water Futures', Keynote Address in the International Conference on Water Sensitive Urban Design: Cities as Catchments, Adelaide, 21–25 November.

Chatterjee, R. and Purohit, R.R. (2009) 'Estimation of Renewable Groundwater Resources of India and their Status of Utilization', *Current Science,* 96(12): 1581–1591.

Cropper, M.L. and Oates, W.E. (1992) 'Environmental Economics: A Survey', *Journal of Economic Literature,* 30(2): 675–740.

Department of Water Affairs and Forestry (2004) 'Development of Internal Strategic Perspectives for the Crocodile Catchment', Pretoria: Department of Water Affairs and Forestry (DWAF), Directorate National Resources Planning.

Dussaillant, A.R., Cuevas, A. and Potte, K.W. (2005) 'Raingardens for Stormwater Infiltration and Focused Groundwater Recharge: Simulations for Different World Climates, Water Science and Technology' *Water Supply,* 5(3–4): 173–179.

Environmental Protection Agency (2006) *Growing Toward More Efficient Water Use: Linking Development, Infrastructure and Drinking Water Policies,* Washington, DC: United States Environmental Protection Agency (EPA).

Esrey, S.A. (1996) 'Water, Waste, and Well-Being: A Multi-country Study', *American Journal of Epidemiology,* 143(6): 608–623.

Frederiksen, H.D. (1998) 'Institutional Principles for Sound Management of Water and Related Environmental Resources', A.K. Biswas (ed.) *Water Resources: Environmental Planning, Management, and Development.* New Delhi: Tata McGraw-Hill.

Geiger, W.F. and Hofius, K. (1996) 'Integrated Water Management in Urban and Surrounding Areas: Findings of the International Workshops in Essen 1992 and Gelsenkirchen 1994 by the German–Dutch IHP Committee to UNESCO Project M3–3a', *Integrated Water Management in Urban Areas,* 3–4: 127–152.

Gerba, C.P., Wallis, C. and Melnick, J.L. (1975) 'Fate of Waste Water Bacteria and Viruses in Soil', *Journal of Irrigation and Drainage Division,* 101(3):1 57–174.

Gijzen, H.J. (2001) 'Low Cost Wastewater Treatment and Potential for Reuse: A Cleaner Production Approach to Wastewater Management', Paper presented at the International Symposium on Low-Cost Wastewater Treatment and Re-use, Cairo, 3–4 February.

Government of India (1999) 'Integrated Water Resources Development: A Plan for Action', Report of the National Commission for Integrated Water Resources Development, Volume 1, New Delhi: Ministry of Water Resources.

Government of India (2005) 'Dynamic Groundwater Resources of India', New Delhi: Central Ground Water Board, Ministry of Water Resources.

Kumar, M.D. (2004) 'Roof Water Harvesting for Domestic Water Security: Who Gains and Who Loses', *Water International,* 29 (1): 43–53.

Kumar, M.D. (2006) *Water Management in River Basins: A Study of Sabarmati River Basin in Gujarat,* unpublished PhD thesis, Faculty of Management, Sardar Patel University, Vallabh Vidyanagar.

168   *M. Dinesh Kumar*

Kumar, M.D., Shah, Z. and Mukherjee, S. (2008a) 'Water, Human Development and Economic Growth: Some International Perspectives', in M.D. Kumar (ed.) *Managing Water in the Face of Growing Scarcity, Inequity and Diminishing Returns: Exploring Fresh Approaches*, proceedings of the seventh Annual Partners' Meet, IWMI-Tata Water Policy Research program, 2–4 April, Patancheru: ICRISAT.

Kumar, M.D., Patel, A., Ravindranath, R. and Singh, O.P. (2008b) 'Chasing a Mirage: Water Harvesting and Artificial Recharge in Naturally Water-Scarce Regions', *Economic and Political Weekly*, 43(35): 61–71.

Kumar, M.D., Malla, A.K. and Tripathy, S. (2008c) 'Economic Value of Water in Agriculture: Comparative Analysis of a Water-Scarce and a Water-Rich Region in India', *Water International*, 33(2): 214–230.

Lawrence, A.I., Ellis, J.B., Marsalek, J., Urbanas, B. and Phillips, B.C. (1999) 'Total Urban Water Cycle Based Management', in I.B. Jollife and J.E. Ball (eds) *Proceedings of the 8th International Conference on Urban Storm Drainage*, vol. 3, Sydney.

Lawrence, A.R., Macdonald, D.M.J., Howard, A.G., Barret, M.H., Pedley, S., Ahmed, K.M. and Nalubega, M. (2001) *Guidelines for Assessing the Risk of Groundwater from On-site Sanitation*, London: Commissioned report (CR/01/142), British Geological Survey.

Mara, D.D. (1997) *Design Manual for Waste Stabilization Ponds in India*, Leeds: Lagoon Technology International Ltd.

Marsden Jacob Associates (2007) *The Economics of Rain Water Tanks and Alternative Water Supply Options*, report prepared for Nature Conservation Council of NSW, Australian Conservation Foundation and Environment, Victoria.

Misra, S. and Eng, F.C. (2007) 'India – Water Supply and Sanitation: Bridging the Gap between Infrastructure and Services'. Online, available at: http://siteresources.worldbank.org/INTINDIA/Resources/SmitaMisra-UrbanWSSPresentationFebruary2007.pdf (accessed 20 July 2010).

Mitchell, V.G., McMahon, T.A. and Mein, R.G. (1997) 'The Utilization of Stormwater and Wastewater to Transform the Supply and Disposal Requirements of an Urban Community', Proceedings of the twenty-fourth Hydrology and Water Resources Symposium, Auckland, 24–27 November.

Mitchell, V.G., McMahon, T.A. and Mein, R.G. (2003) 'Components of the Total Water Balance of an Urban Catchment', *Environmental Management*, 32(6): 735–746.

Molle, F. and Berkoff, J. (2006) *Cities versus Agriculture*, Research Report, Colombo: IWMI.

Mukherjee, S., Shah, Z. and Kumar, M.D. (2010) 'Sustaining Urban Water Supplies in India: Increasing Role of Large Reservoirs', *Water Resources Management*, 24(10): 2035–2055.

National Academy of Sciences (2008) 'Urban Stormwater Management in the United States', brief prepared by the National Research Council on the basis of a report prepared by the Committee on Reducing Stormwater Contribution to Water Pollution, The National Academy of Sciences, Washington, DC.

National Institute of Urban Affairs (2005) 'Status of Water Supply, Sanitation and Solid Waste Management in Urban Areas', sponsored by Central Public Health and Environmental Engineering Organization (CPHEEO) Ministry of Urban Development, Government of India.

Noll, R., Shirley, M.M. and Cowan, S. (2000) 'Reforming Urban Water Systems in Developing Countries', in A.O. Krueger (ed.), *Economic Policy Reform: The Second Stage*, Chicago: University of Chicago Press.

Parr, J., Smith, M. and Shaw, R. (2004) 'Wastewater Treatment Options', Leicestershire: Water and Environmental Health at London and Loughborough (WELL).

Peña, M.R., Madera, C.A. and Mara, D.D. (2002) 'Feasibility of Waste Stabilization Pond Technology in Small Municipalities of Colombia', *Water Science and Technology*, 45(1): 1–8.

Pigou, A.C. (1920) *Economics of Welfare*, London: Macmillan.

Radcliff, J. (2003) 'An Overview of Water Recycling in Australia – Results of a Recent ATSE Study', paper presented at second National Conference on Water Sensitive Urban Design, Brisbane, 2–4 September.

Rooijen, D.J. Van, Turral, H. and Briggs, T.W. (2005) 'Sponge City: Water Balance of Mega City Water Use and Wastewater Use in Hyderabad, India', *Irrigation and Drainage*, 54(1): S81–S91.

Rose, G.D. (1999) 'Community-Based Technologies for Domestic Wastewater Treatment and Reuse: Options for Urban Agriculture', CFP Report No. 27, Ottawa: International Development Research Centre (IDRC).

Rosegrant, M.W., Ringler, C. and Gerpacio, R.V. (1999) 'Water and Land Resources and Global Food Supply', in G.H. Peters and J.V. Braun (eds) *Food Security, Diversification And Resource Management: Refocusing The Role of Agriculture?*, Farnham: Ashgate Publishers.

Sibly, H. and Tooth, R. (2007) 'Bringing Competition to Urban Water Supply', School of Economics and Finance, University of Tasmania.

Swedish International Development Agency (2000) 'Water and Wastewater Management in Large to Medium-sized Urban Centers', Stockholm: SIDA.

Tecco, N. (2008) 'Financially Sustainable Investments in Developing Countries Water Sectors: What Conditions could Promote Private Sector Involvement?' *International Environmental Agreements: Politics, Law and Economics*, 8(2): 129–142.

Tipping, D.C., Adom, D. and Tibaijuka, A.K. (2005) *Achieving Healthy Urban Futures in the 21st Century*, Publications of Ministry for Foreign Affairs, Helsinki Process Publication Series.

Tortajada, C. (2006) Publishing on the Internet, 'Singapore: An Exemplary Case for Urban Water Management—Case Study for the 2006 HDR'. Online, available at: http://hdr.undp.org/en/reports/global/hdr2006/papers/cecilia_tortajada_singapore_casestudy.pdf (accessed 7 January 2011).

Tsuchiya, T. (2004) 'Unaccounted for Water (UFW) Reduction and Control and Water Distribution System Rehabilitation (DSR)', Tokyo: Japanese Bank for International Cooperation.

Tyson, J.M., Guarino, C.F., Best, H.J. and Tanaka, K. (1993) 'Management and Institutional Aspects', *Journal of Water Science and Technology*, 27(12): 159–172.

UN Habitat (2003) *Water and Sanitation in the World's Cities*, London: Earthscan, United Nations Human Settlements Programme.

United Nations Development Programme (2006) *Human Development Report 2006*, New York: UNDP.

United Nations Millennium Task Force and Stockholm International Water Institute (2005) *Health, Dignity, and Development: What It Takes*, Stockholm: UN Millennium Task Force on Water and Sanitation, United Nations Millennium Project and Stockholm International Water Institute.

van Rooijen, D.J., Turral, H. and Briggs, T.W. (2005) 'Sponge City: Water Balance of Mega City Water Use and Wastewater Use in Hyderabad India', *Irrigation and Drainage*, 54(1): S81–S91.

Wong, T.H.F. and Eadie, M.L. (2000) 'Water Sensitive Urban Design – A Paradigm Shift in Urban Design', paper presented at the International Water Resources Association for the Xth World Water Congress, Melbourne, 12–16 March.

World Bank/Government of India (1998) *Urban Water Supply and Sanitation Report, Volume 1, Main Report*, India Water Resources Management Sector Review, Report No. 18321, New Delhi: Rural Development Unit, South Asia Region, World Bank.

World Bank (2007) 'Water Supply Pricing in China: Economic Efficiency, Environment, and Social Affordability', Beijing: World Bank Analytical and Advisory Assistance (AAA) Program China, Addressing Water Scarcity – From Analysis to Action Policy Note.

9 Municipal solid waste management in India

Environmental impacts and institutional reforms

*Prasenjit Sarkhel**

Introduction

In the present decade the urban population of less developed countries (LDCs) have been growing at a remarkable pace. During 2000–05, the average growth rate of the urban population in low income countries was more than twice that of middle income countries and more than three times the figure for high income countries (WDR 2009). One important consequence of the increase in urban population is the rise in urban waste level as well as per capita waste generation owing to concomitant improvement in living standards. Unless properly managed, the burgeoning volume of this waste can impose significant health and aesthetic costs on the city populace. Recognition of these social costs led to the enunciation of environmentally safer norms of disposal and collection. The common thrust of these new initiatives is to arrange for alternative end uses of waste that would prolong the life of landfill sites.

The process of reforming waste management practices was also associated with changes in the institutional delivery mechanism of garbage disposal services. In developed countries, these institutional reforms were seen in the form of contracted out refuse collection and privately operated landfills.[1] Further, stake-holders like households and industry were linked up within the waste collection and disposal chain through economic instruments like user-charges and advance disposal fees. Such a market integrated institutional delivery mechanism, however, is unlikely to work for less developed areas. This is because waste collection and disposal are still non-market activities in this part of the world, and whatever markets exist for the collection of recyclables are informal in nature. Hence, an important agenda for civic authorities in developing countries is to arrive at a proper institutional set up that would sustain the reforms sought by waste management policies.

This conundrum of institutional set up in developing regions can be illustrated by the waste management scenarios in the urban agglomerates in India. Irregular collection of urban waste and its improper disposal in open spaces were one of the major environmental problems in Indian cities. Recognition of the social costs associated with such practices led to the promulgation of the Municipal Solid Waste Management and Handling (MSWMH) Rules (2000) that formulated the best practices of waste collection and disposal for the local bodies in India. The municipal bodies were asked to introduce doorstep collection of segregated waste and replace open dumps by sanitary landfills. Particular emphasis was also laid on the adoption of alternate disposal practices like composting and biomethanation[2] that would divert waste from landfills and delay the capacity exhaustion for an economically meaningful time horizon. This chapter attempts to study the institutional and organizational adjustments that are taking place in India after the issuance of MSWMH Rules (2000) in order to understand the extent of complementarities between environmental policy and institutional reform. To prepare the setting, the following section discusses the trend in waste generation and disposal for developed and developing countries. The waste related policies and institutional arrangements across the high and low income areas are also compared and discussed here. In the next section the stylized facts of urban waste management in less developed economies are then matched and illustrated for India. The institutional evolution following waste management regulations in India are discussed in the following section and the last section offers the concluding observations.

Volume and composition of municipal solid waste: the global perspective

Globally, municipal waste generation is increasing at a high pace with urbanization and improved standard of living. Between 1980 and 2005, on average per capita waste generation in 30 OECD (OECD 2007) countries increased by 7.2 per cent from 387 kg to 528 kg per capita per annum. By 2000, the United States produced 730 kg waste per capita per annum, almost twice the comparable figure for Europe that stood at 414 kg.

The major drivers of this increasing per capita waste generation can be traced back to macroeconomic factors such as economic growth as well as population growth and changes in the population structure. A positive relation between per capita waste generation and proportion of adult population is reported by Van Houtven and Morris (1999) and Johnston and Labonne (2004). Several studies have reported negative relationships between average household size and waste generation rate (Jenkins *et al.* 2003; Hong and Adams 1999). The trend of individualistic lifestyle also results in multiplication of goods that increased the level of post-consumption waste (Tilly 2004).

Reliance on land filling to dispose of this increasing volume of garbage is declining in high-income countries. In fact waste disposal by landfill came down in the United States from 85 per cent in 1985 to around 60 per cent in 2001.[3] Other high income countries like Japan, Denmark and Netherlands that are land scarce have largely substituted landfills by incineration plants.[4] However, incineration as a disposal option has been losing its acceptability over the years due to recognition of its emission potential of dioxins and furans, and extensive pollution regulations are imposed on incineration plants in land scarce countries that operate such facilities (Tilly 2004).[5] Recycling stole the policy emphasis from incineration and the Resource Conservation and Recycling Act (RCRA) (1976) and subsequently Comprehensive Environmental Response, Compensation and Liability Act 1980 (CERCLA) in the United States had been used to devote significant investments for kerbside recycling programs, providing tax rebates or subsidizing commercial recycling programmes and sanctioning grants to local governments for upgrading of their waste management services.

To ensure compliance on the part of the stakeholders of the generation and disposal chain, policy initiatives often took the form of designing incentive compatible economic instruments. At the level of households, for instance, a number of such instruments like unit pricing, advance disposal fee and deposit refund system have been put in place. Unit pricing refers to practice of charging households by the volume of waste, advance disposal fees are charges imposed on manufacturers reflecting the external cost imposed by the end of life disposal of the product, and deposit refund is a two-part instrument that taxes consumption and subsidizes recycling (Kinnaman and Fullerton 2000).

To understand this interplay between various waste disposals options consider the correlation matrix that comes out of waste disposal practices of 30 OECD countries (OECD 2007). To understand the relation between land scarcity and choice of disposal options, the degree of association between population density and waste disposal options is presented in Table 9.1.

Historically landfill was the primary mode of waste disposal in OECD countries. As the opportunity cost of land has gone up, alternative disposal modes like incineration, composting and recycling have started gaining popularity. Therefore, landfill has a significant negative correlation with all these other options, implying that adoption of these alternatives results in higher waste diversion from land filling activities. Selection of a particular option among the array of alternatives depends on a host of factors including the physio-chemical composition of waste determining the private cost of operation, and perceived social cost, and is thus country specific. Often public concern about adverse environmental impacts of incineration has forced the policy makers to replace incineration plants by recycling programmes even when the economic efficiency of the latter was far from optimal in terms of cost recovery (Tilly 2004). However, from technological considerations an increased rate of recycling would imply higher availability of uncontaminated compostable waste. Pre-sorted waste, free from contrary materials, is a vital input for production of good quality compost. Hence, higher rates of recycling provide the necessary impetus for adoption of composting as an alternative disposal option. This explains why incineration displays weak correlation with both recycling and composting whereas composting and recycling are highly correlated among themselves. Finally, the high negative correlation between landfill and population density corroborates the argument of increased land scarcity and the absence of strong correlation with any other alternative disposal options, confirming the conflict of economic drivers of choice of disposal technique with local conditions and social acceptability.

Table 9.1 Correlation between alternative waste processing options (percentage of total waste) and population density in OECD countries[a]

	Composting	Recycling	Incineration	Landfill
Composting	1			
Recycling	0.470(*) (n=20)	1		
Incineration	0.359 (n=22)	0.168 (n=20)	1	
Landfill	−0.650(**) (n=27)	−0.608(**) (n=21)	−0.812(**) (n=23)	1
Population density	0.271 (n=28)	0.273 (n=22)	0.255 (n=23)	−0.453(*) (n=29)

Source: author's calculation.

Notes

* and ** – imply correlation coefficient is significant at 0.05 and 0.01 level (2-tailed) respectively, n = number of observations.

a The number of observations is different for different options as some countries did not choose all the disposal options. For instance, Australia, Greece, Mexico, Ireland and New Zealand chose only composting other than landfill as their disposal options. Countries like Japan and Korea went for both composting and incineration apart from landfilling their waste. Turkey mostly landfilled their waste and recycled only about 1.5 per cent of the total garbage. The rest of the OECD countries used all four options in various proportions.

These material recovery processes were often standardized through nation-wide regulations setting targets for disposal options. A case in point is the European Union (EU) packaging directive (94/62/EC) that imposed 15 per cent recycling targets for materials like glass, plastics, metal and paper (Taveres 2005). These regulations are based on the so called 'waste hierarchy'[6] delineating a sequence of waste disposal options and extended producer responsibility (EPR) whereby the producers are required to finance the recycling and end of life treatment of their products. In response to EPR, producers have clubbed together to form recycling organizations that serve as an interface between waste generators, i.e. consumers and agents involved in ultimate waste disposal, i.e. the municipal bodies. These institutions are called producer responsibility organizations (PRO) that delegate collection and recycling activities to waste management companies, financing them with levies contributed by the members of the organization. Parts of the recycling costs are passed on through the product chain to the customers. These inter-firm co-operations also hailed as 'third generation policy instruments', evolved in the form of *Duales System Deutschland GmbH* (DSD)[7] in Germany, *Eco-Emballages* in France, *Consorzi Obbligatori* in Italy and the packaging covenant in the Netherlands (Whinston and Glachant 1996). The outcome of such voluntary agreements is reported in Table 9.2.

On the other hand, waste generation rates varies from 0.4–0.9 kg per capita per day for low income countries to 0.5–1.1 kg per capita per day for middle income countries and rises to 5.07 kg/day in the case of high income countries.[8] The waste characteristics are also different in low and middle income countries as here the urban refuse is rich in organic and moisture content and hence it is evident that a disposal process involving waste combustion and subsequent energy generation is unlikely to succeed.[9] Traditionally, there is a clear dichotomy between the provision of waste collection and disposal and recycling services in developing countries. Collection and disposal of waste is solely carried out by the municipal bodies while informal institutions like itinerant buyers and rag pickers are engaged in the recycling sector. In fact the low level of income recycling activities is an important source of livelihood in these places and is estimated to provide employment to 1–2 per cent of the workforce in large cities (Furedy 1992). Reviewing waste management practices in low income cities of three regions; namely, Africa, Asia and Latin America and the Caribbean, it is seen that waste disposal practices are mainly dependent on open dumping (See Table 9.3). Composting as an alternative disposal option is eluding the planners as supply of source segregated waste could not be ensured to the waste processing plants resulting in increased cost of operation (UNEP 2005).

In recent times a higher degree of urbanization has generated policy dialogues in developing countries for initiating better management of urban waste. Most of the developing regions have started initiating policies specific to the management of municipal solid waste (MSW) from the latter half of the 1990s. Here, the challenge is grave as the local bodies are typically cash-starved and awareness levels are low. Hence ensuring proper compliance of all the stakeholders to a scientifically feasible disposal option may be a difficult requirement to fulfil. In

Table 9.2 Waste mangement policies in selected European countries

Country	Objectives	Time period	Outcome
France	Domestic packaging: 75 per cent of valorization Municipal waste: 100 per cent of valorization except for ultimate waste.	1992–2002	Attainment of recycling targets was not satisfactory. In 1997 the overall valorization rate reached only 31 per cent of household waste.
Germany	Packaging: between 60 and 70 per cent of recycling Deposit refund scheme and a quota of 72 per cent of rebottling for beverage. Strict hierarchy of treatment techniques. Separate collection of organic waste.	1991–98	Recycling targets were achieved. However, as both the collection and sorting system were completely subsidized huge quantities of recyclables were exported to other European countries causing a recycling glut.
Greece	Packaging recycling – specific objectives of the 62/94/ CE directive: 25 per cent of recycling	1994–2000	Illegal landfilling could not be successfully substituted by recycling, incineration or composting.
Italy	Beverage packaging: recovery rates: 50 per cent of glass, metal etc. and 40 per cent of plastic, composites etc. Recovery from the whole of packaging wastes (between 25 to 45 per cent for recycling) and 35 per cent of separate collection	1988–2002 (regularly postponed)	Recycling targets for glass, metals etc. were reached but after much delay. Plastic recycling reached 31 per cent in 1996, but most of it was not in the domestic packaging category. Weak compliance of the municipalities regarding introduction of separate collection of recyclables.
Netherlands	Packaging waste volume generated in 2000 should not be bigger than in 1986. No more land filling for combustible waste. Minimum of 60 per cent of recycling of packaging waste. No specific goals for municipal waste.	2000	Recycling targets met for most packaging items like aluminium and paper cardboard. The policy failed in case of plastics. Incinerators underutilized and landfilling remained the major disposal mode.

Source: Buclet and Goddard (2000).

Note
Valorization is a generic term which includes recycling, composting, incineration, with all forms of energy recovery (methanization, refuse derive fuels, etc.).

order to be feasible, technological options must have a low cost of adoption, both in the private and the social domain. MSW management has been a non-market activity in these regions and most of the solid waste services provided by the municipal authorities are financed by taxes or fees that are unrelated to the level of waste generation. Hence, the marginal cost of additional units of waste disposal is zero for the resident populace, leading to socially excess generation of waste. To exemplify the issue further, next, the case of India is considered as a typical representative of a developing country.[10]

Urban waste management in India

Presently, the urban populace in India generates 1.15 lakh tonne of MSW per day that amounts to 42 million tonne of garbage per annum (Asnani 2006). Urbanization in India is growing rapidly at 2.7–3.5 per cent per annum and consequently the projected increase in MSW is more than 260 million tonne annually in 2047, i.e. five times the present level.[11] The land requirement for dumping the total quantity of waste would be 1,400 km^2 in the same period (Singhal and Pandey 2001), which is about 7.7 times the area of Kolkata (187.33 km^2).

This grim prognosis is alarming given the fact that traditionally waste management services in India are quite far from optimal. Average waste collection in the Indian cities and states is 70 per cent (Sharholy *et al.* 2008). In addition, the collection activity is largely irregular and involves double handling of waste. The usual practice is to transport the garbage in uncovered vehicles from secondary collection points like roadside vats to the disposal ground, adding to the problem of litter. The predominant mode of disposal has been open dumping (94 per cent), and only 5 per cent of the total waste is taken for composting (CPCB 2000). As the collected waste is not separated at source, disposal of mixed waste at the secondary transfer points or at the final tipping ground creates negative externalities in the form of health and environmental costs. For instance, studies on waste pickers in New Delhi (Huisman 1994), Bombay (Konnoth 1991) and Kolkata (DISHA 1996) have established that they are highly susceptible to respiratory and intestinal diseases – especially for women and children. On the other hand, as the dumping fields are mostly open grounds without any seepage proof lining for leachate collection, they involve a huge risk of groundwater contamination. In fact, analysis of the physiochemical characteristics of groundwater samples from tube wells and bore wells near dumping sites in cities like Jammu, Srinagar, Trivandrum and Coimbatore exhibited excessive concentrations of iron and lead in the water samples and in Kochi and Hyderabad, concentration of chloride and total dissolved solids (TDS) in groundwater exceeded the proposed standards (Kumar *et al.* 2009). In Kolkata the leachate collected from the disposal site also demonstrated that the concentrations of solids, biological oxygen demand (BOD) and chemical oxygen demand (COD) are much higher than the acceptable standard (Mandal 2007).

A number of events during the mid-1990s raised public concern about the social cost of the existing system. First was the deadly pneumonic plague in

Table 9.3 MSW management in developing countries across the region

Regions	Waste generation and collection	Waste disposal methods		Recycling/composting/incineration	Institutions and regulations
		Landfill			
Africa	MSW from Accra, Ibandan, Dakar etc. shows a range of per capita generation rates of 0.5–0.8 kg per day. Putrescible organic contents ranging from 35–80 per cent. Mostly municipal waste collection with median collection coverage ranging from 40–50 per cent.	Most of the landfills are open dumps. Tunisia is the only country to have developed a nationwide sanitary landfill programme.		(a) Recycling or material recovery mostly takes place in the informal sector. South Africa has a deposit system for returnable aluminium and tin cans. (b) Two Industrial composting plants in Dakar, Senegal and Abidjan, Côte d'Ivoire closed for mechanical problems in the 1970s. Community composting efforts are scant and mostly seen in peri-urban areas like suburbs of South African cities in Durban and Pretoria. (c) Incineration would not be cost effective owing to the dominance of moisture and organic content in the waste stream.	National Waste Management Strategy and Action Plan in South Africa (1999)

Region	Waste generation and collection	Disposal technology	Recycling, composting and incineration	Policy and legislation
Asia	Waste generation ranging from 0.4–0.9 kg per capita per day. Average generation rate for the low income countries is 0.64. Collection mostly done by the local bodies with cost representing 80–90 per cent of the total budget. Irregular collection with uncollected waste ranging from 20–50 per cent of the total waste generated.	Mostly Low technology sites with open dumping of waste. Kuala Lumpur for instance uses old tin mines as dumping sites. However, some cities of developing country like Bandung, Jakarta Manila have well operated sanitary landfills	(a) Recycling predominantly done by the informal sector except for Vietnam where recycling is done at the city level and is supported by ministry. In Hanoi for instance the recycling industry is mostly in the hands of family businesses. (b) Composting rarely done and that too on a small scale. Even for large cities in East Asia like Bangkok, and Hanoi mechanical composting plants went out of operation due to high operation and maintenance costs. (c) Incinerators are mostly imported and are not suited to local conditions. Besides high moisture content in the waste prevents it from being cost effective.	In Malaysia the National Environmental Policy guides all programmes towards integrated waste management. The Ecological Solid Waste Management Act (2000) in the Philippines requires all local governments to recycle 25 per cent of the waste collected.
Latin America and the Caribbean	Waste generation ranging from 0.3–1 kg per capita per day. Waste rich in moisture and organic content. Both public and private sector involvement in waste collection.	Landfill as the mode of disposal is dominant and has a rising trend. In large number of cases landfills are maintained by private operators. Majority of the landfills do not have scientific standards.	Informal recycling through scavenger cooperatives. Kerbside recycling practiced only in Brazil and Mexico. Community composting more successful relative to centralized composting. Backyard composting more prevalent in rural and poor area. No incinerator operates in this region.	National laws on MSW formulated in Chile, Honduras, Peru, Columbia and Venezuela but there is a large deficiency in compliance.

Source: UNEP (2005).

Surat that broke out in September 1994. The floodwater from the river Tapti completely submerged the low-lying areas of the city in late August. Even after the floodwater receded, there was no attempt on the part of Surat Municipal Corporation to clean up the filth and dead carcasses of animals. The outbreak of plague demonstrated that the health cost from improper management of municipal waste could be substantial. After about two years, in 1996 Ms Almitra H. Patel filed a writ petition in the Supreme Court alleging that the practice of waste disposal followed by the local bodies in India was faulty and had a negative impact on residents' health. The Supreme Court, in response, formed a committee in 1998 to look into all aspects of solid waste management in Class I cities of India. Based on the committee report the MSWMH Rules were drafted in 1999 and finally came into effect from 29 September 2000. The MSWMH Rules (2000) made it mandatory for all the municipal authorities in the country to abide by the following seven directives:

1   Prohibit littering on the streets by ensuring storage of waste at source in two bins: one for biodegradable waste and another for recyclable material.
2   House to house collection of biodegradable and non-biodegradable waste at pre-informed timings.
3   Street sweeping covering all the residential and commercial areas on all the days of the year.
4   Abolition of open storage depots and provision of covered containers or closed body waste storage depots.
5   Transportation of garbage in covered vehicles to prevent nuisance from litter.
6   Treatment of biodegradable waste using composting or waste to energy facilities according to the prescribed standards.
7   Minimize the waste going to the landfill and dispose of only rejects from the treatment plants and inert materials in the landfill.

A closer look at the directives will reveal that adoption of (6) is mostly contingent upon successful implementation of (1) and (2) respectively. On the other hand, whether an agent actually separates garbage at source will depend on the level of his awareness and the cost of the status quo option, i.e. dumping the waste in the mixed state. The case of major stakeholders in terms of quantity of waste generated, i.e. the households, needs to be understood here. Conventional disposal of mixed waste requires significantly lesser resource (say time) than segregation at source prior to collection. Therefore, in the absence of suitable incentives, households will never separate waste at source (Sarkhel 2009). Treatment facilities that accept mixed garbage will have to compromise with the quality of their product ,and ultimately the disposal option may be abandoned on economical grounds.

The emphasis on composting among other disposal options in MSW Rules (2000) evolved out of its historical antecedents in India. Since the 1960s regulatory initiatives in the MSW sector has been designed to promote composting on a centralized scale (Table 9.4). However, large scale composting projects has consistently encountered financial failures due to high operating costs and lack of marketing avenues for the produced organic manure. In fact a study by UNDP (1991) found that out of 11 subsidized mechanized compost plants set up during 1975–85 with a capacity of 150–300 tonnes, only three are operational in 1991. Even these plants are running far below their installed capacity. The large-scale composting projects failed due to their huge operational and transport costs, lack of market demand and also due to promotion of decentralized composting schemes at the local level with the help of community institutions like NGOs since the 1990s (Zurbrugg *et al.* 2004). Though decentralization tackled the issue of capacity utilization, the quality of compost did not improve as source segregation of waste had not been properly implemented. Moreover, frequent complaints about the odours in compost production from community pits have been one of the major problems with such initiatives (Zurbrugg *et al.* 2003).

This inefficiency in the adoption of disposal processes is further exemplified by the status of compliance with MSW Handling Rules (2000) of the 126 Class I cities in India (Asnani 2006) (Table 9.5). It is interesting to note that though more than 36 per cent of the urban local bodies (ULBs) have introduced segregation of recyclables and primary collection, only 9 per cent of them have set up waste processing facilities. On the supply side, this implies that proper source separation of waste has not been introduced. In the absence of properly sorted waste, the quality of the output of the treatment facilities is likely to be below standard. For instance, comparing the municipal compost of 29 cities in India, Saha *et al.* (2010) finds that compost prepared from segregated household waste contains lesser heavy metal than those processed from open sources like vegetable markets, hotels and slaughter houses. Therefore, the expected revenue from the sale of below standard compost output may even fail to cover the huge fixed cost of the treatment facilities and could be pushed much below the break-even

Table 9.4 Policy initiatives for promotion of composting in India prior to MSW rules (2000)

Year	Policy initiatives
1960s	Ministry of Food and Agriculture offered soft loans to urban local bodies for promoting composting of MSW
1969–74	Fourth five-year plan provided grants and loans to state governments for setting up MSW composting facilities
1974	GoI introduced a modified scheme to revive MSW composting facilities in cities with a population over 0.3 million.
1995	High powered committee under the chairmanship of Professor J.S. Bajaj was constituted. More than 35 composting facilities emerged with private sector participation (PSP).

Source: adapted from Hanrahan *et al.* (2006).

point.[12] By and large, this discourages private investment in disposal facilities. The demand side aspects are equally adverse as there is no clear policy regarding the incentives of such facility operators. For instance, an often-raised point for the poor marketability of compost is the adverse terms of trade of organic manure relative to synthetic fertilizers like urea (Patel 2001).

Regional waste disposal: cooperative management of waste

The initial failure of the local bodies to adopt the norms of the MSWMH Rules (2000) shouldn't come as a surprise if their differences in 'efficiency' level are considered. If the garbage collection and disposal service is produced by the municipalities using capital equipment like tractors and handcarts and conservancy labour as the other input then one can judge the efficiency level of the local body by estimating its distance from the production frontier.[13] Naturally, an efficient municipality would incur a relatively lesser cost to abide by the norms of MSWMH Rules (2000) than those that have failed to utilize the already available capital and labour inputs to their full capacity. There are reasons to suspect that the majority of the local bodies in India had low levels of efficiency prior to the promulgation of MSW Rules (2000). On the basis of the physical and chemical characteristics of the city refuse, it has been estimated that a transport capacity of $320 \, m^3$/day would be required to transport the garbage generated per million of the population. However, a study on 44 Indian cities in the mid-1990s revealed that the majority of them failed to qualify on this account (Bhoyar *et al.* 1996). Another survey of 157 Indian cities displayed that most of the local bodies did not satisfy the prevailing benchmark of optimum workforce requirements in garbage collection and disposal (NIUA 1989).Hence, given the initial state, the failure to comply with the improved waste management mandates is not totally unexpected. One way to overcome this inefficiency barrier is to take advantage of the scale economies inherent in the waste collection and disposal activities. Such scale economies arise from the fact that for a sanitary landfill to be economically viable, waste from at least 0.8–1.0 million population is

Table 9.5 Status of compliance of MSW handling rules 2000 by Class I cities as on 1 April 2004

Sl. no.	Compliance options	Compliance rate (% of ULBs)
1	Storage at source	41.77
2	Segregation of recyclables	36.47
3	Primary collection	38.36
4	Street sweeping	78.1
5	Storage depot	28.4
6	Transportation	53.1
7	Processing of waste	9.18
8	Disposal through sanitary landfill	1.73

Source: Asnani (2006).

required per day.[14] As less than 50 per cent of the urban population in India lives in communities of this size, there is a clear need for urban agglomerates to join together to attain the benefits of scale economies (Water and Sanitation Programme 2007).

Such endeavours towards the development of regional facilities are already visible in some states like Andhra Pradesh, Gujarat, Kerala and West Bengal. The common model for all these states are to develop a number of regional waste disposal facilities covering all the ULBs in the state and then assign a group of local bodies to maintain and operate these facilities (Table 9.6). Keeping in mind the fact that regional facilities are deemed to be optimal from the point of view of scale advantages, a long run agenda would be the sustainability of the project that would involve active participation of all stakeholders involved in the project. The stakeholders include local governments, households, private agencies operating the waste disposal facilities and even the informal sector that is mostly outside the public policy realm. Within local governments a key issue is the obeying of sharing norms and enforcement practices like source segregation of waste within its administrative boundary. However, till date regional facilities are formed by exogenous groups and hence the mechanism of exclusion for noncompliance is not available to ensure quality control on the part of individual municipal bodies. This also implies that local groups will be bereft of the efficiency properties of assortative matching accruing from the process of endogenous group formation.[15] Moreover since there is sufficient heterogeneity in terms of production efficiency across local bodies that have not yet formed the group, the disincentive of pairing with location-wise closest but inefficient partners may actually hinder the process of regionalization. In terms of failure to avail scale economies and loss of potential social benefit from this would involve a social deadweight loss, delaying successful adoption of MSWMH Rules (2000) for a long time.

Table 9.6 Institutional arrangement for regional facilities in India

State	Details of regional facility
Andhra Pradesh	134 local bodies to be grouped into 19 clusters; facilities are to be established and operated by private sectors
Gujarat	141 local bodies to be divided into four to six clusters; 45 sites identified for 130 municipalities
West Bengal	25 to 30 regional facilities would be constructed in the state to cover 126 ULBs including six corporations. One regional facility would serve about five ULBs and each city would share the operating and maintenance cost in proportion to the waste delivered for treatment and disposal.
Kerala	State to be divided into six zones, each with its own landfill site for receiving waste from all the towns in that particular zone

Source: Water and Sanitation Programme (2007) and Asnani (2006).

Concluding observations

For developed and developing countries the common thrust of waste management policies is to make alternate waste disposal options economically viable, thereby reducing waste diversion in engineered landfills. In developed countries due to the dominance of dry recyclables like paper and glass and packaging materials in the waste stream, alternative end use of waste relies on recycling and incineration. Hence, user charges targeted at households and packaging responsibilities for industries have been introduced in many areas of Europe and the United States. At the same time serious attempts have been made to replace open dumps by sanitary landfills in these areas.[16] In contrast local bodies in developing countries like India have lagged behind in implementing at source segregation of waste to facilitate biological processing options like composting for its biodegradable waste component. Adoptions of engineered waste disposal facilities have been thwarted due to prohibitive cost and inefficiency of the local bodies. At the same time in terms of imposing user fees for solid waste services the municipalities are lagging behind due to the non-market nature of waste management services in these areas. As a remedy inter-local body arrangements in terms of common disposal facilities have been proposed to capture the economies of scale inherent in waste disposal. Such ventures are already being piloted in many Indian states.

Whether such arrangements would actually outweigh the impact of dispersed efficiency levels of the participating municipalities is an empirical question. One way to address the question would be to have a measure of the average cost (in) efficiency of the local bodies that are grouped to form regional cooperative and compare it with the per unit cost of garbage disposal when it is jointly produced by all the municipalities. This would remain as a future research agenda.

Notes

* In connection with this chapter the supervisory support of Sarmila Banerjee is gratefully acknowledged. For comments on an earlier draft thanks also goes to Vinish Kathuria. The usual disclaimer applies.

1 However, Bel *et al.* (2007) and Bel and Warner (2008) find no significant difference between private and public cost of provision. In fact, Ohlsson (2003) finds public production to be relatively less costly than that provided by private entities in Sweden. More importantly, cost savings from contracting is observed to have eroded away with time raising question marks about the sustainability of privatization efforts (Bel and Costa, 2006).

2 This is a process used to produce methane gas, which can be used as a fuel, by means of bacteria that feed on the waste, when there is little or no oxygen present. A more general term is anaerobic digestion.

3 The number of landfills in the United States fell from 8,000 in 1988 to about 1,800 in 2006 (Jenkins *et al.* 2009).

4 In these densely populated countries almost 50 per cent of the waste goes for incineration, Japan having the highest figure of 78 per cent (Tilly 2004).

5 For instance, the US Supreme Court issued a law by which incinerator ash failing to pass the toxicity standard must be put into specially designed toxic landfills (Fullerton and Raub 2004).

6 Waste hierarchy refers to ordering of waste management options by which waste prevention/minimization option should take priority over recycling/reuse option and the latter should, in turn, take priority over final disposal activities (i.e. landfill, etc.) (Turner 1995). However, adherence to the waste hierarchy differs across countries in Europe. For instance it is strongly enforced in Germany and Netherlands, but countries like France, Italy and Greece implement a weaker version in the sense that here the strong preference stakeholders are free to choose among the options given in Waste Hierarchy without any strong preference for the sequence (Buclet and Goddard 2000).

7 The acronym 'GmbH' stands for *Gesellschaft mit beschränkter Haftung* which, translated literally, means a 'company with limited liability'. This consortium had the job of organizing and financing differentiated waste collection, performing the required selection of waste types, accomplishing the objectives set by the government. To finance the system a 'green dot' was printed on the packaging itself against a payment.

8 The classification of countries according to income levels is based on the following criterion: US$490 GNP per capita for low income, US$1,410 GNP per capita for middle income and $30,990 for high income countries in 1995 US dollars (Hoornweg *et al.* 1999).

9 Another major impediment towards adoption of incineration is the associated high capital cost. Japan, for instance, spent 45 per cent of its total budget in incineration facilities and only 10 per cent on transportation and disposal of city garbage in 1993 (Hoornweg *et al.* 1999).

10 India can be considered as a representative for developing countries on two aspects: first in terms of per capita GDP (in US$), and second, using the International Monetary Fund's (IMF) definition of developing countries in *World Economic Outlook* issues. According to per capita GDP those with per capita GDP greater than US$10,000 are termed developed while per capita GDP for the developing and LDCs ranges from US$5,000–US$1,000 and greater than US$1,000. For India the per capita GDP at constant prices in 2007 was US$941.557 (World Economic Outlook Database 2008) clearly showing its place in the group of developing countries.

11 Population and waste generation have a strong positive association. Based on the data of waste generation of 59 cities of India collected by the National Environmental Engineering and Research Institute (NEERI) the correlation coefficient between waste generation (tonne/day) and population density comes out to be 0.57. Using the waste generation figures (tonne/day) of 28 cities in Akolkar (2005) and population figures of 2001 census, the correlation co-efficient between the two is found to be 0.87. The correlation coefficient is significant at less than 5 per cent in both cases.

12 In fact due to the unavailability of properly segregated waste the compost processing plant in Kolkata run by M/s Eastern Organic Fertilizer Limited had to cease its operation in 2003. Also there were problems of marketing the produced compost (Chattopadhyay *et al.* 2009).

13 Of course this refers to technical efficiency that can either be input-oriented or output-oriented and can also be derived from the cost and the profit frontier.

14 The economically viable capacity for a sanitary landfill is assumed to be 250–350 tons/day. It is assumed for India the average per capita waste generation per day is 0.3 kg (Zhu *et al.* 2008).

15 Charness and Yang (2008) show that along with exclusion, ensuring sufficient mobility in the form of reappointing members within the same or even different groups can serve as an efficient mechanism for sustaining cooperation.

16 Between 1978 and 2002 there has been an almost eight-fold decrease in the number of open dumps in the United States. These have been replaced by 200 sanitary landfills that receive almost 75 per cent of the nation's waste (Water and Sanitation Programme 2007).

References

Akolkar, A.B. (2005) 'Status of Solid Waste Management in India, Implementation Status of Municipal Solid Waste Management and Handling Rules 2000', New Delhi: Central Pollution Control Board.

Asnani, P.U. (2006) 'Solid Waste Management', in A. Rastogi (ed.), *India Infrastructure Report*, New Delhi: Oxford University Press.

Bel, G. and Costas, A. (2006) 'Do Public Sector Reforms get Rusty? Local Privatization in Spain', *Journal of Policy Reform*, 9: 1–24.

Bel, G. and Warner, M.E. (2008) 'Does Privatization of Solid Waste and Water Services Reduce Costs? A Review of Empirical Studies', *Resources, Conservation and Recycling*, 52: 1337–1348.

Bel, G., Hebdon, R. and Warner, M. (2007) 'Local Government Reform: Privatization and its Alternatives', *Local Government Studies*, 33: 507–515.

Bhoyar, R.V., Titus, S.K., Bhide, A.D. and Khanna, P. (1996) 'Municipal and Solid Waste Management in India', *Indian Association of Environmental Management*, 23: 53–64.

Buclet, N. and Goddard, O. (2000) 'Municipal Solid Waste Management in Europe: A Comparison of National Regimes' in N. Buclet and O. Goddard (ed.) *Municipal Solid Waste Management in Europe: A Comparative Case Study in Building Regimes*, Dordrecht: Kluwer Academic Publishers.

Central Pollution Control Board (2000) 'Status of Municipal Solid Waste Generation, Collection, Treatment and Disposal in Class I Cities', New Delhi: Ministry of Forest and Environment, Government of India.

Charness, G. and Yang, C. (2008) 'Exit, Exclusion and Mergers: Endogenous Group Formation and Public Goods Provision' Working Paper No. 13, Santa Barbara: Department of Economics, University of California.

Chattopadhyay, S., Dutta, A. and Ray, S. (2009) 'Municipal Solid Waste Management in Kolkata, India – A Review', *Waste Management*, 29: 1449–1458.

Direct Initiative for Social and Health Action (DISHA), Centre for Occupational and Environmental Health Society for Participatory Research in Asia, and Centre for Study of Man and Environment (1996) *A Rapid Assessment Survey of the Health and Environmental Impacts of Solid Waste Recycling*, Calcutta: DISHA.

Fullerton, D. and Raub, A. (2004) *Economic Analysis of Solid Waste Policies in Addressing the Economics of Waste*, Paris: OECD.

Furedy, C. (1992) 'Garbage: Exploring Non-conventional Options in Asian Cities', *Environment and Urbanization*, 4(2): 43–60.

Hanrahan, D., Srivastava, S. and Ramkrishna, A.S. (2006) *Improving Management of Municipal Solid Waste in India: Overview and Challenges*, Washington, DC: World Bank.

Hong, S. and Adams, R.M. (1999) 'Household Responses to Price Incentives for Recycling: Some Further Evidence', *Land Economics* 75(4): 505–514.

Hoornweg, D., Thomas, L. and Verma, K. (1999) *What a Waste: Solid Waste Management in Asia*, Washington, DC: World Bank.

Houtven, G.L. Van and Morris, G.E. (1999) 'Household Behavior under Alternative Pay-as-you-throw Systems for Solid Waste Disposal', *Land Economics*, 75(4): 515–537.

Huisman, M. (1994) 'The Position of Waste Pickers in Solid Waste Management', in I. Baud and H. Schenk (ed.) *Solid Waste Management: Modes, Assessments, Appraisals, and Linkages in Bangalore*, New Delhi: Manohar.

International Monetary Fund (various issues) *World Economic Outlook*, Washington, DC: IMF.

Jenkins, R.R., Martinez, S.A., Palmer, K. and Podolsky, M.J. (2003) 'The Determinants of Household Recycling: A Material Specific Analysis of Recycling Program Features and Unit Pricing', Jour*nal of Environmental Economics and Management*, 45(2): 294–318.

Jenkins, R.R., Koptis, E. and Simpson, D. (2009) 'Policy Monitor – The Evolution of Solid and Hazardous Waste Regulation in the United States', *Review of Environmental Economics and Policy*, 3(1): 104–120.

Johnstone, N. and Labonne, J. (2004) 'Generation of Household Solid Waste in OECD Countries: An Empirical Analysis Using Macroeconomic Data' *Land Economics*, 80(4): 529–538.

Kinnaman, T. and Fullerton, D. (2000) 'The Economics of Residential Waste Solid Management', in T. Tietenberg and H. Folmer (eds) *The International Year Book of Environmental and Resource Economics 2000/2001*, Cheltenham: Edward Elgar.

Konnoth, N. (1991) 'Your Clean City at Whose Cost: A Study on the Working Conditions and Occupation Hazards at the Dumping Sites of Bombay', Bombay: Forum for Environmental Concern.

Kumar, S., Bhattacharyya, J.K., Vaidya, A.N., Chakrabarti, T., Devotta, S. and Akolkar, A.B. (2009) 'Assessment of the Status of Municipal Solid Waste Management in Metro Cities, State Capitals, Class I Cities, and Class II Towns in India: An Insight', *Waste Management*, 23: 883–895.

Mandal, M. (2007) 'Leachate from Municipal Solid Waste – Generation, Characteristics and Effects', Unpublished Master of Engineering Thesis, Shibpur: Bengal Engineering and Science University.

National Institute of Urban Affairs (1989) 'Upgrading Municipal Services: Norms and Financial Implications', vols. 1–2, New Delhi: NIUA.

Ohlsson, H. (2003) 'Ownership and Production Costs. Choosing between Public Production and Contracting-out in the Case of Swedish Refuse Collection', *Fiscal Studies*, 24 (4): 451–476.

Organization for Economic Co-operation and Development (2007) *OECD Factbook 2007*, Paris: OECD.

Patel, A.H. (2001) 'Enriching India's Soil', *Down To Earth*. Online, available at: www.downtoearth.org.in/node/123/2001–11–15 (accessed 3 September 2010).

Saha J., Panwar, K.N. and Singh, M.V. (2010) 'An Assessment of Municipal Solid Waste Compost Quality Produced in Different Cities of India in The Perspective of Developing Quality Control Indices', *Waste Management*, 30(2): 192–201.

Sarkhel, P. (2009) 'Source Separation and Organic Waste Disposal: Policy Options for Household Waste Management in Developing Countries' *Arthaniti*, 8(1–2): 50–63.

Sharholy, M., Ahmad, K., Mahmood, G. and Trivedi, R.C. (2008) 'Municipal Solid Waste Management in Indian Cities: A Review', *Waste Management*, 28: 459–467.

Singhal, S. and Pandey, S. (2001) 'Solid Waste Management in India: Status and Future Directions' *TERI Information Monitor on Environment and Science*, 6(1): 1–4.

Tavares, A.F.F. (2005) 'Look What the Cat Dragged in: National Responses to the EU Packaging and Packaging Waste Directive' paper submitted to Subtopic IV (Regulatory Powers of National Governments in a Globalized Economy) of International Institute of Administrative Sciences Conference, Berlin, 20–23 September 2005.

Tilly, S. de. (2004) 'Waste Generation and Related Policies: Broad Trends over the Last Ten Years'. Online, available at: http://ewaste.pbworks.com/f/Economics+of+waste.pdf (accessed 2 May 2010).

Turner, R.K. (1995) 'Waste Management', in H. Folmer, H.L. Gabel and H. Opschoor (eds) *Principles of Environmental and Resource Economics – A Guide for Students and Decision Makers*, Cheltenham: Edward Elgar.

United Nations Development Programme, World Bank and Regional Water and Sanitation Group for South Asia (1991) 'Indian Experience on Composting as Means of Resource Recovery', in *Proceedings of the UNDP/WB Water Supply and Sanitation Program Workshop on Waste Management Policies*, Singapore, 1–5 July 1991.

United Nations Environment Programme (2005) *Solid Waste Management*, Volume I, Nairobi: UNEP.

Water and Sanitation Programme (2007) *Implementing Integrated Solid Waste Management Systems in India: Moving towards the Regional Approach*, Washington, DC: World Bank.

Whinston, T. and Glachant, M. (1996) 'Voluntary Agreements Between Industry and Government: The Case of Recycling Regulations', in F. Leveque (ed.) *Environmental Policy in Europe: Industry, Competition and the Policy Process*, Cheltenham, Edward Elgar.

World Bank (2009) 'World Development Report', Washington, DC: World Bank.

Zhu, D., Asnani, P.U., Zurbrugg, C., Anapolsky, S. and Mani, S. (2008) *Improving Municipal Solid Waste Management in India: A Sourcebook for Policy Makers and Practitioners*, Washington, DC: World Bank.

Zurbrugg, C., Drescher, S., Patel, A. and Saratchandra, H.C. (2003) 'Taking a Closer Look at Decentralized Composting Schemes – Lessons from India', Asian Society for Environmental Protection (ASEP) Newsletter, 1–10.

Zurbrugg, C., Drescher, S., Patel, A. and Saratchandra, H.C. (2004) 'Decentralised Composting of Urban Waste – An Overview of Community and Private Initiatives in Indian Cities' *Waste Management*, 24: 655–662.

10 Environmental cost of biomedical waste management

A case study of Chennai city

S. Srividhya and Paul P. Appasamy

Introduction

The World Health Organization (WHO) Regional Office for Europe convened a meeting on hospital waste management at Bergen, Norway in 1983, which was the first international forum to discuss the issue of biomedical waste (BMW) management. With expansion of health infrastructure in the country, BMW in India is also on the rise. In this background, the purpose of the present chapter is two-fold: (a) to highlight the environmental impacts related to BMW and the need to manage these wastes, and (b) to estimate the costs of managing BMW in a metropolitan city using a case study of Chennai.

The indiscriminate disposal of BMW attracted the attention of the Supreme Court of India, which has from time to time issued instructions regarding the environmentally sound management of solid and hazardous wastes. The Ministry of Environment and Forest, Government of India (GoI) brought out the Bio-Medical Waste (Management and Handling) Rules in 1998 (BMW Rules),[1] which is the primary instrument for regulating BMW in India.

The quantity of BMW generated varies depending on the hospital policies and practices and the type of care being provided. The quantity of the BMW generated in developed countries varies from 1–5 kg/bed/day while the corresponding figure for developing countries is around 1–2 kg/bed/day (Yadav 2001). According to a WHO report, while approximately 85 per cent of hospital wastes are non hazardous, 10 per cent are infectious and the remaining 5 per cent are non infectious but hazardous (Yadav 2001).

In India, generation of municipal solid waste (MSW), industrial hazardous waste and BMW has been increasing due to population growth, economic growth, life style changes and urbanization, etc. BMW is among the most hazardous types of waste and could pose human health risks as it is contaminated with disease carrying pathogens. Therefore, it is essential to implement safe and reliable methods for handling it. However, there are costs involved in BMW handling and disposal. Under the current framework, private collectors transport and dispose wastes from private hospitals while public hospitals dump the waste in the municipal landfills. A substantial amount of BMW is also dumped into the MSW collection points (dustbins) from where rag pickers collect and sell reusable materials.

The chapter is arranged along the following lines. First the potentially harmful environmental impacts of BMW are discussed, followed by the regulatory framework in India. Two case studies are presented next, one covering on-site costs and the other covering off-site costs. Finally, an estimate is made on the costs of managing BMW in the city of Chennai.

Biomedical waste generation in India

It is estimated that hospitals in India have approximately six lakh beds which generate 1,500 tonne of BMW per day. For instance Tamil Nadu (TN), a leading Indian state, accounts for 50,000 hospital beds and generates 120 tonne of waste per day. The number of hospitals in India has increased due to several reasons, including the following:

• Rapid increase in the urban population;
• Increase in income, literacy and longevity creating greater demand for healthcare;
• Proliferation of private hospitals in towns and cities due to inadequate public facilities.

There is a direct relationship between wastes generated by hospitals and the number of hospitals in a city. Poor management of these hospital wastes can cause serious problems to healthcare personnel, patients and the citizens. The generators of BMW have to incur costs to reduce or avoid damage to the environment by investing in BMW management both on-site and off-site. The focus of the present analysis is on both on-site and off-site costs incurred by private hospitals in Chennai in order to comply with the BMW Rules. In addition, in the case of the public hospitals, it is possible to estimate the opportunity costs of not disposing their infectious waste properly in terms of the costs incurred by private hospitals.

Environmental impacts[2]

The improper management of BMW causes serious environmental problems in terms of air, water and land pollution leading to serious health hazards (Karnataka SPCB undated). The nature of pollutants can be classified into three sub-categories; namely, biological, chemical and radioactive. Environmental problems can arise due to the mere generation of BMW and from the very process of its handling, treatment and disposal. Although pollution cannot be mitigated completely, it can be reduced to a large extent through proper management of BMW.

Air pollution

Indoor air pollution

Pathogens present in the BMW can enter and remain in the air in an institution for a long period in the form of spores or as the pathogen itself. Exposure to this contamination can result in hospital acquired infections or occupational health hazards. The patients, attendants and health staff also have a chance of contracting infections caused due to pathogens or spores, which are air borne. However putting the waste properly in covered containers and segregation at source can reduce this type of pollution.

Ambient air pollution

When waste without treatment is being transported outside the institution or dumped openly, the pathogens present in the waste enter the atmosphere. These pathogens then eventually enter drinking water (through leaching and runoff), food-chains, soil, etc. and remain in the air for a long time causing diseases. Among other disposal practices, open burning should be strictly avoided as it emits furans, which can also lead to serious health hazards.

Water pollution

The water pollution from BMW can occur through several channels. First, if the BMW is dumped in low-lying areas (i.e. areas characterized by shallow aquifers) or water bodies, it can also cause severe water pollution through leaching and runoff. Second, the untreated hospital effluent when let into sewers can cause water pollution. Third, the pathogens present in the waste can leach out from landfill sites and contaminate the groundwater or surface water through runoff. Poor landfilling technology (unlined and uncovered) can cause water pollution. Excess nutrient leachate and runoff such as nitrates and phosphates from landfills can cause groundwater pollution and surface water eutrophication. The strict standards for disposal of wastewater from hospitals should be maintained as proper waste management practices reduce water pollution considerably.

Land pollution

The final disposal of all BMW considerably affects land resources. Even in the post-treatment phase wastewater is discharged on land, and hence land pollution is inevitable. However, it can be minimized to a great extent through proper precautions adopted against the following pollution routes. First, open dumping of BMW is a major cause for land pollution. Second, landfilling is also harmful to a limited extent. Third, soil pollution is also caused by infectious wastes, discarded medicines, chemicals used in treatment, incineration ash and other waste generated during treatment processes. Excessive amounts of trace elements and other elements including heavy metals in soil are harmful to crops and are also harmful to animals and human beings. Finally, radioactive waste generated from medical institutions can cause soil pollution. Cadavers, protective clothing and absorbent paper used in the nuclear medicine imaging laboratory are also end up in the environment as solid waste and contribute to soil pollution.

Health hazards

According to the WHO reports, over the last decades global life expectancy has improved consistently. However, deaths owing to infectious diseases are on the rise. A study conducted by the WHO in 1996 revealed that 50,000 people die every day due to infectious diseases. Improper BMW management is one of the causes for increasing incidence of infection diseases, where water, air and land (soil) act as media to spread bacterial, virus-borne and other protozoa-borne diseases (Basavanthappa 2008). Blood, body fluid and body secretions, which are constituents of BMW, harbour most of the viruses, bacteria and parasites that cause serious infection.

Improper disposal of BMW and emissions from incinerators or open burning also leads to exposure to human health hazards. Harmful chemicals such as dioxins and furans can cause serious health hazards to wildlife. Certain heavy metals can affect the reproductive health of the animals.

Regulatory framework in India

According to the BMW Rules and its subsequent amendment in 2003, BMW means 'any waste that is generated during the diagnosis, treatment or immunization of human beings or animals'. The salient features of the BMW Rules are noted in the following:

- The owner/proprietor of the healthcare institution generating BMW should take all possible steps to ensure that the wastes generated are handled without causing adverse impact on human health and environment.
- Every owner/proprietor of the healthcare institution generating, collecting, storing, transporting, treating, and disposing of BMW should obtain authorization from the concerned state pollution control board.
- Every occupier should ensure requisite treatment of BMW at a common waste treatment facility or any other treatment facility.
- BMW should be segregated into containers/bags at the point of generation.
- No untreated wastes should be kept beyond 48 hours.
- The concerned municipal body should continue to pick up and transport segregated non-BMW for disposal at a municipal dumpsite.
- BMW have been classified into ten categories and the method of their disposal has also been prescribed.

All hospitals with more than 30 beds need to comply with the BMW Rules. The regulatory agency is the respective state pollution control board. For instance, the role of the Tamil Nadu Pollution Control Board (TNPCB) is to authorize and implement these rules in the state of TN. The TNPCB monitors whether the hospitals and common biomedical facilities are operating in compliance with the rules. Currently, it is persuading all private hospitals to join the common facility and abide by the rules. If the hospitals do not comply, then legal actions in terms of closure or power cut are imposed on them. However, there is no monetary penalty being imposed at the present time. The TNPCB has also prepared a list of private hospitals that comply with the rules. As a result of the evolving policy framework, all hospitals must bring about an efficient waste management system and train all the staff and people working there on how to segregate and handle waste.

Methodology

This chapter focuses mainly on estimating the costs of managing BMW, which effectively is the cost incurred in order to comply with the BMW Rules. The cost includes both on-site as well as off-site costs. On-site costs can be defined as the costs incurred by hospitals for managing the BMW within their premises. Off-site costs include the costs of transport and disposal of infectious BMW in a central facility and non infectious waste in the municipal landfill. The total off-site cost consists of two components: capital or fixed costs and variable costs. Fixed cost includes a building to house the incinerator, cost of the incinerator and other equipment. On the other hand the variable cost includes electricity and diesel charges, transport costs and wages. The off-site costs are met through user charges paid by the hospitals to the private collectors.

In the present context, one private hospital was chosen to study the extent of on-site costs and one private collector was chosen to analyse the off-site costs in the city of Chennai. The total cost of managing the waste is the sum of on-site and off-site costs. If the private hospital and the centralized BMW management facility follow best management practices, then the total cost of waste management, expressed as the cost per bed per day is the cost of meeting the BMW management standards of India, assuming that the cost per bed per day is similar for most Indian cities. The problem of measuring the environmental damage caused by BMW is beyond the scope of this study. Thus, the present analysis focuses on the costs of meeting the standards (similar to abatement cost studies of pollution control) and not on the associated benefits in terms of lower damages.

The two case studies selected in the present analysis are:

*   Sundaram Medical Foundation (SMF) – for on-site costs
*   Tamil Nadu Waste Management Private Limited (TWML) – for off-site costs

Sundaram Medical Foundation

The SMF has taken the utmost care in dealing with BMW management within their premises. The current method of disposal is preferred to the previous method where they installed an incinerator in the hospital and handled wastes from segregation till final disposal. This incurred heavy capital costs. After the imposition of regulation on incinerator use within residential areas by the municipal authority, hospitals had to remove the incinerator and dispose their wastes in a central facility. This is expected to lead to specialization and cost effectiveness in BMW management in general and also could reduce impacts on the local environment. The centralized facility is expected to result in better handling of the wastes. However, the problem of improper waste disposal persists, as the government hospitals have not tied up with the centralized facility.

The SMF has set up a waste management department, which comes under the housekeeping department. They have well trained employees in their payroll who collect BMW from all five floors of the hospital with the help of a trolley. After collection, the wastes are passed on to the central facility for disposal. The wastes are not stored for more than 48 hours. The central facility collects BMW on a daily basis except Sundays. The burden of BMW expenses on the hospital is negligible. For instance, the BMW expense for SMF is Rs.44,559 per year in 2007–08 prices which amounts to 0.4 per cent of their operations and maintenance budget and 0.25 per cent of their total revenue. The recurring cost is high because of the expense on plastic bags which amount to Rs.13,550 per year, nearly 60 per cent of the total on-site recurring costs. The plastic bags used in the process are non-chlorinated in nature, and can be incinerated.[3]

Tamil Nadu Waste Management Private Limited

TWML started India's first BMW management facility in the private sector, at Dammaiguda, Andhra Pradesh. Every day (except on Sundays) they collect wastes from hospitals, which jointly have a total number of 4,500 beds. A month-wise detailed breakup of the amount of wastes handled by TWML during 2005 is provided in Table 10.1.

However a point of concern is that TWML is operating below capacity. While the incinerator capacity is 60 tonne per month, on an average only 15.3 tonne per

Table 10.1 Quantity of waste handled by Tamil Nadu Waste Management Limited (TWML) in 2005

Month	Incinerated (kg.) quantity	Sterilized (kg.) quantity
February	16,764	1,336
March	15,849	3,556
April	14,323	3,458
May	15,774	4,082
June	15,744	4,082
July	13,657	3,506
August	13,735	3,316
September	14,631	4,993
October	13,699	3,079
November	16,375	2,500
December	17,760	2,340
Total	168,311	36,248

Source: Primary Survey (TWML).

month is incinerated. The capacity utilization could improve only if more hospitals comply with the BMW Rules and join the centralized facility for disposal. Nevertheless, the establishment of a common BMW management facility has improved the BMW handling situation among private hospitals in Chennai through specialization in a cost effective manner. In particular, the pollution caused by multiple incinerators is reduced by having a single facility away from residential locations.

Estimation of costs of managing BMW

In this background, the present analysis intends to analyse the cost structure of BMW disposal among private hospitals in Chennai. The costs are estimated separately for on-site collection and off-site disposal and then from that calculation total costs on per bed per day basis are estimated. The case studies developed here can be extrapolated to estimate the total costs of hospital waste management for Chennai.

The city of Chennai had a population of about 4.2 million in 2001 within the corporation limits while around six million people lived in the metropolitan areas. There were 130 private hospitals with 6,197 beds and several public hospitals with 9,991 beds that have registered with the TNPCB. This however might be an underestimate because of meagre availability of data. During the period of the study most of the private hospitals disposed of their wastes through a central facility. However, the public hospitals treated their infectious wastes on-site and disposed of them in the municipal landfill. The quantity of BMW generated in Chennai in 2007 has been estimated at 16.1 tonne/day.

At present the public hospitals do not utilize the services of the private waste treatment facilities. This non-utilization may result from the price that the private collectors charge. The 'opportunity cost' for public hospitals could be estimated from the present case study. However, the actual cost of disposal may be lower if there is no profit margin.

Case study 1: on-site costs

The SMF, a 150-bedded hospital, is a 'non-profit' organization. It has five floors and 21 rooms. It is one of the best hospitals in terms of BMW management and has received an award from an NGO for its commendable performance. The process of managing BMW starts from segregation at source till disposal of wastes, which is outlined in Figure 10.1.

There are two types of wastes: infectious and non-infectious wastes. Infectious wastes are collected by the private facility while non-infectious waste is given to the municipal corporation. There are costs involved in each step from segregation till collection by the central facility. SMF has an efficient sharps management system. It has seven needle destroyers, which destroy the needles and syringes and dispose the wastes in a black bag, which is then collected by the central facility for landfill. The associated costs are noted in Table 10.2.

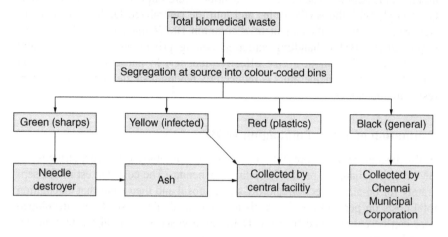

Figure 10.1 Flowchart of biomedical waste disposal in Sundaram Medical Foundation (SMF) (source: Primary Survey, SMF).

It is assumed in the present analysis that boots and gloves are provided to the waste handling staffs as a part of the uniform and thus not included in waste management expenditure. The capital costs are amortized and a simple method of amortization is used. The total capital cost of Rs.52,093 (approximately US$1,166) is divided by the life of the material, which is assumed to be ten years. The average annual capital cost is Rs.5,209 and annualized capital cost per bed is Rs.34.73 (i.e. Rs.5,209/150 beds), and annual capital cost per bed per day is Rs.0.10, which is negligible.

The next step involved calculation of various recurring costs undertaken by SMF, as documented in Table 10.3. It is observed that the total recurring cost is found to be Rs.39,350 per month. The on-site recurring cost is revealed as Rs.23,350 per month. Dividing the figure by the scale of the operation, the on-site recurring cost per day per bed therefore turns out to be Rs.5.18. The total recurring costs can be split into Rs.5.18 bed/day for on-site management of

Table 10.2 Costs of materials needed for BMW on-site management (in 2007–08 prices)

Material	Numbers	Price (Rs./number)	Total (Rs)
Needle destroyer	7	2,500	17,500
Bins	75	95	7,125
Hard plastic bins	–	–	12,718
Trolley	1	1,250	1,250
Shed and electrical work	–	–	13,500
Total			52,093

Source: primary survey (SMF).

Table 10.3 On-site recurring costs (per month) (in 2007–08 prices)

Particulars	Numbers	Price/wages, salaries/ charges (Rs.)	Total (Rs./month)
On-site costs			
Manpower	2	2,500/month	5,000
Plastic bags	–	–	13,550
Disinfectant	30 litre	160/litre	4,800
Subtotal (a)			23,350
Off-site costs			
Charges paid to Chennai Municipal Corporation for general waste	–	–	2,500
Central facility (TWML)	150 beds	3/bed/day	13,500
Subtotal (b)			16,000
Total (a+b)			39,350

Source: primary survey (SMF).

BMW and Rs.3 bed/day for centralized disposal (charges to central facility) and Rs.0.55 bed/day for charges paid to the Chennai municipal corporation. The charges paid to the centralized facility are passed on to the in-patients while the on-site costs are a part of operation and maintenance expenses.

Therefore, the annual total cost of BMW management for SMF turns out to be the sum of the annualized capital cost of Rs.5,209 and the annual recurring cost of Rs.472,200 (Rs.39,350*12), which is Rs.477,409. On the basis of the calculations, the cost of waste management is Rs.8.72 bed/day. The burden of expenses on BMW to total expenses (Rs.107.59 lakh per month) is 4.44 per cent and of the corresponding figure with respect to total revenue (Rs.174.72 lakh per month) is 2.73 per cent.

Case study 2: off-site costs

The quantity of waste generated by the 4,500 beds that TWML (2005) deals with in a particular year amounts to 204,559 kg or 205 tonne.

The process followed by TWML from collection till final disposal is explained with the help of Figure 10.2. Each step is associated with certain costs. The process of disposal has been structured with the objective to minimize or reduce damage to environment.

The main modes of BMW destruction have been sterilization using incinerators and autoclaves. The incinerators are well provided with filters to control air pollution. Incinerators are the best method for treating BMW for two reasons. First, incinerators eliminate the infectious organisms that are present in BMW. Second, the method is economical and substantially reduces the volume of wastes which need to be disposed in a landfill site. The ashes from the incinerator are stored in a

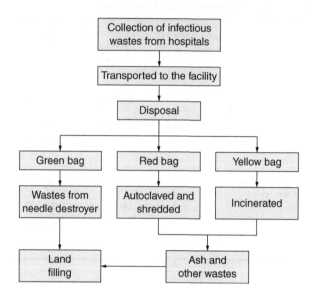

Figure 10.2 Flowchart of final disposal of wastes in Tamil Nadu Waste Management Limited (TWML) (source: Primary Survey, TWML).

secured landfill site. There has been a debate on the use of incinerators because of
the toxicity of the ash and dioxins that they produce which are again harmful to the
environment (WHO 2004). As suggested by the Agarwal (1998), autoclaves could
be a better method as compared to incinerators for BMW management.

Capital cost

The cost of disposing BMW includes both capital costs and recurring costs, the
former is important for determining off-site costs. For TWML, capital costs
include the costs associated with land and building, incinerator (including annual
handling charges), etc. The capital costs calculated for the TWML operation are
presented in Table 10.4. It is observed from the table that the total annualized
capital cost is Rs.1,614,386 (approximately US$36,176) and per day capital cost
is Rs.4,423 (approximately US$99). Since the total number of beds served by
the TWML operation is 4,500, the capital cost turns out to be Rs.0.98 bed/day,
which is negligible.

Table 10.5 denotes the decomposition of recurring/variable cost for the TWML
operation, as revealed by the present survey. The monthly variable cost is found to
be Rs.160,110 (US$3,588) and the corresponding per day per bed figure is Rs.1.2.
Therefore, total cost of off-site disposal constitutes of the total variable cost
(Rs.1.2 bed/day) and the total annualized capital cost (Rs.0.98 bed/day), the sum of
which turns out to be Rs.2.18 bed/day. However, the central facility charges to the
hospital at the rate of Rs.3 bed/day, which sets their profits at Rs.0.82 bed/day.

Table 10.4 Capital costs of TWML (in 2007–08 prices)

Items	Life (in year)	Amount (Rs.)	Amortized annual capital cost (Rs.)[3]
Land and building		14,289,000	1,143,120[1]
Incinerator	15	1,063,000[2]	70,866
Autoclave	15	1,395,000	93,000
Shredder	20	74,000	3,700
Diesel generator	10	470,000	47,000
DM plant and filters	10	129,000	12,900
Transport	10	2,438,000	243,800
Total		19,858,000	1,614,386

Source: primary survey (TWML).

Notes
1 Includes only the interest on the investment on land and building assuming a nominal interest of 12.5 per cent.
2 Includes handling charges of Rs.3.35 lakh.
3 Method of amortization is amortized capital cost=cost of the item/life (in years).

Estimation of total biomedical waste management costs for Chennai private hospitals

From the official data sources on healthcare sector in TN, it is observed that there are 16,188 hospital beds in Chennai (6,197 beds in the private sector hospitals and 9,991 beds under public hospitals). From the estimation of off-site and on-site costs in the present analysis, it can be concluded that the total cost per bed per day is Rs.8.73. It is also assumed that the cost structure of the hospitals is similar, i.e. costs incurred by public hospitals are the same as those of the private hospitals. This assumption enables one to predict the costs of managing BMW in Chennai, and the calculation is reported in Table 10.6.

It is observed from Table 10.6 that the total annual costs of BMW management for Chennai is the sum of private and public hospital costs which stands at Rs.515.82 lakh (approximately US$11,558,992). This is 0.002 per cent of the

Table 10.5 Off-site recurring costs (per month) (in 2007–08 Prices)

Items	Amount (Rs)
Incinerator maintenance	7,500
Autoclave	2,000
Diesel generator and ETP filters	2,000
Vehicle maintenance	9,000
Diesel consumption	59,110
Manpower	80,500
Total	160,110

Source: primary survey (TWML).

Table 10.6 Estimated costs of biomedical waste management in Chennai (in 2007–08 prices)

	Cost per bed per day (Rs.)	Annual cost for private hospitals (Rs. lakh)	Annual cost for public hospitals (Rs. lakh)	Total annual BMW cost (Rs. lakh)
Total on-site cost	5.18	117.17	188.90	306.07
Total off-site cost (central facility)	3.00	67.86	109.40	177.26
Other off-site cost (charges paid to Chennai Municipal Corporation)	0.55	12.44	20.06	32.50
Total cost (a+b+c)	8.73	197.46	318.36	515.82

Source: constructed by the authors.

gross state domestic product of TN in 2007–08 (Rs.304,989 crore – at current prices) and 0.02 per cent of the tax revenue of the government of TN in 2007–08 (Rs.30,988 crore). The hypothetical cost of BMW disposal from government hospitals is estimated to be Rs.3.18 crore (approximately US\$7,126,050) per year. The government can meet this expense either by collecting a fee/surcharge from the patients or from general tax revenues through making a provision accordingly in the budget. Moreover the government need to ensure that hospital staffs, nurses, maids and doctors should be well trained in handling BMW, which is an attainable target.

Conclusion

It is not just industries, but also hospitals and clinics that cause pollution and environmental hazards. This implies that necessary importance should be accorded to this sector as it might otherwise cause considerable damage to the environment and also to human health. Though compliance with the BMW Rules requires hospitals to make necessary investments, their long run implications are far-reaching for society as well as the concerned medical unit itself.

BMW disposal is also increasingly important in the Indian context from another perspective; namely, international trade in health services. Chakraborty and Dilwaria (2011) have shown that medical services export from India is increasing over the period; medical tourism being a dominant form among the category. People from all the continents, including EU, United States, Africa, South Asia, Southeast Asia and West Asia have travelled to India in recent years, due to the high quality of medical treatment (both diagnostic and surgical) available at an affordable price. Chakraborty and Dilwaria (2011) also noted that lack of insurance portability for EU and US citizens is a major problem in expanding the inflow of foreign patients in the country. One way of correcting the present state of affairs would be to ensure that Indian hospitals obtain accreditation by Joint Commission International (JCI)/Joint Commission for the Accreditation of Hospitals and Healthcare Organizations (JCAHO), which is based on all the health related parameters including quality of patient care, accessibility, personal and equipment hygiene, safe BMW disposal and other various processes, etc. Hence better a BMW disposal record and health facilities would be instrumental for an Indian health unit to obtain a better standing both locally as well as globally. However, only a handful of hospitals in India are currently JCI accredited.

While the inflow of foreign patients to Delhi (North India), Mumbai or Ahmedabad (West India) is considerable, a significant number also travel to the southern states of Karnataka, Kerala and TN for their treatment. The present case study for Chennai city brings out an interesting aspect for policy consideration in this regard as well.

The analysis for estimation of on-site costs based on the field survey underlines that per bed per day BMW disposal cost is quite negligible, which can therefore be passed on to the patients. With the economic growth in India in recent period and the associated rising income level, the 'Environmental Kuznets Curve' effects are likely to set in among a significant section of the citizens. In other words, the willingness to pay more for better quality of 'clean and green' health services are likely to increase among the population in the medium and long run, which will make the BMW disposal initiatives sustainable. On the other hand, the estimation analysis involving off-site costs show that the central facility of the TWML is making a normal economic profit in the process of BMW disposal. This finding is also a healthy sign in the urban Indian context.

However, given the economies of scale, the cost structure calculated in a populous city like Chennai (which is also likely to hold good in other metropolitan cities) in the present framework may not be replicated in a relatively smaller city/ town. The high compliance cost there may create perverse incentives not to fully implement the necessary measures. Therefore the government needs to play a proactive role through standardized inspection procedures and necessary penal actions against the violators to ensure safe BMW disposal throughout the country.

Notes

1 The detailed information can be accessed from the Ministry of Environment and Forest web-resources. Online, available at: http://envfor.nic.in/legis/hsm/biomed.html (last accessed on August 4, 2009).
2 This section relies heavily on Karnataka SPCB (undated).
3 The BMW Rules put restrictions on incineration of polyvinyl chloride (PVC) and other related products like plastic bags, given the potential adverse impact on the environment.

References

Agarwal, R. (1998) 'Medical Waste Issues, Practices and Policy: An Indian and International Perspective', presented at Centre for Science and Environment Seminar on Health and the Environment, 6–9 July, New Delhi.
Basavanthappa, B.T. (2008) 'Community Health Nursing', second edition, New Delhi: Jaypee Brothers Medical Publishers (P) Ltd.

Chakraborty, D. and Dilwaria, A. (2011) 'India's Growing Presence in Health Services Trade? Challenges and Policy Options', presented at the third China Trade in Services Congress, 1–3 June, Beijing.

Government of India (1998) 'BMW (Management and Handling) Rules 1998', New Delhi: Ministry of Environment and Forests.

Karnataka State Pollution Control Board (SPCB) (undated) Published Documents on Biomedical Waste Management in Bangalore. Online, available at: kspcb.kar.in/BMW/introduction.asp (accessed 23 October 2010).

Tamil Nadu Pollution Control Board (2005) 'A Note on Biomedical Waste Management', Chennai: TNPCB.

World Health Organization (WHO) (2004) 'Health-care Waste Management', Fact Sheet No. 281, October. Online, available at: www.who.int/mediacentre/factsheets/fs281/en/index.html (accessed 10 March 2011).

World Health Organization (WHO) (2005) 'Management of Solid Health Care Waste at Primary Health Care Centers – A Decision Making Guide'. Online, available at: www.who.in/entity/water_sanitation_health/medicalwaste/hcwdmguide/en/index (accessed 10 March 2011).

Yadav, M. (2001) 'Hospital Waste – A Major Problem', *JK-Practitioner*, 8(4): 276–282.

11 E-waste recycling in India

Bridging the formal–informal divide

Ashish Chaturvedi, Rachna Arora and
Ulrike Killguss

Introduction

The electronics industry is regarded as the world's largest and fastest growing manufacturing industry and hence, electronic waste (e-waste) is also quickly becoming the fastest growing waste stream in the industrialized world. According to the United Nations Environment Programme (UNEP), up to 50 million tonne of e-waste is globally generated each year (UNEP 2007). The recent MAIT-GTZ study notes that about 330,000 tonne of e-waste is generated annually in India and the generation of e-waste is expected to touch 470,000 tonne by 2011 (Chaturvedi *et al.* 2007). The study also reveals that only about 19,000 tonne of the e-waste is recycled, of which 95 per cent is recycled in the informal sector. Empa, the Swiss federal laboratories for materials testing and research, estimate that in Delhi at least 10,000 unskilled workers are employed in recycling and recovery operations (Sinha-Khetriwala *et al.* 2005). The complexity of e-waste flows within India and inadequate record-keeping by industry make an accurate estimation of e-waste difficult (Streiche–Porte *et al.* 2007).

The Basel Action Network (BAN) estimates that 80 per cent of e-waste sent to be recycled is not recycled. It is shipped to other countries. BAN (2005) noted that used appliances, computer equipment and cell phones are being collected and sent to developing nations, under the guise of 'building bridges over the digital divide'. The initiatives assume that the sent equipments, although used, are in working order and will assist people in these poor countries. However, this same report estimates that 75 per cent of the aforesaid equipments received are damaged or broken and are actually useless. Furthermore, imports are often falsely declared to be for charity, going instead to informal recyclers or becoming e-waste within two or three years (Basu 2008). UNEP notes that more than 90 per cent of the globally generated e-waste 'ends up in Bangladesh, China, India, Myanmar and Pakistan' (UNEP 2007).

Electronic wastes can cause widespread environmental damage due to the use of toxic materials in the manufacture of electronic goods (Mehra 2004). E-waste contains more than 1,000 different substances and chemicals, including many toxic ones (Puckett and Smith 2002). These include lead, polychlorinated biphenyls, mercury, cadmium, arsenic, zinc, chromium, and selenium (CIWMB 2002).

The cathode ray tubes (CRTs) in computer and television monitors contain lead, which is poisonous to the nervous system, as do circuit boards. Mercury, a neurotoxin like lead, is used in flat-panel display screens. Some batteries and circuit boards contain cadmium, a known carcinogen (Grossman 2006). An average computer contains 13.8 pounds of plastic (Puckett and Smith 2002). In the e-waste, metals (iron, copper, aluminium, gold and others), plastics and hazardous pollutants comprise over 60, 30 and 2.7 per cent respectively (Widmer *et al.* 2005). Most of the unusable toxic waste ends up in river beds, landfills and on road sides (Goodwin 2008). When disposed, they have the potential to contribute significant levels of toxic materials to the leachate produced in landfills. E-waste contaminants can enter aquatic systems via leaching from dumpsites where processed or unprocessed e-waste may have been deposited (BAN 2005). Similarly, the disposal of acid following hydrometallurgical processes into waters or onto soils, as well as the dissolution or settling of airborne contaminants, can contaminate aquatic systems (Luo *et al.* 2007). Soils at an e-waste recycling slum in Bangalore, India contained up to 39 mg/kg cadmium, 4.6 mg/kg indium, 957 mg/kg tin, 180 mg/kg antimony 49 mg/kg mercury, 2,850 mg/kg lead, and 2.7 mg/kg bismuth (Ha *et al.* 2009). E-waste is a potential source of genetic mutation and may induce cytogenetic damage within the general population exposed to e-waste pollution (Robinson 2009).

The current practices of e-waste management in India suffer from a number of drawbacks such as the difficulty in inventorization, unhealthy conditions of informal recycling, inadequate legislation, poor awareness and reluctance on the part of the corporate to address the critical issues (Joseph 2007). The management of e-waste in India has been discussed in various forums since 2003. The issue has gathered momentum owing to high obsolescence rates of electronic and electrical equipments (EEE), increased disposal rates and enhanced awareness on toxicity and hazard potential due to improper disposal (Chaturvedi *et al.* 2010).

In India, as in other developing countries, waste management is a complex issue due to the presence of the multitude of stakeholders, some of whom are outside the ambit of the law. The strategies for waste management adopted thus far have been, the legislating of norms and policies, awareness generation, incentives and taxation and setting up institutional infrastructure for recycling and disposal (Chaturvedi *et al.* 2010). The allocation of responsibility under existing legislation is another problem area; while certain activities are monitored by the states, the federal government is responsible for others. Moreover, the lack of an efficient enforcement mechanism makes the existing legislation on e-waste management ineffective.

The dominance of the informal sector can be explained by the hazardous, yet efficient methods used in recycling. Recycling is done mainly by the informal sector, in rudimentary backyard recycling set-ups without protective equipment or machinery and with no attention to occupational health and safety measures. The processes include acid baths during metal recovery and open burning of plastics and other materials, which results in pollution of air, groundwater and soil (Buth 2007). The environmental impacts of the informal recycling sector has been widely covered in previous studies (Bridgen *et al.* 2005; Keller 2006; Sepulveda *et al.* 2005; Sarkar 2008). With roughly similar recovery rates as compared to formal recyclers, lower compliance costs and the ability to externalize significant environmental costs (Streiche-Porte *et al.* 2007) enable the Indian informal recycling sector to out-compete the formal sector state-of-the-art recyclers, in bidding for e-waste. The integration of activities in the informal and formal sectors is essential to establish a viable e-waste recycling model for achieving an optimal solution to the recycling practices without compromising on the environment and human health.

Understanding the existing system

E-waste management is recognized as an important issue in developed countries due to its hazardous nature associated with improper disposal as well as the high costs associated with its recycling. The lack of a closed loop approach for electronics and electrical equipments creates significant environmental impacts in both developed and developing countries. The growing interest in urban mining and the utilization of secondary materials associated with increased costs of material extraction from virgin sources makes e-waste a valuable resource. In India electronic waste management is considered a viable business opportunity both in the informal and formal sector. However in the informal sector, this pursuit of secondary materials from e-waste does not follow either environmental or occupational health and safety (OHS) compliance.[1] While most recycling activities carried out in the informal sector involve dismantling and extraction of precious metals, these units use highly polluting technologies posing extensive health hazards to all those involved in the processing of e-waste. However, the scenario is changing with the recent establishment of several formal recycling units that are carrying out an end-to-end recycling of e-waste to produce valuable resources in an environmentally sound manner using the best available technologies (BAT).

Informal sector characteristics

Medina (1998) characterizes the common waste management policies in developing countries as usually centralized and undiversified top-down approaches, not recognizing the needs of the target groups. Hence a capital intensive technocratic solution, focusing on the disposal problem than a resource management problems is often sought, usually oblivious of the contributions of the informal sector. Historically the informal sector played a key role in waste management and recycling in India by reducing the burden of formal agencies. Their widespread and active networks along with manual skills make them economically viable for e-waste recycling.[2] Chaturvedi *et al.* (2007) estimate that the informal sector recycled 95 per cent of the e-waste generated in India. The people working in the informal sector are independent, self-employed producers in urban areas, employing either family members or hired non-family workers or apprentices. Informal sector activities usually require little or no capital, provide low incomes and unstable employment and frequently operate amid unsafe working conditions. The sector consists of entrepreneurs producing legitimate products without proper permits and legal status because they lack the resources and/or the incentives to comply with the burdensome and excessive rules and regulations necessary to become part of the formal economy. Occasionally informality prevails not because entrepreneurs are unwilling to abide by laws and regulations, but rather because they lack the necessary resources to do so (Kuchta-Helbling 2000).

Environment and health implications

When e-waste is disposed of or recycled without any precautions, there are predictable negative impacts on the environment and human health. E-waste contains more than 1,000 different substances, including toxic ones like lead, mercury, arsenic, cadmium, selenium, hexavalent chromium, and flame retardants that create dioxin emissions when burned. Further concerns arise from the sludge from processing which leads to contamination of water bodies and soil due to BFRs (brominated flame retardants), spent fluids/chemicals, traces of polychlorinated biphenyls, etc. (Puckett and Smith 2002).

The other major challenges include the incidence of child labour and OHS-related concerns. It has been increasingly found that child labour is employed in many of the activities associated with the process of e-waste dismantling and segregation. Children form a group of cheap and 'hassle free' workers, and aided by quick learning capabilities can do the minute work quite efficiently with their soft hands. The major OHS concerns during the dismantling activities arise due to the spread of toxic dust, while open burning of wires and printed circuit boards results in emissions of dioxins and furans, lead, cadmium and mercury fumes. Direct contact with chemicals used during the operations, the absence of exhaust pipes in the working environment, improper ventilation and non-usage of personal protection equipments turns the exposure to hazardous chemicals into serious health hazards. Apart from the issues mentioned above, the workers in the informal sector are also exposed to other workplace hazards leading to physical injuries, respiratory disorders, malnutrition, skin diseases, eye irritations, etc. and in some cases long-term incurable diseases. Finally the release of the toxic materials in the environment causes contamination of air, water and soil, leading to adverse health effects.

In general, controlling the pollution created by informal firms is difficult for four reasons. First, by definition, informal firms have few pre-existing ties to the state. Second, such firms are difficult to monitor since they are small, numerous, and geographically dispersed. Third, given the competitive nature informal firms are under considerable pressure to cut costs regardless of the environmental impacts. And finally, informal firms sustain the poorest of the poor. As a consequence, they may appear to both regulators and the public as less appropriate targets for regulation than larger, wealthier firms. Given these constraints, the application of conventional command and control regulation is bound to be problematic if not completely impractical. Hence, pollution control in the informal sector will require innovative approaches (Nas and Jaffe 2004).

Socio-economic implications

Both the socially as well scientifically espoused view on informal waste management system as a problematic and often undesirable segment, and the notion that those involved in these practices warrant opprobrium are not only morally but also empirically wrong. The system and the players involved have proven themselves to be capable of great ingenuity and flexibility in unpromising circumstances (Widmer *et al.* 2005). The e-waste trade chain in India comprises of aggregators who purchase scrap from households and businesses, followed by segregators who dismantle the components manually and sell off to recyclers who process the waste further for extraction of precious metals. The waste aggregators and segregators form an integral and important part of the e-waste trade chain as far as the channelization and collection of the same is concerned. The process is highly networked, with the engagement of skilled workers in sale/purchase and dismantling of e-waste. The aggregators and segregators also possess the necessary skills to reuse the components, thereby extending the products' life cycle which prevents pollution by saving the amount of energy required to make new products, reduces carbon footprints and enhances the penetration of IT and consumer durables among the economically disadvantaged people. Most of the workers are usually illiterate, and belong to rural immigrant families. Many commence their profession at the young age of five to eight years. Even after migrating to cities with the hope of improving their economic standards, they are still at a disadvantaged position in the face of concerns like competition among peers, absence of minimum wages, lack of access to credit, lack of recognition by the authorities and lack of access to social protection schemes, all of which contribute to their vulnerability (Chaturvedi *et al.* 2010).

Formal sector characteristics

Presently there are around 16 formal recycling units located in different parts of the country, registered with the Central Pollution Control Board (CPCB). The formal units perform collection, segregation, shredding and resource recovery. The formal sector employs automated, semi-automated or manual operations for the recycling of e-waste. In India, the formal recyclers lack a robust collection mechanism for e-waste and also lack refineries for precious metals recovery. To date the formal recyclers are exporting the shredded printed circuit boards to refineries in developed countries for resource recovery. The left-over components like glass, plastics, capacitors, etc. are sold off to downstream vendors for further recovery. The recyclers face challenges in the collection of e-waste due to lax regulations, lack of disposal policies, the presence of widely networked informal sector and lack of suitable technologies. The profitability of their entire chain depends on the recovery percentage of precious metals. The formal sector also needs to get clearances for the regulatory authorities for handling of the hazardous wastes. The process of approvals, clearances and certifications is often tedious and time-consuming.

Figure 11.1 highlights the current practices and trade chain of the informal and formal recyclers. As explained earlier, in the informal sector the streams A1, B1 and C1 are usually groups of informal sector workers with highly networked middle-men and scrap dealers engaged in the purchasing, collection and brokering, dismantling, reuse and refurbishment, and recycling for the precious metal recovery. Conversely the formal sector is a unit performing e-waste collection, dismantling, shredding, data destruction and recycling by following environmental and OHS standards.

Integrating the activities of informal and formal recycling

The official e-waste management system in many cities could not be managed without their myriad waste pickers, scrap collectors, traders and recyclers. Although not officially recognized, they often form the very basis of waste collection services, mostly at no cost to local authorities, central governments or residents. Though informal sector activities often take place outside official and formal channels, unlicensed and untaxed, they contribute significantly to the national economy in many ways: formation of new enterprises, evolution of trading networks, capital accumulation and investments, savings in terms of raw materials, transport and energy and last but not the least labour and employment generation. Activities supporting informal sector integration include facilitating credit, skills development and improvements in managerial know-how and marketing to enhance the competitiveness of labour-intensive small-scale activities.

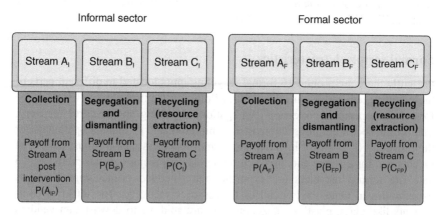

Figure 11.1 E-waste recycling – current scenario (source: constructed by the authors).

The integration of the informal sector aims to utilize its entrepreneurial abilities to create business models that can be accommodated within present economic paradigms. Moreover integrating informal sector workers has the potential to significantly improve their living conditions.[3]

The model shown in Figure 11.2 clearly delineates the activities to be adopted by the two sectors. It is proposed in the model that the two sectors will benefit by developing an inter-linkage and trade-off of the material. In line with the National Environmental Policy (2006) the informal sector needs to be mainstreamed and linked in the formal waste recycling systems. In India, many stringent rules and policies have failed due to the presence of a large number of informal sector workers who consider waste as a resource and opportunity. In terms of the environmental issues and OHS standards, the informal sector needs to be upgraded and trained on safe handling of e-waste. However, the skills of the informal sector in terms of collection, sorting, repair, refurbishing and dismantling need to be treated as a resource for the development of any management system for India. The most important rationale for developing a collaborative model is to level the playing field in sourcing the e-waste from the environment damaging channels to the more environmentally benign channels of recycling. The proposed model is developed by analysing the issues and skills of both the sectors under the broad ambit of sustainable e-waste management, addressing the economic, social and environmental issues.

The model proposes (Figure 11.2) that the informal sector restricts its activities in streams A_1, B_1 involving collection, sorting, repair, refurbishment and dismantling with no resource recovery operations. Even for these activities, the informal sector would need to comply with the legislative norms for handling of e-waste. The dismantled material would be traded with the formal recyclers at a market determined price. The model further suggests that the

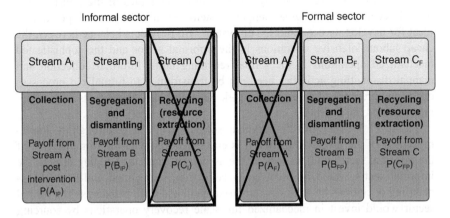

Figure 11.2 Processes to be abstained by the formal and informal sector under the 'proposed model' – post intervention scenario (source: constructed by the authors).

formal recyclers should practice mechanical (automated or semi-automated) dismantling and shredding of the value added e-waste for further processing. Thus the formal sector need not invest in the collection, sorting and dismantling of e-waste but they can make investments in processing of waste for metal recovery. The metal-rich powder can be then sent for final smelting and recovery of precious metals in the state-of-art refinery. Both the sectors will have to share the information on their unit processes, material balance and upstream-downstream vendors with the regulatory agencies for compliance.

It must be recognized that the informal sector, in its present shape and form, cannot do businesses or sign contracts with the formal sector. In order to implement the model, the most crucial step is to make the informal sector embark on the path to 'formalization'. The path to formalization of these units would require a number of stages with different levels of intervention to bring them into main stream activity. Once the clusters of the informal sector are identified, the next stage would be to create groups within the cluster and identify the core business process within each group. The formalization process would also require efforts to create awareness among the group through an extensive awareness campaign on the environmentally sound process highlighting its advantages, simultaneously projecting the environmental and health implications of improper recycling. The awareness programmes should also provide an insight into the economics of recycling using efficient technologies for processing e-waste, especially the printed circuit boards.

Proposed architecture

As mentioned earlier, the role of the informal sector in the value chain of e-waste is well known and continues to remain so due to its employment generation potential. There is a need to integrate the activities of the informal sector into mainstream e-waste recycling by dovetailing the activities of the informal and formal sectors, as the mutual support system developed by such operation is ideal for developing economies. The system will provide a balance between the cheap labour-intensive operations in the informal sector and the sophisticated mechanized operations in the formal recycling units. Informal collection and manual dismantling activities need not be transformed to formalized processes due to the presence of an abundant work force and low labour costs in developing countries (STEP 2009).

Figure 11.3 reveals that the recycling scenario will change through the implementation of the proposed model. It is envisaged that with the formalization of the informal sector units as well as the associated capacity-building efforts, the informal sector would be involved in collection, segregation and manual dismantling operations by following environmental and OHS standards. The formal sector would invest in mechanized full-scale recovery operations by sourcing material from the informal sector associations and acting as a 'buffer' between the informal sector and large scale smelter/refinery.

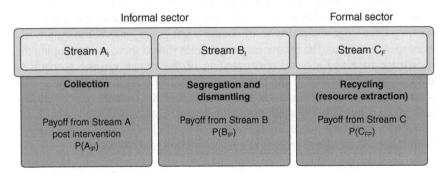

Figure 11.3 E-waste recycling scenario under the 'proposed' model (source: constructed by the authors).

Building blocks of the proposed model

Creation of representative bodies/associations

As per the earlier discussion, the informal sector cannot be integrated in its present shape and form without certain basic elements of formalization. The existence of informal sector entrepreneur clusters makes the creation of associations and bodies to represent the informal recyclers a promising strategy. The main task of these proposed associations is voicing the concerns of their members, resolving their issues and representing them at the national bodies for decision making. The activities in the informal sector are partly profitable due to non-compliance of the regulatory requirements. If the informal sector has to comply with the regulatory norms and conditions laid down by the authorities, the formalization process needs to be incentivized and the association of informal sector workers should be motivated for compliance. Geevan and Oza (2007) points out the following major activities of the informal sector associations, which enhances their relevance:

- Market mediation and supply chain management – forward and backward linkages, the small groups acting in concert for economies of scale and better bargain;
- Helping in developing and marketing of the produce;
- Supply chain management for economic activity;
- Limited engagement with some social issues;
- Better institutional governance – financial management, transparency, accountability, audit and improving economic efficiencies.

Capacity building

The implementation of the proposed model needs awareness and capacity building at various levels; namely, informal sector workers, formal recyclers, governmental bodies, industrial associations and regulatory authorities. The capacity building efforts should aim to address the e-waste related issues, legislative framework and evolving knowledge and expertise within the target group for establishing e-waste management models. The awareness programmes should focus on developing the knowledge base and a better understanding of the current e-waste scenario to address the vulnerability of the hazards associated with improper handling. The tailor-made training tools/modules developed should aim towards creating awareness amongst the recyclers about the environmental impacts and health risks associated with e-waste disposal, enhanced recycling efficiencies and an introduction to good housekeeping and process efficiencies (Arora *et al.* 2008).

Incentives

The economic benefits associated with the recycling of e-waste in the informal sector have to be seen in consonance with the lack of environmental compliance. At present there are no attractive incentives provided for those complying with environmental requirements while the penalties for non-compliance are also limited and usually not implemented. One option to improve the current practices is to offer incentives to those complying with environment and health norms and also promote the marketing of such products/services through a certification mechanism. The system of financing such activity could be through the associations as well as funds financed by the stakeholders in the value chain such as the manufacturers of electrical and electronic equipment as well as formal recyclers. Such a self-financing mechanism will be long standing and motivating for the operations. The package also needs to be made attractive for the informal sector, so that they are drawn towards it. The involvement of associations and other bodies will help in highlighting the issues to the group (Raghupathy *et.al* 2010). The formal recyclers could provide a base for improving the activities in the informal sector by prescribing the norms for the processing and facilitating the informal recyclers to adopt better practices.

Issues and challenges

Some of the major issues and challenges faced during the implementation process can be attributed to the gaps and overlaps in the system. First, the gap in the legal framework which does not specify the role of different stakeholders is a major lacuna in the existing system. No mandatory requirements are imposed on activities that are likely to cause direct or indirect impact on environment or health. This leads to unequal competition between those who comply and those who do not comply with the existing rule of law. In other words there are no rewards for compliance and no punitive action is taken against the erring units.

Second, there is a lack of viable working models amenable for the Indian conditions that emphasize the links between the informal and formal sector. The incentive structure for this collaboration has to be demonstrated through the implementation of a working business relationships as well as through the appropriate contracting mechanisms. For instance, one of the important links in the informal–formal integration is the development of an efficient collection system. In many cases of recycling post-consumer waste like e-waste, the reason for the failure of formal recycling operations is due to the lack of a collection back system. At the same time, the collection of post-consumer waste is managed efficiently through the disparate scrap or junk dealers collecting all sorts of wastes that have recycling potential. The example clearly shows the inefficiencies inherent in the system. The formal sector recyclers do not operate to capacity since there are no (formalized) collection systems, while the informal collection channels work efficiently collecting most of the material which is available as waste.

Third, people working in the informal recycling sector often have a long history of exploitation and oppression. They have not learned to trust each other and organize on a common front, with common opinions and views for negotiation purposes and they are wary of being dominated. Furthermore, informal sector workers are at risk of being dependent on powerful collaborators in order to earn their income. Efforts to organize the informal sector must therefore be particularly careful with regard to attempts by the more powerful groups among the informal sector to abuse support or regulation efforts for their personal interests. As a result there is a need to create a positive public and political attitude towards the informal sector workers. Furthermore, it is necessary to perceive them as benign environmental agents and valued partners, acting together towards common goals for environment protection and social inclusion.

Finally, the integration of activities in the informal and formal sectors is essential to establish a viable recycling model for e-waste recycling. There is a need to dovetail the activities of the informal sector with those of the formal recycling units so as to achieve the optimal solution to the recycling practices without compromising on the environment and human health. Such collaborative models would also meet the broad mandate under the NEP to organize and mainstream the informal sector while facilitating the resolution of problems related to pollution and health hazards.

Notes

1 The MAIT-GTZ e-waste assessment study revealed that 94 per cent of the manufacturers included in the study lack an IT disposal policy for obsolete IT products or e-waste and were not aware of the required practices. Therefore, most of the e-waste was being disposed of to scrap dealers which in turn were sold to the recyclers in the informal sector.
2 The informal sector focuses on cherry picking the precious components for metal recovery and the non-recoverable are disposed off in landfills. A study conducted in Bangalore on precious metal recovery by the informal sector observed that the efficiency of the process adopted there is around 28–30 per cent whereas the gold extraction efficiency is around 99.99 per cent by the smelting companies in developed countries (Keller 2006: 105).
3 The Brickmakers' Project notes four lessons for environmental management in the informal sector: establishing a cooperative with the participation of local unions and political organizations; enforcement of environmental regulations with continuous monitoring; development of low cost clean technologies; and devising workable and replicable business models (Blackman and Bannister 1997).

References

Arora, R., Killguss, U., Chaturvedi, A. and Rochat, D. (2008) 'Whither E-waste in India – the Indo-German-Swiss Initiative' in R. Johri (ed.) *E-waste: Implications, Regulations and Management in India*, New Delhi: TERI Press.

Basel Action Network (2005) 'The Digital Dump: Exporting Re-use and Abuse to Africa', Seattle: BAN.

Basu, S. (2008) 'E-Waste Generation, Mitigation, and a Case Study', R. Johri (ed.) *Implications, Regulations, and Management in India*, New Delhi: The Energy and Resource institute (TERI).

Blackman, A. and Bannister, G.A. (1997) 'Pollution Control in the Informal Sector: The Ciudad Juárez Brickmakers' Project', *Natural Resources Journal*, 37: 829–856.

Brigden, K., Labunska, I., Santillo, D. and Allsopp, M. (2005) *Recycling of Electronic Wastes in China and India: Workplace and Environmental Contamination*, Exeter: Greenpeace International.

Buth, M. (2007) 'The Environmental Impact of E-waste: An International Comparison with a Special Focus on India using the Environmental Kuznets Curve as a Model'. Online, available at: www.ieewaste.org/pdf/135EKC+e-waste-EF.pdf.

California Integrated Waste Management Board (2002) 'Factsheet: Electronic Product Management Issues', Sacramento: CIWMB.

Central Pollution Control Board, Government of India (undated) *Publishing on the Internet*. Online, available at: www.cpcb.nic.in (accessed 10 December 2010).

Chatterjee, S. and Kumar, K. (2009) 'Effective Electronic Waste Management and Recycling Process Involving Formal and Non-formal Sector', *International Journal of Physical Sciences*, 4:893–905.

Chaturvedi, A., Arora, R., Khatter, V. and Kaur, J. (2007) 'E-waste Assessment in India – Specific Focus on Delhi', New Delhi: MAIT-GTZ Study.

Chaturvedi, A., Arora, R. and Ahmed, S. (2010) 'Mainstreaming the Informal Sector in E-Waste Management', paper presented at National Conference on Urban, Industrial and Hospital Waste Management, Ahmedabad, May.

Gao, Z., Li, J. and Zhang, H.C. (2004) 'Electronics and the Environment', IEEE International Symposium, San Francisco, United States, pp. 234–231.

Geevan, C.P. and Oza, A. (2007) 'Promoting People's Organisations and their Federations: Reflections on the AKRSP (India) – Experience', Research Study, Aga Khan Rural Support Programme.

Goodwin, D.A. (2008) 'Evaluating the Environmental Impact of E-waste'. Online, available at: www.helium.com/items/788516-evaluating-the-environmental-impact-of-e-waste (accessed 10 March 2011).

Government of India (undated) *Publishing on the Internet*. Online, available at: www.envfor.nic.in (accessed 10 December 2010).

Government of India (2006) 'National Environment Policy' (NEP), New Delhi: Ministry of Environment and Forests.

Government of India (2008) 'Environmentally Sound Management of E-waste', Guidelines, New Delhi: Ministry of Environment and Forests and Central Pollution Control Board.

Grossman, E. (2006) *High Tech Trash*, Washington, DC: Island Press.

Ha, N.N., Agusa, T., Ramu, K., Tu, N.P.C., Murata, S. and Bulbule, K.A. (2009) 'Contamination by Trace Elements at E-waste Recycling Sites in Bangalore, India', *Chemosphere*, 76(1): 9–15.

Joseph, K. '(2007) Electronic Waste Management in India – Issues and Strategies', Paper presented at the Eleventh International Waste Management and Landfill Symposium, Sardinia, 2007.

Keller, M. (2006) *Publishing on the Internet*, 'Assessment of Gold Recovery Processes in Bangalore, India and Evaluation of an Alternative Recycling Path for Printed Wiring Boards', Diploma Thesis, ETH and Empa. Online, available at: www.empa.ch/plugin/template/empa/*/59244/--/l=2 (accessed 14 May 2010).

Kuchta-Helbling, C. (2000) *Publishing on the Internet*, Background paper on 'Barriers to Participation: The Informal Sector in Emerging Democracies', prepared for the Second Global Assembly: Confronting Challenges to Democracy in the 21st Century, Sao Paulo, November. Online, available at: www.cipe.org/programs/informalsector/pdf/informalEnglish.pdf (accessed 10 May 2010).

Luo, Q., Wong, M.H. and Cai, Z.W. (2007) 'Determination of Polybrominated Diphenyl Ethers in Freshwater Fishes from a River Polluted by E-wastes', *Talanta*, 72: 1644–1649.

Medina, M. (1998) 'Scavenger Cooperatives in Developing Countries', *Bio-Cycle*: 70–72.

Mehra, H.C. (2004) 'PC Waste Leaves Toxic Taste', *Tribune*, 22 March.

Nas, P.J.M. and Jaffe, R. (2004) 'Shifting the Focus from Problem to Potential' *Environment, Development and Sustainability*, 6: 337–353.

Puckett, J. and Smith, T. (2002) 'Exporting Harm: the High-Tech Trashing of Asia', Seattle: Silicon Valley Toxics Coalition, Basel Action Network.

Raghupathy, L., Chaturvedi, A., Mehta, V. and Killguss, U. (2010) 'E-waste Recycling in India – Integrating Informal and Formal Sectors', paper presented at National Seminar on Electronic Waste, Jameshdpur, January.

Robinson, B.H. (2009) 'E-waste: An Assessment of Global Production and Environmental Impacts', Science of the Total Environment, 408:183–91.

Sarkar, A. (2008) 'Occupation and Environmental Health Perspectives of E-waste Recycling in India: A Review', in R. Johri (ed.) *E-waste: Implications, Regulations and Management in India*, New Delhi: Tata Energy and Resource Institute (TERI).

Sepulveda, A., Schluep, M., Renaud, F., Streicher, M., Kuehr, R., Hagelueken, C. and Gereeke, A. (2010) 'A Review of the Environmental Fate and Effects of Hazardous Substances Released from Electrical and Electronic Equipments during Recycling: Examples from China and India', *Environmental Impact Assessment Review*, 30: 28–41.

Sinha-Khetriwala, D., Kraeuchi, P. and Schwaninger, M. (2005) 'A Comparison of Electronic Waste Recycling in Switzerland and in India' *Environmental Impact Assessment Review*, 25: 492–504.

Solving the E-Waste Problem (STEP), (2009) 'Sustainable Innovation and Technology Transfer Industrial Sector Studies', Recycling – From E-waste to Resources, Paris.

Streiche-Porte, M., Bader, P., Scheidegger, R. and Kytzia, R. (2007) 'Material Flow and Economic Analysis as a Suitable Tool for Systems Analysis under the Constraints of Poor Data Availability and Quantity in Emerging Economies', *Clean Technologies and Environmental Policy*, 9: 325–345.

United Nations Environment Programme (2007) 'Global Environment Outlook', Kenya: UNEP.

Widmer, R., Krapf, H.O., Khetriwal, D.S., Schnellman, M. and Böni, H. (2005), 'Global Perspectives on E-waste', *Environmental Impact Assessment Review*, 25: 436–458.

Part IV
Trade and environment

12 Agriculture and environment in India

Policy implications in the context of North–South trade

Amita Shah

Introduction

Sustainable development has increasingly been taken into policy consideration during the last century, with a fair amount of consensus generated over environmental sustainability (Rodrik 2001). However, sustainable development means different challenges as well as developmental outcomes for industrialized economies of the North and the primarily agrarian economies in the South, thereby creating a divide between them (Bond 1996). The sustainable development discussions at various global forums, including the World Trade Organization (WTO), remain mainly confined to evolving broad principles, declarations and, occasionally, specific resolutions (e.g. Agenda 21 of the Rio Summit 1992), rather than ensuring a sustainable global production system. As a result, the world forums aiming to achieve environmental sustainability generally set up different norms for the North and South.

Given that economic growth in the North is partially dependent on the resources in the South, unification of environmental management was inevitable. However in the absence of a common vision for economic growth by the two sets of economies, environmental issues associated with industrial and mining activities, rather than issues pertaining to agriculture, food security, and rural development influencing the livelihood of millions of people in the South, is currently receiving attention. This, in a sense, is almost inevitable given the differences in the natural-resource base, compulsions for utilizing these resources emanating from population growth and dependence on the primary sector, and ability to pay for conservation. For instance, factors governing the utilization rate of natural resources in the South primarily include food and livelihood security concerns, while the same in the North involve rural landscape management and export growth.

Environmental problems in the South emanate mainly from overuse of natural resources like land and water, while the same occur in the North owing to overuse of mechanical and chemical inputs such as machinery, fertilizer and pesticides. While both may result in serious environmental impacts, the developmental implications are different: people in the South misuse natural resources in order to survive or meet basic needs, whereas the same in the North occurs for sustaining a higher growth contour in production and consumption. This dichotomy can either be adhered to by North–South specific norms and obligations as prescribed by WTO, or by evolving a unified perspective not only on environment but also on the aforesaid development concerns.[1]

Given this backdrop, this chapter seeks to review the environmental implications of India's agricultural production in the light of the WTO-agreements, and discuss policy implications for promoting more sustainable farming systems. The analysis is based mainly on the existing literature on various aspects covered by the chapter.

Trade, agriculture and environment: what do the trade theories tell?

Environment and agriculture

Considering environment as a global good, a unified production system, especially for food, may be worked out by addressing the dual objectives of maximizing food production with minimum damage to the environment. Given the broad patterns of natural resource endowment and the technology–environment interface for food production in the North and the South, a possible rearrangement of world food production could achieve it: North and South specializing in production of water-intensive cereal crops and water-saving crops (e.g. oil seeds, dry land horticulture and livestock) respectively. However, this kind of reorganization may not work owing to the fact that the South may lack the requisite purchasing power to pay for the food imports at the price at which North would like to sell. Conversely, the South have serious reservations about being food-dependent, due to adverse political implications.

Another set of constraints emanate from the relative factor endowment in terms of labour and capital. Neither do the North have the requisite labour force to employ for managing extensive farming nor, do the South have adequate capital for enhancing the productive capacities of the depleted land and water resources. Thus, devising an environmentally sustainable unified system for food production is constrained by two sets of forces: (a) relative availability of labour and capital to manage natural resource endowment for productive purposes; and (b) bargaining capacity to influence food prices, and political sovereignty concerns.

Ideally, trade liberalization could help restructuring the world food production system in an environmentally sustainable manner. Presently, the theoretical discourse on trade and environment is at an exploratory stage, where the focus is mainly on examining: how environmental objectives may influence trade or, more ambitiously, whether and to what extent trade can by and large globally ensure a more sustainable food and agricultural production system. Nevertheless, it does indicate possible directions by which a unified system of food production could be explored (Shah and Weis 2004). Trade theory from the comparative advantage perspective attempts to address the environmental sustainability question by considering natural resource endowment (and assimilative capacity) as a factor of production. Several attempts have been made to identify comparative advantage in agricultural production using North–South and South–South models. Before looking into these results, a brief discussion on the contemporary debate on trade and environment with special focus on agriculture or primary production is presented.

There are three major strands of theoretical perspectives on trade and environment. According to economic perspective, free trade leads to a 'win–win' situation as trade induced growth enables the government to tax and raise resources for environmental protection simultaneously increasing demand for environmental good. Environmental economists, in close agreement with the economic perspective argue that trade may not lead to environmental (i.e. resource use) competition because the abatement cost is only a small proportion of the value of output especially in case of industrial production. The main point emerging from these two perspectives is to evolve a domestic policy which puts a correct value to environmental pollution, and to identify the right kind of fiscal and other policy instruments to safeguard environmental sustainability in the long run.

Bhagwati and Srinivasan (1996) argued that the 'win–win' situation necessitates differential environmental standard among countries in the North and South. However this become particularly complex for agricultural trade because of the multi-functionality of agricultural production and use of natural resources thereof (Peterson *et al.* 2004).

Responding to the complexity of the trade–agriculture–environment interface, the ecological economists present a third perspective by taking a more critical view of the conventional trade theory and questioning some of the basic assumptions such as differences in resource endowment, perfect mobility of factors of production, and the absence of any (social/environmental) externalities. Similarly, the theory of unequal exchange questions the stable price of different goods and deteriorating terms of trade for those engaged in primary production and exports (Giljum and Eisenmenger 2003). Essentially, the problem arises because conventional trade theory envisages market prices as the key to understanding how market institutions organize the North–South natural resources transfer. Given that trade, economic growth, and wealth accumulation has always been closely connected with appropriation of natural resources, and that trade negotiations always tend to benefit the side with accumulated power, the volume as well as direction of trade are likely to bring unequal outcomes (Giljum and Eisenmenger 2003).

Though conventional trade theory explains a major part of global trade, the critics argue that the inherent non-interventionist policies enshrined in it fail to explain trade among countries with similar resource endowment, especially, a large volume of intra-industry trade (Datta and Chakrabarti 2001). Hence new trade theories emphasize that apart from differential resource endowment, scale economies, product differentiation, imperfect information flow, negotiating skills, etc. matter significantly in determining the volume as well as direction of trade (Datta and Chakrabarti 2001).

Material resource transfer: some evidence

Global trade trends clearly demonstrate a net flow of primary products from poor to rich countries (Muradian and Martinez-Allier 2001). While exports constitute only a small proportion of southern economies, it may still exert significant environmental pressure because of their high natural resource intensity. Hence agri-environmental issues should be viewed in a larger context, particularly because trade (and the rules governing it) has a critical bearing on shaping up the pace as well as composition of growth among the member countries. The empirical evidence so far suggests that the growth in agricultural trade is more for relatively lower value products (Sawhney 2003). This reflects not only unequal benefits from trade, but may also imply a greater volume of natural resources draining per unit value earned from trade.

Two important policy implications emerge from the asymmetric distribution of natural resources, superimposed by asymmetric payment/compensation structure for environmental damages in the North–South context. The first, refers to reduction in the volume of international resource flows, and the second refers to reducing the intensity of resource use and a de-intensification of resource flows from South to North along with a redistribution of financial flows from North to South (Sachs and Agarwal 2002). This in fact, makes a critical link between trade and sustainable growth (or development) unlike the present framework where trade is linked to growth (and the percolation mechanism following that), whereas resource sustainability, treated as a non-trade concern, is left to the individual countries to take care of through domestic policies.

The fact that a large proportion of agriculture-related environmental damages are mainly local (i.e. within the boundary of an individual country) does not qualify it to be treated as non-WTO matter because of the multi-functionality of agriculture in promoting the social goals. The issues of natural resource sustainability, and long-term prospects for growth, therefore should not be kept outside the realm of trade negotiations as per the current WTO perspective. This is particularly true in a multilateral forum, which essentially hinges on the principle of comparative advantage among the member countries, rather than culminating into a situation of absolute advantage among the few, especially in the North, because of the increased North–South capital mobility. A recent study on ecological footprint demonstrates how environmental externalities have transcended from North to South (WWF 2005). Hence environmental concerns cannot be treated in a disjointed manner, by segregating resources and/or national boundaries.

It is in this context the southern countries need to increasingly engage themselves on environmental issues in trade negotiations rather than evading them in the interest of their short-term goal of achieving greater market access in primary products (Sachs and Agarwal 2002). A better approach would be to keep negotiating for: (a) a level playing field and improved market access in the short run, but more importantly, (b) pleading for evolving a global perspective on trade and sustainable growth in the long run. Though, apparently contradictory, this double-edged approach is necessary in the context of an imperfect world order where historically constructed power relations between North and South (rather than dynamically determined comparative advantage) along with negotiation-skills (without perfect flow of information) significantly influence the volume and direction of agricultural trade. However the negotiating standpoint is not in conflict with the domestic policy reforms essential for ensuring sustainable development.

Agreement on agriculture – commitments and agrarian scenario in India

Till now India has broadly safeguarded her interest under the Agreement on Agriculture (AOA), as observed from the major features of India's commitments summarized by Hoda and Gulati (2002):

- No major commitments for reduction under domestic support or export subsidy.
- Eligible for additional exemptions on investment subsidies, provide input subsidies to resource-poor farmers, gain from special and differential treatment (SDT) in terms of time frame as well as quantum of reduction commitments.
- Applicable limit on distortionary domestic support is 10 per cent as against 5 per cent in the case of developed countries.
- Export subsidies for market promotion, international freight and internal transport are exempt from calculation of export competition measures.
- For export promotion, India has bound its tariff ceiling at very high level (100 per cent for raw commodities; 150 per cent for processed goods; 300 per cent for edible oils; 45 per cent for soya oil).
- Obtained a list of 230 commodities as special products (at six-digit level) vis-à-vis ten in the case of developed countries like the United States.

It may however, be noted at the outset agriculture trade accounts for a small proportion of India's agricultural GDP. In 1998–99, exports and imports accounted for 6.6 and 2.0 per cent of agricultural GDP, which increased from 4.8 and 1.5 per cent over the triennium preceding 1995–96 (Chand 2005). By 2003–04 the share of exports reduced to 5.41 per cent whereas the share of imports increased to 3.57 per cent. While much of the decline in export share could be attributed to declining global prices, evidence suggests that initial gains from trade have receded in more recent period.

This raises the critical issue of the net (welfare) gain from exports, given the resource intensity and potential fear of labour displacement, which even in the initial period showed mixed results (Chand 1999). It may be reiterated that much of the welfare gain from exports is due to increased agricultural production and higher prices to be obtained in the international market. If the price advantage is not available, one needs to revisit the proposition of increasing agricultural production in export-oriented crops as against the ones that have larger developmental implications in terms of ecological balance; spatial distribution and affordability by the poor. There is also an added risk in terms of market fluctuations.

Agriculture and environment in India: evidence and issues

This section reviews the existing evidence on the environmental impact of agricultural production in India. Unfortunately, the available evidence on environmental impact assessment (EIA) for Indian agriculture except certain official statistics on forest and land degradation, depletion of groundwater table, information on air and water pollution caused by multiple sources including agricultural operations, are limited.

Prima facie, the relative neglect of this EIA of India's agricultural sector is a manifestation of the general apathy towards the issue and, also the perception that agriculture, as yet, is not a major contributor to environmental pollution in the country. This perception is often reflected in environmental policies. For instance, the strategy identified by the Ministry of Environment and Forest for meeting the objectives of the Tenth Five Year Plan, has a special thrust on promoting sustainable development, to be achieved by emphasizing the intrinsic linkage between environment management and socio-economic development through *increased access* to natural resources (Khurana 2003). A somewhat similar scenario prevails during the eleventh plan where the central thrust in agriculture is attaining 4 per cent growth mainly by enhancing irrigation facilities, combined with input intensive technologies and diversification to high valued crops (Planning Commission 2009). Hence growth in production continues to be the main thrust of the policy, which otherwise is explicitly committed to environmental concerns.

Before discussing the environmental implications, various important aspects of Indian agriculture are noted in Table 12.1, which indicates deceleration during 1996–97 to 2005–06 for most of the indicators except credit supply, which has registered a phenomenal increase. The deceleration is particularly concerning in light of the fact that the post-2000 period has generally witnessed reasonably good rainfall across the country.

Impact on environment: select evidence

The analysis on the environmental impact of Indian agriculture is based on the existing literature. An account of environmental damages mainly on land and water is presented here, which emanate mainly due to faulty use of natural resources as well as bio-chemical inputs like seed, fertilizer and pesticide. Prima facie, it cannot be denied that use of external inputs like irrigation–fertilizer–pesticides would bring negative externalities like soil degradation, water-logging, depletion of micro nutrients and soil structure, groundwater

Table 12.1 Trend growth rate in various important indicators of agriculture sector in India 1980–81 to 2003–04 (per cent/year)

Detail	1980–81 to 1990–91	1990–91 to 1996–97	1996–97 to 2005–06
Technology*	3.3	2.8	0.0
Public sector net fixed capital stock	3.9	1.9	1.4**
Gross irrigated area	2.3	2.6	0.5**
Electricity consumed in agriculture	14.1	9.4	-0.5***
Area under fruits and vegetable	5.6	5.6	2.7****
Private sector net fixed capital stocks	0.6	2.2	1.2**
Term of trade	0.2	1.0	-1.7**
Total net fixed capital stocks	2.0	2.1	1.3**
NPK use	8.2	2.5	2.3
Credit supply	3.7	7.5	14.4**
Total cropped area	0.4	0.4	-0.1
Net sown area	-0.1	0.0	-0.2
Cropping intensity	0.5	0.4	0.1

Source: Economic Survey (2007–08).

Notes
*Yield potential of new verity of paddy, rapeseed/mustard, groundnut, wheat, maize.
** Up to 2003–04; *** Up to 2004–05.

contamination, etc. The pertinent issue however, is to draw the line of maximum tolerance level whereby (a) damages do not cross a limit of being irreversible; and (b) decline in land productivity does not become perpetual. How does the food-production scenario in India perform vis-à-vis these checks? These questions have been examined with the help of the limited information available on land degradation and the link between soil quality and productivity (Reddy and Bhagirath 2000).

Degradation of land

There is no uniform estimate of wasteland in India. The available estimates by the National Remote Sensing Agency (NRSA) show that around 55.3 million ha in the country in 2005 were in this category, though another NRSA survey estimates the figure to the tune of 64 million ha.

The extent of wasteland however, varies across states. Importantly, wasteland or degraded land consists not only of public or common land but also private land. Among various reasons leading to degradation of private land, lack of soil-moisture is most critical especially in large tracts of dry land regions in the country. It is observed that land degradation is a universal phenomenon across Indian states, which is not particularly associated with a higher level of irrigation, fertilizer use or crop-yield as observed in the case of states like Punjab, Uttar Pradesh (UP), Andhra Pradesh (AP) and Tamil Nadu where the Green revolution (GR) of technology has been widespread from an early stage. Haryana, of course, is a major exception with 63 per cent of its cultivable land being subject to degradation.

Table 12.2 presents various land degradation estimates of, highlighting that nearly 107 million ha of land suffered from some kind of degradation. This

Table 12.2 Estimates of degradation in India

Type of degradation	1990–99		2000–2003	
	M ha	% of total area	M ha	% of total area
Water erosion	107.12	61.70	57.15	53.21
Wind erosion	17.79	10.24	10.46	9.74
Ravines	3.97	2.29	2.67	2.48
Salt affected	7.61	4.38	6.32	5.88
Water logging	8.52	4.91	3.19	2.97
Mines and industrial waste	–	–	0.25	0.23
Shifting cultivation	4.91	2.83	2.37	2.21
Degraded forest	19.49	11.23	24.89	23.17
Special problems	2.73	1.57	0.11	0.10
Coastal sandy areas	1.46	0.84	–	–
Total	173.60	100.00	107.41	100.00

Source: Government of India (2006).

accounts for 32 and 77 per cent of the total reporting area and the net sown area during 2003–04 respectively. Of the total degraded area nearly 53 and 23 per cent are affected due to water erosion and deforestation in that order. It may be noted that the total degraded area is declining over time.

The problem of waterlogging in the latter, of course, is more obvious vis-à-vis the continuous process of degradation, which occurs in the large tracts of low rainfall and/or dry land regions in the country. For instance, while the 'Punjab-crisis' poses a serious problem; it overlooks the fact that a considerable number of subsistence farmers with rain-fed agriculture are sub-optimally utilizing their lands consistently. Hence a substantial part of the recent increase in fallow land (during the post 1980s) is likely to include some of the major dry land regions like Gujarat, Maharashtra and Rajasthan. This, might have happened because 'the small and marginal farmers who opt out of cultivation for a variety of reasons particularly, due to non-viability of farming on the small and degraded holdings, have resorted to the practice of keeping their land fallow' (Sharma 1997).

It is thus, erroneous to assume that the use of external inputs will necessarily result in higher land degradation vis-à-vis subsistence farming, which is often characterized by low irrigation, limited farmyard manure (FYM), inadequate measures for soil moisture conservation, and low adoption of some of the agronomic practices owing to a financial resource crunch. In fact several rain-fed areas in India suffer from acute soil erosion due to poor vegetative cover, continued extension of cultivation on marginal lands and low organic matter content (Marothia 1997).

And yet, it is a fact that the 'Punjab crisis' has indeed reached alarming proportions. While the water table is receding due to overexploitation in major parts of Punjab, the same is rising due to poor quality of groundwater and drainage facilities in the southwestern districts of the state (Sidhu and Dhillon 1997). The pertinent concern is that irrigation-induced land degradation occurred despite the availability of appropriate abatement technologies, implying that it is not the irrigation responsive technology that is at fault. Rather, distorted pricing signals in the absence of requisite institutional arrangements are the root cause of the observed trends of monoculture, overuse of water and a declining yield, especially in the Indo-Gangetic Region. But, much of the damages caused due to misuse of irrigation are reversible by means of the already available technologies, which would not only prevent any further degradation but also help in revitalizing land and water resources for their long-term sustainable use (Sidhu and Dhillon 1997).

The macro level evidences suggest that about one-quarter of the total cultivable area under all the canal projects suffer from waterlogging and soil salinity (Dhawan 1997) though the severity of the problem varies widely across regions. Apart from soil topography conditions, variations in the incidence of waterlogging may also be attributed to the varying degrees of management efficiencies across systems and the institutional framework within which price and non-price factors influence the water use efficiency.

Depletion of groundwater

The situation with respect to groundwater is also quite dismal particularly in the early GR states like Haryana, Punjab and Tamil Nadu. Of course, the official estimates presented in Table 12.3 do not portray the actual gravity of the situation. This is particularly true in the case of several dry land regions where overcoming the damages might take a fairly long time due to unfavourable rainfall as well as soil conditions. It deserves mention that since half the crop acreage that presently benefits from irrigation is based on groundwater resources, any setback in groundwater availability can have serious implications for sustaining the agricultural yield growth (Dhawan 1997).

Although water-economizing devices like drip and sprinkler irrigation offer considerable scope for sustainable use of groundwater, their viability for foodgrain cultivation is yet to be established on a larger scale. Thus, despite this grave situation with respect to land and water resources degradation in early GR regions, the evidence, till at least the early 1990s, suggested that 'yield of wheat and rice have maintained an upward trend in Punjab and Haryana even at a high level. However there has been a stagnation in crop yield in the case of Bihar even at a low level' of degradation (Chand and Haque 1997). This does not mean that total factor productivity (TFP) remains the same as that observed in early phase of GR (Kumar and Joshi 1998). Recent evidence indicates a sharp decline in the TFP of rice and wheat in the

Table 12.3 Over-exploitation of groundwater among selected states

States	No. of blocks having over exploitation	Total no. of blocks	(a) % to (b)
	(a)	(b)	(c)
A. Blockwise assessment			
1 Bihar	0	585	0
2 Haryana	45	108	42
3 Karnataka	6	175	3
4 Kerala	0	154	0
5 Madhya Pradesh	0	459	0
6 Punjab	62	118	53
7 Rajasthan	45	236	19
8 Tamil Nadu	54	384	14
9 Uttar Pradesh	19	895	2
Sub-total	231	3,114	7
B. Others			
10 Andhra Pradesh	6	1,104	1
11 Gujarat	12	184	7
12 Maharashtra	0	1,503	0
Sub-Total	17	2,791	1

Source: Dhawan (1997).

Indo-Gangetic Regions. Two important features of agricultural production in Punjab were noted in the recent period: stagnancy in crop and rapidly declining economic returns from crop yield, caused by mono-cropping, waterlogging and imbalanced use of fertilizer (Ghuman 2001; Singh 2004; Kamra and Abraham 2004). The studies however, do not quantitatively assess the cost of environmental damages.

Imbalanced use of chemical fertilizer

Use of chemical fertilizer has increased from about 70 kg/ha during 1990–91 to about 91 kg/ha during 2002–03 and further to 117 kg/ha during 2007–08. The estimates for 2007–08 however, are based on provisional data on gross cropped area. Notably, fertilizer consumption in India is highly concentrated in two major crops; namely, rice and wheat. Together they constitute nearly two-thirds of the total NPK (nitrogen, phosphorus, potash) use in the country. Similarly, the use is concentrated in states like Punjab, Haryana, AP and Tamil Nadu, UP and West Bengal where the rate of NPK use has already gone beyond 100 kg/ha. The observation implies that the negative environmental impact is likely to be highly localized; hence, highly intensive, rather than widespread, notwithstanding the leaching of nitrate in water covering a larger area.

This raises the issue of improving nutrient management on large tracts of land that are both hungry (in terms of both organic and inorganic fertilizer use) as well as thirsty (in terms of both soil moisture and irrigation). It deserves mention that the current fertilizer pricing mechanism has resulted in accentuating nutrient imbalance. As against the desirable N:P:K proportion of 4:2:1, the actual ratio is 6:2.4:1.

Recent estimates (in Table 12.4) suggest that nearly 30 per cent of the gross cropped area does not receive any chemical fertilizer; application of FYM is likely to be very low. Desai and Rastogi (1995) analysed the use of organic manure in seven villages of the semi-arid regions in AP and Maharashtra, and noted that '40 to 56 per cent of the sample farmers were not using any manure in as many as five (out of nine) years'. Further it was noted:

> Manure was applied to only about one-tenth of the plots (i.e. 15 per cent of the area) every year.... The periodic discontinuation of manure use by many farmers and the pattern of its use probably reflects a severe scarcity of manure and competing alternative uses of organic waste, especially as domestic fuel.
>
> (Desai and Rastogi 1995: 184–185)

Fortunately, the shortage of fuel wood during the 1970s has evoked a positive response from the farmers in terms of widespread development of farm forestry and social forest, which in turn, has been reflected as relative stability in fuel wood prices during 1985–90 (Natarajan 1995). While it is difficult to assess the extent to which these developments might have eased the constraints on availability of FYM, the scarcity syndrome seems to be continuing in large parts of the semi-arid regions. It is possible that the poor and marginal farmers may be facing greater constraints of manure as many of them own limited livestock and also possess limited purchasing power. Hence breaking this barrier is a real challenge for sustaining and accelerating the yield-growth of traditional varieties grown under rain-fed conditions.[2]

Since fertilizer use in India is still moderate as compared to China and many South Asian countries, the problem is not so much of its overuse and the result- ant adverse impact on groundwater (Marothia 1997). Rather, the problem in many parts of the dry land regions is of low, imbalanced and inefficient applica- tion of chemical fertilizers. It is therefore reasonable to argue that poor farmers cannot be made to wait till the chronic scarcity of manure is resolved. The mod- erate application of fertilizer is therefore, necessary if the productivity of the degraded land is to be improved and, diversification from foodgrain production is to be halted in the dry land regions.

Empirical estimates on nitrate contents in surface as well as groundwater suggest that whereas there has been an increase in the intensity of contamination, the level is still below 10 mg/l (milligram per litre) in most of cases (Conway and Pretty 1991), which is fairly low as compared to the United Kingdom (200 mg/l) and the United States (50 mg/l) for intensively cultivated fields. It may be noted that India's share in the global use of NPK is about 9 per cent which is approximately the same as its share in the world's cultivable land (Dev and Painuly 1994). Nevertheless, Dhaliwal and Kansal (1994) note that the negative impact of fertilizer use is more apparent in the case of water as com- pared to land and air.

Table 12.4 Fertilizer use among major crops (2001–02)

Crop	Area ('000 hectares)	% area treated with fertilizer	Consumption kg per hectare
Paddy	37,809	83.5	150.4
Wheat	23,181	90.9	145.6
Jowar	4,467	58.2	98.5
Bajra	7,515	32.8	58
Maize	3,985	64.9	83.5
Total pulses	14,042	34.3	80.5
Total food grains	97,822	70.4	134.6
Total oilseeds	17,201	65.5	98.8
Total fruits	1,662	56.5	257.4
Total vegetable	2,644	82.8	206.1
Total spice and condiments	1,472	71.6	174.3
All crops	136,697	69.3	136.1

Source: fertilizer statistics by Fertilizer Association of India (various issues).

Use of pesticides

The pesticides problem however is more complex. While around 90 per cent of pesticide consumption is concentrated in Punjab, Gujarat, AP, Tamil Nadu, and Maharashtra; the extent of overuse is very high – almost double in several cases (Dev and Painuly 1994). Of the total pesticide use in agriculture (Table 12.5) 84 per cent is concentrated in cotton, rice and vegetables and fruits (Dhaliwal and Kansal 1994). Although pesticide use increased at a phenomenal rate of 10 per cent per annum during 1955–56 to 1989–90, the variation in use is relatively higher during the post GR-period (Desai and Namboodiri 1997).

The types of pesticides used involve another concern area. Nearly half of the pesticides registered with the Indian Pesticides Registration Committee are banned in Western countries like the United States. Of course, this does not mean that all the banned products have the same effect on Indian soils as observed in the United States. However, Indian exports considerably suffer from allegations of pesticide poisoning. The worst sufferers are of course the workers engaged in spraying these chemicals.

Interestingly, a branch of the existing literature indicates that 'if compared internationally, the use of pesticides in Indian agriculture is neither extensive nor indiscriminate' (Chand and Birthal 1997). Moreover, its use is particularly more intense for cotton and certain exported crops like fruits and vegetables rather than in foodgrains.

Notwithstanding these contrary views, evidence suggests the need for proper planning in order to promote and regulate pesticides' use in the country. This perspective receives support from the limited awareness of the farmers regarding the hazardous effects of pesticides as well as the lack of information on environment-friendly alternatives (Gandhi and Patel 1997). In the absence of adequate information and legal framework for responding to the liabilities of the environmental (health) damages caused by pesticide use, there is little incentive for reducing the rate of application. In turn, this highlights the urgency for regulating its use in a more planned as well as informed manner, possibly by

Table 12.5 Proportion of pesticides used on different crops in India

Crop	Pesticides used (%)	Cropped area (%)
Cotton	54	5
Rice	17	24
Vegetables and fruits	13	3
Plantation crops	8	2
Sugarcane	3	2
Oilseeds	2	10
Others (including wheat, coarse cereals, millets and pulses)	3	54

Source: Dhaliwal and Kansal (1994).

increasing the cost of non-compliance (Marothia 1997). People's awareness and local institutions can be of immense help in operationalizing the requisite checks and punitive action in line with developed country practices.

Cost of environmental damages

What is the likely economic cost of environmental damage due to inappropriate use of fertilizer, pesticides and irrigation? Though no systematic study on this aspect exists, a few attempts have been made to gauge the cost of environmental damage in location-specific contexts. For instance, Tisdell (1996) studied three villages in the Midnapore district in West Bengal and showed that the villagers would require about a 50 per cent increase in current income in order to compensate them for the loss of natural resources and environmental deterioration. These estimates are based on a very small sample in a specific context, and the methodologies adopted are often subjective or, too simplistic to address highly complex issues such as the EIA of diverse agricultural systems in the country.

Based on macro analysis, Parikh and Ghosh (1991) estimated that a 10 per cent increase in highly saline soil, may reduce productivity by 2 per cent, resulting in a loss of about Rs.2,500 crore at 1989–90 prices. These estimates are somewhat tentative, as there are serious methodological as well as data limitations for capturing the quality of land.

Alternatively the futuristic scenarios, projecting changes in the extent and nature of input-use in agriculture, can be considered. Based on a consistency model for the Indian economy, Parikh (1991) examines the implications of a projected growth of 4 per cent for the agriculture sector on investment priorities, effective demand, and environment (Table 12.6). The study finds that the future growth of agriculture is likely to be induced mainly by irrigation; impact of fertilizer subsidy (at 30 per cent) and increase in agricultural prices (by 20 per cent) may have only limited impact on growth. The model's projections indicated that attaining a 4 per cent growth will involve an increase in the net sown area from 142.7 million ha to 143.8 million ha along with a corresponding increase in gross irrigated area from 68.4 million ha to 109.6 million ha; with simultaneous rise in consumption of nitrogenous fertilizer from 7.2 million tonne to 14.2 million tonne, which works out to 40.2 kg and 68.7 kg per hectare of gross cropped area, respectively.

The projected increase in the use of irrigation and chemical fertilizer may have a significant bearing on the future state of the environment. The dominant perspective among academicians and policy makers in the country is that the problem of waterlogging or chemical pollution is largely due to an inappropriate application of these inputs (Parikh 1991). Rao (1994) has noted that deforestation presently poses a greater threat than chemicalization of agriculture for agricultural development in India. The policy imperative therefore, is to promote efficient use rather than a blanket reduction in the use of external inputs. With respect to irrigation, it is held that the main environmental problems from irrigation are related to the use of water rather than by the processes of creating

Table 12.6 Agricultural growth under different scenarios

Scenario	Average annual growth rate 1990–2000 (%)			Agriculture/non agriculture		Gross irrigated area (10 ha)	Fertilizer consumption (10 tonnes of N)
	GDP Agri.	GDP Non-agri	GDP	1990	2000	2000	2000
Reference scenario	2.46	6.63	5.41	0.66	0.69	77.8	12.87
Agri. prices increased by 20 per cent	2.49	6.54	5.38	0.81	0.87	80.6	13.19
Agri. investments increased by 50 per cent	2.65	6.28	5.17	0.66	0.69	90.0	14.18
Additional investment in irrigation	3.79	6.77	5.86	0.67	0.57	109.6	14.24

Source: Parikh (1991).

irrigation facilities (Parikh 1991; Dhaliwal and Kansal 1994; Deshpande and Ramakrishna 1990). Overall, the existing evidence on EIA suggests a relatively lower incidence of damages in a developing economy such as India as compared to the developed economies. The thrust therefore is to adopt a policy approach, which is preventive rather than restrictive in terms of promoting productivity for the future growth of the agriculture sector in India.

Food security by regenerating land and water in rain fed/dry land areas

There has been a substantial increase in the productivity of all the major crops since the mid-1980s. The crop yields however, vary significantly across three sets of regions; namely, low, moderate and high labour productivity in agriculture. It may however, be noted that there is significant untapped potential for increasing the yields in states like Bihar, Madhya Pradesh and Orissa that belong to the category of low labour productivity. Relatively better availability of groundwater in these states makes a strong case for prioritizing investment in these regions, which incidentally, also bear a higher burden of poverty.

Development of wasteland, both forest as well as non-forest, has been considered as an important source of food security for the resource-poor households. There has been an increasing realization that shifting the locus of agricultural growth from the hitherto high growth regions under the first phase of GR to the high potential rain-fed areas and also to dry land regions is considered to be pro-growth as well as pro-poor. What is however, missing in the present discourse on the pro-poor growth is that the proposed spatial diversification of agricultural growth may also turn out to be environmentally more conducive. With government support, these regeneration efforts can be channelled for promoting indigenous varieties of food crops, especially coarse cereals and pulses, which are rich in terms of nutrient value as well as bio-diversity.[3]

The policy statement on agriculture (2000), lays special emphasis on blending the twin goals of enhancing productivity with minimum environmental damage, given the crops and state of the technology. This would involve simultaneous efforts in the direction of: (a) realization of the full yield potential of the existing crop-technology mix by adopting a farming systems approach with inbuilt diversity; and (b) increasing the agronomic potential by undoing the damages in terms of degradation of land and water resources.

Emerging policy issues

Agrarian crisis and renewed policy thrust

The recent policy discourse is marked by increasing recognition of the critical role that the agricultural sector in India plays in reducing poverty besides boosting up overall economic growth. The recognition has come at a time when the agricultural sector has started facing yet another crisis, which poses important challenges such as low and fluctuating growth rates over time and space; continued depletion of natural resources and persistent technological stagnation in order to address the problems in drought-prone as well as flood-prone areas, inhabiting a large proportion of agrarian communities in the country. The scenario during the eleventh plan period has only improved marginally. The crisis is being reflected through several channels, noted below:

- Reduced area and production of food grains (the growth rate in production during 1990s being 1.08 per cent, far below the population growth rate);
- Increased area under fallow land;
- Decline in crop productivity during the 1990s (from 2.99 per cent to 1.21 per cent);
- Large proportion of farmers wanting to get out of agriculture (due to non-viability of holdings and input-output prices);
- Overexploitation of land (forest and pastures) and (ground) water resources.

Policy imperatives for future

The discussion so far suggests that the damages are generally severe but not irreversible, except for selected areas of waterlogging and groundwater depletion. Interestingly, a large part of the damage has occurred because of the wrong price signals (input and output), rather than the wrong choice of crops/technology. Hence, the next phase of agricultural growth could be achieved by a relatively moderate shift in crop mix, input use, and agronomic practices – especially in large tracts of dry land agriculture in the country. It may however, be noted that achieving even a moderate shift may require substantial changes in agricultural practices being followed in some of the marginalized regions like dry land, forest and hilly and coastal areas, all facing severe natural resources depletion.

Managing even a moderate shift may therefore, involve a huge task in terms of mobilizing resources for investment in agriculturally laggard areas, modifying the property rights regime as well as the requisite institutional structures, and altering the input-price structure in a manner that compels farmers especially, with irrigation facilities, to improve water use efficiency. All these, primarily need a strong political commitment and will.

Environmental governance

At present there are a number of regulations influencing the use as well as management of natural resources[4] among which two are especially important in the current context. The first relates to the use and conversion of forest land under the Forest Conservation Act (1980), and the other relates to the use of hazardous chemicals as pesticides (Environment Protection Act 1986). Other regulations governing air and water pollution also remain important. Most of the state governments also have specific legislations to control and govern the conversion of agricultural land for non-agricultural use, to facilitate the use of pasture or other community waste land for agriculture (mainly through distribution of land to the landless), to regulate the use of groundwater below a certain threshold level, and also to use surface water (from canal and other water bodies such as community tanks, river, etc.) for irrigation.

While the regulations related to land use are by and large governed by the concerns of equity and diversity, the same for water use mainly concerns the long-term 'sustainability' of resource. Notwithstanding the validity of the underlying rationale, and also the administrative mechanism for ensuring an effective implementation of these regulations, the actual compliance especially in the case of groundwater is found to be abysmally weak. This is due to the fact that groundwater, in most cases, is controlled by the individuals owning the land.

Another important issue relating to weak compliance of environmental regulations pertains to the improper use of pesticides, especially on fruits and vegetables, causing problems of health hazards. Certification of seeds and use of genetically modified organisms (GMO) are yet other dimensions that need greater attention from the viewpoint of environmental governance. Some concern areas are discussed in the following.

Prices and subsidies

Given that India has been a semi-planned economy, regulation of costs and prices have been the most important policy intervention, influencing the agricultural sector. The policy commitment for achieving food security by ensuring the requisite level of aggregate production and its availability through the public distribution system (PDS) has been the guiding motive. The link between aggregate production and distribution is established through procurement of selected agricultural commodities, especially wheat and rice. The minimum support price (MSP) programme is aimed at covering all major crops in the country. However, in practice it focuses on only rice and wheat, and covers selected areas in states such as Punjab, Haryna, western UP and AP. The MSP is based on the notion of covering full cost, which made it go beyond domestic market conditions. Historically, the MSP for wheat and rice were increased at rates below inflation and remained well under import parity prices (Landes and Gulati 2004). Regulation of both input and output prices has been on the one hand instrumental for ensuring aggregate supply, and its actual access among most, if not all, consumers, on the other.

Notwithstanding the laudable policy goals, agricultural pricing and subsidies have remained one of the highly contested issues in India. The main tenor of the debate on output (procurement) prices is that it is a double-edged instrument, which seeks to support both the producers and the consumers. This, indeed, is a very tricky situation since incentives provided to producers fail the objective of supporting the consumers and vice-versa. While this holds good in most cases (including the developed economies in the North), the critical aspect in the case of India is that, a large proportion of consumers in the country are not able to purchase food grains at prices that cover even a 'cost plus' normal profit to the farmers. Thus, a lack of purchasing power among a large number of consumers is the core issue for supporting output prices for the farmers.[5] In the absence of any corrective measure, the phenomenon has culminated into a strange situation of significant growth in the aggregate supply of foodgrains along with massive undernourishment among millions of poor in the country. The scenario has led to a realization that the output price support system needs a major reshuffle not only in the interests of the poor producers as well as consumers within India but, also due to the competitive pressure from the international trade.[6] With over two-thirds of India's workforce still engaged in agriculture and related activities, agricultural productivity augmentation would also increase purchasing power among a large section of the poor. The concern therefore is how to significantly increase agricultural productivity, and what could be the role of price/subsidy versus non-price/technological interventions in achieving this goal?

A plethora of literature exists examining the relative importance of price and non-price factors in the Indian context. The literature broadly indicates that non-price factors, especially technological break-through have been major drivers of agricultural productivity as compared to price-related incentives. While the literature does indicate a relatively crucial role of the non-price factors, the question which needs to be addressed is to what extent, price-support or subsidies are essential for sustaining the increased productivity in agriculture? The next question then would be to know how far these subsidies have caused the environmental damages noted earlier.

The existing literature on the impact of price support to Indian agriculture focuses separately on the aspects of input-subsidy and price support for procuring the output. The former, to a large extent, refers to subsidies for fertilizer, irrigation or power, and other inputs like seeds, farm-equipments, credit infrastructure, etc. especially to small and marginal farmers. Agricultural subsidy especially on irrigation, fertilizer and public distribution of food are the major constituents of the total subsidy (Mehra *et al.* 2003).[7]

The major issue pertaining to agricultural subsidy appears to be the leakages, non-recovery and improper targeting of subsidies, which lead not only to budgetary burdens and misallocation of resources but, also inefficiency and non-sustainability of growth. Mehra *et al.* (2003) noted that the main difficulty, especially in the case of the subsidy to power and irrigation is the state's inability to recover the unsubsidized part of the cost which apparently has outgrown the actual amount of public investment in the sector. Overall the subsidies have grown too large in volume without meeting the objectives, and exerting a negative impact on the economy (Vaidyanathan 2000). This of course, does not suggest that subsidy is entirely undesirable. The concern is rather on the form, structure and governance of subsidy rather than appropriateness of the subsidy per se.

Rationalization of subsidy and environmental concerns

One of the possible ways of redressing the distortions is by incorporating environmental considerations into the subsidy structure in a manner, which enhances efficient rather than intensive use of inputs and natural resources such as land

and water. The total agricultural sector support estimation by Gulati and Naray-anan (2003) demonstrate that Indian agriculture is much less subsidized as com-pared to the same in the EU, implying that India has de-protected a large number of agriculture commodities. The phenomenon becomes clear when alternative estimates using shadow prices are considered (Anand 2000).

Viewed from the policy perspective therefore, India has reached a historical vantage point, from which the country can launch on to a growth path that could simultaneously reinforce resource regeneration, productivity enhancement, and poverty reduction. Ideally, India should be able to move on this path mainly by correcting the domestic distortions in prices and subsidies. If so, she may not need to submit to the externally determined choice of crops, production techno-logy and exports under the current trade negotiations on environment. Arguably undertaking reforms on one's own terms, may work out better than doing so under duress in the context of WTO negotiations. Therefore India's present posi-tion of resisting environmental restrictions to dampen export possibilities may stand justified, provided the country is seriously embarking upon a modified strategy for agricultural growth as discussed above.

Assuming that the country can muster a political commitment, there may still be real problems in mobilizing financial resources within next seven to ten years, so that the historical opportunity, discussed earlier is not lost. The process of trade negotiations may perhaps help in this context. But the present processes of trade negotiations do not seem to be moving into this direction since the central focus continues to remain on increasing the volume of trade, which in turn is treated as welfare enhancing given the conventional neo-classical framework. Rodrik (2001) rightly argued that, 'the problem with the current trade rules is not that they over emphasize trade and growth at the expense of poverty reduction but that they over emphasize trade at the expense of poverty reduction and growth'. While this issue is beyond the scope of the present analysis, it is import-ant to keep track of the contemporary debate on trade which seeks to question the role of trade itself, in promoting sustainability and human welfare, rather than taking it for granted.

The final point however, is that if India fails to consolidate the resources – financial, techno-institutional and political – to effectively adopt a moderate path of growth (along the line of sustainable intensification), it would then be com-pelled to step down into the trajectory of degraded resources, deepened poverty and greater reliance on external markets with potentially high instability in crop production and income–employment among poor households. Of course, the challenges of moving on to a sustainable growth path as discussed earlier, involve an enormous restructuring of the fiscal system, institutions and work ethos or governance. Going by the track record so far, this Herculean goal can be achieved only when changes occur at the macro, meso and micro levels.

The above observations ascertain the fact that promoting sustainable agriculture globally would call for a new growth perspective where environmental as well as livelihood–lifestyle concerns occupies the centre stage. Trade may, at best, play a facilitating role rather than an objective by itself. The trade–environment inter-linkage has so far been actively debated among both academicians and policy makers in the context of trade negotiations. Treating concerns of liveli-hood–lifestyle as integral parts of the present trade–environment discourse is the need of the hour.

Notes

1 This implies environment is a 'luxury' that developing countries can ill-afford. This arguable perspective has created an active debate on adopting differential environ-mental standards across the developed and the developing countries in the context of trade liberalization.
2 The Environment Action Programme (EAP) set up in 1993 by the Government of India has identified seven environmental priorities; of these only one has a direct link with agriculture. This refers to afforestation, wastelands development, soil-moisture conser-vation, and water pollution (Khurana 2003).
3 Promotion of coarse cereals especially in dryland regions therefore, has been viewed as an important strategy for attaining food security among poor households. However, the past experiences in promoting high yielding varieties (HYVs) of jowar, bajri and maize under rain fed conditions are not so encouraging since these new cultivars remain highly vulnerable to the weather induced fluctuations.
4 It deserves mention that India does not have an official policy statement for agriculture since it is included in the concurrent list of sectors to be handled by both the provincial and the central government. Environment on the other hand is a central subject. If there are conflicts between the state agricultural policy and the environmental regulations of the central government, the later prevails upon the former.
5 This is essentially different from the situation prevailing in developed economies like the EU where subsidies are offered to farmers primarily for sustaining their interest in production, which is often at a price far exceeding what most of the consumers within the economies could afford to pay (Oxfam 2002).
6 Landes and Gulati (2004) notes the major limitations of MSP including the absence of linkage with both domestic and world price, resulting in undue inefficiency hurting export potential, etc. Setting MSP linked to domestic and world prices therefore miti-gates some inefficiency associated with the cost of production and environmental externalities.
7 These estimates, based on the basis of domestic supply cost, are likely to be underestimated.

References

Anand, M. (2000) 'Does Trade Liberalization lead to Loss of Comparative Advantage: Empirical Estimates for Indian Agricultural and Industrial Sectors', unpublished paper, New Delhi: National Institute of Public Finance and Policy.

Bhagwati, J. and Srinivasan, T. (1996) 'Trade and the Environment: Does Environmental Diversity Detract from the Case for Free Trade', in J. Bhagwati and R. Hudec (eds) *Fair Trade and Harmonization for Free Trade?*, Cambridge, MA: MIT Press.

Bond, J.W. (1996) *How EC and World Bank Policies are Destroying Agriculture and the Environment: A European and Third World Perspective*, Alkmaar: AgBe Publishing.

Chand, R. (1999) 'Liberalization of Agricultural Trade and Net Social Welfare: A Study of Selected Crops', *Economic and Political Weekly*, 34(52): A153–A159.

Chand, R. (2005) *India's Agriculture Trade during Post-WTO Decade: Lessons for WTO Negotiations*, New Delhi: National Center for Economic and Policy Research.

Chand, R. and Birthal, P.S. (1997) 'Pesticide Use in Indian Agriculture in Relation to Growth in Area and Production and Technological Change', *Indian Journal of Agricultural Economics*, 52(3): 488–498.

Chand, R. and Haque, T. (1997) 'Sustainability of Rice-Wheat Crop System in Indo-Gangetic Region', *Economic and Political Weekly*, 32(13): A26–30.

Conway, G.R. and Pretty, J.N. (1991) *Unwelcome Harvest: Agriculture and Pollution*, London: Earthscan.

Datta, S. and Chakrabarti, M. (2001) 'Trends and Features of North–South Agricultural Trade: Lessons and Cautions for India', in S. Datta and S. Deodhar (eds) *Implications of WTO Agreements for Indian Agriculture*, New Delhi: Oxford and IBH Publishing Co. Pvt. Ltd.

Desai, B.M. and Namboodiri, N.V. (1997) 'Strategy and Sources of Growth in Crop-Agriculture', in B.M. Desai (ed.) *Agricultural Development: Paradigm for the Ninth Plan under New Economic Environment*, New Delhi: Oxford and IBH Publishing Co. Pvt. Ltd.

Desai, G.M. and Rastogi, S. (1995) 'Agricultural Growth in India: An Agro-Climatic Environment Based Perspective', in G.M. Desai and A. Vaidyanathan (eds) *Strategic Issues in Future Growth Fertiliser Use in India*, New Delhi: Macmillan India Ltd.

Deshpande, R.S. and Ramakrishna, K.S. (1990) 'Agro-ecological Problems of Command Area', in Ramchandran (ed.), *Environmental Issues in Agricultural Development*, New Delhi: Concept Publishing House.

Dev, M. and Painuly, J.P. (1994) *Fertiliser and Pesticide Use in Agriculture: Environmental Issues*, Mumbai: Indira Gandhi Institute of Development Research (IGIDR).

Dhaliwal, G.S. and Kansal, B.D. (1994) *Management of Agricultural Pollution in India*, New Delhi: Commonwealth Publishers.

Dhawan, B.D. (1997) 'Latent Threats to Irrigated Agriculture', in B.M. Desai (ed.), *Agricultural Development: Paradigm for the Ninth Plan under New Economic Environment*, New Delhi: Oxford and IBH Publishing Co. Pvt. Ltd.

Fertilizer Association of India (various years) 'Fertilizer Statistics', New Delhi.

Gandhi, V.P. and. Patel, N.T. (1997) 'Pesticides and the Environment: A Comparative Study of Farmer Awareness and Behaviour in Andhra Pradesh, Punjab and Gujarat', *Indian Journal of Agricultural Economics*, 52(3): 519–529.

Ghuman, R.S. (2001) 'WTO and Indian Agriculture: Crisis and Challenges – a Case Study of Punjab', *Man and Development*, 23(2): 67–96.

Giljum, S, and Eisenmenger, N. (2003) 'North–South Trade and the Distribution of Environmental Goods and Burdens: A Biophysical Perspective', SERI Working Paper, Vienna: Sustainable Europe Research Institute.

Government of India (various years) 'Economic Survey', New Delhi: Ministry of Finance.

Government of India (2000) 'National Agriculture Policy', New Delhi: Ministry of Agriculture.

Government of India (2006) 'Third National Report on Implementation of United Nations Convention to Combat Desertification', New Delhi: Ministry of Environment and Forest.

Government of India (2009) 'Eleventh Five Year Plan: 2007–2012', New Delhi: Planning Commission.

Gulati, Ashok and Narayanan, Sudha (2003) *The Subsidy Syndrome in Indian Agriculture*, Oxford, OUP, 2003.

Hoda, A. and Gulati, A. (2002) 'Trade Liberalisation and Food Security in South Asia', paper presented at ICRIER-ICAR-IFPRI conference on Economic Reforms and Food Security: The Role of Trade and Technology, New Delhi, 24–25 April.

Kamra, Om and Abraham, Vinoj (2004) *Punjab Agriculture at the Crossroads*, New Delhi: Jawahar Book Centre.

Khurana, I. (2003) *Environment Management in India: Policies, Practices and Future Needs*, New Delhi: Shastri-Indo Canadian Institute.

Kumar, P. and Joshi, P.K. (1998) 'Sustainability of Rice-Wheat Based Cropping Systems in India: Socio-Economic and Policy Issues', *Economic and Political Weekly*, 33(39): A152–A158.

Landes, R. and Gulati, A. (2004) 'Farm Sector Performance and Reform Agenda', *Economic and Political Weekly*, 39(32): 3611–3619.

Marothia, D. (1997) 'Agricultural Technology and Environmental Quality: An Institutional Perspective', *Indian Journal of Agricultural Economics*, 52(3): 473–487.

Mehra, M., Sinha, M. and Sahu, S. (2003) *Trade-Related Subsidies Bridging the North–South Divide: An Indian Perspective*, Winnipeg: International Institute for Sustainable Development.

Muradian, R. and Martinez-Allier, J. (2001) 'Trade and the Environment: From a Southern Perspective', *Ecological Economics*, 36: 281–297.

Natarajan, I. (1995) 'Trends in Firewood Consumption in Rural India', *Margin*, 28(1): 41–47.

Oxfam International (2002) *Rugged Rules and Double Standards: Trade, Globalization, and Fight against Poverty*, London: Oxfam.

Parikh, K. (1991) '4 Per Cent Growth Rate in Agriculture over the 1990s: Policy Implications and Environmental Consequences', Mumbai: IGIDR.

Parikh, K. and Ghosh, U. (1991) 'Natural Resource Accounting for Soil: Towards and Empirical Estimate of Costs of Soil Degradation for India', IGIDR Discussion Paper No 48, Mumbai: IGIDR.

Peterson, J., Boisvert, R.N. and Gonter, H. de (2004) 'Multifunctionality and Optimal Environmental Policies for Agriculture in an Open Economy', in M.D. Ingco and L. Alan Winters (eds) *Agriculture and the New Trade Agenda: Creating a Global Trading Environment for Development*, Cambridge: Cambridge University Press.

Rao, C.H.H. (1994) *Agricultural Growth, Rural Poverty and Environmental Degradation in India*, Delhi: Oxford University Press.

Reddy, R. and Bhagirath, B. (2000) 'Land Degradation and Food Security in India', paper presented at the National Seminar on Food Scarcity in India: The Emerging Challenges in the Context of Economic Liberalization, Center for Economic and Social Studies, Hyderabad, March.

Rodrik, D. (2001) *The Global Governance of Trade: As if Development Really Mattered*, New York: United Nations Development Programme.

Sachs, W. and Agarwal, H. (2002), *The Jo'burg Memo: Fairness in a Fragile World*, Berlin: Heinrich-Boll-Stiftung.

Sawhney, A. (2003) 'How Environmental Provisions affect Asian Developing Countries', *Management Review*, 15(1): 11–18.

Shah, A. and Weis, T. (2004) 'Trade and Sustainable Agriculture: Review of Evidence and Issues in a North–South Context', unpublished paper, Ahmedabad: Gujarat Institute of Development Research.

Sharma, H.R. (1997) 'Land Reforms: Status and Opportunity' in B.M. Desai (ed.), *Agricultural Development: Paradigm for the Ninth Plan under New Economic Environment*, New Delhi: Oxford and IBH Publishing Co. Pvt. Ltd.

Sidhu, R.S. and Dhillon, M.S. (1997) 'Land and Water Resources in Punjab: Their Degradation and Technologies for Sustainable Use', *Indian Journal of Agricultural Economics*, 52(3): 508–518.

Singh, T. (2004) *Resource Conservation and Food Security: An Indian Experience*, vol. ii, New Delhi: Concept Publishing Company.

Tisdell, C. (1996) 'Agricultural Sustainability and the Environment: Issues and Strategies with Particular Reference to India and Australia', in K.C. Roy, R. Sen and C.A. Tisdell (eds), *Environment and Sustainable Agriculture Development: Concepts, General Issues, Constraints and Strategies*, New Delhi: International Institute for Development Studies and New Age International (P) Ltd. Publishers.

Vaidyanathan, A., (2000) 'India's Agricultural Development Policy', *Economic and Political Weekly*, 35(20):1735–1741.

WWF (2005), *Living Planet Report-2004*, Gland: World Wide Fund for Nature.

13 Is India turning into a pollution haven?

Evidences from trade and investment patterns

Debashis Chakraborty

Introduction

The intensification of certain environment-sensitive economic activities (e.g. mining, ship-breaking), in line with growing international commercial operations in these categories, might bear adverse environmental repercussions in a country in the following manner. First, mislaid thrust on an export-led economic growth model might deplete the stock of natural resources in a developing country/LDC (less-developed country) that traditionally depend considerably on primary items including marine resources, mining and forestry products. Second, the relatively less stringent environmental standards in a developing country/LDC might encourage the players from developed countries to shift their production activities with higher pollution potential in the former location. Alternatively, foreign direct investment (FDI) from the developed countries might come to the developing countries targeting such sectors. As a result, developing countries may specialize in the production of commodities characterized by a higher pollution load and export the final product to developed countries. This leads to an increase of environmental degradation in the South but reduction of the same in the North. The phenomenon of growing degradation in a country characterized by relatively weaker environmental standards/policy, or with lesser willingness and capacity to enforce them through a trade or investment route in this manner is termed as 'pollution haven hypothesis' (PHH) in international trade literature (Lucas *et al.* 1992; Xing and Kolstad 1998; List and Co 1999; Eskeland and Harrison 2003; Cole and Elliott 2005).

Since the adoption of the structural adjustment policies (SAP) in 1991 as per the IMF recommendation, India has followed an outward-oriented growth model. Fuelled by unilateral as well as multilateral reforms since the inception of the WTO in 1995, the importance of external trade and investment in the economy has increased considerably. At present, export of environmentally sensitive goods (ESGs) account for approximately one-third of India's merchandise export basket (Chakraborty 2008). Similarly, the importance of FDI in the strategic sectors, including environmentally sensitive sectors has increased over the years.

Several recent developments necessitate a need to check the existence of the PHH phenomenon in India. Environment-related trade barriers already threaten

Indian exports (Chaturvedi and Nagpal 2007). In addition, both the United States and several European countries are currently exploring the idea of imposing a carbon tax on imports from polluting industries in developing countries like India and China (Sen 2010). Such border tax adjustment (BTA) is argued to be an efficient tool for controlling carbon leakage in countries characterized by less stringent carbon emission regulation (Nanda and Ratna 2010). Chauhan (2011) notes that a recent World Bank document on the Ganga project argues that the share of the most polluting sectors in India's exports has increased considerably during the last decade, with profound implications on health and the environment.

This chapter is organized along the following lines. First, a brief literature survey on PHH is presented, with special reference to the Indian scenario. Second, the importance of the polluting sectors in India's merchandise exports and imports in the manufacturing sector are noted. The FDI inflow in polluting sectors in India and its potential implications on environmental degradation are analysed next. Finally on the basis of the observations, a few policy conclusions are drawn.

Trade, investment and environment degradation: a survey of literature

The instances of merchandise trade-led natural resources overexploitation and environmental degradation are common in international trade. The primary exports often suffer from falling price, and the resulting urge to protect export value leads to an increase in export volume, thereby putting pressure on the environment. For instance, during the 1980s in the post-SAP period Bangladesh attempted to boost shrimp export with a combination of tax breaks and subsidy policies, but the same resulted in environmental degradation in terms of a rise in soil salinity and soil quality related problems, reduction in grazing land and loss of livestock, destruction of mangrove forests, adverse effects on the cropping intensity, etc. (UNEP 1999). Second, the recent decision of Peru to augment oil and gas exploration in the Amazonian forest could be mentioned, which has resulted in an irreversible loss of biodiversity (Finer *et al.* 2008). The iron ore export from India and the potential local environmental consequences can also be mentioned in this context (Sinha undated). Finally, the provision of subsidies in the developed countries often is not restricted to overexploitation within their territories. For instance, the fisheries subsidies provided by developed countries for 'access rights transfer' might lead to the depletion of fish stock in developing countries' waters (UNEP 2004).

Environmental degradation might also occur with direct influence from developed countries in the production and trade process, either by relocation of polluting industrial units or by outsourcing of the most polluting part of the activities in developing countries. The trade or investment decision in these cases is influenced by low labour cost and relatively lax environmental provisions in developing countries. The relocation of American environmentally-sensitive industries to Mexico after the formation of NAFTA can be mentioned here (Gallagher 2004). Second, the growing North–South trade in metal waste and scrap products deserves attention, where the South is increasingly specializing in import and processing of toxic wastes (Lipman 2006). A highly polluting sector like ship-breaking is a case in point, where developing country ports like Alang (India), Chittagong (Bangladesh), Aliaga (Turkey) and Karachi (Pakistan) have emerged as new hubs. Similarly, Basel Action Network (2007) has noted that 'toxic' exports often feature in Japanese regional trade agreements. The environmental consequences are obviously, grave.

The relationship between FDI and environmental degradation is another extensively researched area. The literature on PHH in China is quite rich, given its emergence as a major destination of inward FDI during the 1990s and the debates concerning environmental degradation there. A number of studies have reported the adverse implications of FDI inflow on the environment in China (Cole *et al.* 2008; He 2006), though a section of the literature rejects those findings (Temurshoev 2006). A number of studies also attempt to differentiate the source and destination of FDI in China to explain the observed effects. It is noted that FDI inflow in China from Southeast Asian developing countries is generally motivated by weaker province-level environmental levies, while joint ventures from developed countries (e.g. United States, United Kingdom and Japan) are attracted by stronger environmental levies regardless of the pollution intensity of the industry concerned (Dean *et al.* 2004). It was also observed that FDI inflow from the OECD countries has intensified pollution in several ASEAN countries (Mukhopadhyay 2006; Merican *et al.* 2007). Moreover, it can be mentioned that countries like Papua New Guinea, the Philippines and Indonesia had relaxed their environmental standard for enhancing FDI in the mining sector (CUTS 2003).

The existence of PHH can also be established through the relationship between FDI outflow and environmental degradation. For instance, analysing the outward FDI flows of various industries within the German manufacturing sector, Wagner and Timmins (2008) observed robust evidence of PHH for the chemical industry, which is one of the polluting sectors. Aminu (2005) demonstrated that 'dirty' FDI outflow is positively correlated with environmental policy in 11 OECD countries.

However, PHH has been rejected by a number of studies with the argument that factors like capital abundance, technology differences, infrastructure, etc. are far more important as compared to environmental policy in determining trade and FDI patterns (Birdsall and Wheeler 1993; Letchumanan 1998; Kahn 2003). It is argued that FDI may facilitate the adoption of modern technologies and best environmental practices in the production process and ensure better knowledge transfers, through labour training, skill acquisition, introducing alternative management practices, etc. The rejection of PHH in several countries can be explained from the fact that trade may ensure environmental sustainability by providing incentives to upgrade production conditions. For instance, the need to ensure compliance with stringent environmental conditions in developed countries for export often might compel the developing countries and LDCs to improve their existing level of environmental standards which could further be aided by the transfer of environment-friendly technologies. While responsible multinational corporations (MNCs) can contribute in this regard, the 'pioneer' local firms can also adopt necessary steps. It is observed that in line with the growing demand for 'cleaner' and 'greener' production process, the number of ISO 14000 certifications across developing countries has gradually increased over the last decade (Boys and Grant 2010).

However, developing countries often react to the policies undertaken by the North, instead of adopting proactive policies. For example, leather firms in India have modified their pollution abatement system and reduced the use of carcinogenic and other harmful chemicals in the production process considerably since the late 1990s, owing to the stringent environmental standards and sanctions imposed in Germany (Chakraborty and Singh 2005). However, there is a limit to which the environmental instruments adopted by developed countries can be effective. If the developed countries continue to impose higher environmental standards on their developing counterparts' exports as a trade policy tool, then it might lead to a suboptimal outcome (Sankar 2006).

Several studies have been undertaken in the Indian context to analyse the impact of trade and investment patterns on the environment. The literature reports adverse environmental repercussions resulting from the operations of transnational corporations during the 1980s (Jha 1999), i.e. during the pre-liberalization period. Higher FDI inflow in relatively more polluting sectors in the period after liberalization in 1991 has also been noted (Singh 1997; Gamper-Rabindran and Jha 2004). Mathys (2004) has argued that activities in the polluting sectors have increased in India with the advent of globalization of the economy. The observation has been supported by Chattopadhyay (2005), which through an analysis of India's export basket noted an increase in the proportional share of polluted products there. Nevertheless, several studies through the analysis of India's export basket/state-wise/sector-wise FDI inflow patterns have rejected the existence of an explicit PHH phenomenon in the recent period (Mukhopadhyay 2004; Jena et al. 2005; Mukhopadhyay and Chakraborty 2005; Chaturvedi and Nagpal 2007; Dietzenbacher and Mukhopadhyay 2007).

Environmental governance in India

Before moving to the discussion on international trade and investment patterns, a brief note on environmental governance on production in India will not be inappropriate here. The Central Pollution Control Board (CPCB) has identified 17 categories of industries as highly polluting industries in India; namely, (1) aluminium smelting, (2) caustic soda, (3) cement (capacity of 200 tonne/day and above), (4) copper smelting, (5) fermentation (distillery), (6) dyes and dye intermediate, (7) fertilizers, (8) integrated iron and steel, (9) leather processing including tanneries, (10) pesticide formulation and manufacturing, (11) petrochemicals, (12) basic drugs and pharmaceuticals manufacturing, (13) pulp and paper (having capacity of 30 tonne/day and above), (14) oil refineries, (15) sugar mills, (16) thermal power plants and (17) zinc smelting. Pandey (2005) estimated the pollution load in India by taking the data for the 17 categories of polluting industries from the CPCB and generating their pollution intensity by matching it with the World Bank Industrial Pollution Projection System (IPPS) database. The analysis identified iron and steel, paper, and the aluminium industry to be the top three polluting industries in India. Analysing the number of factories closed down in recent years, Chakraborty (2009) noted that thermal power, pharmaceutical, cement and leather are among the major polluting sectors. The CPCB (with the help from state pollution control boards) monitors the environmental compliance of medium- and large-scale units under the 17 most polluting categories of industries on a regular basis. Based on the pollution potential (red/orange/green) and size (based on the value of capital investment) of the industry, pollution control boards decide on the frequency of sampling (on-site visits) to verify pollution abatement compliance (UNDP 2009). Table 13.1 reports the sectoral distribution of the surveyed and defaulter units in the country. The table indicates that coverage of the units under these industries has increased substantially since 2003–04. In addition, the industrial units in general are also subject to regular checks on their emission/effluent concentration depending on their pollution potential.

Table 13.1 Compliance status in the 17 polluting categories of industry in India

Polluting sector	1999–2000		2000–01		2001–02		2002–03		2003–04	
	A	B	A	B	A	B	A	B	A	B
Aluminium	7	0	7	0	7	0	07	0	7	0
Caustic	25	0	25	0	25	0	25	0	33	0
Cement	116	4	116	0	116	0	116	0	205	6
Copper	2	2	2	1	2	0	2	0	4	0
Distillery	177	27	177	11	177	2	177	2	209	3
Dyes and dyeing industries	64	2	64	0	64	0	64	0	102	2
Fertilizer	110	3	110	3	110	1	110	1	124	2
Iron and steel	8	6	8	6	8	4	8	4	19	4
Leather	70	0	70	0	70	0	70	0	94	4
Pesticide	71	2	71	1	71	0	71	0	111	1
Petrochem	49	0	49	0	49	0	49	0	75	1
Pharma	251	1	251	0	251	0	251	0	401	10
Pulp and paper	96	6	96	1	96	0	96	0	136	2
Refinery	12	0	12	0	12	0	12	0	16	0
Sugar	392	38	392	11	392	2	392	1	462	3
TPP	97	23	97	19	97	15	97	14	151	15
Zinc	4	0	4	0	4	0	4	0	6	0
Total	1,551	114	1,551	53	1,551	24	1,551	22	2,155	53

Source: compiled from annual reports of Ministry of Environment and Forests (various years).

Notes
A – Total number of units.
B – Defaulting units.

In order to secure greater adoption of environmentally sound production, financial assistance is currently being provided to the industrial sector for operationalization of Common Effluent Treatment Plants (CETPs). While central and the state governments each provide a subsidy of 25 per cent of the total project cost of installing the CETP, the remaining cost is met partly by loan from financial institutions and partly through members'/entrepreneurs' contribution. Major industrial clusters with operational CETPs presently include firms from several polluting categories such as pharmaceuticals, chemicals, textile bleaching and dyeing, distillery, dye and dye intermediate, pesticides, plastic, paper, engineering industries, leather sector, etc. (Toxics Link 2000). The observed quality of effluent discharged from the CETP underlines the benefits for the environment (Chakraborty 2009).

Apart from the unilateral attempts, India's commitments to multilateral environmental agreements (MEAs) have also augmented its environmental governance. Presently, the hazardous substances management division (HSMD) within the Ministry of Environment and Forests (MoEF) takes care of India's commitments under the Basel Convention (1992), Rotterdam Convention (2004) and Stockholm Convention (2004). The purpose of enactment of the Hazardous Wastes (Management and Handling) Rules (1989), which were amended in 2000, is to reduce the waste generated or recycled or reused. The MoEF has identified nearly 200 zones in the country as hazard-prone industrial pockets, and has conducted hazard analysis for most of them (MoEF undated). Moreover, financial assistance has been provided to several industry associations and state-run institutions for conducting training programmes on hazardous waste management, with a focus on setting up of common treatment, storage and disposal facilities (TSDFs) for proper treatment and disposal of hazardous wastes to ensure environmental sustainability. There is a need to analyse whether the government initiatives have been reflected in the trade pattern.

Trends in merchandise trade

Empirical studies have shown that pollution-intensity in the trade pattern of developing countries may increase over time (Grossman and Krueger 1995; Low and Yeats 1992; Akbostanci *et al.* 2004) and the contention is also supported in the Indian framework (Chattopadhyay 2005). In the present context, the pollution intensity from trade is measured in the following manner. First, the presence of products from the 17 highly polluting industries in India's export basket has been measured, an increase in which also implies potentially adverse environmental implications for domestic environment. Second, the evolving proportional presence of the waste and scrap imports in the total import basket has been calculated. An increase in the same implies higher processing of hazardous wastes in the country, with potential consequences for the environment.

It is observed from India's external sector performance over 1999–2009 that, while merchandise exports have increased 4.5 times, the same for commercial services has increased 6.2 times. Figure 13.1 shows that India's share in global

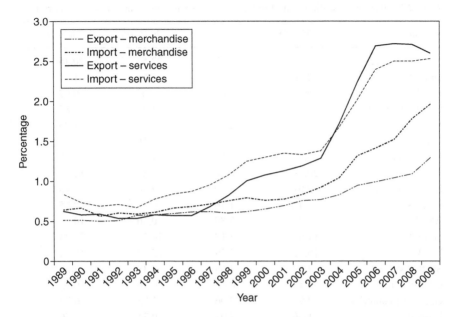

Figure 13.1 India's increasing presence in global merchandise and services trade (per cent) (source: constructed from International Trade Statistics data for various years).

merchandise exports has increased from 0.51 per cent in 1999 to 1.3 per cent in 2009, while the corresponding figures for services are 0.62 per cent and 2.61 per cent in that order. However, the growth rate of merchandise imports has increased at a higher rate as compared to exports, thanks to the growing energy demand for the country.

The evolving composition of India's region-wise export and import direction can be understood from Tables 13.2 and 13.3 respectively. The analysis is important from the fact that PHH often involves outsourcing of polluting sector activities from the developed countries to the developing countries. However, it is observed from both the tables that the share of the EU as well as the United States and Canada are declining in India's trade basket. On the other hand, the share of the developing countries in East Asia (e.g. China, South Korea) and the oil-rich economies in West Asia (e.g. United Arab Emirates, Saudi Arabia) are on the rise. At the macro level, this development does not support a clear drive towards PHH.

The commodity level analysis by Chakraborty (2009) however reveals a mixed picture. For instance, it is observed that proportional exports of several non-ferrous metals like nickel, aluminium, lead and zinc (the domestic production of which all have environmental consequences) to the EU and the US market have increased. On the other hand, the leather sector has faced a number

Table 13.2 Region-wise direction of India's exports (percentage share in total exports)

Region	1997–98	2001–02	2005–06	2009–10
EU countries (27)	26.84	23.17	22.53	20.16
Other WE countries	2.00	1.57	1.58	1.33
East Europe	0.03	0.04	0.05	0.07
Southern Africa	1.41	1.06	1.88	1.85
West Africa	1.30	2.39	1.84	1.76
Central Africa	0.26	0.21	0.16	0.20
East Africa	1.40	1.27	1.39	1.97
North America	20.59	20.76	17.82	11.56
Latin America	2.01	2.19	2.90	3.46
East Asia	1.48	1.16	0.97	0.95
ASEAN	7.09	7.89	10.10	10.16
WANA	11.08	13.18	16.19	22.03
NE Asia	15.67	13.29	15.74	16.12
South Asia	4.69	4.68	5.38	4.69
CAR countries	0.13	0.16	0.16	0.15
Other CIS countries	2.94	2.06	1.05	0.79
Unspecified	1.06	4.93	0.24	2.76

Source: calculated from India's trade data obtained from Ministry of Commerce.

Table 13.3 Region-wise direction of India's imports (percentage share in total imports)

Region	1997–98	2001–02	2005–06	2009–10
EU countries (27)	26.23	20.71	17.43	13.34
Other WE countries	6.76	5.82	4.72	5.96
East Europe	0.02	0.01	0.02	0.02
Southern Africa	1.51	2.88	1.77	3.54
West Africa	3.18	0.93	0.78	3.41
Central Africa	0.08	0.01	0.01	0.09
East Africa	0.24	0.29	0.15	0.13
North America	9.97	7.16	6.96	6.64
Latin America	1.38	1.96	1.79	3.59
East Asia	3.79	2.71	3.54	4.52
ASEAN	8.19	8.53	7.30	8.96
WANA	15.74	6.17	7.28	28.18
NE Asia	12.18	12.87	15.51	18.57
South Asia	0.59	1.15	0.95	0.57
CAR countries	0.09	0.06	0.05	0.07
Other CIS countries	1.98	1.38	1.93	2.05
Unspecified	8.06	27.38	29.82	0.35

Source: calculated from India's trade data obtained from Ministry of Commerce.

of sanctions and restrictions in the EU and the United States since the late 1990s (Chakraborty and Chakraborty 2007), as a result of which its proportional exports to these developed countries are subject to fluctuating trends.

Indian exports

Table 13.4 reports the evolution in export pattern of India's polluting sectors as identified by the MoEF. However, in addition to the 17 most polluting categories of industries, two additional product groups; namely, wood, and articles of wood and textiles, are included in the current analysis. The reason behind their inclusion is that the production process in both the sectors has considerable environmental implications. For analysing the evolving trade dynamics, the period of observation is divided into two equal periods: 1996–2002 and 2003–09. It is observed that the average value of exports from the polluting sectors has increased considerably for all sectors in the second period. Moreover, the proportional share of the polluting sectors in India's export basket has increased from 22 per cent in the first period to 33 per cent in the second period, which is a matter of grave concern. However, the observation does not conclusively indicate presence of PHH in India.

Indian imports

Sharma (2005) has reported that the import of several waste items in India since the late 1990s has led to the creation of several toxic waste zones in the country (e.g. Vapi and Vadodara in Gujarat, Thane-Belapur in Maharashtra, Patancheru-Bollarm in Andhra Pradesh). The analysis further noted that during the 1980s and 1990s, import of hazardous waste for processing or re-use as raw material was permitted. However at present wastes cannot be re-exported after 30 days. This procedural change and the consequent problems in exporting sometimes prompt exporters to dump such waste products at the sea-ports, leading to serious environmental degradations. India is also increasingly turning into a global e-waste recycling hub (Krishna 2003). Considering the import pattern of several toxic waste and scrap products, Greenpeace (1998) has also raised concerns over the environmental implications of allowing greater import of these categories. Though regulatory measures to control pollution on this front are being implemented, concern areas do remain. For instance, the Draft Hazardous Materials (Management, Handling and Transboundary Movement) Rules, 2007 specify that if 60 per cent of any waste is recyclable, then it would not be considered as waste but a material fit for import (Dastidar 2007). Understandably, such regulatory measures may grossly underestimate the very calculation of waste items.

Table 13.5 shows the proportional presence of the imports of select hazardous waste and scrap products in the overall import basket of India during 1996–2002 and 2003–09. It is observed that while import of several polluting categories like waste and scrap of primary cells and batteries, cadmium, hard zinc spelter, etc.

Table 13.4 India's exports in select polluting sectors

HS code	Sector description	Average export value (1996–2002) Millions	Average export value (2003–09)	Simple average annual export growth (1996–2009) %
17	Sugar and sugar confectionary	165.51	567.11	104.08
22	Beverages, spirits and vinegar	28.00	68.85	13.33
2,520 + 2,523	Cement and gypsum	71.88	207.49	15.10
27	Oil refineries and petrochemicals	1,008.92	16,966.19	132.56
2,815	Caustic soda	8.05	18.34	21.82
30	Drug and pharmaceuticals	890.65	3,236.82	17.27
31	Fertilizers	9.72	33.93	62.72
32	Tanning and dyeing extracts	476.60	997.30	8.95
3,808	Pesticides and insecticides	236.57	681.54	14.44
41 + 42	Leather and leather articles	1,215.48	1,914.98	5.40
44	Wood and articles of wood	32.26	117.77	13.01
47 + 48	Pulp and paper	139.16	424.55	15.53
50–60 (barring 52)	Textiles	2,135.70	4,250.19	8.47
72 + 73	Iron and steel	1,794.09	8,336.70	18.17
74	Copper	138.50	1,746.59	33.83
76	Aluminum	270.49	780.24	17.27
79	Zinc	5.57	258.93	178.28
Per cent share of the polluting sectors in total export		22.00	33.00	–
Total export		39,212.75	123,048.87	14.22

Source: calculated from World Integrated Trade Solution (WITS) data.

Table 13.5 India's imports in select polluting sectors

HS code	Product description	Average import value (1996–2002)	Average import value (2003–09)	Simple average annual import growth (1996–2009)	Major sources (1996–2009) (average share in total import in parentheses)		
		Millions		Per cent	1	2	3
262011	Hard zinc spelter	1.16	0.17	72.07	US (31.48)	UAE (11.09)	Saudi Arab (9.63)
262019	Other ash and residue containing mainly zinc	10.65	15.52	13.97	US (21.43)	UAE (13.48)	Saudi Arab (10.69)
262030	Brass dross containing copper, zinc, etc.	6.57	29.25	127.28	US (21.76)	Australia (11.76)	UK (9.31)
262090	Other ash and residues of metals/metallic compounds	0.30	0.89	1,470.77	Indonesia (27.32)	Egypt (22.22)	Australia (19.15)
7204	Ferrous waste and scrap; remelting	349.10	1,506.33	17.77	USA (14.98)	UK (14.97)	UAE (10.75)
7404	Copper waste and scrap	134.76	301.66	10.25	UAE (18.46)	UK (16.03)	US (14.28)
7503	Nickel waste and scrap	0.71	5.16	145.44	Germany (15.18)	UAE (11.90)	UK (9.44)
7602	Aluminium waste and scrap	65.74	319.63	33.02	UAE (17.76)	Saudi Arab (13.63)	UK (12.38)
7802	Lead waste and scrap	6.27	29.21	32.71	UK (35.02)	US (10.17)	Australia (9.43)
7902	Zinc waste and scrap	22.75	46.76	21.26	Germany (11.75)	Belgium (11.49)	US (10.79)
8002	Tin waste and scrap	0.19	0.29	79.02	UAE (27.97)	Germany (13.68)	Singapore (11.78)
810510	Waste/ scrap of cobalt and cobalt alloys	11.61	18.73	6.37	Belgium (19.85)	Canada (15.05)	France (10.53)
810710	Waste/scrap of cadmium and its alloys	0.78	0.66	1,213.36	South Korea (25.27)	Mexico (16.94)	Russian Fedn (9.39)
811220	Waste/scrap of chromium and chromium based alloys	1.25	3.64	20.23	Russian Fedn (35.86)	UK (21.63)	Germany (11.83)
811291	Waste/scrap of hafnium, indium, niobium, rhenium, thallium and other base metals	0.13	0.04	89.53	Australia (34.69)	UK (21.41)	US (18.86)
854810	Waste/scrap of primary cells, batteries and electric accumulators, and spent primary cells, batteries and spent electric accumulators	1.52	1.11	22.82	UAE (31.37)	US (7.46)	UK (6.13)
	Per cent share of the polluting sectors in total import	1.29	1.24	–	–	–	–
	Total import	47,720.42	18,4463.53	17.24	–	–	–

Source: calculated from World Integrated Trade Solution (WITS) data.

have declined in the second period, the same for all other categories have increased. Interestingly, it is observed that the waste and scrap products not only originate from traditional developed markets like the United Kingdom and the United States as predicted by the PHH, but also are increasingly coming from several advanced developing countries like United Arab Emirates, Saudi Arabia, Singapore, Mexico, etc. A silver lining is that the proportional share of the selected commodities in India's import basket has decreased marginally in the second period. However, this proportional decline has been caused by the rapid rise in India's oil import in recent years. Therefore, environmental concerns from waste and scrap import might be a major challenge for India in coming days.

Emergence as a ship-breaking hub

Globally, the PHH phenomenon can be strongly traced in ship-breaking operations, which are cited as 'hazardous wastes' under the Basel Convention. SCRIBD (undated) has noted that the combined effects of the factors like wage increase and protests from local environmentalists in the 1960s and 1970s caused ship-breaking activities to move from the United States and the United Kingdom to the then less industrialized countries like Spain, Italy and Turkey. Japan also underwent a similar process. Presently, India, Pakistan, Bangladesh and China are among the major destinations for this purpose.

Understandably, the growing business in Indian ship breaking yards has been accompanied by rising pollution (BAN 2004). Greenpeace (2000) has noted the adoption of several 'brown' practices like dumping of toxic materials in the sea or on nearby agricultural land, poor worker safety, release of residual oil in the sea, etc. for disposing ship-breaking waste, etc. in Alang port. The study concluded that the area around Alang port is becoming increasingly contaminated with polluting materials like asbestos dust, lead, arsenic, chromium, organotins, dioxins, etc. The International Metalworkers' Federation (2006) also reported the release of hazardous wastes like asbestos, fibres, dust, heavy and toxic metals (e.g. lead, mercury, cadmium, copper, zinc), organometallic substances (tributyltin), polyvinyl chlorides (PVC), welding fumes, volatile organic compounds, compressed gas, etc. in the environment from Indian ports. Though the CPCB has classified these activities as per the Basel Convention as hazardous, their continuance even in a lesser degree poses a major challenge to environmental management given that pollution generated from this sector bears profound environmental and health implications both for humans and animals. For instance, Puckett (2003) has noted that around 25 per cent of the workers employed in one Indian ship-breaking region are likely to suffer from cancer by asbestos exposure alone.

Investment patterns

The FDI coming from abroad has played a crucial role in facilitating the economic growth process in India in several sectors with forward and backward linkage effects (NCAER 2010). While in 2002, FDI flows expressed as a percentage of gross fixed capital formation (GFCF) stood at 3.0 per cent, the same has increased to 9.6 per cent in 2008. It is observed from various issues of World Investment Report (UNCTAD) that FDI stocks expressed as a percentage of GDP has increased in India from 3.7 per cent in 2000 to 9.9 per cent in 2008. Similarly, proportional FDI inward stock in India has increased from 0.22 per cent in 2000 to 0.83 per cent in 2008. Hence there is a need to analyse whether the increasing FDI inflow has been marked with any environmental consequences.

Environmental regulations on FDI inflow in India

In India, entrepreneurs are required to obtain clearances on pollution control and environment for setting up an industrial project from the MoEF in the polluting sectors (e.g. petrochemical complexes, petroleum refineries, cement, thermal power plants, bulk drugs, fertilizers, dyes, paper). In addition, setting up of industries in certain locations, which are considered ecologically fragile (Aravalli Range, coastal areas, Doon Valley, etc.) are restricted, and MoEF takes the final decision in these cases. The clearance granted explicitly checks whether the proposed project involves import of hazardous or banned items or follows a process which is detrimental to the environment (e.g. import of plastic scrap or recycled plastics). The foreign investment proposals are also subject to similar procedural steps. The stringency on granting environmental clearance can be understood in the light of the Bhopal Gas Disaster in 1984, caused by the methyl isocyanate leak from a chemical plant, which resulted in deaths as well as delayed effects on health and environment on a massive scale.

Despite the stringency, there exist certain exemptions to the general provisions. First, if the proposed investment is less than Rs.1,000 million, exemption on environmental clearance is permitted for certain sectors, barring pesticides, bulk drugs and pharmaceuticals, asbestos and asbestos products, integrated paint complexes, mining projects, distilleries, dyes, foundries and electroplating industries, etc. Second, entry in a sector reserved for small-scale units, with investment of less than Rs.10 million, is allowed without any environmental clearance. Third, state governments are entitled to grant environmental clearance for certain categories of thermal power plants. Finally, the potential investors are free to decide the location of their plant, subject to the existing regulations of the government. For instance, the plant location has to be at least 25 km away from the standard urban area for cities with population of more than a million, or within the defined 'industrial area'. However, industries with relatively lower pollution load, e.g. electronics, computer software and printing are currently exempt from such locational restriction (SIA 2003).

FDI inflow in India

From the *SIA Statistics* published by Department of Industrial Policy and Promotion (DIPP), the FDI inflow data in the country can be accessed. Table 13.6 looks into the cross-sector inflow in proposed FDI in general and the polluting sectors in particular during August 1991–March 2002 and April 2002–March 2009.

Table 13.6 Proposed FDI inflow in select polluting industries

Industry code	Polluting sector	1991–2002		2002–09		
		IEMs (%)	LOIs (%)	IEMs (%)	LOIs (%)	LOIs + DILs (%)
1	Metallurgical industries	15.053	0.631	25.489		7.842
2	Fuels	6.863	24.532	5.220		6.118
3	Boilers and steam generating plants	0.003	0.000	0.026		0.000
18	Fertilizers	2.238	0.000	0.159		0.000
19	Chemicals (except fertilizers)	16.024	31.456	6.999		12.196
21	Dye stuffs	0.032	0.048	0.023		0.000
22	Drugs and pharmaceuticals	1.120	4.722	0.426		3.335
23	Textiles	11.622	6.378	2.436		28.520
24	Paper and pulp	3.833	3.072	1.043		0.350
25	Sugar	24.310	12.545	3.219		0.000
26	Fermentation industries	0.779	1.184	0.792		0.000
31	Leather and leather products	0.119	2.690	0.026		0.158
35	Cement and gypsum	6.929	0.774	6.604		0.359
36	Timber products	0.171	0.906	0.025		0.000
Share of FDI in polluting sectors		89.096	88.938	52.487		58.877
Total FDI inflow (Rs. crore)		968,977	107,350	3,974,321		22,851

Source: calculated from data provided in various issues of SIA Statistics.

Note

The two periods represent August 1991 to March 2002 and April 2002 to March 2009 respectively.

The proposed FDI figure includes industrial entrepreneur memorandum (IEMs), letters of intent (LOIs) and direct industrial licences (DILs) (*SIA Statistics* various issues). It is observed from the table that the average proportional share of proposed FDI in the identified polluting sectors has declined during the second period. While proposed FDI in several polluting sectors like metallurgical industries and in service sectors like telecom has increased, the same in chemicals, sugar, etc. has gone down, causing the overall decline.

However, from Table 13.7 a different dynamic involving implemented IEMs can be noted. It is observed that the proportional share of implemented IEMs has increased in the second period considerably. The increase is caused by higher inflow in sectors like fuels, fertilizers, etc. which was not possible during the 1990s due to the policy regime in the country. The unilateral measures to reform the investment climate in the new millennium have ensured higher FDI inflow in general, but with an inclination towards pollution generating sectors.

Figure 13.2 looks into the origin of the FDI inflow in the country over the period January 2000–February 2011 with the data provided in *SIA Newsletter*. It is observed from the figure that the top ten sources account for 80.92 per cent of the total FDI inflow during this period. Interestingly, a considerable proportion of the investment originates from offshore tax havens like Mauritius (41.81 per cent) and Cyprus (3.66 per cent). FDI from developed countries like the United States (7.38 per cent), United Kingdom (4.96 per cent), Netherlands (4.36 per cent) and Japan (4.11 per cent) comes next. The recent Indian initiatives to enter

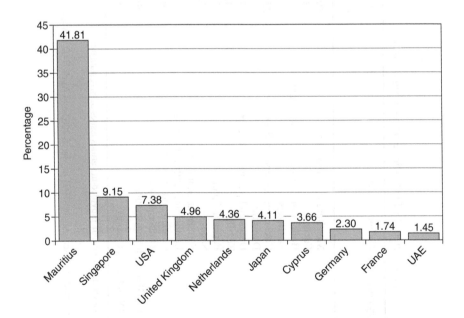

Figure 13.2 Top ten sources of FDI inflow in India (January 2000–February 2011) (per cent) (source: constructed from 'SIA Newsletter' data various years).

Table 13.7 Implemented FDI inflow in select polluting industries

Industry code	Polluting sector	1991–2002		2002–09	
		IEMs (Rs. crore)	Share (%)	IEMs (Rs. crore)	Share (%)
1	Metallurgical industries	19,298	10.654	11,424	12.017
2	Fuels	3,431	1.894	32,113	33.781
3	Boilers and steam generating plants	17	0.009	0	0.000
18	Fertilizers	546	0.301	3,166	3.330
19	Chemicals (except fertilizers)	35,403	19.545	9,135	9.610
21	Dye stuffs	7	0.004	45	0.047
22	Drugs and pharmaceuticals	2,768	1.528	918	0.966
23	Textiles	24,543	13.549	6,554	6.894
24	Paper and pulp	3,162	1.746	2,629	2.766
25	Sugar	1,422	0.785	9,448	9.939
26	Fermentation industries	8	0.004	434	0.457
31	Leather and leather products	67	0.037	21	0.022
35	Cement and gypsum	10,081	5.565	5,372	5.651
36	Timber products	191	0.105	244	0.257
	Share of FDI in polluting sectors	100,944	55.728	81,503	85.737
	Total FDI inflow (Rs. crore)	181,136		95,062	

Source: calculated from data provided in various issues of SIA statistics.

Note
The two periods represent August 1991 to March 2002 and April 2002 to March 2009 respectively.

into comprehensive economic cooperation agreements (CECA) with east and west Asia can be explained in light of the FDI coming from Singapore (9.15 per cent) and United Arab Emirates (1.45 per cent). The analysis however does not reveal any major upsurge in polluting FDI from OECD countries in India, in line with the Southeast and Chinese experience.

Environmental vulnerability in several Indian States is a major problem area. Looking at the cross-state scenario, the government's Planning Commission (2000) had noted that the compliance with existing environmental standard has been very low, particularly in the case of Assam, Bihar, Haryana and Punjab. Pandey (2005) had identified Maharashtra, Gujarat, Uttar Pradesh, Tamil Nadu, Bihar and Andhra Pradesh among the major polluting states. Mukherjee and Chakraborty (2009) show that Punjab, Haryana, Uttar Pradesh and Bihar need to ensure better environmental governance. Table 13.8 in the present context analyses the state-wise implemented FDI scenario, to understand whether FDI in India is increasingly targeting the polluting states. It is observed that in the recent period, implemented IEMs in Gujarat have increased considerably. Among the polluting states, FDI inflow is coming to Haryana, which however includes FDI in a number of service sectors as well. Therefore, no clear trend of FDI inflow towards more polluting states emerges.

Relationship between FDI inflow and pollution: an empirical analysis

According to PHH, the foreign investors may be tempted to come to a territory, which is characterised by lax environmental standards (reflected in higher pollution levels). For this purpose, the current empirical analysis assumes that the pollution level in a state is influenced by the FDI inflow within its territories. It can be argued from the Environmental Kuznets Curve (EKC) hypothesis, that the pollution level may also be a function of the location of the state in the economic plane, as reflected from its income. Here per capita net state domestic product (PCNSDP) is considered for representing income level of a state, data for which is collected from various issues of the 'Economic Survey' (GoI various issues). Implemented IEM figures are taken as explanatory variables, which are collected from the April issues of the 'SIA Statistics'. Since, the definition of FDI inflow in India has undergone a change since 2002 (Jena *et al.* 2005), the implementation related IEM data is considered only from 2002–03 to 2006–07. Environmental pollution is incorporated in the model with respect to three air pollutants; namely, sulphur dioxide (SO_2), nitrite (NO_2), and suspended particulate matter (SPM). The disaggregated data on these three pollutants is obtained from the online resources of CPCB, where their concentration for each state at various industrial and residential areas is reported. The annual average of the concentrations reported in all the stations located in industrial areas within the ith state is considered here as the pollution level for a particular pollutant in the tth year. The following proposed functional relationship is estimated in the present analysis:

$$\log P_{it} = \alpha_i + \beta_1 \log FDI_{it} + \beta_2 \log FDI_{it}^2 + \beta_3 \log Y_{it} + \beta_4 \log Y_{it}^2 + SD + \varepsilon_{it} \quad (13.1)$$

where,

Log is natural logarithmic transformation

P_{it} is the annual average concentration of a particular pollution indicator (NO_2, SO_2 and SPM) for state *i* during time period *t*.

α_i is unobserved specific effects in state *i*

FDI_{it} is the implemented FDI inflow in state *i* during time period *t*.

FDI^2_{it} is the square of implemented FDI inflow in state *i* during time period *t*.

Y_{it} is the PCNSDP in state *i* during time period *t*.

Y^2_{it} is the square of PCNSDP in state *i* during time period *t*.

SD represents the state dummies.

ε_{it} is an error term.

The regression results are summarized in Table 13.9. It is observed from the table that the average pollution level in a particular state is not being significantly influenced by FDI inflow. In other words, existence of PHH in terms of implemented FDI destination across Indian states cannot be conclusively ascertained.

Future policy considerations

There has been a conscious effort in India over the last decade to enhance environmental quality, both by strengthening the legal framework as well as the enforcement mechanism. However concerns over potential environmental degradation, in particular due to activities related to international commerce, still remain. World Bank (2006) has noted that India's environmental institutions and regulatory regime need to be strengthened through incentives provided to the industries complying with greener norms on one hand and devolution of more powers to local governments to control pollution on the other. Moreover, the actual coverage of estimating polluting units is still a major problem. On one hand, there exist a number of uncovered units within the 17 categories of most polluting industries already identified. There is also a growing need to extend the coverage towards the newly emerging polluting sectors on the other (Chakraborty 2009).

In addition to the unilateral measures to enforce compliance in India, the stringent environmental requirements in the EU and the United States like sanitary and phytosanitary measures (SPS), technical barriers to trade (TBT) standards, registration, evaluation, authorization and restriction of chemical substances (REACH), hazard analysis critical control point (HACCP), etc. have motivated several Indian exporting units to considerably reduce their pollution load. Chakraborty (2009) has noted that the compliance cost to comply with foreign standards has been high, but not prohibitive in nature. Through a firm level survey in the leather sector, the analysis further noted that several exporting firms are moving towards cleaner production methods. This is indeed a healthy development. However, concern areas still remain, which are noted in the following.

First, the increase in the share of highly polluting sectors in the export basket is indeed a cause of worry, which might lead to an increase in higher emissions during the domestic production process. Second, increase in the waste and scrap import

Table 13.8 State-wise implemented FDI scenario

State/union territory	1991–2002		2002–09	
	FDI (Rs. crore)	Share (%)	FDI (Rs. crore)	Share (%)
Andaman and Nicobar Islands	0	0.000	0	0.000
Andhra Pradesh	13,215	7.296	4,998	5.258
Arunachal Pradesh	0	0.000	9	0.009
Assam	1,032	0.570	310	0.326
Bihar	65	0.036	103	0.108
Chhattisgarh	1,197	0.661	424	0.446
Chandigarh	258	0.142	0	0.000
Dadra and Nagar Haveli	1,053	0.581	560	0.589
Daman and Diu	2,228	1.230	119	0.125
Delhi	634	0.350	12	0.013
Goa	670	0.370	143	0.150
Gujarat	31,882	17.601	47,982	50.477
Haryana	10,138	5.597	6,906	7.265
Himachal Pradesh	355	0.196	1,431	1.505
Jammu and Kashmir	602	0.332	801	0.843
Jharkhand	1,610	0.889	451	0.474
Karnataka	8,237	4.547	1,880	1.978
Kerala	1,005	0.555	14	0.015
Lakshadweep	0	0.000	0	0.000
Madhya Pradesh	9,327	5.149	431	0.453
Maharashtra	26,855	14.826	6,416	6.750
Manipur	0	0.000	13	0.014
Meghalaya	11	0.006	62	0.065
Mizoram	0	0.000	0	0.000
Nagaland	0	0.000	0	0.000
Orissa	1,606	0.887	247	0.260
Pondicherry	268	0.148	63	0.066
Punjab	5,813	3.209	980	1.031
Rajasthan	10,810	5.968	2,489	2.618
Sikkim	0	0.000	15	0.016
Tripura	0	0.000	72	0.076
Tamil Nadu	9,367	5.171	3,504	3.686
Uttar Pradesh	16,527	9.124	8,710	9.163
Uttaranchal	113	0.062	2,034	2.140
West Bengal	26,258	14.496	3,878	4.080
Total implemented FDI inflow	181,136		95,057	

Source: calculated from data provided in various issues of SIA Statistics.

Note
The two periods represent August 1991 to March 2002 and April 2002 to March 2009 respectively. The FDI figure represents IEMs.

Table 13.9 Regression results for SO_2, NO_2 and SPM concentration and IEM implemented

Explanatory variable	Dependent variables		
	SO_2	NO_2	SPM
Constant	3.42 (0.35)***	−0.78 (0.33)**	2.21 (0.33)**
IEM implemented	3.64 (3.87)	3.56 (3.61)	−3.99 (3.98)
IEM implemented^2	−1.80 (1.93)	−1.79 (1.80)	1.99 (1.99)
PCNSDP	−5.25 (4.09)	0.04 (4.57)	−5.35 (4.38)
PCNSDP^2	2.32 (2.05)	0.23 (2.27)	2.70 (2.18)
Andhra Pradesh	−0.06 (0.04)*	0.05 (0.02)**	−0.17 (0.02)***
Bihar	0.27 (0.03)***	0.58 (0.04)***	0.28 (0.06)
Gujarat	0.50 (0.04)***	0.04 (0.03)	−0.08 (0.38)**
Haryana	0.46 (0.04)***	−0.09 (0.02)***	0.01 (0.04)
Karnataka	0.21 (0.05)***	0.12 (0.04)***	−0.33 (0.03)***
Kerala	0.37 (0.07)***	−0.36 (0.04)***	−0.40 (0.05)***
Madhya Pradesh	0.27 (0.02)***	−0.05 (0.05)	−0.06 (0.40)***
Maharashtra	0.40 (0.05)***	−0.01 (0.02)	−0.16 (0.03)***
Orissa	dropped	dropped	dropped
Punjab	0.36 (0.05)***	dropped	−0.22 (0.07)***
Rajasthan	dropped	0.10 (0.04)**	dropped
Tamil Nadu	0.39 (0.03)***	dropped	−0.31 (0.03)***
Uttar Pradesh	dropped	0.19 (0.04)***	dropped
West Bengal	0.07 (0.02)***	0.36 (0.03)***	−0.11(0.03)***
F-statistic	682.85	666.76	415.76
Observations	70	70	70

Source: computed by the author.

Notes
The autocorrelation and heteroscadisticy corrected standard errors are reported in parentheses.
***, ** and * represent significance at 1, 5 and 10 per cent respectively.

also might lead to worsening of environmental quality in a significant manner, as the resulting pollutants could eventually pollute groundwater and degrade soil, etc. Third, the emergence of several developing countries like Singapore, United Arab Emirates, etc. as the sources of polluted product groups raises another concern, given the recent South-centric trade blocs entered by India (e.g. Indo-ASEAN FTA, India–South Korea CEPA, etc.). In the absence of adequate care, hazardous imports under FTA preference (i.e. lesser duty) from these developing countries might add to environmental degradation in India. Fourth, an increasing share of implemented FDI in highly polluting sectors might bear adverse environmental consequences for the future. Finally, although greater FDI inflow to relatively more polluted states is not being noticed, concentration in selected states itself might lead to serious environmental concerns in the future. For instance, it can be noted that the Alang port or the Vapi industrial cluster are located in Gujarat (GPCB 2010), which is a major recipient of FDI. Therefore, any future government strategy to avert environmental disasters needs to closely monitor the pollution-quotient in international trade and investment patterns as well.

References

Akbostanci, E., Tunc, G.I. and Turut-Asik, S. (2004) 'Pollution Haven Hypothesis and the Role of Dirty Industries in Turkey's Exports', ERC Working Paper No. 3, Department of Economics, Middle East Technical University.

Aminu, A.M. (2005) 'Foreign Direct Investment and the Environment: Pollution Haven Hypothesis Revisited', paper presented at the Eighth Annual Conference on Global Economic Analysis, Lübeck, Germany, 9–11 June.

Basel Action Network (BAN) (2004) 'BAN Comments and Proposals for Resolving Basel Convention Ship-breaking Issues', For Consideration by the Intercessional Working Group on the Legal Aspects of Ships for Scrap and the Open-Ended Working Group of the Basel Convention. Online, available at: www.ban.org/Library/BAN_Submission_shipbreaking_jan04.pdf (accessed 14 May 2009).

Basel Action Network (BAN) (2007) 'Basel Non-Compliance Notification Report', Country Violation: Japan. Online, available at: www.ban.org/Library/Japan_JPEPA_BNN2007_1.Final.pdf (accessed 6 February 2008).

Birdsall, N. and Wheeler, D. (1993) 'Trade Policy and Industrial Pollution in Latin America: Where are the Pollution Havens?' *Journal of Environment and Development*, 2(1): 137–149.

Boys, K.A. and Grant, J.H. (2010) 'ISO 14000 Standards: Voluntary Environmental Governance as a Trade Facilitation Strategy?', Paper Presented at the Agricultural and Applied Economics Association 2010, Denver, 25–27 July.

Central Pollution Control Board (undated) Data on Air Quality. Online, available at: www.cpcb.nic.in (accessed 21 March 2011).

Chakraborty, D. (2008) 'Impact of Stringent Environmental Measures on India's Exports', Paper Presented at the International Conference on 'Empirical Issues in International Trade and Finance', Indian Institute of Foreign Trade, Kolkata, 23–24 December.

Chakraborty, D. (2009) 'Sanctions and their Effects on Trade Flows and Environment: The Indian Experience', Unpublished Thesis, Jawaharlal Nehru University.

Chakraborty, P. and Chakraborty, D. (2007) 'Environmental Regulations and Indian Leather Industry', *Economic and Political Weekly*, 42(19): 1669–1671.

Chakraborty, P. and Singh, J. (2005) *Leather Bound: A Comprehensive Guide for SMEs*, New Delhi: The Energy and Resources Institute.

Chattopadhyay, S. (2005) 'Dirtier Trade for India? The Story of Globalization', *Contemporary Issues and Ideas in Social Sciences*, 1(3): 1–24.

Chaturvedi, S. and Nagpal, G. (2007) 'Case Study of India', in N. Kumar and S. Chaturvedi (eds.) *Environmental Requirements and Market Access: Reflections from South Asia*, New Delhi: Academic Foundation.

Chauhan, C. (2011) 'Indian Exports from Polluting Firms Rising', June 20, *Hindustan Times*, New Delhi.

Cole, M.A. and Elliott, R.J.R. (2005) 'FDI and the Capital Intensity of 'Dirty' Sectors: A Missing Piece of the Pollution Haven Puzzle', *Review of Development Economics*, 9(4): 530–548.

Cole, M.A., Elliott, R.J.R. and Zhang, J. (2008) 'Growth, Foreign Direct Investment and the Environment: Evidence from Chinese Cities'. Online, available at: www.ceauk.org.uk/2008-conference-papers/Cole-Elliott-Zhang.doc (accessed 9 October 2008).

Consumer Unity and Trust Society (CUTS) (2003) 'How Mining Companies Influence the Environment', Briefing Paper No. 1, Jaipur.

Dastidar, A.G. (2007) 'India a Global Dumping Yard? The New Rule Defines Hazardous Waste merely as "Material"', 29 November, *Hindustan Times*, New Delhi.

Dean, J.M., Lovely, M.E. and Wang, H. (2004) 'Foreign Direct Investment and Pollution Havens: Evaluating the Evidence from China', Office of Economics Working Paper, US International Trade Commission.

Dietzenbacher, E. and Mukhopadhyay, K. (2007) 'An Empirical Examination of the Pollution Haven Hypothesis for India: Towards a Green Leontief Paradox?', *Environmental and Resource Economics*, 36(4): 427–449.

Eskeland, G.S. and Harrison, A.E. (2003) 'Moving to Greener Pastures? Multinationals and the Pollution Haven Hypothesis', *Journal of Development Economics*, 70(1): 1–23.

Finer, M., Jenkins, C.N., Pimm, S.L., Keane, B. and Ross, C. (2008) 'Oil and Gas Projects in the Western Amazon: Threats to Wilderness, Biodiversity, and Indigenous Peoples'. Online, available at: www.plosone.org/article/info:doi/10.1371/journal.pone.0002932 (accessed 19 May 2010).

Gallagher, K.P. (2004) *Free Trade and the Environment: Mexico, NAFTA, and Beyond*, USA: Stanford University Press.

Gamper-Rabindran, S. and Jha, S. (2004) 'Environmental Impact of India's Trade Liberalization'. Online, available at: http://unpan1.un.org/intradoc/groups/public/documents/APCITY/UNPAN024230.pdf (accessed 23 November 2006).

Government of India (undated) 'Export Import Data Bank', New Delhi Ministry of Commerce. Online, available at: http://commerce.nic.in/eidb/default.asp (accessed 2 March 2011).

Government of India (undated) 'Hazardous Waste Management', Hazardous Substances Management Division, Ministry of Environment and Forests, Government of India. Online, available at: http://envfor.nic.in/divisions/hsmd/hsmd.html (accessed 2 March 2011).

Government of India (various years) 'Annual Reports', New Delhi: Ministry of Environment and Forests.

Government of India (various years) 'Economic Survey', New Delhi: Ministry of Finance.

Greenpeace (1998) 'Toxic Waste – Poisons from the Industrialised World'. Online, available at: www.ban.org/Library/GPIndia1998–9.PDF (accessed 20 August 2006).

Greenpeace (2000) 'Shipbreaking: A Global Environmental, Health and Labour Challenge', A Greenpeace Report for IMO MEPC 44th Session. Online, available at: www.greenpeace.org/raw/content/international/press/reports/shipbreaking-a-global-environ.pdf (accessed 20 May 2011).

Grossman, G.M. and Krueger, A.B. (1995) 'Economic Growth and the Environment', *Quarterly Journal of Economics*, 110(2): 353–378.

Gujarat Pollution Control Board (GPCB) (2010) 'Comprehensive Environmental Pollution Abatement Action Plan Vapi Industrial Cluster – Gujarat', Gandhinagar: GPCB.

He, J. (2006) 'Pollution Haven Hypothesis and Environmental Impacts of Foreign Direct Investment: The Case of Industrial Emission of Sulfur Dioxide (SO_2) in Chinese Provinces', *Ecological Economics*, 60(1): 228–245.

International Metalworkers' Federation (2006) 'A Survey on Working and Socio-Economic Conditions of Shipbreaking Workers in India', IMF-FNV Project in India. Online, available at: www.imfmetal.org/files/06042810465779/Shipbreaking_survey.pdf (accessed 12 June 2009).

Jena, P.R., Sahu, N.C. and Rath, B. (2005) 'Does Trade Liberalisation Create Pollution Haven? An Indian Experience', Paper Presented at the 'International Conference on Environment and Development: Developing Countries Perspective', JNU, New Delhi, 7–8 April.

Jha, V. (1999) 'Investment Liberalization and Environmental Protection: Conflicts and Compatibilities in the Case of India', Occasional Paper No. 1, Cross Border Environmental Management Project, Copenhagen: Copenhagen Business School.

Kahn, M.E. (2003) 'The Geography of US Pollution Intensive Trade: Evidence from 1958 to 1994', *Regional Science and Urban Economics*, 33(4): 383–400.

Krishna, G. (2003) *E-Waste: Computers and Toxicity in India*, Sarai Reader: Shaping Technologies.

Letchumanan, R. (1998) 'Trade, Environment and Competitiveness: Testing the "Pollution Haven Hypothesis" from Technology Perspective', UNU Working Paper No. 43, Tokyo: United Nations University.

Lipman, Z. (2006) 'A Dirty Dilemma: The Hazardous Waste Trade'. Online, available at: http://hir.harvard.edu/environment/a-dirty-dilemma (accessed 20 July 2007).

List, J.A. and Co, C.Y. (1999) 'The Effects of Environmental Regulations on Foreign Direct Investment', *Journal of Environmental Economics and Management*, 40(1): 1–20.

Low, P. and Yeats, A. (1992) 'Do 'Dirty' Industries Migrate?', in P. Low (ed.), *International Trade and the Environment*, World Bank Discussion Paper No 159, Washington, DC: World Bank.

Lucas, R.E.B., Wheeler, D. and Hettige, H. (1992) 'Economic Development, Environmental Regulation and the International Migration of Toxic Industrial Pollution: 1960–88', in P. Low (ed.) *International Trade and the Environment*, World Bank Discussion Paper No 159, Washington, DC: World Bank.

Mathys, N.A. (2004) 'In Search of Evidence for the Pollution-Haven Hypothesis', Université de Neuchâtel, Division économique et sociale. Online, available at: www.hec.unil.ch/nmathys/mem.pdf (accessed 20 July 2007).

Merican, Y., Yusop, Z., Noor, Z.M. and Hook, L.S. (2007) 'Foreign Direct Investment and the Pollution in Five ASEAN Nations', *International Journal of Economics and Management*, 1(2): 245–261.

Mukherjee, S. and Chakraborty, D. (2009) 'Environment, Human Development and Economic Growth: A Contemporary Analysis of Indian States', *International Journal of Global Environmental Issues*, 9(1 and 2): 20–49.

Mukhopadhyay, K. (2004) 'Impact of Trade on Energy Use and Environment in India: A Input–Output Analysis', Paper Presented for International conference 'Input–Output and General Equilibrium: Data, Modeling and Policy Analysis', at the Free University of Brussels, Brussels, September.

Mukhopadhyay, K. (2006) 'Impact on the Environment of Thailand's Trade with OECD Countries', *Asia-Pacific Trade and Investment Review*, 2(1): 25–46.

Mukhopadhyay, K. and Chakraborty, D. (2005) 'Is Liberalization of Trade Good for the Environment? Evidence from India', *Asia-Pacific Development Journal*, 12(1): 109–136.

Nanda, Nitya and Ratna, R.S. (2010) 'Carbon Standards and Carbon Labelling: An Emerging Trade Concern', ARTNET Policy Brief No. 29, Bangkok: United Nations Economic and Social Commission for Asia and the Pacific (ESCAP).

National Council of Applied Economic Research (2010) 'FDI in India and its Growth Linkages', New Delhi, Sponsored by Department of Industrial Policy and Promotion, Ministry of Commerce and Industry, Government of India.

Pandey, R. (2005) 'Estimating Sectoral and Geographical Industrial Pollution Inventories in India: Implications for using Effluent Charge Versus Regulation', *Journal of Development Studies*, 41(1): 33–61.

Planning Commission (2000) 'Evaluation Study on Functioning of State Pollution Control Boards', Government of India, New Delhi.

Puckett, J. (2003) 'Recycling: No Excuse for Global Environmental Injustice', Basel Action Network. Online, available at: www.ban.org/Library/whyban.pdf (accessed 20 May 2011).

Sankar, U. (2006), 'Trade Liberalisation and Environmental Protection Responses of Leather Industry in Brazil, China and India', *Economic and Political Weekly*, 41(24): 2470–2477.

SCRIBD (undated) 'Ecological Restoration and Planning for Alang-Sosya Ship-breaking Yard, Gujarat'. Online, available at: www.scribd.com/doc/50270578/1/global-scenario-of-ship-breaking (accessed 17 May 2011).

Secretariat for Industrial Assistance (SIA) (2003) 'Manual on Foreign Direct Investment in India: Policy and Procedures', New Delhi: Department of Industrial Policy and Promotion, Ministry of Commerce and Industry.

Sen, A. (2010) 'India Girding itself for US, EU Carbon Tax', *Economic Times*, 14 April, New Delhi.

Sharma, D.C. (2005) 'By Order of the Court: Environmental Cleanup in India', *Environmental Health Perspectives*, 113(6): A394–A397.

'SIA Newsletter' (various issues) Secretariat for Industrial Assistance (SIA), New Delhi: Department of Industrial Policy and Promotion.

'SIA Statistics' (various issues) Secretariat for Industrial Assistance (SIA), New Delhi: Department of Industrial Policy and Promotion.

Singh, K. (1997) *The Reality of Foreign Investments: German Investments in India*, New Delhi: Madhyam Books.

Sinha, S. (undated) 'Economic Analysis of Impact of Surface Iron Ore Mining on Natural Resources and Economy of Iron Ore Mining Belt of Eastern India'. Online, available at: http://coe.mse.ac.in/eercrep/fullrep/cpr/CPR_FR_Suranjan_Sinha.pdf (accessed 24 May 2011).

Temurshoev, U. (2006) 'Pollution Haven Hypothesis or Factor Endowment Hypothesis: Theory and Empirical Examination for the US and China', Working Paper No. 292, Charles University, Prague.

Toxics Link (2000) 'Common Effluent Treatment Plant: A Solution or a Problem in itself'. Online, available at: www.toxicslink.org/docs/06038_CETP_Report.pdf (accessed 20 May 2011).

UNDP (2009) 'Analysis of Existing Environmental Instruments in India', United Nations Development Programme: New Delhi.

United Nations Conference on Trade and Development, 'World Investment Report' (various issues), New York and Geneva: UNCTAD.

United Nations Environment Programme (UNEP) (1999) 'Environmental Impacts of Trade Liberalization and Policies for the Sustainable Management of Natural Resources: A Case Study on Bangladesh's Shrimp Farming Industry', Geneva: UNEP.

United Nations Environment Programme (UNEP) (2004) 'Analyzing the Resource Impact of Fisheries Subsidies: A Matrix Approach', Geneva: UNEP.

Wagner, U.J. and Timmins, C. (2008) 'Agglomeration Effects in Foreign Direct Investment and the Pollution Haven Hypothesis'. Online, available at: www.econ.duke.edu/~timmins/wagner_timmins_fdi.pdf (accessed 21 September 2008).

World Bank (undated) 'World Integrated Trade Solution'. Online, available at: http://wits.worldbank.org/wits (accessed 19 May 2011).

World Bank (2006), *India: Strengthening Institutions for Sustainable Growth*, Country Environmental Analysis, Washington, DC: World Bank.

World Trade Organization (WTO) (various years) 'International Trade Statistics', Geneva: WTO.

Xing, Y. and Kolstad, C. (1998) 'Do Lax Environmental Regulations attract Foreign Investment?', Monograph, Santa Barbara: University of California.

Editors' conclusion

Environmental management in India: past policies, present lessons and future course

Sacchidananda Mukherjee and Debashis Chakraborty

Correcting past mistakes in policymaking?

The analysis presented in the 13 chapters of the present volume clearly indicates that economic growth does not necessarily translate into sustainable development, and India is no exception to this trend. It would be interesting to evaluate the evolving nature of Indian environmental governance framework in this light.[1] As discussed in the introduction of the volume, the approach followed by the Ministry of Environment and Forest (MoEF) in India during the 1980s and the 1990s for ensuring environmental sustainability relied heavily on the involvement of the government agencies (e.g. firm level inspection) for pollution abatement in various spheres; namely, air pollution, water pollution, land degradation, etc. as well as protection of forest and wildlife. Though the framework laid due emphasis on enhancing public awareness through regular arrangement of training programmes, private participation in this sphere however was not encouraging. For instance, the National Environmental Awareness Campaign (NEAC) was launched in July 1986, but the problem of deforestation or air and water pollution remained a major concern area during the same period.

The environmental awareness among industries in particular remained stagnant throughout the 1980s, which led to an increase in the number of public interest litigations lodged by environmental advocacy forums since the late 1990s (Rajamani 2007). It is widely acknowledged that the involvement of the judiciary contributed significantly to enhancing environmental quality across Indian states (Sahu 2007; Sawhney 2003; Prasad 2004). However, Faure and Raja (2010) note that environmental management by the legislative and executive organs still provides the best solution, in the light of the informational advantage enjoyed by them. The observation makes a strong case for more informed as well as sensitive decision-making by the government, preferably by involving the private stakeholders during various stages of environmental management. Media, the fourth estate, could also play an important role in environmental protection. Media coverage of pollution incidents in sensitive areas (e.g. industrial estates/clusters) could function as informal regulations and the sensitization could put pressure on polluters to adopt 'greener' policies (Kathuria 2007). Informal regulation could also be effective to control pollution from unorganized sectors where local communities could monitor the environment and put pressure on polluters to undertake necessary control measures.

Since the late 1990s, the need for ensuring greater public–private partnership for environmental management in India started receiving greater emphasis. Sankar (1998) stressed the need to provide an enabling environment to community-based organizations, so that they can participate in the management of local commons and more importantly in the enforcement of environmental laws and rules. Several successful models have emerged in the following period, though criticisms were not uncommon (Forsyth 2005; OECD 2006). The government initiative in 2006 to launch the National Environment Policy (NEP) through a process of in-depth consultation with experts, as well as with diverse stakeholders can be considered as a culmination of its deliberations on the public–private partnership front (MoEF 2006). The NEP differed significantly from the earlier policies in that it intended to ensure people dependent on particular natural resource obtain better livelihoods from the conservation initiatives. The steps involved in the NEP for integrating a particular section of the population in environmental management initiatives are as follows:

•   For securing better wildlife conservation, expansion of the protected area (PA) network of the country has been proposed, but the same needs to be performed though participation of local communities, concerned public agencies, and other stakeholders, who might have an involvement in the procedure and outcome.
•   The conservation and use of wetlands needs active participation of all relevant stakeholders including local communities, for better maintenance of hydrological regimes and conservation of biodiversity.
•   Need to ensure access to environmental information for stakeholders including concerned local players has been recognized, which will enable them to evaluate ground-level compliance with environmental standards and other requirements. Any shortfall between the policy and practice noticed by the environmentally conscious stakeholders or civil society organizations would then motivate them to undertake required actions, leading either to eventual compliance or to necessary penal procedures.
•   The government needs to undertake extensive consultations every three years with groups of diverse stakeholders (e.g. researchers, experts, community based organizations, industry associations, voluntary organizations), and on the basis of the feedback the NEP needs to be regularly updated.

Lessons from the present scenario

Has the responsibility conferred to the stakeholders by the NEP delivered yet in enhancing environmental quality in India? The time period lapsed since introduction of the policy document is relatively small to undertake any detailed empirical analysis on that front. Nevertheless, it would be an interesting exercise to evaluate the lessons learnt from various vibrant sectors of the economy in the recent period in light of the shifting focus by the government on public–private partnership. The present volume enables one to analyse the future reform requirement prescribed in the 13 chapters included in the present volume for different economic activities and sectors, and understand the role of public–private partnership therein.

The first part of the present volume, i.e. agriculture and primary activities, contains three chapters. The first chapter on non-point source (NPS) pollution of groundwater notes that farmers' groundwater quality perceptions vary across the villages but interestingly mimic the actual groundwater situation. However, their willingness to support local government initiatives in protecting groundwater shows different results. The observation leads to the policy prescription for provision of agricultural information and education along with basic agricultural extension services, which would induce the farmers to protect groundwater from NPS pollution, i.e. ensure better stakeholder participation. The second chapter on shrimp aquaculture stresses the need for reforms both at the policymaking as well as information facilitation level. First, the study noted that aqua-clubs presently do not coordinate with non-members within the watershed, which debars them from efficiently incorporating environmental considerations in their activities. Second, public–private partnership is prescribed through restructuring of national and state level coastal zone management authorities by including all the stakeholder organizations. Third, the government responsibility to estimate the extent of soil degradation through field surveys and need to integrate the operations of the key institutes working in this area were pointed out. The third chapter on the monsoon trawling ban on marine fisheries notes that the 'effectiveness' of the policy is ambiguous. The findings imply that the ban in the present format is perhaps insufficient to rejuvenate fish stocks and greater micro management in terms of regulation of mesh size, etc. might provide better effectiveness. Nevertheless in the short run, the ban poses a better solution than indiscriminate fishing.

Four chapters are included within the second part, concerning manufacturing activities. The fourth chapter notes that despite implementation of several corrective measures, pollution in the Noyyal River Basin is not adequately controlled. The underlying reason for this 'institutional failure' is the adoption of a 'command and control approach' (CAC), which rather infuses pervasive inefficiency, 'ad hocism' in decision-making and an absence of adequate incentives for the economic agents to carry out their responsibilities to reduce pollution. The observation motivates the analysis to recommend introduction of 'market-based instruments (MBIs) such as, 'Pigouvian tax' and 'tradable pollution permits', by factoring in 'site-specific' institutional and behavioural aspects at the local level. The fifth chapter on the environmental costs of coal-based thermal energy generation stressed the need to improve generating efficiency for reducing per unit coal requirement, adoption of technology mix and instruments like carbon tax, emissions trading, etc. The sixth chapter on the estimation of environmental cost and economic impacts of topsoil removal in selected regions of Tamil Nadu for brick-making reveal that the revenue from the sale of soil more than offsets the loss in yield and soil nutrients in the short run. While the farmers' decision can be rationalized in the short run, based on the belief that soil is an infinitely renewable resource both in terms of quality and quantity they spent only a meagre proportion of the revenue on remedial measures to improve the fertility status of the soil. This is a major concern area for the future. Finally, analysing the environmental impacts during hydropower plant construction and operational phase, the seventh chapter notes a different kind of potentially negative consequences involving the local people, flora, vegetation, fauna and habitats, etc. which should be appropriately mitigated and compensated, with ongoing monitoring and adaptive management.

The service sector is showing a sharply rising growth path over the last decade, and four chapters are included under the third part, which discusses service-related environmental management. The role of environmental geography is stressed in the eighth chapter, which notes that integrated urban water management (IUWM) would be economically more viable in water-scarce regions. The analysis also points out major future challenges for the authorities including the coordination of the agencies concerned with development and allocation of water resources at the level of river basins, determining the optimal level of wastewater treatment (WWT) where the real costs do not exceed the net social welfare, and ascertaining the economic viability of metering and making communities aware of the health benefits of using good quality water so as to increase their willingness to pay for water supplies, etc. The ninth chapter indicates the inefficiency of the local bodies in ensuring efficient municipal solid waste (MSW) disposal. As a remedy, the analysis proposes inter-local body arrangements in terms of common disposal facilities to ensure the economies of scale inherent in waste disposal. Through an on-site and off-site estimation exercise, the tenth chapter reports that the per bed per day biomedical waste (BMW) disposal cost in Chennai is quite negligible, making the model sustainable. However, given the indivisibility of the fixed and capital costs, the cost structure calculated in a populous city like Chennai may not be replicated in a relatively smaller city and therefore the government needs to ensure safe BMW disposal in these locations through standardized regulatory procedures and necessary penal actions. The eleventh chapter on e-waste disposal recommends a mix of policy measures; namely, strengthening the gap areas in the legal framework clearly specifying the role of different stakeholders, devising incentive mechanisms for compliance, integration of activities in the informal and formal sectors to establish a viable recycling model for e-waste recycling, etc. to rectify the inefficiencies inherent in the current system.

The last part covers the issue of international trade, and the two chapters here focus on trade in agricultural commodities and the trade–investment–environment linkage in polluting sectors respectively. Analysing the input usage pattern for various crops, the twelfth chapter notes that despite the presence of various regulations, actual compliance in the case of groundwater and pesticide usage is found to be abysmally weak. The analysis also notes the recent rise in agricultural subsidies, and concludes that sustainable development can only be ensured through an enormous restructuring of the fiscal system, institutions, and work ethos or governance, at all levels. The thirteenth chapter observes that export of potentially polluting sectors as well as waste and scrap import in the country has increased over the period, which is a major concern area. Moreover, an increasing foreign direct investment (FDI) trend in the polluting sectors deserves the attention of the policymakers. Though currently no regional concentration in FDI inflow in dirty sectors is noticed, the government nevertheless needs to maintain an efficient regulatory mechanism on this front.

The observations and policy prescriptions undertaken by the above analysis based on both case studies through field surveys as well as empirical models relying on secondary data are indeed thought-provoking. First, it becomes clear that despite the role accorded to public–private partnership in NEP (2006), there is still considerable scope to enhance the same in various sectors like shrimp aquaculture and others. Second, the basic NEP objective of involving stakeholders for important feedback and inputs would be defeated if no information access is provided that group. The response of the stakeholders in practical situations of NPS groundwater pollution or soil degradation due to topsoil removal for brick-making purposes underlines the same in no uncertain terms. It is clear from their responses that the overall environmental sustainability concern comes nowhere during their decision-making process. Third, government involvement is sought practically in all the sectors covered, ranging from low-skill based shrimp aquaculture to capital-intensive power sector or hydropower generation. Greater government involvement has been prescribed for ensuring better compliance (BMW, pesticide usage in agriculture), removal of 'ad hocism' in decision-making (river pollution), integration of similar tasks being undertaken by multiple agencies (IUWM, MSW, shrimp aquaculture), strengthening the gap areas in current legal framework (e-waste management), micro management of policies (marine fisheries, agriculture), etc. In addition, MBIs like Pigouvian tax, tradable pollution permits, carbon tax, etc. have been recommended in several areas including controlling surface water pollution, power generation, etc.

The adoption of a regulatory role by the government, ensuring environmental governance with informational advantage, is widely supported in the literature. Following a conscious taxation policy is, however, an entirely different policy space. Taxation policy to secure sustainable environment is indeed practiced in various parts of the world, and several successful examples can be quoted (Chelliah *et al.* 2007; Knigge and Görlach 2005). But the key question is, would the same strategy provide an efficient solution for India?

An eco-tax is a price-like instrument which assigns a price to the 'unpaid factor' of production, translating the 'polluter-pays-principle' into practice. Economic instruments in environmental policy try to correct prices in order to internalize externalities. The environmental tax reform is a specific policy approach, which raises taxation of 'bads' such as resource use or emissions and reduces other taxes on 'goods' such as labour that are felt as a burden so that the total tax revenue remains constant. The taxation and/or fiscal incentives or setting up of tradable pollution permits generally work through price signals. However, price signals function most efficiently when the market is allowed to operate freely. In the absence of an effective tax administration or pollution control authority, the system might be subject to malfunction and could only generate revenue to the government at the cost of environment. Under the present CAC-based approach adopted in India for environmental management, the penalties for non-compliance are not related to the degree of compliance (Chelliah *et al.* 2007). Understandably the system not only encourages corruption and rent-seeking activities but also results in large scale environmental degradation. The other factor inhibiting introduction of MBIs is that all pollution prevention and control legislations come under criminal law (Chelliah *et al.* 2007). Before following a strong MBI regime, these concern areas need to be considered.

An associated concern involves the potential shifting of the environmental taxes. In EU-25 which have efficient tax administration, at the national level, eco-taxes generate only 6.6 per cent of total tax revenues, of which three-quarters comes from energy taxes and the rest primarily from transport (registration and circulation) taxes (*The Economist* 2007). In India, taxes from petroleum products alone provide 20–25 per cent of tax revenues of the state governments and 5–10 per cent of revenue comes from vehicles, passenger and goods taxes. There is a high possibility in India that a further increase in eco-taxes might simply shift the burden of taxes to more environmentally damaging activities. For instance, potentially polluting industrial units (e.g. textile bleaching and dyeing, tanneries, electroplating, etc.) which are within the organized sector might simply outsource parts of their most polluting process to the un-organized sector at the cost of organized employment. It is to be noted that the labour laws or environmental laws do not apply to the latter sector. So, ultimately the cost might be transferred to the labour, rendering the government eco-tax initiative with best intentions at least partially ineffective. Given the present system of tax administration in India, environmental taxation is unlikely to introduce a one-point solution in the system. Nevertheless, environmental fiscal reform is definitely a consideration that the country needs to tackle in the near future (Sankar 2009).

While a quantity-based instrument, e.g. tradable pollution rights, can also lead to improvement in environmental quality, there are several legal as well as institutional obstacles to introduce such a policy measure in Indian framework. The legal system in the country does not permit the creation and assignment of property rights for environmental resources (Chelliah *et al.* 2007). The Supreme Court of India however interprets Article 21 of the Indian constitution dealing with the right to life as the right to clean air and water, i.e. a wholesome environment (GoI undated). The state is viewed as a trustee of natural resources like air, water in rivers and lakes, forest resources, etc. To sum up, adequate attention needs to be given to the potential outcome before implementing any such policy measure in the country.

Recent government policies: the drive to a sustainable future?

The institutional reforms in India either undertaken in recent years or currently being explored for ensuring environmental sustainability include both judicial and regulatory measures. On the former front, the National Green Tribunal Authority (NGT) can be mentioned, while the National Environmental Protection Agency (NEPA) is to be quoted as an example of the latter. On a theoretical level, both steps mark a distinct improvement over the existing judicial and regulatory framework and a brief description of them would not be inappropriate here.

On the judicial front, the NGT was established under the National Green Tribunal Act, 2010 for the effective and expeditious disposal of cases relating to environmental protection and conservation of forests and other natural resources, including the enforcement of any legal right relating to the environment and giving relief and compensation for damages to persons and property, etc. NGT replaces the National Environmental Appellate Authority (NEAA), constituted under the NEAA Act, 1997 and National Environmental Tribunal Act (NETA), 1995. While NEAA lost its importance with limited achievements (Rosencranz and Sahu 2009), NETA was never implemented. The NGT is a specialized body to handle environmental disputes involving multi-disciplinary issues and includes members from various fields. It is proposed that the NGT have five locations in India. The tribunal has been mandated to ensure the final disposal of applications or appeals within six months of filing of the same, for providing speedy environmental justice.

With the rising economic growth and emergence of a vibrant entrepreneur class, the number and complexity of project proposals received for environmental clearance by the MoEF has increased manifold in the recent period. To complicate the matter, the inadequate capacity and resources of the Central Pollution Control Board (CPCB) and State Pollution Control Board (SPCB) to ensure compliance with environmental regulations has emerged as a serious concern area (MoEF 2009). In this background, to implement the long-awaited regulatory reform, in September 2009, the MoEF has brought out a discussion paper for the creation of a National Environment Protection Authority (NEPA). NEPA would be a professionally managed body, with members from various knowledge disciplines (e.g. economics, law) and truly autonomous of the MoEF, both from a financial and a regulatory standpoint (MoEF 2009). Once implemented, NEPA will essentially assume responsibility for the issuance of environmental clearances (presently undertaken by the MoEF) and national stewardship for compliance and enforcement of environmental laws (presently done by the CPCB). However, it is argued that the separation of policy-making from regulation through creation of NEPA should not separate political commitment/accountability from governance (Lele *et al.* 2010).

In short, with the implementation of the proposed reforms in the near future, environmental management in India will be considerably streamlined. While legislation and policy-making would still be dealt by the MoEF, adjudication will be the responsibility of the newly formed NGT. On the other hand, regulation, monitoring and enforcement will be the responsibility of a new NEPA, with the deeper objective of comprehensive and effective implementation of the Environment (Protection) Act, 1986. The underlying philosophies of NEPA include 'polluter-pays principle' and the 'precautionary principle', which in effect should be able to partially achieve the objective of eco-taxation.

But, however strong the legal framework might be with introduction of NGT and NEPA, their efficient implementation would still remain subject to their enforcement by the regulator and the response of the economic agents. Interestingly, it is observed that the MoEF actions over the last year send an ambiguous signal on the future of environmental governance, which makes arriving at any straightforward conclusion on that front difficult.

To stress the above-mentioned point, three instances can be quoted on the achievement front, which underlines the commitment of the regulators to ensure environmental sustainability. First, the MoEF has regularly revoked environmental clearance for the violating factories, thereby maintaining a credible threat perception for the offenders. For instance, clearance was revoked for a major cement factory in May 2011 on the ground that it was established in a wetland with a high density of bird. The petition by the local farmers opposing the factory played a key role in this regard, which underlines the responsiveness of the system (HT 2011). Second, in mid-2010 charges of illegal mining were levelled against certain influential lobbies in the state of Karnataka, following which the export of iron ore and other minerals were banned with immediate effect (HT 2010). Finally, the government is presently nurturing the idea of imposing a tax on the turnover of the tourist facilities around 600 protected areas, indicating consideration of innovative steps to ensure sustainability (Chauhan 2011a).

Three specific incidents would however also underline the concern areas. First, in 2010 it was revealed from the response to a request from civil society activists under the Right to Information Act that a leading firm, which operated a large aluminium smelter plant and nine captive power plant units in the Jharsuguda district of the state of Orissa was functioning without the necessary clearances from the Orissa State Pollution Control Board (OSPCB). The event under the present environmental governance framework defies explanation (Sahu 2010). Second, Chauhan (2011b) reported that while the statutory Forest Advisory Committee (FAC) rejected a proposal of iron ore mining in 595 acres of forest land in Chiria by the Steel Authority of India Limited (SAIL), Jharkhand, within the MoEF a different viewpoint might exist. This indicates the need to strengthen the independence of the proposed NEPA in a legal sense in no uncertain terms. Third, the government has recently decided to go forward with the restoration of Asia's largest freshwater lake, Wullar (in the state of Jammu and Kashmir), which was long overdue. However, the decision has emerged as a debatable issue because of the fact that the restoration would require that around 20 lakh willow trees need to be cut in the process (Chauhan and Ashiq 2011). In other words, the resulting environmental benefit is likely to be lower than the projected figure.

To sum up, the discussions undertaken in the present volume indicate that while the seriousness of the government agencies in enhancing environmental quality is strongly felt, the system is far from being perfect and future concern areas do remain. Three sets of general recommendations emerge from the discussion of the volume. First, the recent strengthening of the regulatory framework through NGT and NEPA are commendable, but that development in no way reduces the importance of the civil society in securing a sustainable environment. Therefore, what is required is the involvement of stakeholders with greater autonomy to function and adopt necessary procedures to ensure due action against the polluting units/entities in the agricultural and manufacturing, services and other similar important spheres. The initiatives taken up by the Supreme Court Monitoring Committee on environment with active involvement of local people can play a significant role in checking the menace of environmental pollution. For instance, the Local Area Environment Committee (LAEC) under the Supreme Court Monitoring Committee on Hazardous Waste could be mentioned here. Such a step would not only be applicable for point sources of pollution but also for NPS where it is difficult to identify the exact sources (e.g. through the active involvement of farmers). In addition other innovative forms of public–private partnership, in line with the capacity of the local population to participate in the decision-making process, needs to be devised and successfully implemented. Moreover, the government must also play a key role in this context by ensuring access to key environmental information to the stakeholders, with periodic updates.

Second, the problems associated with standard setting needs to be deliberated upon. The emission (or effluent) standards are currently set for respective pollutants without due care for the assimilation capacity of the media which receives the treated effluent. In other words, the emission (or effluent) standards are often not in line with the ambient standard, which results in large scale pollution of rivers, degradation of land and engendering of the marine ecosystem. Barring the exception of a few states and also a few industries, the effluent (or emission) standard is same for all states (Appasamy *et al.* 2001). Though on a theoretical front this harmonization of standards can be supported in a federal structure, there is a serious practical limitation to its application. For instance, it has been observed that even if all the industrial units located in a river basin of industrial cluster meet the effluent standard, there might not be enough water in the river to assimilate the same and meet the designated ambient standard (best desired use). Therefore, the current scenario calls for the imposition of at least state-specific environmental standards immediately, and later in a time bound manner a move to the creation of river basin specific effluent standards. Another viable alternative could be the imposition of a total maximum daily load (TMDL) based standard, based on the assimilative capacity of the receiving media (say, river). Environmental standard setting in this manner, with special consideration of the scenario prevailing in a particular region, will contribute significantly to securing sustainable development for the country as a whole as well.

Finally, any government decision on an environmental front has to be based on a detailed *ex ante* and *ex post* environmental impact assessment (EIA). Absence of an EIA in environmental policymaking may lead to disasters on several other fronts, and the resultant effect on the environment might turn out to be ambiguous.

The Indian focus in this respect should be guided by the urge to move towards a green economy in the context of sustainable development and poverty eradication, as is being discussed under the United Nations Conference on Sustainable Development (UNCSD) forums. 'Green economy' is an outcome-oriented concept, aimed at improving human well-being without undermining the resource-base that current and future generations depend on for their livelihoods. The associated measures not only promote 'green sectors', but should also support 'greening' of traditionally 'brown' sectors (e.g. energy, agriculture, transport, housing sectors). The greater focus on 'green economy' would further facilitate the government target to release green GDP data from 2015 (Ramesh 2011).

The recent government initiatives on this front include the first phase of the national resource accounting projects of the Ministry of Statistics and Programme Implementation (GoI) for accounting natural resources – encompassing eight projects spread across eight states: West Bengal (air and water), Tamil Nadu (land and water), Goa (environment and forest), Karnataka (land and forest), Andhra Pradesh and Himachal Pradesh (air and water), Madhya Pradesh and West Bengal (mineral extraction), Madhya Pradesh and Himachal Pradesh (land an forestry) and Meghalaya (land and forest)) (MoS&PI undated). Apart from the government initiative, the initiatives taken by institutions like The Energy Resources Institute (TERI, previously TATA Energy Research Institute) and Green Indian States Trust (GIST) is worthy of mention here (TERI 1999). The commendable initiatives taken up by the GIST under the Green Accounting for Indian States and Union Territories Project (GAISP) deserve special mention. The studies conducted under this project attempt to account for natural resources depletion (Haripriya *et al.* 2005, 2006; Kumar *et al.* 2006, 2007). Though, the Government of India has brought out its 'Compendium of Environmental Statistics' regularly since 1997 and states have also brought out their 'State of Environment Reports', given the present system of environment statistics, it is difficult to adopt an integrated environmental accounting framework in India. Hence, there is a need for more case studies to generate the coefficients of environmental impacts of various economic activities. We believe that the chapters included in the current volume, which are extremely relevant in that context both for the academia and the policymakers, will contribute significantly in this regard.

Note

1 For a comprehensive discussion on the evolution of Indian laws and institutions for environmental protection see Sankar (1998).

References

Appasamy, P.P., Nelliyat, P., Jayakumar, N. and Manivasagan, R. (2001) 'Economic Assessment of Environmental Damage: A Case Study of Industrial Water Pollution in Tiruppur', Environmental Economics Research Committee (EERC) Working Paper Series: IPP-1. Online, available at: http://coe.mse.ac.in/eercrep/fullrep/ipp/IPP_FR_Paul_Appasamy.pdf (accessed 12 July 2010).

Chauhan, C. (2011a) 'Cess on Wildlife Tourism on Cards', 3 June 2011, *Hindustan Times*, New Delhi.

Chauhan, C. (2011b) 'Panel says No, but Ramesh Okays Mines for SAIL', 10 February 2011, *Hindustan Times*, New Delhi.

Chauhan, C. and Ashiq, P. (2011) '20 Lakh Trees to be Cut to Restore Wullar lake', 3 June 2011, *Hindustan Times*, New Delhi.

Chelliah, R.J., Appasamy, P.P., Sankar, U. and Pandey, R. (2007) *Ecotaxes on Polluting Inputs and Outputs*, New Delhi: Academic Foundation.

Faure, M.G. and Raja, A.V. (2010) 'Effectiveness of Environmental Public Interest Litigation in India: Determining the Key Variables', *Fordham Environmental Law Review*, 21(2): 239–294.

Forsyth, Tim (2005) 'Building Deliberative Public–Private Partnerships for Waste Management in Asia', *Geoforum*, 36(4): 429–439.

Government of India (undated) 'The Constitution of India'. Online, available at: http://aptel.gov.in/pdf/constitutionof%20india%20acts.pdf (accessed 17 May 2011).

Government of India (2006) 'National Environment Policy 2006', Ministry of Environment and Forests, Government of India, New Delhi.

Haripriya, G., Sanyal, S., Sinha, R. and Sukhdev, P. (2005) 'The Value of Timber, Carbon, Fuelwood, and Non-Timber Forest Products in India's Forests', Monograph 1, Green Accounting for Indian States Project (GAISP), Green Indian States Trust (GIST): Chennai.

Haripriya, G., Sanyal, S., Sinha, R. and Sukhdev, P. (2006) 'The Value of Biodiversity in India's Forests', Monograph 4, GAISP, GIST: Chennai.

Hindustan Times (2010) 'Bad News for Bellary Bros: Iron Ore Export Banned', July 29, New Delhi.

Hindustan Times (2011) 'Ramesh Scraps Green Clearance to Nirma Factory', May 11, New Delhi.

Kathuria, Vinish (2007) 'Informal Regulation of Pollution in a Developing Country – Evidence from India', *Ecological Economics*, 63(2–3): 403–417.

Knigge, M. and Görlach, B. (2005) 'Effects of Germany's Ecological Tax reforms on the Environment, Employment and Technological Innovation', Ecologic Institute, Berlin.

Kumar, P., Sanyal, S., Sinha, R. and Sukhdev, P. (2006) 'Accounting for the Ecological Services of India's Forests: Soil Conservation, Water Augmentation, and Flood Prevention', Monograph 7, Green Accounting for Indian States and Union Territories Project (GAISP), Chennai: Green Indian States Trust (GIST).

Kumar, P., Sanyal, S., Sinha, R. and Sukhdev, P. (2007) 'Accounting for freshwater quality in India', Monograph 8, GAISP, Chennai: GIST.

Lele, Sharachchandra, Dubash, Navroz K. and Dixit, Shantanu (2010) 'A Structure for Environment Governance: A Perspective', *Economic and Political Weekly*, 45(6): 13–16.

Ministry of Environment and Forest (2006) 'National Environment Policy 2006', Government of India. Online, available at: http://envfor.nic.in/nep/nep2006e.pdf (accessed 25 March 2011).

Ministry of Environment and Forest (2009) 'Towards Effective Environmental Governance: Proposal for a National Environment Protection Authority', Discussion Paper for Comments, New Delhi: Government of India.

Ministry of Statistics and Programme Implementation (MoS&PI) (undated) Natural Resource Accounting Project. Online, available at: www.mospi.nic.in/mospi_new/site/inner.aspx?status=3&menu_id=100 (accessed 15 May 2011).

Organization for Economic Co-operation and Development (2006) 'Environmental Compliance and Enforcement in India: Rapid Assessment', Paris: OECD.

Prasad, P.M. (2004) 'Environmental Protection: The Role of Liability System in India', *Economic and Political Weekly*, 39(3): 257–269.

Rajamani, L. (2007) 'Public Interest Environmental Litigation in India: Exploring Issues of Access, Participation, Equity, Effectiveness and Sustainability', *Journal of Environmental Law*, 19(3): 293–321.

Ramesh, Jairam (2011) 'The Way to a Green GDP', Lecture Delivered at the India Today Conclave, 18 March 2011. Online, available at: http://moef.nic.in/downloads/public-information/Way%20to%20Green%20GDP.pdf (accessed 25 May 2011).

Rosencranz, Armin and Sahu, Geetanjoy (2009) 'National Green Tribunal Bill, 2009: Proposals for Improvement', *Economic and Political Weekly*, 44(48): 8–10.

Sahu, G. (2007) 'Environmental Governance and Role of Judiciary in India', PhD Thesis, University of Mysore, Mysore (Institute for Social and Economic Change, Bangalore).

Sahu, P.R. (2010) 'No Pollution clearance: Vedanta runs 10 Units', September 9, *Hindustan Times*, New Delhi.

Sankar, U. (1998) 'Laws and Institutions relating to Environmental Protection in India', Paper Presented at the Conference on 'The Role of Law and Legal Institutions in Asian Economic Development', Erasmus University, Rotterdam, 1–4 November, 1998. Online, available at: www.mse.ac.in/pub/op_sankar.pdf (accessed 5 April 2010).

Sankar, U. (2009) 'Ecology, Environment and Sustainable Development in Indian Fiscal Federalism', Working Paper No. 47, Chennai: Madras School of Economics.

Sawhney, Aparna (2003) 'Managing Pollution', *Economic and Political Weekly*, 38(1): 32–37.

Tata Energy Research Institute (TERI) (1999) 'Pilot Project on Natural Resource accounting in Goa (Phase 1)', TERI Project Report No. 99RD61, TERI, Goa.

The Economist (2007) 'Ecotaxes: Are Taxes the Best Means to Cut Greenhouse Emissions?' 23 April 2007. Online, available at: www.economist.com/node/9063277?story_id=9063277 (accessed 10 May 2010).

Index

Page numbers in *italics* denote tables, those in **bold** denote figures.

'green economy' 276
Green GDP 276
greenhouse gases (GHGs) 16n5, 100, 107, 115n1
Green Indian States Trust (GIST) 276
green jobs, recycling sector 14
Greenpeace 251, 254
green revolution (GR), 3, 234
gross domestic product (GDP) 1, 15, 22, 223, 255, 276
gross fixed capital formation (GFCF) 255
gross national product (GNP) 45
ground level ozone 113
groundwater: deep aquifiers, quality of 26; depletion 228–9; factors influencing farmers' willingess to protect 38–9; farmers' perceptions about quality 35, 37; integrated development of surface water, groundwater and catchments 159–61; nitrate (NO₃) concentration 21, 22, *23*, 28, 29, *32*, 35, 40; 'precautionary approach' 30; shallow aquifiers, quality of 24, *25*, 26; status of nonpoint source pollution 22–8, *23*, *25*; status of nonpoint source pollution (in Tamil Nadu) 26–8; *see also* nonpoint source (NPS) water pollution
Gujarat: nonpoint source groundwater pollution in 22; pesticide use 231
Gulati, A. 223, 238, 239n6
Gunatilake, H.M. 122
Guo, Z. 122–3
Gupta, M. 110
Gupta, R.K. 112
GWQP (groundwater quality) 35, 37
gypsum 89

Haastrecht, E. van 68, 79n3
hardpan problem, topsoil 133n2
Haryana: fertilizer consumption 229; groundwater depletion 228; land degradation 226; nonpoint source groundwater pollution in 24
hazard analysis critical control point (HACCP) 260
hazardous substances management division (HSMD), MoEF 248
Hazardous Wastes (Management and Handling) Rules (1989) 248
Hazardous waste and scrap imports 251
health hazards: biomedical waste management 192; municipal solid waste 177, 179

Hicks–Kaldor compensation criterion 96
high court 97
high tide line (HTL) 48, 57
high yielding varities (HYVs) 239n3
Hoda, A. 223
Houtven, G.L. Van 172
Human Development Index (HDI) 15
hydropower generation 12–13; construction phase 136, 139, 140–1, **143**, 145; EIA case study 136–46; environmental impacts 135–47; operational phase 136, 139, *141*, **144**; quarrying 140–1; rapid impact assessment matrix *see* RIAM (rapid impact assessment matrix); site-preparation phase *139*, **142**
hydrological regimes 268

ICAM (integrated coastal area management) 46, 59, 61
IETPs (individual effluent treatment plants) 90, 92, 93
Institutional failure 269
imperfect information flow 221
indiscriminate fishing 269
incineration 172, 173, 184n4, 184n5, 185n9, 198
Indian growth paradigm: whether explosive growth or sustainable development 1–5; whether improvement of environmental governance 7–9; legal framework, evaluation 5–6
Indian Pesticides Registration Committee 231
Indira Gandhi Nehar Yojna (IGNP) 160
individual effluent treatment plants (IETPs) 90, 92, 93
indoor air pollution 190–1
industrial entrepreneur memorandum (IEMs) 257
industrial pollution 54; government intervention 85–6; Noyyal River Basin case study *see* Noyyal River Basin (Tamil Nadu), industrial pollution case study
Industrial Pollution Projection System (IPPS) database, World Bank 247
informal regulation 267
Inorganic manure/fertilizer 132
integrated coastal area management (ICAM) 46, 59, 61
integrated urban storm water management (IUSM) 161